Who's Who Of Stage and Screen

Who's Who Of Stage and Screen

C. Elizabeth Lalla

Who's Who of Stage and Screen.
Lalla, C. Elizabeth

The photographs contained in this book have been supplied by the featured artists' representatives and all material has been released for inclusion in this book. Additional photos supplied from the private collection of Judith A. Moose.

Library of Congress Cataloging – in – Publication Data

C. Elizabeth Lalla
Who's Who of Stage and Screen - 1st Edition
ISBN 1-4184-9558-1
    1. Television – Non-fiction
    2. Motion Pictures – Non-fiction
    3. Acting – Non-fiction

FIRST EDITION

Acknowledgments

As a teenager I collected "Movie Magazines" full of pictures and stories about the "Stars." They were great fun to read and collect, but something was missing. My interest in the entertainment field went far beyond the "Stars," I wanted to know more about the "known, but not recognized" actors and actresses. I searched magazines, books and newspapers, but found little information on them. Eventually I gave up looking, but never forgot the desire to know more about everyone on the credits list.

One day, I was suddenly and vividly inspired to put together books with pictures, profiles and resumes of everyone from the well known to the not so well known to the unknown. The inspiration was God-given and I thank God for entrusting me with the idea and inspiration for my books.

I wish to thank the actors and actresses for granting their permission to be included in "Who's Who of Stage and Screen," along with their managers, agents and publicists. Without them, my books would be only a dream.

I also wish to thank my typist, editor and assistant, Donna Grant for her willingness to work long hours and sacrifice her personal time to help me achieve my goals.

A special thanks goes to Denise Smith for her faithful encouragement and support, her wonderful sense of humor (your laugh makes me laugh) and her timely reminders to "take a break." Thanks, my friend.

Finally, thanks to family and friends who supported me, believed in me and helped make my dream a reality.

6

Contents

8

James Garner

James Garner

Profile

One of Hollywood's most popular actors, Academy Award-nominated and Emmy Award-winner James Garner has long been regarded as one of America's foremost and distinguished actors, continually maintaining his popularity over time. He played the role of "Duke" in the 2004 hit movie, "The Notebook," and lent his voice to the character "Pat" in "The Land Before Time X: The Great Longneck Migration." Since 2002 he has played the role of Jim Egan in the hit TV series "8 Simple Rules for Dating my Teenage Daughter." He starred in "The Divine Secrets of the Ya Ya Sisterhood," as Chief Justice Thomas Brankin in CBS's one-hour legal drama series "First Monday" and starred in the original miniseries Mark Twain's "Roughing It" for the Hallmark Channel. Audiences heard him as the voice of Commander Rourke in Disney's 2001 summer hit "Atlantis: The Lost Empire." In 2000 he starred in "Space Cowboys" opposite Tommy Lee Jones and Donald Sutherland for actor/director Clint Eastwood and in the Showtime telefilm "The Last Debate," based on the novel by PBS's Jim Lehrer. He also co-starred in the four final episodes of "Chicago Hope" for CBS-TV and lent his voice to the character 'God,' in Carsey-Werner's animated series "God, The Devil and Bob."

Continuing to easily transition between film and television, Garner has starred in many projects for both mediums over the past few years. In 1999 he starred in the CBS made-for-television movie "One Special Night," which set a ratings record. The love story reunited him with his "Americanization of Emily" and "Victor/Victoria" co-star Julie Andrews. The same year he starred as a high-powered lawyer in the TNT made-for-television movie "Legalese," which brought him his third SAG Award nomination.

In 1997, he starred in the Paramount Pictures film, "Twilight," with Paul Newman, Susan Sarandon and Gene Hackman for director Robert Benton; in the HBO Original Motion Picture "Dead Silence" with Marlee Matlin and Lolita Davidovich; and then opposite a stellar cast, including Sissy Spacek, Sam Shepherd, Sonja Braga and George Carlin in the critically-acclaimed miniseries "Larry McMurtry's Streets of Laredo," the follow-up to "Lonesome Dove."

In 1996 he starred with Jack Lemmon in the Warner Bros. film "My Fellow Americans." Since 1994, Garner has starred as Jim Rockford, one of his best known and loved characters, in seven two-hour made-for-television movies of "The Rockford Files" for CBS Television. The first show, which aired in November 1994, was rated the highest made-for-television movie of the 1994-95 season. This marked the second year in a row that Garner appeared in the number one made-for-television movie.

One of Garner's most touching performances to date came in the Hallmark Hall of Fame Presentation "Breathing Lessons," the highest rated made-for-television movie of the 1993-94 season, for which he earned an Emmy nomination and a Golden Globe nomination. Also in 1994, Garner brought to the big screen another of his unforgettable characters, co-starring with Mel Gibson and Jodie Foster in the Warner Bros. film "Maverick," which grossed over $100 million domestically.

Throughout Garner's career, he has received recognition for performances ranging from his sensitive portrayal of 'Murphy Jones' in "Murphy's Romance," which earned him an Academy Award nomination for Best Actor in 1985, to the misguided and over-reaching business tycoon 'F. Ross Johnson' in "Barbarians at the Gate," for which he received a Golden Globe Award and an Emmy nomination in 1993 for Best Actor in a Miniseries or Special. Garner's accolades include both Emmy and Golden Globe nominations for Best Actor for his role in the 1984 telefilm "Promise" with James Woods. "Promise," produced by Garner-Duchow Productions won five Emmy Awards including one for Garner as Executive Producer of that year's Outstanding Television Drama.

In 1989 Garner-Duchow produced The Hallmark Hall of Fame Presentation "My Name is Bill W." The telefilm received seven Emmy nominations. Garner was nominated for Best Supporting Actor as well as Executive Producer of the Most Outstanding Television Drama of the year.

Coming from a background with no ties to show business, Garner was born on April 7, 1928 in the mid-sized city of Norman, Oklahoma. His father Weldon Bumgarner, was of European ancestry and his mother, Mildred, was one-half Cherokee. When Garner was five his mother died and he and his brothers Jack and Charles went to live with relatives. At 14 he left home, did odd jobs, and at 16 signed on for a stint in the Merchant Marines.

In the meantime his father had moved to Los Angeles. Garner followed, helping his father in the carpet-laying business while attending Hollywood High School. He eventually got a job modeling swimsuits, but before his career got started, he found himself in the Army with the distinction of being Oklahoma's first draftee to the Korean conflict, during which he was awarded a Purple Heart. After the war he returned to the U.S. and eventually moved back to Los Angeles.

When a friend offered him a small part in a Broadway production of "The Caine Mutiny Court Martial," he took it. That part led to a $150-a-week contract with Warner Bros. His first on-camera appearance was with Clint Walker on the TV series "Cheyenne." His feature film debut came in "Toward the Unknown." Next, he gave an acclaimed performance as Marlon Brando's friend in the hit film "Sayonara," which led to his first big break – the starring role in the television series "Maverick," which brought him true stardom.

Since then, he has starred in roughly 40 films, including "The Children's Hour," "The Great Escape," "The Americanization of Emily," (his personal favorite), "Grand Prix," "Cash McCall," "Move Over, Darling," "Support Your Local Sheriff," "The Skin Game," "The Thrill of it All" and "Victor/Victoria."

On television, he played one of the world's most famous private detectives, "Jim Rockford," in "The Rockford Files" from 1974-1980, for which he won an Emmy Award in 1977, and starred in the series "Nichols." His other television roles include the miniseries "Space," HBO's "Glitterdome" and 1990's Hallmark Hall of Fame Presentation "Decoration Day" for which he received an Emmy nomination and a Golden Globe Award for Best Actor in a Miniseries for Special.

In total Garner has received one Academy Award-nomination, 15 Emmy nominations with two wins, 13 Golden Globe nominations with four wins, 2 People's Choice Awards and 3 Screen Actors Guild Award nominations. He was also the recipient of a Clio Award for his Polaroid commercials.

Away from acting, he is involved with auto racing. From 1967-69, he owned a racing team called American International Racing, it's members driving at such sites as Daytona and Sebring and in off-road races like Baja. He has also driven the pace car at the Indianapolis 500 on three occasions in 1975, 1977 and 1985.

Garner is involved with many humanistic causes. He helped organize Martin Luther King's March on Washington for Civil Rights in 1963, and went to Vietnam in 1967 to visit the troops. He is a member of the National Support Committee of the Native American Rights Fund and the National Advisory Board of the United States High School Golf Association. He has been involved with the "Save the Coast" movement to stop offshore drilling in California and is most recently involved with Save the Children. In 1986, Garner was inducted into the Oklahoma Hall of Fame. He was made Ambassador of Cultural Arts for the State of Oklahoma in November of 1989. He won the Most Valuable Amateur Trophy at the AT&T Golf Tournament in February 1990. He was inducted into the Cowboy Hall of Fame in Oklahoma City, Oklahoma in March 1990. In 1993 he received the Western Heritage Award for Lifetime Achievement in Film and Television from the Gene Autry Museum and in 1995 he received an Honorary Doctor of Humane Letters Degree at the University of Oklahoma.

A gifted and ardent golfer Garner lives in Los Angeles with his wife, Lois. They have two daughters, Kim and Gigi.

Scene from *The Notebook*

James Garner Contact

PMK/HBH
8500 Wilshire Blvd. Suite 700
Beverly Hills, CA 90211
Phone: 310-289-6200

Debra Jo Rupp

Debra Jo Rupp

Profile

From a starring role in FOX-TV's long-running hit television series, "That '70s Show," to memorable performances on Broadway and in film, Debra Jo Rupp brings boundless energy, comedic prowess and limitless talent to every role she undertakes.

Debra is currently starring in "That '70s Show," in which she portrays 'Kitty Forman,' the endearing, yet high-strung mom. Set in suburban Wisconsin in 1977, the show follows the growing pains and hilarious antics of the Forman family as they deal with the rapidly changing times. *Entertainment Weekly* listed Debra Jo's 'Kitty' as one of the great performances of 1999, the *Boston Herald* named her the best sitcom mom on TV, and according to the *Los Angeles Times*, "If FOX's 'That '70s Show' is thriving, one shouldn't overlook the parents played by Kurtwood Smith and Debra Jo Rupp." Voted a "Fall Favorite" by *TV Guide*, "That '70s Show" stirs up a sense of nostalgia and is a glaring reminder of the decade's outrageous fashion.

"In 1977, I looked like a capon chicken dressed up in denim jumpsuits, and now I finally get on a series that airs longer than six episodes, and I *still* look like a capon chicken dressed up in denim jumpsuits! I hope and pray that we get to the '80s very, very soon – those shoulder pads helped out the hip issue tremendously!" laughs Debra Jo.

In addition, Rupp was the voice of the schoolteacher, 'Mrs. Helperman,' in the Emmy award-winning ABC animated series, "Teacher's Pet," which also featured the voices of Nathan Lane and Jerry Stiller. Debra has also completed work on the feature film of "Teacher's Pet."

In the can is the ensemble feature, "Jackson," written, directed, executive produced and edited by JF Lawton (scribe of "Pretty Woman" and "Under Siege"). The bittersweet drama spans a day in the life of two homeless men (Barry Primus and Charlie Robinson) and offers a rare glimpse at the faces and souls of the very people who are normally ignored and avoided. Rupp plays the pivotal role of a kindly cafeteria manager who makes a basic connection with the pair and is the one person who treats them with respect and dignity at a poignant and uplifting moment when they need it most. "Jackson" is expected to make the festival circuit.

Born in Glendale, California and raised in Massachusetts, Debra Jo made her stage debut in the third grade. "My Brownie troop did a little production. We were flappers doing the Charleston with all the fringe and these huge flowers in our hair, and then we had to turn around, take the flower off, wrap a blanket around our shoulders and become Indians. I couldn't get the flower off and someone took my blanket, so I burst into tears and ran off the stage (my mom found me in the parking lot). I kind of figured it couldn't go downhill from there and, believe me, that's been comforting through the years."

While Debra Jo intended to study drama in college, her parents, who were adamantly against her pursuit of acting, sent her to the best liberal arts college they could find, the University of Rochester in New York, which specifically did not offer drama. "A month before I started, I got a letter from the college announcing their new drama department," recalls Debra Jo, who credits fate for stepping in at the right time. "The blood drained from my dad's face, and I lit up like a Christmas tree." Throughout college, she participated in numerous plays and, upon graduation, was encouraged by her drama professors (all two of them) to head to New York. "Mom made me promise never to waitress (we don't know what that was about), and Dad rented a U-Haul and drove me there. Very quietly," she grins.

Her big break came ten years later with the starring role in Cynthia Heimel's acerbic play about modern-day relationships, "A Girl's Guide to Chaos." "It was as though the play were written for me – the way I act, the way I talk, and the wardrobe I wished I could afford," says Debra Jo, whose performance garnered rave reviews. Her other Broadway credits include "Frankie and Johnnie in the Claire de Lune" as 'Frankie,' and "Cat on a Hot Tin Roof" as 'Sister Woman' with Kathleen Turner and Charles Durning.

For television, Debra Jo has starred in over a dozen sitcoms, including "Davis Rules," "If Not For You," "The Jeff Foxworthy Show" and "The Office." She has also had memorable recurring roles as Phoebe's sister-in-law on "Friends" and Jerry Seinfeld's booking agent on "Seinfeld." In addition, she has appeared in such telefilms as NBC's "In the Line of Duty" with Tim Daly; FOX's "The Invaders" with Scott Bakula; and the HBO miniseries, "From the Earth to the Moon," directed by Sally Field.

For the big screen, Debra Jo made her feature film debut in the box-office hit, "Big," opposite Tom Hanks. Additional film credits include Dan Aykroyd's wife in "Sgt. Bilko"; "Death Becomes Her" with Goldie Hawn; "Clockwatchers" with Toni Collette and Parker Posey; and "Lucky Thirteen" with Lauren Graham.

When she's not ruling the roost on "That '70s Show," she finds other ways to channel her energy. "I've been busy fixing up my home. 'Kitty' and I own the same appliances. I've learned about plumbing, caulking, painting, and how to kick the refrigerator," says Debra Jo, who also enjoys refinishing furniture, needlepoint and hanging out with her two silky terriers – McPheeters and McCallister – when she's not obsessing on video games or surfing the net.

Despite her continued success and hectic schedule, however, she has not lost sight of her roots. "My long-term goal has always been to build a house back in Massachusetts before I'm too old to shovel snow," says Debra Jo, who is now doing just that. She looks forward to one day living closer to her sisters (one a figure skating coach, and the other a computer programmer). "And of course, returning to New York and the theatre is the big, big dream."

Scene from *That 70's Show*

Debra Jo Rupp Contact:

Nancy Iannios Public Relations
8225 Santa Monica Blvd.
Los Angeles, CA 90046
Phone: 323-650-0300

Paige Brooks

Favorite Quote

"If God brings you to it, he will bring you through it."

Paige Brooks

Profile

Paige Brooks has been successfully pursuing a career as a professional international model and actress. She is also an accomplished dancer and singer, studying and performing since the age of three. A native of Mobile, Alabama, Paige is the daughter of James, a corporate attorney, and Greta, a former educator.

After graduating with honors from UMS-Wright Preparatory School, this Presidential Scholar pursued scholarship opportunities in New Orleans, finally deciding upon Tulane University for her college education. While at Tulane, she continued her semi-professional career as a ballerina, coupling her love of dance with that of acting and modeling. Despite the strong call of the stage, Paige decided to focus her efforts on broadcast journalism and graduated with a B.A. in Communication/Broadcast Journalism from the Newcomb College of Tulane University. She then prepared to tour the world and make her dreams a reality.

While pursuing those dreams, Paige has lived around the globe with stops in New York, Miami, New Orleans, Philadelphia, France and Milano, Italy. She is represented by agencies worldwide including: Wilhelmina (New York), Ricardo Guy (Milano), Michele Pommier (Miami), T.H.E. (Washington, D.C.), San Diego Model Management (San Diego), and Network Entertainment (Los Angeles).

In 1998, one of her dreams came true when Paige had the honor of representing her home state of Alabama in the *Miss USA Pageant*, where she was a Finalist and Swimsuit Winner. With this honor, came many opportunities including a move to Los Angeles. Today, Paige is continuing her career efforts in Los Angeles, where she currently resides and considers the "last stop" on her world tour.

Throughout her career, this Wilhelmina Model Search Winner has graced the covers and pages of numerous international magazines including *Cosmopolitan, Glamour, Modern Bride, Seventeen, Vogue, WWD,* Italian *Practica*, London's *That's Life* (2 covers), French *Maxi*, and *Beverly Hills* [213] (cover story, interview and cover shot). Paige was interviewed and photographed by world-famous photographer, Don Thompson, for his new magazine, *The Green Room*. She also has walked the runways of famous designers such as Halston, Oscar de la Renta, St. John, Anna Sui, Carmela Sutera, Victor Alfaro, Jim Hjelm, Carolina Herrara, Viviene Tam, Oleg Cassini, Betsey Johnson, Nicole Miller, and Ralph Lauren.

In addition to her many successes in the world of modeling, Paige has had the opportunity to host numerous programs and events. She has hosted the Venus International Model Search competition live at the House of Blues with Danny Bonaduce. Paige also adds to her repertory: host of the first web-a-thon in history for Click2Asia.com, host and spokesperson for IGIA/Tactica International, host for Hughes Space and Communications programming, KYOU-TV anchor and reporter, and international spokesperson for the Zebra Double-Up Putter for golf enthusiasts around the world. She has appeared in film, television, and countless commercials including David's Bridal, Candies Shoes, Burlington Coat Factory, Good Morning America, and her feature film debut performance in John Grisham's *The Client*.

Paige also appeared in *Men in Black II* with Will Smith and Tommy Lee Jones starring as "Princess Lauranna, Queen of the Universe." She has been featured in numerous magazines, newspapers, and websites and on radio stations around the world as a result of the film's release in July 2002.

Most notably, Paige was the "cover story" on the home page of *Internet Movie Database (IMDB)*, the film industry's premiere website. Paige has also been featured as a "Barker's Beauty" on "The Price Is Right," television's longest-running game show, voted the "#1 Game Show of All Time" by *T.V. Guide*. In addition, she appeared in a CBS Promo for the "Miss USA Pageant"…naturally.

Paige sings with "The Swank Pharaohs Jazz Band" and can be heard at various clubs throughout the Los Angeles area including The Mint, Lava Lounge, Knitting Factory, and The Derby.

In her spare time, Paige enjoys ballroom dance, salsa, aerobics, gourmet cooking, and jiu jitsu. She is an active member of The Junior League of Los Angeles, sings in her church choir, and volunteers to cook dinner each week for her church Bible study. She also loves sharing her life with her two cats: Pontchartrain and Xerxes. Rounding out her many talents and abilities, Paige studies Spanish at Santa Monica College, with hopes of one day speaking fluently.

Paige Brooks

Acting Resume
SAG/AFTRA

FILM/TELEVISION

Men in Black II	Principal/Princess Lauranna	Barry Sonnefield, Director
Hollywood Homicide	Principal/Yoga Professional	Ron Shelton, Director
Cash Cowboy	Starring/Julie	Shamus Murphy, Director
Runners	Co-Starring/Phyllis Greenbaum	Carlo Gustaff, Director
The Client/TV Series	Principal/Michelle	Daniel Attias, Director

Modeling Resume

PAGEANTS

Miss Hawaiian Tropic 1994
Miss Alabama USA 1998 (also Swimsuit Winner)
Miss USA 1998 – Finalist
Miss Beverly Hills 2000

AGENCIES

Wilhelmina	New York (Former Model Search Winner)
Ricardo Guy	Milano, Italy
T.H.E.	Washington, D.C.
Michele Pommier	Miami
San Diego Model Management	San Diego
Network Entertainment	Los Angeles

PRINT

Editorial:

Vogue
Glamour
Women's Wear Daily
Cosmopolitan
Seventeen
French Maxi
London's That's Life (2 cover shots)
Italian Practica
Beverly Hills [213] (cover story interview and cover shot)
The Green Room (interview and multi-page photo layout)
Fashion Market
The Philadelphia Inquirer (numerous cover shots)
Danielle - New York
Designer Circle - New York
Star City Clothing Company - New York
Simultaneous - Milan
Vertigo – Paris

Bridal:

Modern Bride
Elegant Bride
Bridal Guide
Bride's
Domo Adami-Milano
David's Bridal
Sweetheart Bridal New York
Le Bon Bridal

Swimwear/Lingerie

Ralph Lauren
Authentic Fitness/Speedo
Jantzen Swimwear
Catalina Swimwear
Liz Claiborne/Sirena Swimwear
Mayo Swimwear of Turkey
La Gemme Lingerie of South America

ADVERTISEMENTS/CATALOGUES (partial list):

Domallo, Bieff Basix, Nina Austin, Janine of London, Visage, Mesmerize, Jenny Helene, Bianca Nero, Japanese Aroma Spa - Los Angeles, Arizona Iced Tea, Crown Casino, Bunnie's Juice Bar, Victor's International, Parisian, Maison Blanche, Srawbridge & Clothier, Henry Margu International, Fashion Bug, Boscov's, DuPont, Apligraph, Spindle River Western Wear, *Pageantry*, Jeep, Gayfer's, Scala Gowns, Vivian Chang, Peep, Fashion 1001 Nights, Lord & Taylor, *Fashion Images*, C'YA in CA, Diva, My Fashion, Jin Taylor, Fashion Show Online, Bette Paige, Donna Vinci, Billy Wolff (book cover), CBS.

RUNWAY
Fashion:
Halston
St. John
Anna Sui
Oscar de la Renta
Candies Shoes
Nicole Miller
Betsey Johnson
Westcott
Oleg Cassini with Robin Leach
Victor Alfaro
Carolina Herrera
Viviene Tam
Vogue - Fall Shows New York
Seventeen
Episode
Bebe
Fashion Show Online/FSO
The Shops at Bal Harbour
Macy's Herald Square – New York
Saks Fifth Avenue
Bloomingdale's
Neiman Marcus

Bridal:
Modern Bride
Jim Hjelm
Eden
Carmela Sutera
Ian Stuart
Domo Adami-Milano

Swimwear/Lingerie:
Cosmopolitan- Gottex Swimwear
Jantzen Swimwear
Catalina Swimwear
Sirena Swimwear
Ralph Lauren
Authentic Fitness/Speedo
Jezebel Lingerie
Manhattan Beachwear/Surfside
Venus Swimwear

FIT MODELING
Bianca Nero
Marcello Soltan
Domallo
Streets Ahead
Star City Clothing Company
P. Star Clothing Company
David's Bridal
Manhattan Beachwear

Ian Stuart Bridal
Domo Adami Bridal
Fashion Forms Lingerie
Jezebel Lingerie
Intapp Lingerie
So Low Lingerie
Authentic Fitness/Speedo

CONVENTIONS (partial list)
Narrator/Demonstrator/Spokesperson/Host
Proficient in Ear Prompter and Teleprompter

National Organization of Orthopedic Surgeons, National Organization of Drug Stores, COMDEX (3 years), National Bar and Restaurant Convention, E3 (5 Years), ACC, National Auto Parts (Napa Auto Parts), Plastek, Tapley Entertainment, BreakAway Films, ISAM, Infocom, ASHP, CES, Minot Area Development, Jillian, MAGIC (semi-annually), Venus International Model Search - Master of Ceremonies for seven events (with Danny Bonaduce for Finals)

Paige Brooks Contact:

Wilhelmina Models
300 Park Ave. South
New York, NY 10010
Phone: 212-473-0700
Website: www.paigebrooks.com

Paul Dunleavy

Paul Dunleavy

Profile

Paul Dunleavy, a telecommunications technician for Charles Schwab in Jersey City, N.J., leads an amazing double life. By day he's doing his job as technical support on the trade floor. But once he steps off the floor, Dunleavy enters the world as a professional actor. He has appeared on hit television shows, including "Law and Order: Special Victims Unit," "Oz," and "Sex and the City." He is landing lead roles in independent films such as "Back to Manhattan," and "Drawing Conclusions." He thanks his acting coach John Eyd of The Actors Training Institute, where he studied method acting, for his successes.

Paul is a native of Jersey City. This former U.S. sailor also has an amateur boxing background. He has participated in the nationally known Toughman Competition and has also participated three times in Golden Glove competitions. He continues to use his boxing background as an avenue to raise money for his favorite charity the Make-A-Wish Foundation, where he is also a volunteer. Paul has his sights on becoming a fulltime actor one day. Paul says "Life is not about where you start out, it's where you finish that matters."

Paul Dunleavy

Resume

THEATRE

Steve Bayner Show	Participant – (Hypnotized Man)	Steve Bayner Productions
Variety Show	Elvis Impersonator	RCL Cruise Lines

TELEVISION

Guiding Light	Nurses – Husband	CBS
Law and Order (SVU)	Mob Defendant – (Featured)	Studios USA
OZ	Softball Player – (Featured)	HBO
Sex in the City	Photographer	HBO
Law and Order (SVU)	Detective	Studios USA
Sports Section	Guest – Interview	Cablevision – Metro NY

FEATURE FILM

Mona Lisa Smile	Photographer	Mike Newell
Kate and Leopold	Crowd Participant	Otis Production
Changing Lanes	Pedestrian	Paramount Productions

INDEPENDENT FILM

Sledge	Lead (Danny Kelly)	Director – Lance J. Reha
Drawing Conclusions	Lead (Garret Ward) Ex-Con	Director – Lance J. Reha
Survival Brooklyn	Principal (Wise guy)	Director – Kenneth Kushner
The Fire Within	Principal (John Garber, Corr. Officer)	Director – Lance J. Reha
Back To Manhattan	Lead (Paulie—Mobster)	Director – Robert O'Reilly
Motel	Principal (Norm-Hitman)	Director – Marcus Bleeker
Anthony's Foundation	Principal (Joey Protein)	Director – Leo Di'Stefano
Boxing Documentary	Principal (Boxer)	Director – Christopher Lallo

SPORTS HISTORY

Toughman Contest	Participant	Adorable Promotion, Inc.
Semi Pro Football	Wide Receiver	NJ Oaks / NJ Raiders
3 Time NJ Golden Gloves	Boxer-Ring 20	Kearny NJ
2 Time NJ Diamond Gloves	Boxer-Ring 20	Kearny NJ

EDUCATION

Actors Training Institute (John M. Eyd) (On-going)
Introduction to Stanislavski (Stella Adler)

Creating The Character (Sanford Meisner Technique)
Method Acting (On-going)
Scene Studies (On Camera)
Weist Barron (Penelope Hirsh) – Scene Studies

United States Military – United States Navy
Ships Steam Propulsion, Machinist Mate School
Ships Firefighter Training

SKILLS

Boxing, Weight Training, Jogging, Football, Baseball, Softball, Basketball, Bicycling, Golfing, Bowling, Billiards, Swimming, Snorkeling, Wave Runner, Horseback Riding, Bartender, Construction Foreman, Singing, Wish Granting—(Make-A-Wish-Foundation)

MISCELLANEOUS

1995 Chevy S-10 Pickup (Green), 1998 Mazda 626 (Bronze), Business Attire, Bicycle, Football Uniform, Boxing Gear (Trunks, Gloves, Shoes, Robe), Jewelry

Paul Dunleavy Contact

E-mail: ptd5@yahoo.com

Parry Shen

Parry Shen

Profile

Parry Shen was seen as high school overachiever, 'Ben Manibag' in MTV Films' "Better Luck Tomorrow." Directed by Justin Lin, the film was the first acquisition of an Asian-American film from the Sundance Film Festival and MTV Films' first acquisition ever. Film critics, Roger Ebert and Elvis Mitchell (*Chicago Sun-Times* and *NY Times*) stood up to defend the film and its subject matter when the picture sparked heated debate during its Q&A sessions at the renowned festival.

Shen was also seen in Columbia Pictures/Revolution Studios' comedy, "The New Guy" opposite DJ Qualls ("The Core") and Zooey Deschanel ("The Good Girl"), also 20th Century FOX's "First Daughter" starring Katie Holmes and "The Hazing" with Brad Dourif and Brooke Burke. Television credits include: "Tru Calling," Navy NCIS: Naval Criminal Investigative Service," "Asia Street Comedy," "Sabrina the Teenage Witch," "The King of Queens," "Buffy the Vampire Slayer," "Party of Five," "Suddenly Susan" and "Caroline in the City."

Parry Shen is a Queens, New York native. He graduated from the State University of New York at Buffalo with a degree in Marketing and minors in Media Studies and PR/Advertising. To get his bearings in California, Shen spent several years working as a Dorm Parent at a boarding high school in Ojai, California which enabled him to receive free room and board, while touring nationally with the Asian-American Theatre Company, here*and*now. On weekdays before the students got out of school, he commuted 160 miles per day to Los Angeles for auditions.

At one point, Shen was about to give up on acting when he accepted a waiter position at Applebee's Restaurant. On his very first day, he was tracked down at the neighborhood eatery and informed he had landed a role in "The New Guy." He was whisked away nine hours later for a two-month shoot in Austin, Texas. Shen worked three hours at the restaurant and has a $20.13 paycheck still waiting for him!

Besides teaching High School Drama part time, Shen has guest lectured alongside fellow industry alums James Foley ("Glengarry Glen Ross") and Peter Riegert (Traffic) to Drama and Media Studies students at his alma mater, SUNY Buffalo.

Parry Shen

Resume

FILM

FIRST DAUGHTER	Supporting	20th Century Fox/Regency
BETTER LUCK TOMORROW*	Lead	MTV Films/Paramount Pictures
THE NEW GUY	Lead	Columbia Pictures/Revolution
THE HAZING	Lead	Honey Creek Pictures
THE DEVIANTS	Lead	Green Band Pictures
SHRIEKER	Lead	Full Moon Pictures
STARSHIP TROOPERS	Featured	Columbia TriStar

*(Dramatic Competition: Sundance Film Festival 2002, Toronto Int'l Film Festival 2002)

TELEVISION

TRU CALLING	Recurring	FOX
NAVY NCIS: NAVAL CRIMINAL INVESTIGATIVE SERVICE	Guest Star	CBS
ASIA STREET COMEDY	Various Characters	International Channel
THE KING OF QUEENS	Guest Star	CBS
BUFFY THE VAMPIRE SLAYER	Co-Star	WB
SABRINA THE TEENAGE WITCH	Guest Star	WB
THE WILD THORNBERRYS	Guest Star	NICK
THE PRIVATEERS (Pilot)	Series Regular	SYN
DAMAGED GOODS (Pilot)	Recurring	FOX
AN AMERICAN TOWN	Guest Star	FOX
COUSIN SKEETER	Guest Star	NICK

THEATRE

ONE COLD DARK NIGHT	Various Leads	Wells Fargo Radio Theatre
hereandnow THEATRE COMPANY	Various Leads	U.S. National Tour
A NICKEL'S WORTH	Jared	East LA College
P.J. MAXWELL-MYSTERY TRAIN	Various Leads	Fillmore Mystery Train
BRIGHTON BEACH MEMOIRS	Eugene	Katherine Cornell Theatre
BILOXI BLUES	Eugene	Katherine Cornell Theatre
LEGEND OF THE RED BEAN SOCIETY	General Tso	The Buffalo Black Box
BUFFALO, 14261	Geek/Cool Guy	Katherine Cornell Theatre

TRAINING

Howard Fine Studio	Howard Fine/Heidi Davis/Uta Hagan	Los Angeles
The Groundlings	Chase Winton	Los Angeles
Playhouse West	Robert Carnegie	North Hollywood
Theatre Minor	SUNY Buffalo	Buffalo, NY
Master Scene Study Workshop	Jason Alexander	Burbank

LANGUAGES Fluent in Chinese (Cantonese), Conversational Spanish

SPECIAL SKILLS
Rock Climbing, Rappelling, Inline (figure) Skating, Puppeteer, Snowboarding, Jet Ski, Firearms, Juggling, Lifeguard, able to recite the entire alphabet backwards in under 5 seconds.

Premiere of *Better Luck Tomorrow*

Parry Shen Contact:
Stone Manners Agency
8436 W. 3rd St., Suite 740
Los Angeles, CA 90048
Phone: 323-655-1313
Website: www.parryshen.com

Kelly Taylor

Kelly Taylor

Profile

There is something <u>unusual</u> about Texas-born Kelly Taylor.

In today's youth-driven Hollywood, where "twenty-something" actors labor at staying pubescent, Kelly is a throwback to "Classic Hollywood." Reminiscent of the good old days when stars like Elizabeth Taylor, Sophia Loren and Ava Gardner had curves and character...Kelly Taylor is a <u>woman</u>.

Still in her twenties, she's an old soul, with a deep well of talent, faith, discipline and desire that burns like the Texas sun. Think Catherine Zeta-Jones, Mira Sorvino, Sean Young, and Alyssa Milano all in one.

Kelly is a worker. During the time she has been in L.A., Kelly has had leads in 17 diverse Independent films. In "American Lottery" Kelly played a drug cartel leader, in "The Most," a Roman vestal virgin, in "The Vice of Living," a lovesick drug dealer, in "Deadly Games," a spy, and in "Pygmalion," a professional killer. Rounding it off, Kelly plays a C.E.O. in "Absolutely Beautiful," a mental patient in "Painful Memoirs," a criminal in "Sinless Deception," and in "St. Peter: The Rock," Kelly plays 'Mary Magdalene.'

In her own words: "I'm always in the right place at the right time." This sounds idealistic after some of the cards Kelly has been dealt. Kelly's mother passed away when Kelly was only 15, and Kelly was viciously attacked on her first day in the City of Angels, after the long drive from Houston. Nevertheless she always looks for light and she has found it in the darkest places. In a childhood spiked with challenges her unique character was forged of steel, spirit and compassion. Kelly remarks, "I was always the one who stayed strong when things were falling apart."

Her mom's long bout with cancer left her previously comfortable family devastated financially. Kelly states, "My Dad was shattered. The insurance only covered 80% of the expenses. Long story short, we were hungry." At 13, Kelly was granted a hardship license, so she could drive her siblings to school, and her mother to the hospital. She stood in line to get them financial aid and took a part time job. She made it through.

Kelly found her inner strength through spirituality. It propelled her to being a top earner, selling computers to corporate America, although she didn't even know what a mouse was before she got the job. A few years later, Kelly took that money, got in her car and headed for L.A. She says, "I knew that my future was in the film industry and I had to follow my heart's desire. I trusted God to put me in the right hands: I opened a training manual looking for an acting teacher, and chose John Sarno, and later, "Star Maker" Jay Bernstein referred me to Ivan Markota. It was my luck that they turned out to be the best." Kelly has also sung backup for Enrique Iglesias, with no voice training to speak of. Kelly enthusiastically states, "Yeah, I can do it! I never say, I can't!"

Kelly Taylor

Resume

SAG

FILM (Partial List)

American Lottery	Lead - Cindy Capone	Drug Cartel Leader	Dir. Ismail Hossain
Cupid's Arrow	Lead - Alex Meyers	Professional Killer	Dir. Edward J. Lawrence
Painful Memoirs	Lead - Susan Kristoff	Mental Patient	Dir. Justin Jaquesmotte
Absolutely Beautiful	Lead - Katherine Oxford	Powerful CEO	Dir. Scott Owen
Sinless Deception	Lead - Julie Dawson	Seductive Criminal	Dir. Samantha Fonti
Pygmalion	Lead - Pygmalion	The Perfect Woman	Dir. Edward J. Lawrence
California Issues	Lead - Sai McCoy	Trendy Show Host	Dir. German Forno
Movin' Up	Lead - Erica Reed	Popular Cheerleader	Dir. J. C. Crew
Glamour Girl	Lead - Naomi Roberts	Naïve Supermodel	Dir. Art Sanders
Deadly Games	Lead – Vivian Hayworth	Betrayed Spy	Dir. Bruce Bilson
Flaming Hot Master Lounge	Supporting	Futuristic Earth Girl	Dir. James Diebold
Local Boys	Supporting	Enchanted Surfer	Dir. Ron Moler
Reasonable Doubt	Principal	Party Animal	Dir. Eric Delabarre
Played	Principal	AK47 Armed Bartender	Dir. Michael Valenzuela

TELEVISION (Partial List)

St. Peter: The Rock	Lead - Mary Magdalene	Biblical Lady	History Channel
The Most	Lead - Vendela	Roman Vestal Virgin	History Channel
Only Joking	Lead - Kelly Maxwell	Witty Customer	FOX
The Vice of Living	Guest Star - Martha	Lovesick Drug Dealer	Telemundo
Let's Talk About Sex	Supporting	Live Co-Host	ABC
The Donner Party	Co-Star	Starving Pilgrim	History Channel
The Hunters	Co-Star	Supernatural Vampire	CBS
Moesha	Principal	Deranged Stalker	UPN Television
The Parkers	Principal	College Student	UPN Television

THEATRE (Partial List)

A Midsummer Night's Dream	Lead - Helena	Channelview Theatre
The Crucible	Lead - Abigail	Channelview Theatre
Cat on a Hot Tin Roof	Lead - Margaret	Channelview Theatre
A Streetcar Named Desire	Lead- Blanche	Channelview Theatre
A Rose for Emily	Lead - Emily	Galena Park School of Art
Hello, From Bertha	Lead - Bertha	Galena Park School of Art
In the Boom Boom Room	Lead - Susan	Galena Park School of Art

TRAINING (Partial List)

Improv/Comedy	The Groundling
Motion Picture and TV Acting	Van Mar Academy/Ivan Markota
Scene Study/Camera Technique	John Sarno Actor's Studio
Voice-Over and Looping	Kalmenson and Kalmenson

Voice Training   Lisa Popeil Voice Works

<u>SKILLS</u>
Languages: Fluent in Spanish
Singer: Soprano - Low C# to Super High G (3½ Octaves)
Dance: Choreographed Performances, Social Dancer, Club, Rave, Salsa, Ballroom, Hip-Hop, Country
Dialects: Standard American, NY, Southern and Southwestern U.S., Standard British and Australian
Looping and Voice-Over: Narrative, Commercial and Character Voices, Radio Broadcasting Internship
Sports: All Winter & Water Sports, Kickboxing, Firearms, Snow Boarding, Snow Skiing, Bungee Jumping,
Sky Diving, Horseback Riding, Volleyball, Tennis, Racquetball, Bike Marathons, Hiking, Fishing, Roller Skating, Photography, Drawing, Writing, Billiards, Parasailing

Commercials, Industrials, Music Videos, Voice-Over, Print Work,
Affiliations, Special Events, Etc

Demo Reel Available Upon Request

Kelly Taylor Contact:

Cavaleri & Associates
178 S. Victory Blvd; Suite 205
Burbank, CA 91502
Website: www.kellytaylor.biz

Christy Moore

Favorite Quote:

"Leap and the net will appear."

Christy Moore

Profile

Christy Moore is a passionate and dedicated actress. She got her start in the musical "Guys and Dolls" six years ago and hasn't stopped since. Christy has continued to study her craft while working in television, film, and on stage. Her work includes hosting the highly rated show, "Comedy Night School." Christy holds a Bachelor of Arts Degree in Psychology and continues her education through film and music classes.

She can be seen in "Making the Grade," "Characters" and "Gifted."

Christy Moore

Resume

SAG Eligible

FILM/TELEVISION

COMEDY NIGHT SCHOOL	Host	Gordon Tynes Productions
LEGION OF RYU	Keely/Lead	Legion Films
I LOVE YOU	Michelle/Lead	One More Second Productions
G.P.F.	Laura/Lead	Dir. Thor Trammel
MAKING THE GRADE	Madeline/Lead	Dir. J. Anthony D'Aguiar
CHARACTERS	Darcy/Principal	Dir. Jason Sorrell
SWEETS	Marcie / Principal	Dir. Ren Morrison
KING PATHETIC CREEP	Damsel in Distress/Principal	Dir. Todd Thompson
VIRGINS	Cinderella Girl/Featured	Dir. Glenn Mobley
GIFTED	Club Girl/Featured	Dir. Bob DeRosa
SHEENA QUEEN OF THE JUNGLE	Cult Member/Featured	Corsica Productions

THEATRE

OUR TOWN	Emily	Sands Theatre
SHAKERS	Carol	Orlando Fringe Festival '01
THEY CALL ME MITZI	Elaine	Orlando Fringe Festival '00
FOURPLAY	Vera	Performance Space Orlando
THE RIMERS OF ELDRITCH	Patsy	Seminole Comm. College
TELL US WHAT WE'VE WON	Lexi	Play de Luna
THE HOLDING	Julie	Play de Luna

COMMERCIALS/INDUSTRIALS

MILLER LITE	Spokesmodel/Principal	GMR Productions
SONNY'S	Sexy Babe/Principal	Alphawolf Productions
SKY T.V.	Fun Loving Teen/Principal	Television Arts, Inc.
CONVERGYS	Customer Support Rep/Principal	Beyond Reality Productions
VERIZON WIRELESS	Trendy Hairdresser/ Principal	EMM Group

THEME PARKS/LIVE CONVENTION

BILL AND TED ALMIGHTY	Charlie's Angel	Universal Studios Florida
STAR WARS WEEKENDS	Queen Amidala	Disney MGM/Lucas Films
FANTILLUSION!	Cinderella/Ariel/Belle	Tokyo Disneyland
FANTASMIC!	Ariel/Belle/Snow White	Disney's MGM Studios
DISNEY'S INTERNATIONAL SONGBOOK	Belle/Snow White	Disney's Epcot

EDUCATION/TRAINING

UNIVERSITY OF CENTRAL FLORIDA	Bachelor of Arts Psychology
FULL SAIL PRODUCTIONS	Casting Seminar with Bob Kahn
ART'S SAKE ACTING STUDIO	Scene Study & Meisner with Yvonne Suhor (Most Memorable Award)
ART'S SAKE ACTING STUDIO	Working Actor & Meisner with Yvonne Suhor
ART'S SAKE ACTING STUDIO	Advanced Intensive Meisner with Yvonne Suhor
ART'S SAKE ACTING STUDIO	British Dialect (Cockney) with Simon Needham
DISNEY MGM STUDIOS	British Dialect (R.P.)

SPECIAL SKILLS

Dance (Hip-Hop, Jazz, Ballet), Horseback Riding (English and Western), Ice Skating, Rollerblading, Water-skiing, Cheerleading, Bartending, Snorkeling, Cliff diving, Waving (left and right)
Dialects: British, Irish, Southern

Christy Moore Contact:

Manager Laura Walsh
Central Artists
3310 West Burbank Blvd.
Burbank, CA 91505
Phone: 818-557-8284

James Caan

James Caan

Profile

One of the most versatile actors in motion pictures, James Caan is best known for his Academy Award nominated performance as Sonny Corleone in "The Godfather" and for his Emmy-nominated portrayal of football star Brian Piccolo in "Brian's Song."

Appearing in more than 50 feature films over the course of his career, Caan also earned great recognition starring in Rob Reiner's highly successful and critically acclaimed film "Misery," a psychological thriller based on the novel by Stephen King and in "For The Boys," a romantic drama co-starring Bette Midler. He was equally praised for his performance as a brain damaged football star in Francis Ford Coppola's "The Rain People," garnering him the Best Actor Award from the San Sebastian Film Festival. He also received the Actor of the Year honor from the National Association of Theatre Owners for his role in "The Gambler."

Born in the Bronx and raised in Queens, New York, Caan knew early on that he did not want to follow in his father's footsteps and work in the family meat business. He entered Michigan State University at age sixteen to study economics and to play football.

Caan transferred to Hofstra University to study law and during a spring break was interviewed by, and accepted to Sanford Meisner's Neighborhood Playhouse. He then won a scholarship to study with Wynn Handman, and went on to get the first four jobs he auditioned for in the theatre.

Caan began his career on stage in the 1961 off-Broadway production of "La Ronde." He followed with a powerful slate of guest appearances in virtually every major television series of the day.

In addition to the previously named titles, Caan's other film credits include "Cinderella Liberty," "Funny Lady," "A Bridge Too Far," "Thief," "T.R. Baskin," "Slither," "Silent Movie," "Rollerball," "The Killer Elite," "Another Man, Another Chance," "Comes A Horseman," "Gardens Of Stone," "Alien Nation," "Flesh and Bone," "The Program," "Honeymoon In Vegas," "Eraser," and "Mickey Blue Eyes."

He also starred in "The Yards," for Miramax Films, opposite Joaquin Phoenix, Mark Wahlberg and Charlize Theron, and Artisan Entertainment's "The Way of the Gun," in which he co-starred with Benicio Del Toro. He directed, as well as starred in, the critically acclaimed film "Hide In Plain Sight."

Caan was also seen in MGM/UA's "City of Ghosts," with Matt Dillon, and in the New Line Cinema comedy "Elf," in which he co-stars with Will Ferrell, and Lars von Trier's "Dogville," co-starring Nicole Kidman.

James Caan can currently be seen starring as Ed Deline in the NBC Drama, "Las Vegas."

James Caan Contact:

Rogers & Cowan
1888 Century Park East Fifth Floor
Los Angeles, CA 90067
Phone: 310-201-8800

Niecy Nash

Niecy Nash

Profile

Niecy Nash was sitting in her grandmother's living room at the tender age of 5, when she first witnessed an elegant black actress grace her television screen. From the sight of the luminous Lola Falana, Niecy decided "I am going to become that woman!"...A beautiful and glamorous actress, which she has successfully done (picking up the nickname "Lola" along the way). She is living out the dream of every Hollywood actress, and has starred in three TV projects! Her work includes hosting Style Network's home-makeover series, "Clean House" as well as starring in two series on Comedy Central: "Reno 911!," a thirty minute unscripted comedy and the animated series Kid Notorious a.k.a. the "Robert Evans Show." Though born and raised in Los Angeles, Niecy has never considered herself an "LA Girl," she is too honest and real for that stereotype. After spending much of her childhood in St. Louis, she returned to Los Angeles at the age of nine, with her future already determined and the quest to become a performer dominating her life. Throughout school and especially during high school she put most of her time and energy into improving her performance skills. She excelled particularly in dramatic interpretation, prose and poetry, winning numerous high school Forensic competitions.

Niecy continued her education at Cal State Dominguez Hills, where she majored in Theatre. She graduated with a BA, a husband, a baby...and a mission. Soon after graduation, determined to make a name for herself, Niecy made a fateful decision to call a casting director for whom she had auditioned months earlier. When he answered the phone she said, "I don't know if you remember me. I'm Niecy Nash, I'm broke, I've got a baby, and I need a job." He told her to come down to his office and audition for his new movie. Needless to say, she blew them away and landed her first paid gig in a scene opposite Whoopi Goldberg in "Boys On The Side." Since that significant day, Niecy has turned in stunning performances in many feature films. She co-starred in Robert Altman's "Cookie's Fortune" opposite Glenn Close, Julianne Moore and Liv Tyler, "The Bachelor" with Chris O'Donnell and the indie feature "Em & Me." Niecy also co-starred in "Malibu's Most Wanted" alongside Jamie Kennedy, Anthony Anderson, and Taye Diggs. Her television credits are another testament to her talent. Included are recurring roles in CBS's "Presidio Med," "That's Life," "Popular," and "City of Angels." In addition, she has had guest-starring roles on "NYPD Blue," "One on One," "Judging Amy," "Reba," "Girlfriends," "That's so Raven," and the Emmy Award winning comedy, "The Bernie Mac Show," where Niecy played Bernie's sister Auntie Benital.

Niecy Nash Contact:

Shannon Barr Public Relations
3619½ Crest Dr.
Manhattan Beach, CA 90266
Phone: 310-546-5069

Michael Stever

Michael Stever

Profile

   Michael has worked extensively in the theatre for over fifteen years. College years found Michael pursuing majors in writing, communications and media production. Since then, he has come to officially call New York City his home and has racked up some pretty impressive theatrical and TV credits of his own. He has worked as a production manager on the epic documentary film "Broadway; The Golden Age." Past credits also include the role of Joe Hardy in NETwork's National Tour of "Damn Yankees," Diesel in a Berlin-based Broadway production of "West Side Story," Mortimer Brewster in "Arsenic And Old Lace" opposite theatre legends Betty Garrett and Carole Cook at the prestigious Papermill Playhouse, "The Radio City Christmas Spectacular," not to mention a hilarious fight scene opposite the notorious Traci Lords in an episode of the Sci-Fi series "Super Force." Along with performing Michael has also been sharpening his writing skills. He has finished his first play, a dark tale of Vampirism in 16th century Romania. He has also done several feature length screenplays, 2 of which are collaborations with actress Morgan Brittany whom many remember as the villainous Katherine Wentworth on the hit TV series "Dallas." Michael is also a great fan of Fay Wray and anything to do with King Kong.

Michael Stever

Resume

OFF BROADWAY

Masquerade	Singer/Dancer	Rios Moore Prod./Paris Club Kapt. Banana - SoHo

NATL./EUROPEAN TOURS

Damn Yankees '97-'98	Joe Hardy	NETworks L. L. C.
Mame w/Morgan Brittany '96-'97	Ralph Divine/Patrick	Bit League Theatrical/NYC
West Side Story/Berlin sit-down '96	Diesel/Riff	WolfGang Bocksch Concerts/ Berlin

THEATRE/MUSICALS/REVUES

Arsenic and Old Lace w/Betty Garrett & Carole Cook	Mortimer	U.C.O. Prod./Oklahoma City
Radio City Christmas-M. Beach SC '99	Singer	Radio City Prod./NYC
Grease	Kenickle	TriArts Prod./Sharon Playhouse CT
A Mid Summer Night's Dream '99	Oberon	A.C.B.T.-Atlantic City
A Shirley Jones Christmas '98	Lead singer/dancer	University of Central Oklahoma
Oliver w/Aileen Quinn	Bow St. runner- pauper	Papermill Playhouse / Millburn NJ
The Will Rogers Follies	Wrangler/Indian solo	Gateway/Candlewood Playhouse
South Pacific	G.I.	Papermill Playhouse/Millburn NJ
Hello Hollywood Hello	Singer/Dancer	Don Arden/MGM Grand/ Reno
West Side Story	Riff	Ron Cisneros/Showstoppers Prod.
A Chorus Line	Al	"
Chicago	Ensemble	"
Edwin Drood w/Helen Reddy	Barker	Sacramento Civic Light Opera
Carousel w/Peter Reckell	Ensemble	"
Best Little Whorehouse in Texas w/Juliet Prowse	Aggie	"

FILM/TELEVISION

Super Force w/Traci Lords	Mike (principal alien- abductee)	Universal Studios FL/ Viacom T.V.
Quick Cable Fables	Principal	Sacramento Cable Foundation
New Generations – teen news program	Lead Anchor	KXTV Channel 10/Sacramento
History of Broadcasting	Anchor-interviewer	Sacramento Cable Foundation

EMCEE/DEMONSTRATOR

Toy Fair '96 – '97	Demonstrator	Hasbro Co./Parker Bros.
Superstar Television	Emcee	Walt Disney Co./Orlando FL

TRAINING

Scene Study, Musical Theatre, Technique, Vocal Workshop – Betty Buckley
Cold Reading, Technique, Scene Study – Mel Johnson CSA

48

Voice	Betty Buckley/Ron Raines - NYC/Doug Houston – Broadway Dance Center
	Doris Butch – Orlando Comm. College/Sheila Sparr – Reno/Jeri Clinger –
	Sacramento
Dance	Jazz – Chet Walker, Ballet – Gabriella Darvash/Broadway Dance Center
	Ron Cisneros – Jazz, Tap, Ballet/Sacramento

SPECIAL SKILLS
Tennis, Bicycling, Swimming, Ice Skating, Rollerblading, Snow Skiing;
Stick shift driver, Stage Combat, Deep-guttural demon voice

Michael Stever Contact:

Showho Productions
422 West 56th St.
New York City, NY 10019
Phone: 212-582-6072

Shirley MacLaine

Shirley MacLaine

Profile

The dazzling star of almost 50 motion pictures, Shirley MacLaine is a multi-talented personality who has entertained millions all over the world in some of the most memorable film roles of the motion picture industry. She acts, sings, dances, writes, produces, directs, travels and takes an active part in human causes. And she does it all with equal expertise. Always interested in new challenges, in 1999 she expanded her achievements by becoming a motion picture director on the critically-acclaimed independent film "Bruno," in which she also plays a major role with co-stars Kathy Bates, Gary Sinise, Jennifer Tilly, Brett Butler and 10-year-old Alex Linz in the title role. The following year she embarked on another challenge with her own website, www.shirleymaclaine.com, which drew more than 20,000,000 in its debut weeks on the internet. Her latest critical triumph came with the title role of famed cosmetics queen Mary Kay Ash in the CBS telemovie, "Hell On Heels: The Battle of Mary Kay."

A dancer and singer at age three, Shirley was thrust into stardom when she was the understudy for Carol Haney on Broadway in "The Pajama Game." Haney broke her ankle and Shirley went on, drawing the attention of legendary film producer Hal Wallis, who was in the audience and immediately signed her to a Paramount Pictures contract.

MacLaine won an Academy Award for Best Actress in 1984 for "Terms of Endearment," after receiving nominations for "Some Came Running," "The Apartment," "Irma La Douce," "Turning Point" and, as a producer, 'The Other Half of the Sky." Additionally, she has received 10 Golden Globe Awards, two Venice Film Festival Awards, two Silver Bear Awards and a Golden Bear Award from the Berlin Film Festival and numerous other international accolades. Her television appearances have also brought her numerous Emmy Awards.

Returning to the stage in 1974 in a one-woman musical revue, she won critical acclaim and has played to sold-out audiences continuously in New York, Los Angeles, Las Vegas, Atlantic City and theatres throughout the country, as well as highly successful tours of England, Australia and major cities throughout the world.

An internationally best-selling author, Shirley has nine popular published books, including "Out On A Limb," which she also co-wrote as a successful miniseries starring Shirley as herself, on ABC Television. Her current book, "The Camino," which chronicles her 30-day journey on foot on the historic Santiago de Compostela pilgrimage through Northern Spain, marks her ninth best seller.

In 2001, Shirley united with three other icons of the screen, Elizabeth Taylor, Debbie Reynolds and Joan Collins, in a comedy titled "These Old Broads," written by Carrie Fisher. In 2003/2004, she starred in "Carolina" for Miramax and in "The True Story of the Salem Witch Trials," a CBS miniseries. Watch for Shirley in the soon to be released movie "Bewitched," based on the hit TV sitcom "Bewitched."

Shirley MacLaine Contact:

Dale C. Olson
7420 Mulholland Dr.
Los Angeles, CA 90046
Phone: 323-876-9331
Website: shirleymaclaine.com

Sheri Lawrence

Favorite Quote:

"Close your eyes, take my hand and see your beauty through my eyes."

Sheri Lawrence

Profile

Sheri was born and raised in New Jersey, now living in Florida for the past four years. She started her modeling career five years ago and has now fulfilled her childhood dream of acting. As a child she would write a scene, borrow some of her parent's clothing and together with her friends would act out the sketch. She's been involved in several local movie productions, music videos and commercials. Some of her roles consisted of playing the part of a doctor, nurse, scam artist, golfer, minion, femme fatale, tourist, spy, business rep and voice-overs. Sheri also dabbles in writing comedy skits. Ms. Lawrence has been credited with her Dr. Goodwrench sketch, which was recently performed at a local comedy club in St. Petersburg, FL.

She has a loving husband, two beautiful daughters and was blessed with a darling granddaughter. Sheri and her granddaughter modeled together for a Florida tourism ad. Although she had a late start with her filming career, she is thrilled to contribute her talents to the entertainment industry. She has also voiced an interest in producing and directing. With family support, love and encouragement she will continue to follow that dream.

When she's not working you might find her enjoying a day at the beach with family and friends, bowling in league tournaments or struggling with her golf game.

Sheri Lawrence

Resume

TV/FILM
Feature Films:

Reconciled	Monk	SRU Ventures LLC
I Am Vengeance	Nurse	Richard R. Anasky Productions
Bok Choy	Hetty Pitts	IMEX Productions
Live, Cry, Shampoo & Die		Yitibit Films
We're Coming to Help	Congresswoman Irene Weston	JD Casey Prods./Joe Casey
008	Female Spy	Hocus Focus Prods./ Jason L. Liquori
South Florida	Lead Doctor	Grimaldo/Trabucco Productions/Louis Grimaldo
Scammers	Lead Scam Artist/Sherry	Naked Zebra Prods./ Gregory Bearor
Scammers	Voice-Over	Naked Zebra Prods./ Gregory Bearor
Short Film: Perspective	Waitress/Flo/Associate Producer	IKO Productions
Filthy*	Female Lead/Fermentia	The Tinker Winns Productions, Inc.
TV Show: The Spot	Guest Appearance	Sam Hallenbeck Producer
*2003 Crystal Reel Award	Lead Actress/Short Film Category	

COMMERCIALS (Partial List)*

The Villages	Principal On Camera, MOS/Golfer	DreamWorks Prods.
The Villages	Principal On Camera, MOS/Tourist	DreamWorks Prods.
Island Gypsy Bed & Breakfast Motor-Yacht	Tourist/Guest	Island Gypsy Prods./ Chris Quinn
FlavorWave Oven (Infomercial)	Audience Member (Speaking)	Reliant Interactive Media
Thunderstick Mixer (Infomercial)	Audience Member	Reliant Interactive Media

*Conflicts Full List Available Upon Request

MUSIC VIDEOS

Stage Light Lover	Featured Female	Windsong Prods./William Rogers
Stage Light Lover	Minion Character	Windsong Prods./William Rogers
My City Life/Papi Frishko	Nurse	ANM Productions

THEATRE

HMO Mall Dentist/Comedy	Author	The Flor-Idiots Sketch Comedy Troupe/Mary Jane Heath Productions

SKETCH

Sketch Comedy Troupe	Writing Skits	The Flor-Idiots Sketch Comedy Troupe/Mary Jane Heath Productions

54

MODELING (Partial List)*

Cadillac	Spokesmodel/2002-2003	Gail and Rice Prods.
Buick	Spokesmodel/2003	
Malibu Rum	Spokesmodel/2002	Yo Soy Irini Productions, Inc.
Diet Rite Promotion	Spokesmodel/2003	Yo Soy Irini Productions, Inc.
Michael Caristo Photography	Stock Model	Florida Tourism Magazines
Dunedin Fine Arts Center	Stock Model	Commercial Print
Miracle Skin	Stock Model/2002	Texas Product Marketing Promotions

*Complete List Available
Upon Request

BACKGROUND

Associate Producer
Marketing/Promotions
Clearwater TV

TRAINING

Passaic County School of Dance/Vocal	Tampa, Florida
Phillips Actors Studio Workshop	Tampa, Florida
Rogers Actor's Workshop	
Trinity Players Acting Workshop	Richey Suncoast Theatre/Charles Skelton, President

SKILLS/ACTIVITIES

Dance: Jazz, Tap, Swing, Ballroom; Accents: New Jersey, New York, Italian; Voice-Over Writing: Comedy Skits; Web Design/Computer Skills, Drama Club, Modeling; Tournament Bowling, Golf, Boating, Tennis; EMS volunteer; participant in numerous fund raisers.

PROFESSIONAL MEMBERSHIPS

Florida Talent Team, Florida Motion Picture and Television Association (FMPTA), IndieClub/Tampa Chapter, Trinity Drama Club

REFERENCES

List available upon request

Sheri Lawrence Contact:

Email: sherilawrence@tampabay.rr.com
www.geocities.com/sherimodel/enter

Hector Elizondo

Hector Elizondo

Profile

Four-time Emmy nominee, Hector Elizondo, received the prestigious Emmy Award for Outstanding Supporting Actor in a Drama Series in 1997 for his portrayal of Dr. Phillip Watters on CBS' "Chicago Hope." He feels, "Watters is a multifaceted person and we are peeling the onion one layer at a time to reveal his inner-most feelings, as well as demons." Elizondo jokes, "I have little in common with Dr. Watters in real life. However, we both love basketball, boxing and playing the guitar." Hector is an accomplished musician and singer, performing on the conga and guitar.

Elizondo is one of those rare actors who continue to move back and forth freely between starring roles on Broadway, television and feature films. He was nominated for a Golden Globe Award for his portrayal of a hotel manager in the mega feature hit "Pretty Woman."

Hector's film credits include: "The Princess Diaries 2: Royal Engagement," "How High," "Tortilla Soup," "The Princess Diaries," "Pretty Woman," "Runaway Bride," "Beverly Hills Cop III," "Getting Even With Dad," "Frankie and Johnny," "Final Approach," "Necessary Roughness," "Taking Care of Business," "The Flamingo Kid," "Nothing in Common," "Young Doctors in Love," "American Gigolo," "The Fan," "Leviathan," "Report to the Commissioner" and "The Taking of Pelham 1-2-3" among others. "Pretty Woman" is one of his most renowned performances, winning him a Movie Award as well as nominations for both a Golden Globe and an American Comedy Award.

In addition to his big screen success, Elizondo starred in the critically acclaimed Broadway revival of Arthur Miller's "The Price," alongside Eli Wallach at the Roundabout Theatre.

Hector's numerous television appearances began with guest starring roles on now classic episodes of "Columbo," "All in the Family" and "Kojak." He quickly moved on to numerous television projects opposite such leading ladies as Michelle Pffeifer, Sophia Loren, and Candace Bergen. He played the starring role in the ABC miniseries of Scott Turow's "Burden of Proof." Hector received another Best Supporting Actor nomination for his riveting performance opposite Anne Bancroft in the two-character drama "Mrs. Cage," for PBS's acclaimed series, "American Playhouse."

A native New Yorker, Elizondo first gained recognition on the New York stage for his portrayal of God in "Steambath," which earned him an Obie Award. High praise followed for his Broadway roles in Neil Simon's "Prisoner of Second Avenue," "The Great White Hope," and "Sly Fox," for which he received a Drama Desk Award nomination.

Hector is especially proud of his involvement in the prestigious LA Theatre Works, a group of forty top actors who are devoting their time and talent to reinstating classic radio drama as a contemporary art form for National Public Radio (N.P.R.). Hector co-hosted the Environmental Media Awards with the poet Laureate Maya Angelou, with the keynote speaker being Mikhail Gorbachev.

Hector received the Diversity Award's prestigious "Integrity Award" as well as Nosotros' "Lifetime Achievement Award" for the quality of roles he has chosen during his career. Hector has done many voice-overs and narrations including Ken Burn's critically acclaimed PBS documentary series, "The West," as well as "NOVA," "The American Experience," and served as the host of the CBS special, "Mysterious Man of the Shroud."

Hector is often asked to be a guest speaker and serve as a role model for children. He is an avid supporter of The Alzheimer's Association, Amnesty International, The Creative Coalition, Pediatric Aids, and The Boys and Girls Clubs of East Los Angeles.

Scene from *The Princess Diaries 2*

Hector Elizondo Contact:

William Morris Agency
One William Morris Place
Beverly Hills, CA 90212
Phone: 310-859-4000

Trent Gill

Trent Gill

Profile

Trent Gill was born in Terre Haute, Indiana on Nov. 1, 1982. His family moved to Naperville, Illinois in 1991, where Trent attended Hill Middle School and was a serious athlete. He played baseball, football and was an All-State wrestler. His family moved to California in 1997 when Trent was fifteen and his sports obsession was soon replaced by his new love of acting. He was immediately recruited by an agent and began his career in commercials, appearing in several national spots such as McDonald's, Gateway, Dominos Pizza and Nike. Trent also has filmed an abundance of independent films before landing the role of "Jim" on MTV's "Undressed." He is a huge fan of horror movies and collects "Halloween" memorabilia. He lives in Burbank with his parents and siblings. His sister (Tia) also enjoys acting, while his brother (Travis) is an aspiring musician. Trent also has a passion for playing the guitar and takes music lessons.

Trent Gill

Resume

SAG/AFTRA

FILM	ROLE	DIRECTOR
LITTLE BLACK BOOK	Dan	Nick Hurran
POINT OF ORIGIN (with Ray Liotta)	Marty	Tom Sigel/HBO
SECOND CHANCE	Sam	David Wittkower
NIGHT BREAKS	Kenneth	Eddie Siebert
PARENTAL GUIDANCE	Nick	Sebastian Apodaca
IDENTITY UNKNOWN	Dean	Bill Pettijohn
ALCATRAZ AVENUE	Young David	Tom Edgar
HOLLYWOOD SIGN	Teen Prodigy	David Greenberg
OLD SOULS	Robert	David Kern

TELEVISION

NYPD Blue	Guest Star	ABC
Grounded For Life	Guest Star	WB
RENO 911!	Recurring	Comedy Central
THE GEORGE LOPEZ SHOW	Guest Star	John Pasquin / ABC
8 SIMPLE RULES	Guest Star	James Widdoes / ABC
7th HEAVEN	Guest Star	Joel Feigenbaum / WB
MAYBE IT'S ME	Guest Star	Bryan Gordon / WB
SO LITTLE TIME	Co-Star	Richard Correll / FOX
THAT 70's SHOW	Co-Star	David Trainer / CBS
JUDGING AMY	Co-Star	Arvin Brown / CBS
UNDRESSED	Recurring (Jim)	Tim Andrew / MTV
UNDERWORLD (Pilot)	Series Regular (Nick)	Todd Tucker
IT'S A MIRACLE	Guest Lead	Jim Lindsay / PAX
DREAMS CAN COME TRUE (Pilot)	Guest Lead	Barry Glaser

THEATRE

NEXTSTAGE	Lead	Chris Berube
STUART LITTLE	Lead	Dave Calvert
YOU CAN'T TAKE IT WITH YOU	Lead	Dave Calvert

COMMERCIALS   Extensive List Available Upon Request

TRAINING

Acting	Young Actors Space (Diane Hill-Hardin, Jamie Donnelly, Gary Spatz), Weist-Baron-Hill (Andrea Hill), Simply Acting (Andrew Magarian), Mary McCusker (Private Acting Coach)
Commercials	Aaron Marcus (New York), Susan Cash
Improvisation	Children's Theatre Improvisation (Chicago)

SPECIAL SKILLS

Accents	Midwestern, Southern
Sports	All-State Wrestling, Football, Baseball, Basketball, Swimming, Rollerblades, Billiards and Guitar

Trent Gill Contact:

Commercials Unlimited
Phone: 310-278-5123

Janice Lynde

Janice Lynde

Profile

Janice Lynde is a consummate industry professional who, while continuing to be in demand as an actress, has become one of the field's most sought after teachers. She has had a recurring role on the Showtime series "Resurrection," as well as co-starring in that same network's original movie "One Kill" which headlined Anne Heche. In that film, Ms. Lynde played the pivotal role of Sam Shepard's wife.

Janice's entrance into show business came at an early age when she toured as a child concert pianist. Later one of the many scholarships she won brought her to New York where the famed Actor's Studio accepted her. Ms. Lynde soon found a welcome venue for both her musical and thespian abilities: Broadway, where she starred in "Butterflies Are Free," "Applause" and "Pippin" directed by the legendary Bob Fosse.

Other stage highlights include an Obie Award for her work in the Joe Papp production "Sambo," originating the role of Carnelle in "The Miss Firecracker Contest," as well as receiving three Dramalogue Awards for best actress.

Television soon beckoned, where Ms. Lynde joined the original cast of the popular daytime drama "The Young And The Restless." Her portrayal of Leslie Brooks garnered an Emmy nomination, as well as four wins as "the most popular female star" in Daytime TV's annual readers' poll.

Janice's prime time credits include "The Odd Couple," "Quincy," "Dear John," "Who's The Boss," "Sledge Hammer" and "Night Court." Famed producer Norman Lear also created a television pilot specifically for her entitled "Roxy."

Small screen roles span such shows as "Nothing Sacred," "Promised Land" and "Touched By An Angel." Additionally Ms. Lynde has appeared in the television movies "Doing Time on Maple Drive" featuring Jim Carrey, ABC's "Question Of Sex" directed by Tom Skerritt and "Life of the Party" opposite Ann-Margret.

A sampling of feature film work consists of Garry Marshall's "Pretty Woman," "Missing Pieces" top lining Eric Idle, Robert Wuhl and directed by Leonard Stern, as well as "Letter to Dad."

Behind the camera Ms. Lynde has directed a documentary entitled "Still Young And Foolish." It tells the story of how Tony-winning composer Albert Hague escaped Nazi Germany for safety and artistic triumph in America.

As faculty at AFI, she imparts the actors' techniques in insightful, supportive ways. The analysis and interpretation of scripts are amongst her fortes. Ms. Lynde's specialty is fortifying the essential communication skills which filmmaking requires for success. She also gives seminars with noted teacher Joan Darling on "Directing The Actor," as well as having the unique distinction of being a frequently invited guest to Robert Redford's Sundance Institute.

Janice Lynde Contact:

The Artists Agency
1180 South Beverly Dr., Suite 301
Los Angeles, CA 90035
Phone: 310-277-7779

Ben Affan

Ben Affan

Profile

Ben was born May 25, 1980 in Casablanca, Morocco. When he was 17 his family migrated to the United States. He graduated from Sarah J. Hale high school in New York in 1999. He then moved to Orlando, FL where he attended Valencia Community College as a Business Major. To overcome his shyness, he started studying acting. After about seven months of attending acting schools, he began actively pursuing his dream of finding work as an actor. Ben has appeared in the films, "A Simple Gesture," "The Spell of Silence," "The Exchange" and "Passenger Removed" and the TV pilot "The Edge." He has also done theatre and commercials and can speak fluent Moroccan, Arabic and French.

Ben Affan

Resume

FILM

Aeolian Harp	Waiter	Yellow Bus Productions
A Simple Gesture	Paulo	Valencia Productions
A Day In Life	Photographer	Filmera Productions
The Exchange	Brian (lead)	Full Sail Productions
Passenger Removed	Detective	Filmera Entertainment Productions
The Marionette	Featured Extra	World Gate Entertainment
The Spell of Silence	Student (Featured)	4 D Pictures

THEATRE

Happily Never After	Prince Charming	Valencia Productions
The Ferris Wheel	John	Valencia Productions

TELEVISION

Astonishing News	News Reporter	Nippon TV Productions
Animal Planet	Extra	Animal Planet (Universal Studios)
Music Video	Extra	Corporate Advertisement Video
Music Video	Extra	Jeremy Hall (Lock Down)

COMMERCIALS

Cheez Doodles	Roman Guard	ACNE Film

MODELING

Nexus	Model	Nexus Hair Show
Nelly's Fashion Show	Model	Shy Figaro Show

INDUSTRIALS

Government Industrial Video	Principal	Mark Karvolty (Director)
Counter Terrorism	Principal	New River Productions Group
FATS Incorporated Firearms Training Video	Principal	Lael Camak / (USMC) US Marine Corp.
National Terrorism Preparedness Training Video	Principal	Mark Cogently / Media group management

EDUCATION/TRAINING

Act III Acting Studio	Karen J. Rugerio
Act III Acting Studio	Karen J. Rugerio
Art's Sake Studio	Yvonne Suhor
The Westside players of Valencia	Dr. Koory

LANGUAGES

Moroccan, Arabic, French, English (All fluent), and some Spanish.

SPECIAL SKILLS
Basketball, Baseball, Tennis (Challenging Levels), Billiards, Swimming, Singing, Soccer, Hiking, Cars (manual/automatic), Bikes (speed/automatic). Dialects (Arabic, French, Italian, and Spanish). Weapons (AK47, 9MM handguns, MP5).

Natashia Williams

Natashia Williams

Profile

Natashia Williams stars as the tough and sexy Shane, one of three female ex-cons pressed into service for a clandestine government agency and charged with bringing lowlifes to justice on NBC's action adventure comedy series "She Spies."

Williams says she absolutely loves her character, "Shane gives me an outlet for my aggressions; it's road rage that's OK." A lover of spy movies from a young age, Williams says she has some similarities with Shane, "There is a little bit of her in all of us. The love of excitement and a little bit of danger can turn boredom around pretty quick."

It was somewhat by mistake that we are even graced with Williams' presence on "She Spies." "I signed up for typing in high school, but was misplaced and ended up in drama class," Williams says. The teacher was so impressed with her work that she gave a tape to an agent and Williams started going on auditions. She landed a few commercials, which led to guest starring roles on television series like Damon Wayans' "My Wife and Kids" and "Son of the Beach." Williams' biggest role came as a series regular on The Olsen Twins' latest series, "So Little Time," playing Teddy, the neighbor. Not that she'll need that skill anytime in the near future, but Williams did eventually learn how to type.

Williams was born in Pontiac, Illinois, and her family moved to Los Angeles when she was in her teens. "It was a lot different than the Midwest," Williams remembers, "but there were more opportunities for everyone in my family in L.A." Her new "She Spies" family members are a big part of Williams' life now. "I'm having a great time with everybody on the show. We are all giving 110%." Williams laughs when she talks about getting in shape for the rigorous demands of the show, "I have a track background, but I'm doing more kickboxing now – a lot more kickboxing!"

Williams is happy about helping to bring the character of Shane to her full potential. "The writers have really given all of the "She Spies" women their own personalities, just like all of us have our own personalities in real life. It will be fun to watch each character grow as I get to know Natasha and Kristen better." "She Spies" is created by NBC Agency President and Creative Director Vince Manze and NBC's Vice President of On-Air Advertising Joe Levecchi, both of whom also serve as the series' executive producers, along with Jeff Reno & Ron Osborn ("The West Wing," "Moonlighting," "Duckman").

Williams tries to take it easy in her free time. "I'm giving everything I have to Shane; there's not much left for me at the end of the day. It's a really good feeling though." Williams' birthday is August 2nd.

Natashia Williams Contact:

Lisa Sorensen Public Relations
12522 Moorpark St.
Studio City, CA 91614
Phone: 818-761-0430

Richard Norton

Richard Norton

Profile

Richard Norton is a Martial Artist/Movie Star with over 60 films to his credit. He has worked alongside such named actors as Chuck Norris, Jackie Chan, Rutger Hauer, Joan Chen, Lance Henriksen and Patric Bergen.

Richard's career began in 1979 while on tour with singer Linda Ronstadt when he visited California and started training with his old friend Chuck Norris. Chuck offered Richard the role of "Kyo" in "The Octagon" (1980). Richard would later appear in Norris' "Eye for an Eye" (1981) and "Forced Vengeance" (1982) and since has guest starred in over 15 episodes of Norris' top rated television series, "Walker, Texas Ranger."

In 1984, Richard was invited to Hong Kong to co-star with Jackie Chan in "Twinkle, Twinkle Lucky Stars." He later starred with Chan in "City Hunter," making Richard one of only two western martial arts stars ever to be invited back to Hong Kong by Jackie to work on a number of projects, which in itself is a remarkable testimonial of the respect Mr. Chan has for Richard's acting and acting abilities.

Six years later, New Line Cinema theatrically released Chan's "Mr. Nice Guy," once again co-starring Norton and marking the third reunion of Richard and Jackie with longtime friend and star of CBS's "Martial Law," Director/Actor Samo Hung. Aside from Mr. Nice Guy, Richard's latest projects include starring in the action /sci-fi thriller "Nautilus" for Royal Oaks Entertainment, producing and starring in "Under The Gun," an action drama, "Amazons and Gladiators" for Paramount/Lion's Gate, another lead in soon to be released psychological drama "Mind Games" and most recently the action/drama, "A Man called Rage" where Richard starred alongside Lance Henriksen and Sherilyn Fenn.

Acting aside, Richard is also very sought after for his expertise behind the camera as a 2nd Unit Director/Stunt Coordinator/Fight Choreographer. He recently returned from working on the Warner Bros. syndicated television series, "The New Adventures of Robin Hood." He also worked as 2nd Unit Director/Stunt Coordinator on the feature films, "Amazons and Gladiators" for Paramount/Lion's Gate, another lead in the psychological drama "Mind Games" and the action/drama, "A Man Called Rage" and "Heavens Pond" starring Kip Pardue (Driven) and Tara Read (American Pie).

Richard's biggest accomplishment to date though, is landing the lead role of Sam Hill in the television series called "The Sam Hill Chronicles," with filming the principle photography in Melbourne, Australia. Richard will also serve as a producer on the series.

Richard has studied acting in Los Angeles at the American Theatre Arts, The Actors Center and with drama coaches Zina Provendie (former MGM Chief acting coach), Sharon Madden, Kate McGregor Stewart and Paul Elliot Currie.

Richard Norton

Resume

SAG

ACTOR – FILMOGRAPHY

Dream Warrior (2002)	Lead
Mind Games (2002)	Lead
Amazons and Gladiators (2001)	Lead
Redemption (2001)	Lead
The Rage Within (1999)	Lead
Nautilus (1998)	Lead
Path of the Dragon (1998)	Lead
Tex Murphy Overseer (1998)	Lead
Black Thunder (1997)	Lead
Soul of the Avenger (1997)	Lead
Strategic Command (1997)	Lead
Mr. Nice Guy (1998)	Lead
Fugitive X: Innocent Target (1996)	Lead
Tough and Deadly (1995)	Lead
Under the Gun (1995)	Lead & Prod.
Cyber Tracker (1994)	Lead
Death Fight (1994)	Lead
Direct Hit (1994)	Lead
Rage and Honor (1993)	Lead & Asst. Prod.
Rage and Honor II (1993)	Lead & Asst. Prod.
City Hunter (1992)	Lead
Iron Heart (1992)	Lead
Lady Dragon (1992)	Lead
Raiders of the Sun (1991)	Lead
China O'Brien (1990)	Lead
China O'Brien II (1991)	Lead
Future Hunters (1989)	Lead
Sword of Bushido (1989)	Lead
Hyper Space (1989)	Lead
Blood of Heroes (1988)	Featured
Not Another Mistake (1985)	Lead
The Fighter (1987)	Lead
Return of the Kick Fighter (1987)	Lead
Equalizer 2000 (1986)	Lead
Millionaire's Express (1986)	Featured
Jade Crystal (1986)	Lead

GymKata (1985)	Lead
Twinkle Twinkle Lucky Stars (1985)	Lead
American Ninja (1985)	Lead
Forced Vengeance (1985)	Featured
Force Five (1981)	Lead
The Octagon (1980)	Featured

TELEVISION - SERIES

Walker, Texas Ranger (1993-2001)
15 Episodes
New Adventures of Robin Hood (1997-2000) – 50 Episodes
Rising Sun
Kung Fu-The Legend Continues

STUNTS/FILMOGRAPHY

Dream Warrior (2002) – 2nd Unit Dir/Stunt Coordinator
Amazons and Gladiators (2001) – 2nd Unit Dir/Stunt Coordinator
The New Adventures of Robin Hood (1997-2002) – 2nd Unit Dir/ Stunt Coordinator
GymKata (1985) – Stunt Coordinator
Under The Gun (1995) – Fight Coordinator
Death Fight (1994) – Fight Coordinator
Guardian Angel (1994) – Fight Coordinator
Walker, Texas Ranger – Fight Coordinator
Not Another Mistake – Fight Coordinator
Raiders of the Sun (1992) – Fight Coordinator

Richard Norton Contact:

Cavaleri & Associates
178 S. Victory Blvd., Suite 205
Burbank, CA 91502
Phone: 818-955-9300

Bob Tella

Favorite Quote:

"Nothing's impossible."

Bob Tella

Profile

Bob Tella was born in Medford, Massachusetts. He thought he only wanted to be a singer but as time went on, he realized a good vocalist would act the song he sings and not just stand there and sing the song. So he studied acting with Spiro Veloudous at the Lyric Stage Theatre in Boston and film & television acting with Susan Willet and Angela Peri at Boston Casting and Ken Cheeseman at Collinge Pickman Casting in Boston. Susan Willet used to be a casting director in Los Angeles with her casting partner Mary Jo Slater. Susan moved back to Boston and Bob was lucky enough to take her class and learn about her experiences casting actors in Los Angeles and how to hone his auditioning skills and how to be truthful in front of the camera. Ken Cheeseman is a working actor and works quite frequently in television and film. Working with him helped Bob tremendously on how to work with the camera.

In the past, Bob has been working with student films and in the theatre. He worked on "The Human Stain" up in the Berkshires and thought it was great to watch Sir Anthony Hopkins, Gary Sinise and Nicole Kidman work in front of the camera. He also worked on "Mystic River" directed by Clint Eastwood in Boston. Bob thought watching Eastwood behind the camera was like attending a Master Class!

Bob's favorite quote is "Nothing's impossible." He heard that said by Barbra Streisand in a movie awhile back and he adopted that phrase for himself. It pushes him to do his very best no matter how hard the task may seem at hand.

In his off time Bob loves to go hunting for antiques. He's always hoping he will find a Picasso behind an ugly old painting.

Bob Tella

Resume

SAG/AFTRA

FILM

Call Her	(Student film) Co-Starring	Jeffery	Kevin Ott-Director – Boston University
The Art Critic	(Student film) Co-Starring	Derek	Charles Castell – Director-Boston Unv.
Break Fast at Tiffany	(Student film) Co-Starring	Sam	Charles Castell – Director-Boston Unv.
Into The Black	Featured	Officer Odin	Green Monster Films – Mark Powers-Director
Mystic River		State Trooper	Clint Eastwood/ Director-Warner Bros.
The Human Stain		College Staff	Robert Benton-Dir.
Passionada		Towns Person	Sandyo Productions
Moonlight Mile		Towns Person	Brad Silberling-Dir.
What's The Worst That Can Happen?		Patrolman	MGM-Sam Weisman

STAGE

All My Sons	Frank Lubey	Jerry Lebel-Theatre Company of Saugus
Closer Than Ever	Ensemble	Nancy Lemoine-Theatre Co. of Saugus
GodSpell	Ensemble Nancy	Lemoine-Theatre Company of Saugus
Starting Here, Starting Now	Ensemble	Jerry Lebel-Theatre Company of Saugus
Jesus Christ Superstar	Various Characters	Brian Toomey-Next Move Theatre
Broadway in Song	Ensemble	Nancy Lemoine-Theatre Co. of Saugus
1940's Cabaret Act	Ensemble	Jerry Lebel-Theatre Company of Saugus
Grease	Teen Angel	Nancy Lemoine Theatre Co. of Saugus
Into The Woods	Rapunzel's Prince	John Safina-Chelsea Community Theatre

RADIO & VOICE-OVER

Sang on WHDH Radio for the promotion of Soda Products
Voice-Over Horror/Mystery CD Kevin Collins/Director-Producer-TCH Productions

MISCELLANEOUS

Performed in a cabaret group – A Touch of Broadway

TRAINING

Acting for Film-Ken Cheeseman-Collinge Pickman Casting, Boston, MA
Acting for Film-Susan Willet, Angela Peri-Boston Casting
Vocal Performance Workshop-Boston Center for the Art-Jere Shea
Advanced Monologue and Scene Study with Spiro Veloudous, Lyric Stage, Boston, MA

Acting for Film/Advanced Acting for Film-Actor's Workshop, Boston, MA
Acting for Film Workshop-Kevin Fennessy Casting, Cambridge, MA
Vocal performance studies with Mili Bermejo, Berklee College of Music
Berklee College of Music-B.A. Vocal Performance, Boston, MA

SKILLS
Proficient at Medical & Legal Terminology, Vocalist, Piano, Sight Reading

Bob Tella Contact:

www.lovethyjob.com/bobtella

Holly Fields

Favorite Quote:

"Make It Happen."

Holly Fields

Profile

You've seen her carrying her own opposite such actors as Michael J. Fox, Christopher Walken, Tobey Maguire, and Jennifer Aniston just to name a few. Madonna, Chris Carter, Burt Reynolds and Christopher Guest have hired her among many other greats. You've seen her face, but you may not know her name...yet.

Holly Fields was born into Hollywood royalty. Her great aunt and uncle were the infamous Slim and Howard Hawks. Slim was known for being a socialite gracing the cover of *Vogue* Magazine several times and Howard Hawks was known for being one of the greatest directors ever, directing "Gentlemen Prefer Blonds," "Scar Face," "His Girl Friday," "To Have or Have Not," etc.

Holly had entertaining in her blood from day one. She began her acting career at the tender age of 6 in Sacramento, California, when she understudied Molly Ringwald in "Through the Looking Glass." Her parents, wanting the family to have a normal life, moved to a small ranch in Garland, Texas, where Holly and her brother and sister grew up riding horses and playing sports and exploring the acres of land in their backyard. They were allowed to do theatre as a hobby as long as they kept up their grades.

Her parents gave in after seeing how much she loved acting and let her take it more seriously. By age 11 she had become a theatre veteran along side her brother touring the United States in national theatre productions and being cast in the Broadway hit "Annie." Soon after, she was starring in local TV shows, national television and radio commercials and modeling for Nieman Marcus, Jordash Jeans, Bloomingdales and many others.

At age 13, with Molly Ringwald's father's encouragement, Holly was allowed to come out to Los Angeles for one month as a summer vacation. A week after landing in LA she met Christopher Guest and Michael McKean and they hired her on the spot for their movie "The Big Picture." At the same time she was cast in the Warner Brothers/CBS pilot "Fort Figueroa" starring opposite Charles Haid. While she was in LA, her father was told he was being transferred back to California. Her parents decided to move their family to a small town outside of San Francisco. So Holly went back and forth working on many movies and TV shows when school permitted. She had many guest star, recurring, and regular roles on shows including "It's Garry Shanding's Show," "Married With Children," "Blossom," "Evening Shade," "Quantum Leap," "Macgyver," "Growing Pains," and "Touched By An Angel."

At age 14, proving equally adept with drama, she held her own along side Sarah Jessica Parker and Jane Kaczmarek in the Emmy winning "Equal Justice" where she played a child heroin addict who becomes a hooker to support her habit which ends in a deadly overdose. From people seeing her work she won the lead roles in "The Suzanne Somers Story 'Keeping Secrets'" with a sensitive portrayal playing the young Suzanne Somers and Joanna Kern's daughter in the award winning miniseries "The Big One, The Great LA Earthquake."

Holly graduated 2nd in her high school class and opted to move to LA fulltime. That year proved a good year for her when after a meeting with Joe Dante, he cast her as his female lead along side 'Ed's Julie Bowen and Paul Rudd in his Emmy nominated film "Runaway Daughters." She went right into her next film starring along side Christopher Lloyd in "Mr. Payback." This was the first interactive movie ever made. Thinking it would be the wave of the future in movie making, Sony Pictures signed Holly and the other leads on to do the sequels to "Mr. Payback." Unfortunately, even with the creator of "Back To the Future," Bob Gale, as the director and writer, the interactive movies didn't catch on as much as Sony had hoped and the 2nd and 3rd were never made.

Holly has gone on to play the leads in many other films including Artisan's cult hit "Wishmaster 2" where she plays the part of Morgana who wakes up one day to find the fate of the world on her shoulders and the independent film "Roomies" where she plays an innocent young southern girl who moves to Los Angeles and becomes corrupted. Along with these movies she has "Hip, Edgy, Sexy, Cool" that's been winning awards in the film festivals and the cult hit "Interceptor Force" among others.

In addition to filming "Sunflower," Holly has also filmed emotion-turning roles on "JAG" and "Charmed" and worked on the CD ROM of "Spiderman 2" as the voice of Black Cat/Felicia Hardy along side Tobey Maguire and Willem Dafoe. She is preparing for her next role as a girl who falls into the dark world of stripping and drugs in the edgy drama "Amateur Night." She is still working on her singing when she has time. She was signed to a record deal with Avex Tracks 3 in 1999 with a girl group she put together with Joey Carbone and toured in Japan with them in 2001. She has also recorded songs with Robby Nevil and Apartment 26 among others. In her time away from acting she loves to paint, write music and hang out with her animals and friends.

Holly at the premiere of *CQ*

Holly Fields

Resume

TELEVISION

The O.C.	Guest Star	FOX
JAG	Guest Star	CBS/Bellisarius Prods.
FORT FIGUEROA	Series Regular	CBS/Luis Valdes
SUNDAY FUNNIES	Series Regular	NBC/Gerry Cohen
HULL HIGH	Series Regular	NBC/James Keach/Kenny Ortega
EQUAL JUSTICE	Recurring	CBS/Michael Rhodes/ Bill Corcoran
CHARMED	Guest Star	WB
BRIMSTONE	Guest Star	FOX/Peter Horton
SABRINA THE TEENAGE WITCH	Guest Star	ABC
TOUCHED BY AN ANGEL	Guest Star	CBS/Terrance O'Hara
THE SENTINEL	Guest Star	UPN/Bruce Bilson
BRAND NEW LIFE	Guest Star	NBC/Eric Laneuville/Chris Carter
MACGYVER	Guest Star	ABC/Michael Caffey/ Winkler Prod.
QUANTUM LEAP	Guest Star	Alan Levy/Don Bellasario
IT'S GARY SHANDLING'S SHOW	Guest Star	HBO/Alan Raifkin/Alan Zweibel
EVENING SHADE	Guest Star	CBS/Reynolds/Bloodwirth/ Thompson
EMPTY NEST	Guest Star	NBC/Steve Zuckerman/Witt Thomas Harris
BLOSSOM	Recurring	NBC/Gil Junger/Witt Thomas Harris
MARRIED....WITH CHILDREN	Guest Star	FOX/Linda Day
GROWING PAINS	Guest Star	ABC/John Tracy
FALCON CREST	Guest Star	CBS
THE SUZANNE SOMERS STORY(MOW)	Lead	CBS/Luiz Valdes
THE GREAT LA EARTHQUAKE (MOW)	Lead	NBC/Larry Ellkin
SCANDAL IN A SMALL TOWN (MOW)	Lead	ABC/Anthony Page
THE DAY MY KID WENT PUNK (MOW)	Lead	NBC/Alan Levy/Don Bellisario

FILM

SUNFLOWER	Lead	Dir. Cathy Ziehl
FANTASY WORLD	Lead	Dir. Michael Baumgarten
BEEHIVES	Lead	Dir. Jim Brakowski/Indie
KINGS HIGHWAY	Lead	Mandalay Entertainment
ROOMIES	Lead	Dir. Olive Robbins/Indie
INTERCEPTORS	Supporting	Dir. Philip Roth/Ken Olandt/Indie
WISHMASTER II	Lead	Dir. Jack Shoulder/Wes Craven/ Artisan
HIP, EDGY, SEXY, COOL	Lead	Dir. Erin Priest/Robert Martin/Indie
RUNAWAY DAUGHTERS	Lead	Dir. Joe Dante/Debra Hill/ Showtime
MR. PAYBACK	Lead	Dir. Bob Gale/Sony Pictures

THE BIG PICTURE	Featured	Dir. Chris Guest/Aspen Film Society
BLUE	Featured	Dir. Salome Braziner/Hershel Weingard
COMMUNION	Featured	Dir. Phillippe Mora
SEED PEOPLE	Lead	Dir. Peter Manoogian
FIRST ENCOUNTER	Lead	Dir. Redge Mahaffay
SPIDERMAN II (CD ROM)	Lead	Paramount

THEATRE

ANNIE	Lead	Casa Manyana Theatre
CHRISTMAS CAROL	Lead	National Tour
THE SOUND OF MUSIC	Lead	DRT
THROUGH THE LOOKING GLASS	Lead	Sacramento Repertory Theatre
GYPSY	Lead	GRT
WORKING	Lead	DRT

SINGING FOR FILM & TELEVISION, SOUNDTRACKS & ALBUMS AVAILABLE UPON REQUEST

Holly Fields Contact:

Manager: Toni Benson
Phone: 310-786-1936

Edward Asner

Edward Asner

Profile

Versatile, committed, eloquent and talented are all adjectives that describe actor/activist Edward Asner. Perhaps best known for his comedic and dramatic crossover as the gruff but soft-hearted journalist Lou Grant, the role he originated on the landmark TV newsroom comedy "The Mary Tyler Moore Show" and continued in the newspaper-set drama "Lou Grant," which earned him five Emmys and three Golden Globe Awards. Asner received two more Emmy and Golden Globe Awards for the miniseries "Rich Man, Poor Man" and "Roots." His prolific and much honored acting career demonstrates a consummate ability to transcend the line between comedy and drama.

One of the most honored actors in the history of television, Edward Asner has been the recipient of seven Emmy Awards and 16 nominations, as well as five Golden Globe Awards and served as National President of the Screen Actors Guild for two terms. He was inducted into the TV Academy Hall of Fame in 1996. Asner received the Ralph Morgan Award from the Screen Actors Guild in 2000, presented periodically for distinguished service to the Guild's Hollywood membership. In March, 2002, he was again honored by the Guild as the 38th recipient of the prestigious Life Achievement Award for career achievement and humanitarian accomplishment, presented annually to an actor who fosters the highest ideals of the profession.

In addition to his professional versatility, Edward Asner has consistently served and committed himself to the rights of the working performer in addition to advocating for human rights, world peace, environmental preservation and political freedom. A passionate and informed spokesperson for the causes he supports, Asner is a frequent speaker on labor issues and a particular ally for the acting industry's older artists. Some of the many honors he has received throughout his career include the Anne Frank Human Rights Award, the Eugene Debs Award, Organized Labor Publications Humanitarian Award, American Civil Liberties Union's Worker's Right's Committee Award and the National Emergency Civil Liberties Award.

Edward Asner has more than 100 TV credits, which include starring in the series "Off The Rack," "The Bronx Zoo" and "Thunder Alley." Numerous guest appearances include recent roles in "Dharma & Greg," "Curb Your Enthusiasm" and "ER." Besides commercials and various books on tape, he has lent his voice to popular cartoon shows such as "The Simpsons" and "Spiderman." Asner's dozens of motion pictures include "They Call Me Mister Tibbs," "Fort Apache The Bronx" "Daniel," "JFK," "The Bachelor," "Missing Brendan" and he starred in the highest rated television miniseries in the history of Italian TV viewing, "Giovanni XXIII," based on the life of Pope John XXIII. Asner was one of the stars of "Elf" for New Line Cinema and he has completed two TV movies: "The Man Who Saved Christmas" with Jason Alexander and "The King and Queen of Moonlight Bay" for the Hallmark Channel.

Edward Asner Contact:

Innovative Artists
1505 Tenth St.
Santa Monica, CA 90401
Phone: 310-656-0400

Rockmond Dunbar

Rockmond Dunbar

Profile

Rockmond Dunbar can currently be seen starring in the critically acclaimed Showtime original series "Soul Food," in which he portrays "Kenny," a hardworking family man and entrepreneur.

The essence of Rockmond is as intriguing as his name and as captivating as his on-screen presence. Named by *TV Guide* one of "Television's 50 Sexiest Stars of All Time," this Renaissance man has hypnotized his audience not only theatrically but also in all realms of art. From his provocative mixed-media exhibit, "ARTHERAPY," to his powerfully unforgettable guest appearance in Dylan McDermott's directing debut of "The Practice," Rockmond is undoubtedly one of Hollywood's hottest new up-and-coming artists.

His journey began with a series regular role in Steven Spielberg's "Earth 2" strapped under his belt. Once Rockmond arrived on the Hollywood scene, it was only one short month before he landed a recurring role on the now expired TV series, "Good News." To his credit, he now has over 9 guest starring roles on such shows as "Felicity," "The Pretender," "Two Guys and a Girl," "G. vs. E," and most recently the UPN series "Girlfriends." He also managed to book a series regular role for "Radio Silence" (Zalman King Productions) and a recurring role for "Bloomington Indiana" (Warner Brothers Television).

This talented, theatrically trained actor experienced yet another career boost when he secured four leading roles in various independent films, one of which debuted at the Sundance 2000 film festival and released in 2001, "PUNKS," Executive Produced by Babyface, and produced by Tracey Edmonds. Rockmond has also performed lead roles in "Love The Way," which premiered in June 2001 at the Acapulco Film Festival, "Sick Puppies," "Misery Loves Company," and "Whodunit."

Remarkably enough, Rockmond also claims writing, producing and directing titles to his credit. He just completed his script for a television drama series entitled, "Solitaire," which he is expected to executive produce and most recently made room on his plate to produce and direct a project for Showtime, which is slated to air mid 2003.

Rockmond is gaining favorable notices as a quality actor from producers, directors and audiences across the country. Once you experience his talents as an actor and artist you will understand why this young man is destined for great success.

Rockmond Dunbar Contact:

Lisa Sorensen Public Relations
12522 Moorpark St.
Studio City, CA 91604
Phone: 818-761-0430

Rachel Langley

Favorite Quote:

*"We don't need to see the top of Don's head, it's already been established
in the previous shot that he has a top to his head..."*
Marilyn Monroe on the set of "Bus Stop.

Rachel Langley

Profile

Actor, painter, writer, muse...Rachel Langley, a New York transplant from Rhode Island has been involved in the arts for numerous years. Over those years she has acted both in film and off-Broadway, some of her favorite roles include "Vicki" in "Noises Off" and "Marjorie" in "Extremities." Her greatest concentration now lies in creating compelling, cutting edge films both in short and feature length, while utilizing different techniques and collaborating with highly talented artists in all related fields to bring these projects to fruition. Her latest accomplishments in the industry include the 35mm production of her latest shot screenplay "Six Tulips" which has debuted at the Tribeca Film Center. On the acting front, she has had the privilege of lead roles in the short films "Love Child," "Henro" and the title role in a short she wrote entitled "Breaking Down Delilah." Rachel also made her feature film lead debut in the film "Getting Out of Rhode Island."

She never made a decision to be an actress. It was in her blood from day one. From the time she was small she was always acting or dancing and putting on some type of show. She feels it's a love/hate relationship, but there are no other choices. Acting and the industry is her passion. Her hobbies are watching people and watching city life. It's where she finds inspiration to write, to act, to paint, to live. Nothing is impossible. Her life is a dream to her right now and though there is so much more to accomplish, she could die tomorrow and know she did what she was meant to do.

Rachel Langley

Resume

FILM/TV

Wilted	Lead	Dir. Steve McMahon
Semantics of Suburban Despair	Supporting	Dir. Rob Myers
The Me Factor	Lead	Dir. Saul Braun
Molly's Bar	Lead	Dir. Danielle Leiser
Art of the Chip	Lead	Dir. Moira Boag
The Audition	Supporting	Dir. Bob Mead
Henro**	Lead	Dir. Ken Spassione
Love Child	Lead	Dir. Larysa Kondracki
Breaking Down Delilah	Lead	Dir. Duane Langley
Visible Past	Supporting	Dir. Will Gilmore
Amateur	Lead	Dir. April Hayes
Getting Out of RI*	Lead	Dir. Christian de Rezendes
Larry's Home Video	Supporting	Dir. Scott Caseley
Rivercrossing	Featured	Dir. Jake Diamond
Normal	Lead	Dir. Richard Griffin
Home Sweet Hoboken	Featured	Dir. Yoshifumi Hosoya

*This film was named Best Unseen Indie Film of 2002 on Filmthreat.com and official 2003 selection of BareBones Int'l FF, Back Alley FF, Black Point FF
**This film was an official nominee for the Seton Hall Film Festival 2002

INDUSTRIAL/COMMERCIALS   Conflicts Available Upon Request

THEATRE

God.com	One	The Producer's Club, NYC
Agony's Crash Comedy Group	Various characters	Kraine Theatre, NYC
Laugh Track Comedy Troupe	Various characters	Don't Tell Mama, NYC
Manhattan Towers*	Mona/Bambi	Don't Tell Mama, NYC
2 Steps in Left Direction	Penny	Dixon Place, NYC
A Bedroom Farce	Brenda	NADA, NYC
The Taming of the Shrew	Tranio	Hudson Shakespeare Co, NYC
The Golden Age	Vanessa Meyer	El Bohio, NYC
Comedy of Errors	Courtesan	Hudson Shakespeare Co, NYC
Extremities	Marjorie	Theatreworks, RI
Noises Off	Vicki	Pawtucket Players, RI

*Appeared in production from Spring 2001-Winter 2002

TRAINING

Longform Scenework & Improvisation	John O'Donnell, Upright Citizens Brigade (Fall '03)
Acting	Abra Bigham, NYC
Improvisational Theatre	Creative Acting Company, NYC
Screenwriting	Douglas Katz, Gotham Writers Workshop, NYC
Theatre Conflict Workshop	Hunter College, NYC
Scene Study	Studio One, RI
Actor Voice & Movement	Perishable Theatre, RI

SPECIAL SKILLS

Character improvisation, sketch comedy, Marilyn Monroe impersonation, Italian cook, computer geek, screenwriter, poetry, painting, founder Film Star & Company, founding member of AMT Collective

Rachel Langley Contact:

Peter Coe Talent Agency
Phone: 212-613-5792
Website: www.rachellangley.com

Elizabeth D'Onofrio

Elizabeth D'Onofrio

Profile

Elizabeth D'Onofrio, actor and instructor has worked alongside fellow actors Mathew Modine, Marg Helgenberger (CSI), Ben Stiller, and her brother Vincent D'Onofrio (Law and Order, Criminal Intent). Ms. D'Onofrio began her studies in New York City with Sonia Moore (Moscow Art Theatre) at the American Center for Stanislavski Theatre. She continued them with Sharon Chatton of the Actors Studio. Ms. D'Onofrio's film credits include, "Household Saints," "The Whole Wide World," "Ace Ventura," "The Velocity of Gary," Dr. Alex in the Indie Film, "Slice," "Lunch Box," and "Dear Angry."

Elizabeth along with her partner, Lis Anna, currently has a film production company, "Blue Rumor Productions, LLC," where she produced and played the lead in "The Chocolate Fetish," and Aunt Eddy in "Waiting for Jilly." She worked in several plays at the American Center for Stanislavski Theatre in New York City, such as: Tennessee Williams' "27 Wagons Full of Cotton," "The Fugitive Kind," and "This Property is Condemned." She has also worked Off-Broadway in Luigi Pirendello's American debut of "The Life I Gave You." Her resume consists of many Off-Off Broadway plays, Summer Stock, and she originated the role of Cissy in a Los Angeles Production of "Timing."

Ms. D'Onofrio gives instruction in the art of method acting which includes sensory work, improvisation, and preparing for a character. She is currently teaching "Acting As A Creative Art" classes at Brevard College and Blue Ridge Community College in Brevard, NC. Elizabeth has previously held classes at The Transylvania Arts Council in Brevard and at Gallery 31 in Asheville. Her acting seminars have been very successful. She has held Cold Reading, Scene Study, and Auditioning for Film workshops and seminars in the following North Carolina cities and film studios: Greensboro, Hendersonville, Blue Ridge Motion Picture Studio in Asheville, Film Studio in Charlotte, Talent One in Raleigh, The Atlantis Maritime Film Festival in Atlanta Beach, The River Run Film Festival in Brevard and Winston/Salem. Elizabeth has also traveled out of state for seminars she held at Women in Film, Callas, TX, and in Charleston, SC.

Elizabeth D'Onofrio

Resume

SAG/AEA/AFTRA

FILM

Waiting for Jilly	Blue Rumor Prods.	Indie Short	Aunt Eddy
The Chocolate Fetish	Blue Rumor Prods.	Indie Short	Christine
Lunch Box		Indie Feature	Bethel
Dear Angry		Indie Short	Nurse
Slice		Indie Feature	Dr. Alex Sanders
The Velocity of Gary, w/Vincent D'Onofrio, Salma Hayek			Dorothy (Homeless Woman)
"The Whole Wide World," w/Vincent D'Onofrio, Renee Zellweger			Mrs. Smith
"Ace Ventura II, When Nature Calls			Geri (Tourist Mom)
"My Name is Lisa Petrie"	American Film Institute		Elizabeth
"My Kids"	NYU student film		Amy

LA THEATRE

"Timing" originated role of Cissy The Globe Playhouse, CA

NEW YORK THEATRE

"The Life I Gave You" by Luigi Pirandello	The Classic Theatre, NY	
Fathers Day" one-act From "Holidays	Italian American Rep. Co. NY	Marianna Paolucci
"Hands" by Valerie Owen	Trinity Church Theatre, NY	Felicia/Deborah
"Lunchtime" by Leonard Melfi	Hoboken Theatre Festival, NJ	Avis
"This Property is Condemned" w/Vincent D'Onofrio	American Stanislavsky Theatre, NY	Willie
"Orpheous Descending" by Tennessee Williams	American Stanislavsky Theatre	Carol
"27 Wagons Full of Cotton" by Tennessee Williams	American Stanislavsky Theatre	Flora

REGIONAL THEATRE

"Yuppies and Yufu's	Transylvania Arts Council, NC	5 characters One-woman performance
"Passion" by Peter Nichols	Nomad Theatre, Boulder, CO	Kate
"Italian American Reconciliation" by John Patrick Shanley	Nomad Theatre	Janice
"Danny and The Deep Blue Sea" by John Patrick Shanley	Nomad Theatre	Roberta
"The Dark at the Top of the Stairs" by William Inge	Rhinebeck Barn Theatre, NY	Flirt

TRAINING

American Stanislavsky Theatre, (Four year program) – graduate 1983 NYC
Sharon Chatton of The Actors Studio – (workshop for professional actors) – NYC & L.A., 1983-1996.

SPECIAL INTERESTS AND SKILLS
Martial Arts, Instructor of Scene Study Classes, and Cold Reading Seminars
Currently Producing Indie Films with Blue Rumor Productions, LLC, "Waiting for Jilly," "The Chocolate Fetish" and "Faded Dreams and Faded Jeans."
Wrote and performed, Yuppies and Yufu's, a one-woman show.
Co-founder and VP of Bella Visione Film Society and The RiverRun Film Festival.

Elizabeth D'Onofrio Contact:

Email: eliza1023@aol.com

Mike E. Pringle

Mike E. Pringle

Profile

Mike Pringle's career began in 1989 in Philadelphia, PA where his first acting teacher was John Barth. He learned a great deal about the business from him, including excellent auditioning techniques. The skills he gained from Barth he still uses today.

In his "rookie" year he appeared on the local talk show "AM Philadelphia." Later that year he landed a spot on the national TV show, "America's Most Wanted," and that was done without an agent. Mike says, "The secret word is networking."

During the following years he went through a long dry spell. He believes it was a mistake telling everyone about his goals. During that time, he worked in a retail store where a co-worker hung up on anyone who called for him. He missed many auditions due to her actions. So now, Mike's advice to anyone new to the "Biz" is, "don't tell everyone what you are up to, only a select few, and get a cell phone or pager if you're always on the go." Another cause for his dry spell was lack of good representation.

Mike's career picked up when a kid's show, based on a popular board game and toy line, was in development for national television. They wanted actors with extensive children's theatre experience, but even though Mike didn't have much experience in that field, he was called for an audition. Out of thousands of submissions, the casting director narrowed it down and saw that Mike's resume had something he liked. Mike says, "Wait for no one, just do it. You never know what can happen." His current representative is excellent. She is Debra Phelps of Quiet Tip. She has acquired more work for him in one year than he did in five years with his other representatives. He has had an audition for "All My Children," thanks to Debra.

In 1996, Kurt Fitzpatrick invited him to an audition for his independent film called "Kin," and he was cast in the movie as a supporting player. Other films soon followed including, "Please Don't Burn My Beaver," "The Mommy Track," "Without a Badge," "Countdown to Extinction: Virgins Blood" and "Youth of the Nation."

Later projects include "Merc Force," and "UFAC." "Merc Force" is a science fiction comedy created by the multi-talented Jim Panetta. "UFAC" is a science fiction family comedy that Mike wrote and directed. Mike's current goals are to do animation voice-overs (he loves cartoons!) and to appear in TV Guide's Fall Preview as a cast member of a new series, standing among the other stars with his name spelled correctly.

Mike E. Pringle Contact:

Quiet Tip Management
Debra Phelps
NY Phone: 212-715-1839
PA Phone: 215-342-2272
Website: www.inmikescorner.com

Jeffrey DeMunn

Favorite Quote:

"It is better to sleep with a sober cannibal than a drunk Christian"

Jeffrey DeMunn

Profile

Jeffrey DeMunn was born in Buffalo, New York and graduated from Union College. He studied at the Bristol Old Vic in England and toured with the National Shakespeare Company. His films include "The Lucky Ones," "The Majestic," "The Green Mile" and "The Shawshank Redemption." He has also had the guest-lead on "Law & Order," "Gideon's Crossing," "The Fugitive" and "The Practice." In addition he has had many roles on Broadway and Off-Broadway. Jeffrey is married, has two children and lives in upstate New York.

Scene from *The Green Mile*

Jeffrey DeMunn

Resume

FILM

THE LUCKY ONES	Simon	Loren-Paul Caplin, Dir.
THE MAJESTIC	Mayor Ernie Cole	Frank Darabont, Dir.
THE GREEN MILE	Harry	Frank Darabont, Dir.
THE X-FILES (Fight the Future)	Bronshweig	20th Century Fox
BLACK CAT RUN	Bill Grissom	Citadel Films
HARVEST	Jake Yates	Goldheart Pictures
ROCKET MAN	Wick	Disney
PHENOMENON	Ringold	Disney
THE SHAWSHANK REDEMPTION	D.A.	Columbia
BLAZE	Tuck	Disney
THE BLOB	Sheriff Geller	TriStar
BETRAYED	Flynn	MGM
NEWSIES	Mayer Jacobs	Disney
FRANCES	Clifford Odets	Universal
RESURRECTION	Joe MacCauley	MCA/Universal

TELEVISION

EMPIRE FALLS	Horace	HBO
OUR TOWN	Editor Webb	Showtime/PBS
NORIEGA	Papal Nunzio	Showtime
CITIZEN X*	Andre Chikatillo	HBO/WB
STORM OF THE CENTURY	Robbie Beals	ABC
PATH TO PARADISE	Sam Simon	HBO
NIGHT SINS	De Palma	CBS
HIROSHIMA	Oppenheimer	Showtime
ALMOST GOLDEN	Rosenfeld	Lifetime
EBBIE	Jake Marley	Lifetime
DOWN CAME A BLACKBIRD	Rob Rubenstein	Showtime
BARBARIANS AT THE GATE	Grennus	HBO
WHO SPEAKS FOR JONATHAN	Frank	Cannell
BY DAWN'S EARLY LIGHT	Harpoon	HBO

SERIES GUEST-LEADS: LAW & ORDER (NBC), LAW & ORDER: SVU (NBC), GIDEON'S CROSSING (ABC), THE FUGITIVE (CBS), THE PRACTICE (ABC)

BROADWAY

OUR TOWN	Editor Webb	Booth Theatre
THE PRICE	Victor Franz	Royale Theatre
K2**	Taylor	Brooks Atkinson Theatre
BENT	Horst	New Apollo Theatre
COMEDIANS	Phil Murray	Music Box Theatre
HEDDA GABBLER	Tesman	Roundabout Theatre
SPOILS OF WAR	Andrew	Music Box Theatre
SLEIGHT OF HAND	Dancer/Geoffrey	Cort Theatre

OFF-BROADWAY

GUN-SHY	Duncan	Playwrights Horizons
ONE SHOE OFF	Leonard	Second Stage Company/NYSF
THE HAND OF IT'S ENEMY	Howard Bellman	Manhattan Theatre Club
THE COUNTRY GIRL	Bernie Dodd	Chelsea Playhouse
A MIDSUMMER NIGHT'S DREAM	Bottom	NYSF/Delacorte Theatre
A PRAYER FOR MY DAUGHTER***	Jack	NYSF
MODIGLIANI	Modigliani	Astor Place Theatre

*Emmy nomination/Cable Ace Award
**Tony Award nomination
***Drama Desk nomination

Jeffrey DeMunn Contact:

Davis/Spylios Management
244 West 54th St., #707
New York, NY 10019
Phone: 212-581-5766

Yeni Alvarez

Favorite Quote:

"Reach for the moon, even if you don't make it, you'll still be among the stars."

Yeni Alvarez

Profile

As an actress with great versatility, Yeni Alvarez has developed a successful career in television, film and stage. With the success of her sitcom, she entered the lives of 6.5 million Spanish-speaking households every Sunday as Anita Beltran, a young outgoing law student, who brings her Chicano newlywed husband into her parents' super Cuban household, in the hilarious Columbia/TriStar and Sony Pictures comedy "Los Beltran."

Audiences may remember Yeni Alvarez as the sassy hostess of "Miami Hoy," a TV magazine show, which premiered through MediaOne. She also garnered attention for her portrayal of Alina, a young Cuban girl who left her country on a raft, seeking a better life in the US, in the critically acclaimed feature film "Libertad," featured in many festivals across the U.S.

Born in Cuba, but raised in Miami, Florida, Yeni studied in the Young Actor's Workshop and at Marymount Manhattan College in New York City, and then back to Miami for her Bachelor's of Fine Arts Degree in Theatre from Florida International University.

Seeking new challenges, Yeni moved to Los Angeles in January 1999 and within one and a half months landed the pilot for "Los Beltran," which after two hugely successful seasons gained national attention for doubling the ratings for the Telemundo Network. "Los Beltran" received a Golden Eagle Award, Imagen Award and the Alma Award for "Outstanding Television Series," as well as two consecutive nominations for the GLAAD Awards against shows like "Sex in the City" and "Will and Grace."

Her projects include a guest star role on "Resurrection Blvd." for Showtime and a leading role in the film "Rogues" on its way to Sundance. She continues to live and work in Los Angeles, where she filmed, (opposite Jose Solano from Baywatch), the romantic comedy "In Hot Pursuit."

Yeni Alvarez

Resume

FILM

Rogues	Starring	Dir. Laurel Wetzork
In Hot Pursuit	Starring	Dir. Davah Avena
Brothers and Sisters	Starring	Dir. Jonathan Williams
Prisoner of Fate	Starring	Dir. Rakeda Ervin
Freedom	Starring	Dir. Norton Rodriguez
A Waste of Time	Starring	Dir. Franco Barbetti

TELEVISION

Without A Trace	Guest Star	CBS Productions
Judging Amy	Guest Star	CBS Productions
Resurrection Blvd.	Guest Star	Viacom
Los Beltran	Series Regular	Columbia TriStar
Sabado Gigante	Guest Star	Univision
Morelia (Soap)	Recurring	Univision
De Pelicula (Ent. Show)	Starring	Univision
Disney Superbowl Halftime Show	Co-Star	Walt Disney Prods.
Estamos Unidos (Pilot)	Starring	CIM Productions
Detectives	Starring	Falcon Productions
Miami Hoy (Ent. Show)	Hostess	MediaOne

THEATRE (partial list)

Paquito's Christmas (Musical)	Angela (Supporting)	Doolittle Thtr/Luis Avalos Dir.
Cuba and his Teddy Bear	Lourdes (Lead)	Arthur Hartunian
The Witless Lady	Finea (Lead)	Bilingual Found. of the Arts
Tropical Passion (Musical)	Lulu (Lead)	ALBA Productions
Las Impuras	Anita (Co-Lead)	Hispanic Theatre Guild
Dona Rosita La Soltera	Ayola (Co-Lead)	Hispanic Theatre Guild
Imagenes de Garcia Lorca	Various	Avante Theatre
The Good Times Are Killing Me	Sharon (Lead)	Coconut Grove Playhouse
Through Rosalinda's Eyes	Rosalinda (Lead)	Starving Artists Productions
LIC on Broadway (Musical)	Various Leads	LIC Theatre, NY
Oh, Grow Up! (Musical)	Various Leads	LIC Theatre, NY
The Handsomest Man	Diana (Lead)	Black Sheep Theatre Co

Commercials – List available upon request

TRAINING

BFA in Theatre, FIU; Robert Burgos (Acting Coach); Counterforce Actor's Workshop, Dan Chemau; Young Actor's Workshop, Bernard Rachelle; Prometeo Acting Group, Teresa Maria Rojas; Animation Voice-Over Workshop, Andrea Romano; Voice-Over Seminar, Mario Martin; FIU Mainstage Players; Coconut Grove Playhouse Summer Conservatory, Judith Delgado; Society of American Fight Directors, David Boushey; Hispanic Theatre Guild; Royal Chessmen; LIC Play Productions, Yetta Tropp; Black Sheep Theatrical Group, Neighborhood Productions.

SKILLS
Sing, Dance (Salsa, Merengue, Cha-cha, Mambo), Karate, Stage Combat, Stunts, Firearms, Swords (Rapier and Dagger, Broad Sword), Swim, Sports, Weight Training, Aerobics, Horseback Riding, Billiards, Jet Ski, Bilingual (Fluent in Spanish); Dialects – Cuban, Italian, New York, Argentinian, French, Hispanic; Voice-Over, Animation, and Dubbing.

Demo and voice-over tapes available upon request.

2004 Animal Avengers Fashion Show

Yeni Alvarez Contact:

Zanuck, Passon & Pace
Agent Michael Zanuck
4717 Van Nuys Blvd., Suite 102
Sherman Oaks, CA 91403
Phone: 818-783-4890
Website: www.yenialvarez.com

Danny DeVito

Danny DeVito

Profile

Danny DeVito, a bright funny man and marvelous floor-prowling storyteller, has been called the most likable person in Hollywood. As an actor, producer and director he has been called one of the entertainment industry's most versatile players.

DeVito wrote, directed and produced several short films in his early Hollywood years, before his emergence as a feature-length filmmaker in 1984, when he directed "The Ratings Game" for Showtime/The Movie Channel. In 1987 DeVito directed his first feature for theatrical release, "Throw Momma from the Train." That led to other directing projects: "The War of the Roses," "Hoffa" and "Matilda." DeVito also stars in "Death to Smoochy," which he directed with Robin Williams and Edward Norton. The film bears the DeVito trademark of darker comedic themes. In 2003 he directed "Duplex" starring Drew Barrymore and Ben Stiller.

In 1992 DeVito added another dimension. He partnered with producers Michael Shamberg and Stacey Sher to form Jersey Films, which has produced 18 motion pictures, including "Erin Brockovich," "Man on the Moon," "Pulp Fiction," "Out of Sight," "Get Shorty," "Hoffa," "Matilda," "Living Out Loud" and "Drowning Mona."

In 2000, yet another dimension emerged. Jersey Television was launched with the TV series "Kate Brasher" (CBS). Jersey also produced "UC Undercover" (NBC) and "The American Embassy" (FOX).

Though two films co-starring DeVito won the Academy Award for best picture ("One Flew Over the Cuckoo's Nest" and "Terms of Endearment"), it was the part of Louie De Palma that propelled him into national prominence as star of the hit television show "Taxi." In a 1999 readers' poll conducted by *TV Guide*, DeVito's Louie De Palma was voted number one in "TV's Fifty Greatest Character's Ever."

DeVito has also starred in many films not produced by Jersey. They include "Junior," "Renaissance Man," "Jack the Bear," "The Big Kahuna," "The Virgin Suicides" and "Heist."

Following "Taxi" and before the creation of Jersey Films, DeVito starred in such films as "Batman Returns," "Twins," "Romancing the Stone," "Jewel of the Nile," "Ruthless People" and "Tin Men."

DeVito attended Our Lady of Mt. Carmel grammar school and Oratory Prep School in Summit, New Jersey, but appeared in only one school play, as St. Francis of Assisi. After graduation, he pursued several odd jobs, always with the idea of acting in the back of his mind.

Finally he applied at the American Academy of Dramatic Arts in New York and was accepted. "They had fencing and a speech class," he said mockingly, "so you don't talk funny."

Graduating two years later, he made the rounds of open auditions "where you squeeze in with scores of other faceless actors and 15 minutes later ask the guy next to you, 'Hey, what's the name of this play?'"

Unable to get work, Danny bought a round trip-ticket and headed for Hollywood, where, he was sure, casting directors and chic people were gathered around pools waiting for him to walk into their lives. Not knowing Los Angeles, he took a bus to the part of town where he thought they made films and wound up spending his first night in California at an old downtown hotel.

After years of unemployment, Danny returned to New York. He called an old friend and former American Academy professor who, coincidentally, had been seeking him out for a starring role in one of three one-act plays presented together under the title of "The Man With the Flower in His Mouth."

Soon Danny was into big money ($60 a week), and other stage performances followed in rapid succession. Among his credits were "Down the Morning Line," "The Line of Least Existence," "The Shrinking Bride" and "One Flew Over the Cuckoo's Nest."

In 1975, under a grant from the American Film Institute, Danny and his wife, actress Rhea Perlman, wrote and produced "Minestrone," which has been shown twice at the Cannes Film Festival and has been translated into five languages. Later they wrote and produced a 16-millimeter black-and-white short subject, "The Sound Sleeper," which won first prize at the Brooklyn

106

Arts and Cultural Association competition. Danny and Rhea appeared together in five episodes of "Taxi."

DeVito carries his success well. Never forgetting that there were more difficult times, he maintains a healthy sense of perspective. As "Taxi" character Louie De Palma, would say, "If you don't do good today, you'll be eatin' dirt tomorrow."

Danny DeVito and Andy Kaufmann in scene from *Taxi*

Danny DeVito Contact:

Stan Rosenfield & Associates
2029 Century Park East, Suite 1190
Los Angeles, CA 90067
Phone: 310-286-7474

Allan Hale

Favorite Quote:

"The only ones that don't make it are the ones that quit!"

Allan Hale

Profile

Allan Hale is originally from Germany where he lived until the early 1980's. Raised in a military family, Allan's mother is German and his father is an American retired from the U.S. Army. He is the younger of two brothers, born on the 7th of July 1970.

This versatile actor gained experience in film, television and stage through dedication and perseverance. His ambition for acting evolved naturally when he was a young child. Family support for the profession without another skill or trade to rely on was not available. So, he made long term plans to achieve his goals and accomplish his dreams.

Allan joined the Marine Corps and served on active duty for four years, from 1989 to 1993. This experience taught him how to sing, clean, and be organized. Besides developing his discipline and maintaining physical fitness, the Marine Corps established an excellent base for his path. He was trained extensively in combat, law enforcement, and special security operations and was chosen to provide security for Marine One. Allan Hale may be seen in old news footage with Former Presidents George H. W. Bush or Bill Clinton near "Marine One," the Presidential Helicopter. Allan traveled worldwide on Presidential Missions, meeting many Heads of State, as a Security Specialist for Marine One Helicopters.

In 1993 Allan Hale worked for The Department of State in Washington, D.C. as a Special Operations Unit, Diplomatic Security Officer. He provided security at the State Department for Secretary of State Warren Christopher and escorted such dignitaries as Nelson Mandela. Allan lived and worked in Australia from 1995 to 1997 and in Moscow, Russia from 1997 to 1999 as a security specialist for the United States Government.

Allan's work on the set of "Born on the Fourth of July" directed by Oliver Stone in 1989 fueled his inspiration to achieve success in the entertainment industry. Ten years later, upon completing his duties at the U.S. Embassy in Moscow, Allan returned to Dallas, Texas. He intensively pursued learning the business of entertainment and further developed his acting abilities. The skills he acquired from his previous work experience would prove to be beneficial as he trained at KD Studios in Dallas and The Actors Place at the studios of Las Colinas. Traveling between Dallas, Austin and Los Angeles, Allan Hale developed business relationships with those in the industry and learned a lot from his mentor, Bill Erwin, a film & television star since the late 1940's. Allan also gained a lot of experience working on the set of "Walker, Texas Ranger" for twelve episodes.

Allan Hale moved to Los Angeles prior to the "Pilot Season" in 2001. He acquired an agent and began his career auditioning along with thousands of seasoned professionals. His skills obtained from previous work experience facilitated a position as a personal assistant to Will Boroski, CEO of Summit Pictures. Allan actively fulfills his passion in the industry as an actor, writer, and a producer. He stands by his motto: "The only ones that don't make it are the ones that quit!" This motto stands true for anything you may pursue in life.

Allan Hale

Resume

FILM

Codename: Walkure	Co-Starring	Dir. Matt Poitras
Tucked Away	Supporting	Dir. Billy Senese
Anacardium	Stand-In	Dir. Scott Thomas
The Lorwich Findings	Stand-In	Dir. David Howard
Born on the 4th of July	Convention Member	Dir. Oliver Stone
American Pie II	Band Camp Audience	Universal Pictures
Serving Sara	Shocked Monster Truck Show Patron	Dir. Reginald Hudlin
The Riff	Black Tie Jazz Club Patron	Dir. Mark W. Allen

TELEVISION

Politics (Pilot)	Starring	Dir. Clarke Lindsley
Cold War Even (Pilot)	Co-Starring	Dir. Clarke Lindsley
MTV-Japan-Yuki Koyanagi	Supporting	Dir. Yuu Nakai
Walker, Texas Ranger (12 Episodes)	Featured/Stand-In	Dir. Michael Preece
CNN International (1990-1993)	U.S. Marine Guarding "Marine One"	Turner Broadcasting
Hell Yes, I'm a Redneck! (Pilot)	Crazy Western Dancer	Gameshow Network
Mother of the Year 1992	Bodyguard	Dir. Hank Haynes

COMMERCIALS

Village Lincoln Mercury of Irving	Featured	Radiovision
Boardwalk Land Development	Principle / Regional / VOC	Spur Media / Rick Patterson
Personal Injury Attorney	Principle / Regional / VOC	Invision / Billy Senese

INDUSTRIALS

Durango Saddle Company	Principle	Zone 7 Productions
Majestic The Game.com	Principle	Majestic Productions
The Actors Place	Voice-Over	Dir. Will Boroski
Mary Kay Cosmetics	Featured	Dir. Margie Aguilar

THEATRE

Comedy Special	Bob Hope	Dir. Karen Zeske
A Christmas Carol	Ghost / Past	Dir. Karen Zeske
Dealing A Dose of Death	Host	Dir. Tim Newkirk
Who Wants To Be A Murderer?	Bob from Denver	Dir. Tim Newkirk
The Prince Who Couldn't Speak	Wizard of Thinkology	Dir. George Morrow

TRAINING

Voice-Over	Randy Tallman
Commercials	Clarke Lindsley / Tom Logan
Master Level Training	Clarke Lindsley / Will Boroski
Advanced Scene Study	Elizabeth Rothan / Shiela Anderson / KD Studios

WORKSHOPS

Andy Henry / Bill Dance / Bill Erwin
Ed Johnston / Eric Castro / Greg Sacks
Heidi Janssen / Jackie Margey / Marilyn Pinzur
Meryl O'Loughlin / Michael Hothorn / Rachael Harris
Susan Wiltfang / Tara Johnson

SPECIAL SKILLS/ACHIEVMENTS/DOCUMENTATION

◆ Current U.S. Passport/Class A Commercial Drivers License/Concealed Weapons Permit
◆ Former U.S. Marine Presidential Security Specialist/State Department Diplomatic Security
◆ Medical First Responder/Water Rescue Swimmer/Firefighting & Hazardous Materials Certified
◆ Counter Intelligence / Knife Fighting / Safe Manipulation & Penetration Certified
◆ Repelling / Horseback Riding / Snow & Water Ski

WORK HISTORY

1999 – 2003

Field Marketing Manager, TLC Productions
◆ Executed marketing campaigns for various clients in North Texas and Los Angeles.
◆ Recruited, hired, trained and managed staff on numerous branding campaigns.
◆ Developed strategies to achieve client goals.

1999 – 2003

Personal Assistant, William Boroski – Producer/Director, Summit Pictures
◆ Provided fluidity for the business and personal affairs of an energetic businessman.
◆ Logistics and support of every nature was accomplished in an organized manner.
◆ Gained a wealth of knowledge and experiences within the entertainment industry.
◆ Assisted with the progress of scripts and fundraising for independent films.

1993 – 1999

Special Security Operations Unit Officer, U.S. Department of State
◆ Managed security requirements for the construction of a Secure Chancery Facility in Moscow, Russia (1997-1999).
◆ Completed reports and created documents for review by other government entities.
◆ Provided government security services in Australia (1995 – 1997).
◆ Transported, controlled and destroyed highly classified documents and materials.
◆ Manipulated and penetrated GSA Safes and file cabinets.
◆ Provided protection for High Level U.S. Government Officials and escorted foreign dignitaries visiting the State Department (1993 – 1995).
◆ Top Secret, SBI, SCI, Polygraph Clearance.

1989 – 1993	*Presidential Security Officer, U.S. Marine Corps*

◆ Provided security for former President George Bush worldwide on Marine One.
◆ Top Secret, SBI, Yankee White Clearance.

ADMINISTRATION

◆ Ten years of administrative experience for a government client at major installations and facilities worldwide. Additionally, 3 years of administrative structure provided in the entertainment industry.
◆ Received the ISO 9002 Quality Improvement Award for organizational and administrative skills.
◆ Research and Analysis skills are fully developed for assignments that require attention to detail.

EDUCATION

◆ 54 Semester Hours, Business Curriculum, University of Maryland
◆ Law Enforcement Academy, United States Marine Corps
◆ Diplomatic Security, U.S. Department of State
◆ Special Security Operations, U.S. Government

SPECIAL SKILLS

◆ Terrorism Counteraction
◆ Surveillance / Counter Intelligence
◆ Investigations / Reports & Presentations
◆ Concealed Handgun Permit / Current Passport

Allan Hale Contact:

Dianne Hooper
Starcraft Talent
1516 North Formosa
Los Angeles, CA 90046
Phone: 323-845-4784

Paul Molinaro

Paul Molinaro

Profile

Paul was born in New Jersey in 1965. "Having lived a disease free life until after college, it was during medical school that Paul was badly infected with the acting bug. He started sneaking into New York City on weekends to study and after graduating from New Jersey Medical School in 1991, while his physician buddies went off to do residencies, Paul entered the full-time program at The Neighborhood Playhouse School of the Theatre where he studied with Sanford Meisner.

Realizing that he couldn't just let the medical degree go to waste, and that he needed money, Paul moved to Southern California and became a part-time Family Practitioner. Practicing part-time allowed Paul plenty of time to continue his studies at Playhouse West and several other schools in Hollywood as well as build his resume.

Never seeming to be satisfied with pursuing one goal at a time, Paul decided on one more career and began law school. He is now in his second year at Chapman University School of Law, which, not surprisingly, has a strong undergraduate film program.

With regard to his acting credits Paul is most proud of performing as James R. Douglas since 1993 in one of Los Angeles' longest running theatrical productions, "Welcome Home Soldier: A Tribute to Vietnam Veterans." Paul can still be seen in this play on the first Saturday of every month at The Playhouse West in North Hollywood."

114

Paul Molinaro

Resume

TELEVISION (Title/Role/Producer/Location)

Madison Heights (2 episodes)	ER Doctor (Key Supporting)	Peter Robinson, PBS	Los Angeles
Nothing to Lose	Game Show Co-Host	MTV	Los Angeles
The Kerry Mortell Show	Joey (Lead)	Mortell Prods	Santa Monica
My Back Yard	Louie (Key Supporting)	Cox Prods	Hollywood

FILM/VIDEO (Title/Role/Director/Location)

Sensitive Johnson	ER Doctor (Key Supporting)	Chris Valenti, SJ Prods	Los Angeles
The Lonelys	Larry (Key Supporting)	Henry Barrial	Los Angeles
DV8	Mr. Money (Key Supporting)	Scott Russell	Los Angeles
Hangman	Suspect (Supporting)	Ben Coltrane, BT Prods	Los Angeles
The Teddy Bear Syndrome	Timmy (Supporting)	Kacee DeMasi	Los Angeles
Thoughts on L.A.	Bill (Lead)	Bobby Duncan	Hollywood
Hitchhiker	Tom (Lead)	Aki Takemura	Los Angeles
Lunatic	Jimmy (Key Supporting)	Brian Dill	Los Angeles

THEATRE (Title/Role/Director/Location)

The Battling Brinkmires	George Brinkmire	Tony Savant	Hollywood
Hardstuff	Jon	Robert Carnegie	Hollywood
In Search of Iron John	Woodie	Scott Trost	Hollywood
Mental Floss	Multiple Characters	Chris Berube	Highland Park
Sticks and Stones	De Palma	Robert Carnegie	Hollywood
Welcome Home Soldier*	James R. Douglas	Robert Carnegie	Hollywood

Currently running in its eleventh year at The Playhouse West Theatre, with Paul as James since October 1993

DRAMATIC TRAINING/EDUCATION
Playhouse West (seven years), Hollywood
   Acting with Robert Carnegie, Jeff Goldblum, Tony Savant and Scott Trost
Neighborhood Playhouse School of the Theatre (1991-92 full time program), New York City
   Acting with Sanford Meisner, Martin Barter, Richard Pinter and Ron Stetson
   Ballet and Modern Dance with Barbara Cole and Bert Terborgh
   Speech and Voice with Jacklyn Maddux and Gary Ramsey
   Singing with J. Ronald Shetler
Margie Haber Cold Reading Workshops (starting 11/00), Los Angeles
   Cold Reading with Courtney Burr
Herbert Berghoff (H.B.) Studio, New York City
Hollywood Improv Players, Hollywood
Idiot Savants Improvisation Workshops, Highland Park, CA
Theatrical Education Workshop, Ridgewood, NJ

OTHER EDUCATION

Lafayette College	B.A. Biology	Easton, PA
New Jersey Medical School	M.D. Medicine	Newark, NJ
Chapman Univ. Sch. of Law	J.D. Law (2nd year student)	Fullerton, CA

SKILLS/SPORTS

Physician – practicing for over 10 years, expert in medical sciences, experienced in script consultation
Law – expert in legal terminology, current first year law student
Firearms – expert, life memberships in National Rifle Association and California Rifle & Pistol Association
Motorcycles – owner of mint condition 1985 Verago 700, can also drive a fork-lift like nobody's business
Natural New York / New Jersey accent
Sketch comedy writer and performer with strong comedy/improvisation background

Paul Molinaro Contact:

Website: www.actorsbone.com

Susan Blakely

Susan Blakely

Profile

Susan Blakely first gained international recognition as an actress for her starring role in the famed miniseries "Rich Man Poor Man," for which she won The Golden Globe for Best Dramatic Actress. She was also nominated for two Emmys for her performance in the miniseries. A winner again, Blakely received the Best Actress Award from the California Independent Film Festival, for her starring role in the movie "Hungry Hearts."

"Hungry Hearts," written and produced by Glenn Benest and Timothy Wurtz premiered at the Hollywood Film Festival, the Palm Springs Film Festival of Festivals, the New York Film Festival, and swept the awards at the California Independent Film Festival, winning Best Picture, Best Actress (Blakely), Best Actor (Greg Gardner), and Best Director, (Rolf Schrader). It was also selected as one of the top films for the Houston Film Festival and the Ft. Myers Film Festival in Miami.

Blakely stars in "Hungry Hearts" in a dark comedy which deals with the lives of four elegant women who have decided that they have had enough of the good life because it wasn't as good as they had hoped.

Blakely starred in the world premiere of "Diva!" at the La Jolla Playhouse, for playwright Howard M. Gould. Blakely's work in "Diva!" won high praise in the *San Diego Union Tribune* that said, "Blakely's performance never lets up. Her 'Deanna' is a force of nature...amoral, unstoppable...Blakely seduces us with her charm...Blakely's elegant, arrogant 'Deanna' is the engine that drives the show."

Adding to the success of the San Diego/La Jolla opening, Blakely is set to star in the Broadway production of "Diva" in 2004.

Blakely also recently completed starring in the film "LA Twister," which is to be released in 2004.

The multi-talented actress, Blakely has a number of interests and has recently created a new line of jewelry, which she designed for her website. SB Designs, consisting of semi-precious jewelry, which has received widespread national media attention, will be available on www.susanblakelydesigns.com in November, 2004.

Blakely, has starred in HBO's "Chain Of Command," with Roy Scheider, "Gut Feeling," "A Mother's Testimony," and "The Perfect Nanny."

Blakely is currently set to star opposite French superstar Thierry Lhermitte ("The Dinner Game") next year in a comedy that takes place at a Colorado ski resort. The film, which is entitled, "Dudes," was written by Patrick Read Johnson based on a story by Robert Hernreich, Billy Staobs and Annah Scully. Charlie Matthau is set to direct the snowboarding screwball comedy. It will be the first film produced under the UpStart Films banner, a screenplay development company in which she is a partner that was established by Stephen Jaffe and Daniel Howell.

Blakely, who Fred Silverman once called "one of television's all-time best actresses," starred in NBC's "Race Against Fear," as the mother of an aspiring Olympic track star played by Ariana Richards ("Jurassic Park"). This is the third time Blakely has played Richards' mother in a TV movie. The first two times were in the Emmy-Award-winning film (Best Picture), "The Incident" and the sequel, both of which also starred Walter Matthau and Harry Morgan. "Race Against Fear" was produced by O'Hara – Horowitz as part of their "Moment of Truth" series for NBC Television.

Blakely also starred in 1998 in the Lifetime Cable feature "Color Me Perfect," a movie starring the multi-talented Michele Lee.

Prior to that Blakely joined the international cast of "Seven Sundays" for Academy-Award-winning director Jean-Charles Tachella ("Cousin, Cousine"), in a comedy about two Europeans who come to Florida to find their dream. It starred Blakely, Thierry Lhermitte, Italy's Maurizio Nichetti ("Icicle Thief"), Molly Ringwald, and Rod Steiger.

Blakely starred as the naive spy-lover opposite Barry Bostwick in "Russian Roulette," which also starred E.G. Marshall and Jeff Altman. She portrays a Kansas schoolteacher who's seen as a tourist who gets caught in a web of KGB-CIA intelligence. The film was shot entirely on location in St. Petersburg, Russia (formerly Leningrad). Greydon Clark directed the David Reskin script. Stephen Jaffe and Patricia Lynch produced "Russian Roulette," the first American-Russian co-production to be filmed in Russia since the historic collapse of Communism.

Blakely's feature film career began with starring roles in two classics, one from the Oscar-winning team of Merchant-Ivory, "Savages," and the other "The Lords Of Flatbush," in which she starred with three other relative newcomers, Sylvester Stallone, Henry Winkler, and Perry King.

Blakely worked right along side of the New York "undercovers" (police) to prepare for a film, which brought her strongest praise from critics for her solid performance in, "Report To The Commissioner." After that role, the critics no longer referred to her with the cliché, "model-turned actress."

Blakely appeared in three films with Stallone, including the role of his wife in "Over The Top." She also gained international recognition in two very popular films "The Towering Inferno," which also starred Paul Newman, Steve McQueen, Fred Astaire, and William Holden, and "The Concorde," where she played the network anchorwoman opposite Alain Delon and R.J. Wagner.

Before she became an actress, Susan Blakely was one of the world's top fashion models, gracing the covers of *Vogue*, *Bazaar* and *Cosmopolitan* magazines. She was seen in hundreds of commercials, as one of the star-models of the Ford Agency. She was the only model to appear on the cover to *TV Guide*. During her busy schedule she would insist on taking time out from that lucrative career to study acting with the great teachers, Lee Strasberg, Sanford Meisner and Warren Robertson.

Blakely is regarded, according to one entertainment writer, as "one of the classy stars of many fine movies for television, including two with Walter Matthau, "The Incident," directed by Joe Sargent, and "Incident In Baltimore" directed by Academy Award Winner, Delbert Mann." Blakely also starred as Eva Braun opposite Academy Award winner, Anthony Hopkins, in his Emmy-Award-winning portrayal of Hitler, in George Schaefer's classic film, "The Bunker," written by John Gay.

Blakely's range is impressive as her roles go from leads in highly rated movies for television and cable, such as "Dead Reckoning" and "Blackmail" (USA Cable), two films of the "action-thriller-women-in-jeopardy-genre," to the popular screwball comedy, "Make Me An Offer," in which she played the hottest real estate agent in the nation's richest city, Beverly Hills. Credit was given by her critics across the nation for her ability to go from those films to the touching portrayal of a battered wife, in "Wildflower," Diane Keaton's debut as a director.

Perhaps her most memorable performance, dubbed "Magnificent" by the *New York Times*, was her portrayal of the late 30's film star, Frances Farmer, in "Will There Really Be A Morning," (3 Hour Special on CBS) for which she was again nominated for a Golden Globe as Best Dramatic Actress.

Blakely's love of comedy has been rewarded twice with the highly successful movie spoof, "My Mom's A Werewolf," in which she starred in the title role. Blakely's bumbling "werewolf-mom" caught people off-guard. Her nimble comic talent, something she had studied so hard to perfect, showed her in extreme contrast to the heavy dramatic roles for which she has been best known. Blakely also starred in ABC'S comedy pilot, "Dad's A Dog," produced by Barry Kemp ("Coach"), "The George Carlin Show," and "Step By Step."

Blakely grew up in cities all over the world as an "Army Brat," in Frankfurt (where she was born), Seoul, Arlington, Honolulu, and many others. Her parents lived in Honolulu where they were avid golfers. Her father, the late Col. Larry Blakely, retired from the Army to pursue his passion for golf. Blakely's mother, Weezie, a former art teacher, is an accomplished golfer, formerly of St. Joseph, Missouri.

Blakely is married to Stephen Jaffe, former television and film producer, who is now the chairman of Jaffe & Company, Strategic Media, a national media consulting firm, specializing in legal, medical, crisis management and corporate public relations. They reside in Beverly Hills with their dog "Sophie."

Susan receives Best Actress Award at Los Angeles Independent Film Festival for *Hungry Hearts*

Susan Blakely Contact:

Jaffe & Co., Inc.
Phone: 310-275-7327
www.susanblakelydesigns.com

Scott Levy

Scott Levy

Profile

Born in New Jersey and raised in Central Florida, Scott served in the U.S. Marines before pursuing dual degrees in Film Production and Audio Engineering. He began acting in film school, where his distinct style and charisma got him drawn into acting in his classmates' short films. Scott used his film and sound background to work as an audio engineer for George Lucas' Skywalker Sound in Marin County, California, but couldn't stay away from acting. After working on such films as "The Lost World: Jurassic Park," James Cameron's "Titanic" and with the encouragement of his Academy-Award-winning co-workers, Scott moved to Los Angeles to pursue a career in front of the camera.

Scott has trained and worked with theatre groups, both as an actor and a writer. His film credits include "The Matrix Parody, The Helix...Loaded," "Demon Under Glass" and "The Attic Expeditions." His television appearances include the sci-fi pilot, "The Privateers" and commercials for Jeep. Scott currently lives in Los Angeles, California.

122

Scott Levy

Resume

FILM

		DIRECTED BY
The Helix...Loaded	Lead	Alec Raven Cruz
Demon Under Glass	Lead	Jonathan Cunningham
The Attic Expeditions	Supporting	Jeremy Kasten
Marking Time (Short)	Star	Mary Liz Thomson
Night Vision	Lead	Akos Szemenyei
Provider	Lead	Jeremy Kasten
That Was Then	Lead	Calvin To
One Hit Wonder	Supporting	Lawrence Schecter
Better Never Than Late	Supporting	Kenn Scott
Storm Catcher	Featured	Anthony Hickox

TELEVISION

The Privateers (Pilot Presentation)	Lead	David Duncan
Angel	Featured	James Whitmore, Jr.
Jag	Featured	Ray Austin
The X-Files	Featured	Chris Carter
Buffy The Vampire Slayer	Featured	Daniel Attias

THEATRE

A Few Good Men	Kaffee	Annie Russell Theatre
Biloxi Blues	Eugene	Annie Russell Theatre
The Villafonte Method	Brad	The Artists' Gym
Deep Furrow	Steve	The Artists' Gym
The Machine	The Technician	The Artists' Gym

TRAINING

Billy Hornbuckle	Scene Study / Method
Jeff Rubens	Camera Technique
Jeff Sable	Business of Acting
Steve Cardwell	Improv / Comedy
Joey Garza	Commercials

SKILLS

U.S. Marine Corps, Expert Pistol & Rifleman, Hand To Hand Combat, Scuba Diving, Skydiving, Rappelling, Sword Fighting, Surfing, Soccer, Weight Training, Hiking, Swimming, Fishing, Camping, Snowboarding, Guitar, Running, Skating, Snorkeling, Jet Skiing, Computer Skills, Biking, Skateboarding, Bowling, Audio Engineering

Scott Levy Contact:

The Lliteras Group
Phone: 310-478-8398

Valentina Cardinalli

Valentina Cardinalli

Profile

Valentina has been acting since she got her start in the Belleville Theatre Guild at the age of 8. At 12, she was "discovered" by Casting Agent Anne Taite. She moved to Toronto a few years later and with help from the Edward G Agency she landed the starring role in a sitcom called "Doghouse" (actually, the Dog got top billing, but Valentina didn't mind one bit, she was just glad to be in the show!). She also had a supporting role in the feature film "PCU," co-starred for three seasons on Disney's "Road to Avonlea," and had recurring guest star roles on TV's "Ready or Not," "Maniac Mansion" and "Tales from the Cryptkeeper" (two seasons). She has appeared in numerous TV commercials and V.O. spots.

Theatre will always be her first love. Her list of credits includes every type of acting from serious to comedic, improv to puppetry. After graduating from Earl Haig (Claude Watson Program for the Arts), Valentina learned of her acceptance to the American Academy of Dramatic Arts. She packed her bags and moved to the Big Apple, where she graduated from the Academy and is currently pursuing her life-long passion.

Valentina Cardinalli

Resume

SAG and ACTRA (Canadian Union)
Dual Citizen (American/Canadian)

FILM

A BEAUTIFUL MIND	Principal-Joyce	Universal & DreamWorks/Ron Howard
RIDING IN CARS WITH BOYS	Principal-Braces Girl	Columbia Pictures/Penny Marshall
P.C.U.	Principal-Signer	20th Century Fox/Hart Bochner
BRAINCANDY	Principal-Burger Boss	CBS/James Parriot

TELEVISION

MATT WATERS (pilot)	Principal-Student	Paramount/Kelly Makin
READY OR NOT (5 episodes)	Recurring-Daisy	Global/Alyse Rosenberg
TALES FROM THE CRYPTKEEPER (2 seasons)	Recurring-Camille	ABC/Nelvana
I'LL NEVER GET TO HEAVEN	Principal-Lorraine	CBC/Steven Scani
DOGHOUSE	*Series Reg-Annabelle*	**Paragon/YTV/Various**
ROAD TO AVONLEA (3 seasons)	Recurring-Jane Spry	CBC/Disney
AIDS CARE: AIDS SCARE	Principle-Teenager	CBC/Ron Meraska
THE JUDGE	Principal-Defendant	CFTO/Peter Moss
MANIAC MANSION	Principal-Nerd Girl	YTV/Atlantis

THEATRE - Recent Work Only - Complete List Available Upon Request

THE BALLAD OF PHINEAS GAGE	Nurse	Drama Works/HERE/Gretchen VanLente
THE SCIENCE SHOW	Lauren	Dandelion Prod. NTPA/Seth Rienhiert
THE DRINKING GAMES	Staycee	Showcase/THE PUBLIC/Murphy Guliotti
POINT OF YOU	Drama-Various	Showcase/Various Locations/ Jeff Love
THE SPLINTER GROUP	Comedy-Various	Found. Member/Theatre for the New City
THE TEMPEST ON MARS	Narrator/Puppeteer	Bread and Puppet Theatre/ Lincoln Cent.

Best Young Actress supporting role in a Cable Series at the Academy of Television Arts and Sciences (Hollywood)

INDUSTRIALS & COMMERCIALS - Complete List Available Upon Request
Commercials include: Quaker Life Cereal, UNO Card & Cheer Fabric Softener
Industrials include: Better Sportsmanship, How to Report Child Abuse & The Surprise Party

TRAINING
GRADUATE OF THE AMERICAN ACADEMY OF DRAMATIC ARTS (AOS DEGREE)
GRADUATE OF EARL HAIG S.S. Claude Watson Program (Drama Major & Gifted Student)
Extensive acting, voice, movement, improv., mask, puppet, & storytelling workshops with teachers
Robert Derosier, Paula Citron, Neil Freeman, Sears & Switzer, & more.

SPECIAL SKILLS & AWARDS
The Gordon C. Johnson Playwriting Award, Achievement & Effort in 10th grade Dramatic Arts,
Backstage Support (Sears Drama Festival), Highest Achievement in Performing Arts (1989)
Skills Include: Ice Skating, Painting, Drawing, Sculpting, Pottery, Sewing, Chess, Writing, Skiing,
Biking, Research, Sign Language (fluent), Puppetry and being a good Mommy.

DEMO REEL AVAILABLE UPON REQUEST

Valentina Cardinalli Contact:

Website: http://communities.msn.com/valentina

Ashlie Brillault

Ashlie Brillault

Profile

At a mere four years of age, Ashlie Brillault was organizing and directing neighborhood productions of her favorite movie, "Cinderella." Since then, she has immersed herself in an unyielding passion for the art of acting. Her effort and enthusiasm paid off when she landed the role of Kate on the Disney Channel's highest rated show "Lizzie McGuire" and reprised her role in the highly successful "The Lizzie McGuire Movie," which was released in April of 2003.

Ashlie was born and raised in Long Beach, and inherited the laid-back and down-to-earth Southern California attitude. At an extremely young age, her mother noticed the passion and excitement Ashlie had for performing and got her feet wet by introducing her to the world of modeling. She landed her first modeling job at the age of three and continued to model in many print ads, fashion shows and was a regular in K-Mart's national advertising campaigns. At the age of six, Ashlie decided she no longer enjoyed, "having her hair curled" and desired something more interactive, so she began acting classes at the Beverly Hills Acting School. The owner of this renowned school noticed Ashlie immediately in a cattle call of nearly 1000 girls, zealously pursued her, and guaranteed that she would be signed in her first showcase, which she was...

With great support of her mother and father, Ashlie continued her pursuit in the performing arena...with countless dance, singing and acting classes. Meanwhile she also excelled in her school drama classes and gave stellar performances in many school plays. Though Ashlie was very shy in school, once she stepped onto a stage, it belonged to her and any trace of her shyness quickly disappeared. She aced her first ever television audition, leading her to a co-starring role on the new Disney show "Lizzie McGuire." As Lizzie's nemesis, Ashlie's character is the popular, pretty and utterly snobby junior high student we all love to hate. Another testament to her acting ability is the fact she can portray this character's attributes with great sincerity, while they are so opposite of her generous spirit and kind soul.

Following the momentous success of the television show, Disney created "The Lizzie McGuire Movie." Ashlie jumped at the chance of filming a movie, packed her bags, and traveled to both Canada and Rome for the filming. She relished in the opportunity to improve and diversify her acting skills on this new adventure. She counts the experience of working on her first feature film and working abroad, as one of the best experiences in her life so far.

Though acting is her passion and love, Ashlie thinks it is important to be a regular teenager, and always finds time to be with her two younger sisters, hang out with her friends, go to the beach and the movies. She excels in school, is dedicated to getting good grades and eventually graduating from college.

Charity work is also a top priority in Ashlie's life. She recognizes her tremendous blessings and feels a strong need to give back to her community. She resides as a board member of "Kids with a Cause," an organization that works on different projects with low-income families, inner city youth, foster kids and cancer patients. In addition, she is involved with the "Ronald McDonald House, Long Beach Child Cancer Center," and speaks at local high schools in connection with the "DARE" organization. Though acting keeps her busy, she finds the time to participate in at least one charity event a week. With grace, charisma, and beauty this exceptional young actress will continue to light up the screen for countless years to come...

Ashlie Brillault Contact:

Shannon Barr Public Relations
3619½ Crest Dr.
Manhattan Beach, CA 90266
Phone: 310-546-5069

Keith David

Keith David

Profile

A Korean war veteran running a pool hall in Harlem...A guide to the underworld with an elegant walk and a haunting laugh...A Moslem cleric stranded on an alien planet...No matter what role he's playing, the combination of Keith David's full-bodied, baritone regal presence and solid theatrical training is sure to result in an impressive performance.

Very few actors working today possess Keith's extraordinary range of talent as evidenced by his body of work. Keith has completed work on the movie "Crash" and the sequel to "Agent Cody Banks." He also co-stars with Vin Diesel in "The Chronicles Of Riddick." He has appeared on the ABC series "The Big House and also co-starred with Ice Cube in the hit "Barbershop." Other credits include "Hollywood Homicide," "Requiem For A Dream," and "Pitch Black." Prior to that, Keith was featured in "There's Something About Mary" and "Armageddon." He received a daytime Emmy nomination for his work in Showtime's "The Tiger Wood's Story." Other releases include "Dead Presidents" and Spike Lee's "Clockers."

Keith is proud to have narrated Ken Burns' millennium project "Jazz" for PBS. He was honored with another Emmy nomination for his work. He is the narrator for Burns' most recent work, "Mark Twain" and the upcoming "Horatio Drive." Keith was the lead character on the animated series version of the comic book "Spawn" for HBO, as well as the lead in the Disney animated series "Gargoyles." Keith can be heard commercially on behalf of BMW, UPS, the U.S. Navy and X-Box.

Such a demanding schedule is nothing new to Keith. Immediately after his graduation from the Julliard School he was hired as an understudy for the role of Tullus Aufidius in Shakespeare's "Coriolanus" at Joseph Papp's New York Public Theatre. Ironically, ten years later he co-starred in the same role opposite Christopher Walken and was the recipient of the Actor's Equity St. Claire Bayfield award. In 1992, Keith was recognized with a Tony nomination for best supporting actor in a musical for co-starring with Gregory Hines in the Broadway production of "Jelly's Last Jam." Several years later he starred on Broadway in August Wilson's "Seven Guitars." Keith has performed his jazz/cabaret act at New York's legendary Hotel Delmonico and the venerable Cinegrill in Los Angeles. He fulfilled a lifelong ambition by portraying "Othello" at the New York Shakespeare Festival.

Keith David gained wide attention in 1986 for his role as King in the Oscar winning film "Platoon." He has starred with Gene Hackman and Sharon Stone in the "Quick And The Dead" and with Richard Gere and Kim Basinger in "Final Analysis." Keith has also worked with notable directors including Clint Eastwood ("Bird"), Steven Spielberg ("Always") and John Carpenter ("The Thing" and "They Live").

Born in Harlem, NY and raised in East Elmhurst, Queens, Keith sang in the all borough choir as a boy. He knew he wanted to act at the age of nine when he appeared as the cowardly lion in his school's production of "The Wizard Of Oz." He later attended New York's famed High School of the Performing Arts and then graduated from Julliard. There he studied under such voice and speech teachers as Robert Williams and Edith Skinner.

In addition to the wide variety of modern characters he has played, Keith says he still loves the classics. "Heightened, elevated text always really interests me...the kind of stuff you don't get to say everyday," he explains. He says that when he first started acting, he would bring his own personality to the characters he portrayed. Now, however, that approach has changed. "I want to be a character actor. I want to discover the character and play him."

Keith David Contact:

Lisa Sorensen Public Relations
12522 Moorpark St.
Studio City, CA 91604
Phone: 818-761-0430

Jenine Mayring

Favorite Quote:

"Laughter is the best defense against the universe."
Mel Brooks

Jenine Mayring

Profile

Who's that redhead?

A distant relative of composer Johannes Brahms, it's no wonder Jenine Mayring made her way into the performing arts. A native New Yorker, Jenine got her first big break at the Mayring dinner table and has been performing ever since.

Ms. Mayring is a graduate of Brooklyn Technical High School, one of the top three high schools in New York City. Following in the footsteps of actor John Turturro, Jenine received her Bachelor of Arts degree, majoring in Theatre Arts, from the State University of New York at New Paltz.

Born and raised in New York City, Jenine is grateful her parents exposed her to the arts at a very young age. Originally theatrically trained, Ms. Mayring crosses over from stage to film to TV and beyond with effortless ease.

A true Gemini at heart, Jenine has also performed as a Theatrical ASL Interpreter. She studied American Sign Language (ASL) at Gallaudet University in Washington, D.C. and toured with the acclaimed New York Deaf Theatre in "StorySign" for two consecutive years.

Ms. Mayring currently lives in Los Angeles, where she performs nearly every week as a singer and dancer with award-winning Director John Pieplow. The award-winning band "John Pieplow" has taken LA by storm and is currently in the recording studio working on their first CD with Producer Alan Mason at Chalice Recording Studio.

Who's that redhead? Find out more at www.mayring.com.

Jenine Mayring

Resume

FILM

HEADLINERS	Lead	Dir. Kevin Collins
THE OFFERING	Lead	Dir. Luke Heyne
NOISE	Lead	Dir. Seth Manheimer
SPANISH FLY	Supporting	Dir. Will Wallace
HORROR SHOW	Supporting	Dir. Stefan Hering
TO BE SOMEBODY	Supporting	Dir. Juan Aguero

TELEVISION

A DAY IN THE LIFE OF US (pilot)	Star	Time Warner Cable
GOOD MORNING AMERICA	Cast of Pocahontas II	ABC-TV

OFF BROADWAY

A MIDSUMMER NIGHT'S DREAM	Helena	Samuel Beckett Theatre
TWELFTH NIGHT	Viola	Wings Theatre
THE CELEBRATION	Tatiana Alexeyevna	Producers Club Theatre
SORRY, WRONG NUMBER	Mrs. Stevenson	Shepard Theatre
NOISES OFF!	Belinda/Flavia	Interborough Rep. Theatre
FERAL MUSIC	Interpreter	HERE (tiny mythic)

REGIONAL THEATRE

STORYSIGN	Performer/Interpreter	New York Deaf Theatre
PEOPLE LIKE US	Janet/Lee	Plays for Living
ANNUAL CHILDREN'S SHOW	Elizabeth	Shadowland Theatre
CAMINO REAL	Marguerite	Parker Theatre
THE "OR" Bit	Sally	Bloomsburg Theatre

COMMERICIALS – conflicts available upon request

TRAINING

B.A. Theatre Arts: State University of New York at New Paltz

Acting Technique: Ron Marquette (NY)/Carol Fox Prescott (LA)

Soap/Film Technique: Linda Laundra (NY)

Dance: Broadway Dance Center (tap-NY)/Oscar Ramirez (salsa-LA)

On-Camera Commercial: Weist Barron (Ed Ferron/Frank Spencer-NY)

Improvisation: Beverly Brumm (NY)/ Gary Austin (LA)

Shakespeare: Luane Davis (NY)/ Roy Doliner (NY)

Voice: Arthur Williams (NY)/Wendy MacKenzie (LA)

Stage Combat: Diana Banks (NY)

Speech/Dialects: Kate Ingram (NY)

SPECIAL SKILLS

Language: Various Dialects/Character Voices/American Sign Language (fluent)
Sports: Horseback Riding/Figure Skating/Inline Skating/Wave Runner/Weight Lifting/Tennis
Action: Stage Combat/Tae Kwon Do/Kick-Boxing/Firearms (hand guns/rifles)
Misc: Dual Passports (USA/German)/Ear Prompter/Tele-Prompter/Child & Animal Friendly/ 40" legs

Jenine Mayring Contact:

Website: www.mayring.com

Richard Mamola

Richard Mamola

Profile

Richard Mamola was born January 13, 1961 and raised in Lodi, New Jersey. As a young boy, he had dreams of becoming a professional baseball player. He played many sports including baseball, football, wrestling and tennis. Many of his athletic dreams were cut down when he had an accident and broke his hip in three places. He was sixteen at the time and did not walk without the aid of crutches for ten months. For many years after that, he was limited in the sports that he could play. He graduated Lodi High School in 1978. During high school he had "five minutes of fame" when he was asked to choreograph a disco dance for the drama class. They sold out the entire auditorium to standing room only for three nights and that is still a school record.

He continued on to The University of Southern Connecticut State College where he studied pre-veterinarian medicine. His work as a bartender, along with some grants and loans paid for his schooling. After three years in college he decided that veterinarian medicine was not for him. He continued to bartend and did not really know where his life was heading. Having lots of fun along the way, he worked many jobs some of which were selling cars, life insurance and loading trucks for UPS.

Then one day he decided to join the United States Air Force. He signed the paper work and was scheduled to report to basic training within 6 months. Before his entry into the Air Force, he was determined to party and have a great time. While at a restaurant, he met the girl who would eventually become his wife. He had such a great time for the four months before he had to report to duty, that there were many times he hoped he could back out, but he was always the type to stay true to his word and fulfill his commitments so off he went to basic training. Looking back on basic training he would say that there were many great experiences he cherished, but while he was going through them he did not think so. After basic training was over he received his orders to report to Okinawa, Japan. Not having signed up for overseas duty, this came as a shock and he was scared. Talking to his future wife on the phone, they decided to get married and she would accompany him to Kadena Air Base, Okinawa, Japan. They spent 3½ years on the Island of Okinawa going through good times and some bad times but always staying strong and gaining strength in their marriage.

After leaving the Air Force they came home to Park Ridge, New Jersey where Richard began to work as a data analyst. Shortly after their return they had twin girls and their family was started. He had moved up the ladder in his computer career and had started to make some money. They bought their first house and four years after their daughters were born they had a son. Things were getting better and better for him and his company so they decided to rent their first home and purchase a new home. They moved into their new house and things were going very nicely. He was now a Network Engineer in the computer field with a business degree.

One night he stumbled on to the set of a movie and was bitten by the acting bug. Since then he has taken many classes with TVI Actors Studio, including Commercial Technique and Advanced Acting. He has played many side parts and he was a member of the Bergen County Players Theatre. He has played as an extra on the hit HBO television series "The Sopranos" and "Law and Order." He had the pleasure of meeting James Gandolfini on the set of "The Sopranos." Ironically, Richard's wife and Gandolfini grew up in Park Ridge, New Jersey.

He played a lead role in an independent film "A Family Affair" which he is proud to announce was accepted into the New York International Film Festival and the Las Vegas Film Festival. The director of "A Family Affair" Chris Vallone has finished his short film "The Agent" where Richard played the lead. This film won Best of Show at the Putnam Valley Film Festival and The Pioneer Theatre in New York City. He also played a principal role in a movie by Rob Riley "Back to Manhattan" which was submitted to the Rad Festival.

Currently, he is continuing to pursue his acting career. The short film "The Agent" is being made into a full feature film. All involved are working to get the proper funding and backing to make it a success. He now lives in Pennsylvania where he has come across many contacts in the acting industry. Richard says, "Hope you see me on the big screen!"

Richard Mamola

Resume

FILM

A FAMILY AFFAIR	Vito (Lead)	Chris Vallone, Dir.

(NY and LAS VEGAS Independent International Film Festival 2002)

SOLOMON'S TWIST	The Gentleman (Principle)	Joshua P. Locantore, Dir.
BACK TO MANHATTAN	Kenny (Principle)	Rob Riley, Dir.
COSANOSTRA	Santo (Principle)	Peter D'Amato/Al Linea
THE MENTOR	Angelo (Principle)	Pete Delorenzo, Dir.
TIME TO LIVE TIME TO DIE	Tony (Lead)	Salvatore Lauriola, Dir.

THE AGENT	Rich (Lead)	Chris Vallone, Dir

(Putnam Valley Film Festival Best of Show)

ROOT OF ALL EVIL	Agent Slater (Lead)	Chris Vacarelli, Dir.
LUCKY CHIPS	Tony (Principle)	Peter D'Amato, Dir.
THIS THING OF OURS	Featured	Danny Provenzano, Dir.
BROOKLYN GAMES	Featured	Phil Brandt, Dir.
KATE AND LEOPOLD	Featured	James Mangold, Dir.

TELEVISION

SOPRANOS	Stand-In	HBO Promo Unit
SOPRANOS	Featured	HBO
LAW and ORDER	Court Officer	NBC

COMMERCIALS
Listing available upon request

TRAINING

Valerie Kingston	Advanced Acting	TVI Actors Studio
Jeff Barber	Commercial Technique	TVI Actors Studio
Bertrand Quonia	Acting Technique	

SPECIAL SKILLS
Okinawa Karate, Baseball, Football, Bowling, Tennis, Skiing, Ice Skating, Fishing, Camping, Bartender, Computer Networking, Valid Driver's License, Dance the Hustle!

Richard Mamola Contact:

Email: rich@richardmamola.com
www.richardmamola.com

Antonio Saillant

Antonio Saillant

Profile

Antonio Saillant is a fulltime engineer, but likes saying he's an actor posing as an engineer. It keeps him in character.

He was born in Washington Heights, NY and is the product of Cuban and Italian parents. Antonio and his friends ran with the wrong crowds and were surrounded by death and drugs, but Antonio eventually broke away and chose another path by which to make a name for himself. In high school his older brother let him borrow his weights, so he could work out and he began playing football and baseball and also joined the track team. He joined the drama class, but due to the ribbing he received from teammates and the practice schedules, he dropped drama. Antonio studied hard, went to college and became an engineer with an Aerospace Engineering Degree.

About 10 years ago Antonio and his brother were in a car accident and before he knew it, the one person he looked up to, admired and from whom he always got the best advice was gone. This was a life-changing event for Antonio. He gave up everything, even a career in baseball when the Mets and Yankee scouts wanted to sign him. Just when he thought his life was getting back on track he found out his sister was HIV positive. He believes he has to be strong and keep going in order to help his family. As Antonio remembers back, there was always something that he enjoyed and that made him feel alive and that was acting. You can describe Antonio as warm, talented and lighthearted, but serious about the task at hand. He has the inner strength, personal confidence and power to prevail against all odds. Look for Antonio in "Jersey Girl," directed by Kevin Smith.

Antonio Saillant

Resume

TELEVISION

All My Children	Bouncer – Roadhouse Bar	Angela Tessinari, Director
All My Children	Blue Collar	Conal O'Brien, Director
The Sopranos/HBO	Casino Gambler	David Chase, Director
Monday Night Mayhem	Football Team Owner	Ernest Dickerson, Director
As The World Turns/CBS	Airport Traveler	Marla Wagner, Director

FILM

Jersey Girl	Wedding Guest	Kevin Smith, Director

TRAINING

Harold Guskin	How to Stop Acting	Acting Coach
TVI Actors Studios	Cold Readings Overview	Valerie Kingston
TVI Actors Studios	The Art of Audition	Andra Reeve / Director of Primetime
TVI Actors Studios	Auditioning Technique	Rob Decina / Casting Dir. / Guiding Light
T. Schreiber Studio	Acting, Body Dynamics	Terry Schreiber & Carol Reynolds
AIA Actor's Studio	Monologue Workshop	Michele Pulice / Casting Director
AIA Actor's Studio	Cold Reading Workshop	Michele Pulice / Casting Director
AIA Actor's Studio	Monologue Workshop	Paul Weber / VP of Talent – MGM
AIA Actor's Studio	Cold Reading Workshop	Paul Weber / VP of Talent – MGM
AIA Actor's Studio	How to Produce Your Own Independent Film	John Putch / Director, Producer
AIA Actor's Studio	Improvisational Class	John Michalski / Actor, Director, Writer
AIA Actor's Studio	Acting for Commercials	Patrick Pankhurst / Casting Associate
AIA Actor's Studio	Monologue Technique	John Henry Richardson / Director
AIA Actor's Studio	The Art of Audition	Mark Paladini / Casting Director
AIA Actor's Studio	Mastering The Actor Within	Linda Phillips-Palo / Casting Director
AIA Actor's Studio	Interacting	Robert Forster / Actor
Scott Powers Productions	Daytime Drama Course	Joe Cotugno / Director of "One Life to Live"

EDUCATION
New York Institute of Technology, Old Westbury Campus, New York
Degree: Bachelor of Science, Engineering
Special Courses: Communications Law, Film & TV Production

State University of NY at Farmingdale, Farmingdale, NY
Major: Aerospace Technology

John Jay College of Criminal Justice
Special Courses: Criminal Law, Law and Evidence & The Investigative Function

SPECIAL SKILLS
Baseball (semi-pro), Football, Weight Training, Wrestling, Track, Aviation Background, Auxiliary
Policeman, Firearms, Streetwise, Automobile (standard & automatic).

LANGUAGES
English & Spanish

Antonio Saillant Contact:

Cunningham, Escott, Dipene & Associates
257 Park Avenue South, Suite 900
New York, NY 10010
Phone: 212-477-1666

Julie Ann Emery

Julie Ann Emery

Profile

Julie Ann Emery was born and raised in the small town of Crossville, Tennessee. The daughter of a dairy farmer and a computer analyst, she caught the acting bug performing in her first school play at age 16. After playing lead roles at the local Community Theatre, she attended Webster Conservatory in St. Louis to study acting.

Julie Ann went on to appear on stage across the country including Chicago and New York. Her critically acclaimed performances paired her on stage with such actors as Rue McClanahan, Sally Struthers, and John Schuck before television whisked her away to Los Angeles.

She made the leap onto the small screen playing opposite Eric Paladino on the long running series "ER" where she will be seen again this season. She went on to join the cast of "Stephen Spielberg Presents Taken" the hit miniseries on the Sci-Fi channel. Other television appearances include "First Monday" (with James Garner, Joe Mantegna, and Dean Stockwell), "The Drew Carey Show" (opposite Ryan Stiles), "Providence," and "CSI: Miami." This emerging young actress then caught the eye of writer/director Rod Lurie ("The Contender," & "Last Castle") who invited her to join the cast of "Capital City," a pilot for ABC, alongside Peter Fonda, Tom Berenger, and Mary Steenburgen.

Julie Ann most recently finished shooting Rod Lurie's new pilot "Lines of Duty," also for ABC, and in contention for the network's Fall 2003 schedule. She is currently preparing to return to the stage in Rebecca Gilman's "Boy Gets Girl" alongside Nancy Travis at the Geffen Playhouse in Los Angeles.

Julie Ann at the premiere of *The Grudge*

Julie Ann Emery

Resume

TELEVISION

LINES OF DUTY (ABC Pilot)	Series Regular	Dir: Rod Lurie
CSI: MIAMI	Guest Star	Dir: David Grossman
PROVIDENCE	Guest Star	Dir: Mike Fresca
CAPITOL CITY (ABC Pilot)	Recurring	Dir: Rod Lurie
THE DREW CARY SHOW	Guest Star	Dir: Bob Koherr
FIRST MONDAY	Recurring	Dir: Lou Antonio
ER	Recurring	Dir: Richard Thorpe

MINISERIES

TAKEN (Episode 4, 5, 6)	Amelia	Dir: Felix Alcala, Bryan Spicer, Thomas Wright; EP: Steven Spielberg

MOW

ANOTHER PRETTY FACE	Lead	Dir: Reynaldo Villalobos

THEATRE – Los Angeles

BOY GETS GIRL (Geffen Playhouse)	Harriet	Dir: Randall Arney

THEATRE – New York (Selected Lead Roles)

TWELFTH NIGHT	Olivia	Dir: Hank Schoebe
HOT L BALTIMORE	The Girl	Dir: Marita Woodruff
CAESAR & CLEOPATRA	Cleopatra	PT Studios
A FUNNY THING HAPPENED...	Philia	National Tour

REGIONAL THEATRE – Chicago (Selected Lead Roles)

GYPSY	Louise	* Jeff Nomination *

NEW WORKS

SEVENTEEN (Produced by Jeffrey Kramer, Honey Sanders, Kelly Gonda)	Lola Pratt	Mus. Dir. Jack Lee

TRAINING

Webster Conservatory, B.F.A. in Theatre
Acting: Belita Moreno, John Swanbeck and Nancy Scanlon, Penny Templeton, Warner Laughlin

Julie Ann Emery Contact:

Lasher/McManus/Robinson/Kipperman
1964 Westwood Blvd., Suite 400
Los Angeles, CA 90025
Phone: 310-446-1566

Hans Hernke

Hans Hernke

Profile

California/Orlando actor, Hans Hernke was born in Menasha, Wisconsin, November 6, 1981. He lived there for 13 years of his life.

He then moved to Florida in 1995. His acting career launched in 1999 when he started doing theatre for high school and his church. He then got his first agent, Central Florida Talent Agency after submitting a headshot and small resume to them. He started to take commercial and film-acting classes at KVG Studios in Orlando headed by actor Ken Grant. His very first job was a music video for the band "Creed," shot at the Hard Rock Cafe. He then started landing more work in films, including "Held For Ransom," an independent thriller starring Dennis Hopper and Zachary Ty Bryan. He also began landing work in dozens of commercials for Universal Studios and TV shows for Nickelodeon such as "Taina" and "Noah Knows Best." His career began to flourish. Being urged by industry friends, he joined the Florida Motion Picture and Television Association in 1999.

He has enjoyed working on productions every single month and loves to make new industry friends and contacts. He stresses more then anything to actors and actresses that networking is the key to getting places in this industry. Throughout his high school years, his acting career was going very well, he won many awards for drama, and his senior year, he won the coveted "Directors Cup for the Performing Arts." From there on, he continued to pursue his career in the film and television industry, especially acting and directing. He graduated May 2001 from The Master's Academy High School. He was accepted into Vancouver Film School in August 2001 to study acting, but shortly after starting school, he was feeling that maybe this school wasn't the place for him. He packed his bags and headed home September 10th 2001, the day before the terror attacks! There was definitely a reason for him coming home so early he came to find out.

After the September 11th terrorist attacks, work in Florida started getting very slow and depressing. He began working at a small movie theatre in Winter Park, Florida called Carmike Cinemas. His boss, Koko Mihilas was a great encouragement to him, telling him not to give up, and to keep going for your dreams. She would often tease him and tell him she will be his Soap Opera fan club manager whenever he got on a Soap! His career, however, fell into a depression, there was just simply no industry work in Orlando for anyone. Sometimes he felt like quitting the whole thing all together but, he hadn't given up hope yet, it was a learning and growing experience for him. He learned that if you have time on your hands...use it to network and educate yourself more in the industry. He also made time to join with the Screen Actors Guild as well. During this time period, he was asked by his former drama teacher to be the first alumni of the high school to direct and produce a dinner theatre show for The Master's Academy.

In February 2002, he directed a one-act murder mystery comedy play called "Murder Well Rehearsed." It was a very challenging and exciting experience for him. The experience sparked the director's side of him, it was something he really felt comfortable doing. He decided to join the New York Film Academy on the Universal Studios back lot at Universal Studios, Hollywood. There he would learn to direct, produce, shoot and edit his own films. So in August 2002 he decided it was time for him to restart his life, he packed his bags again, with the help of his father and mother, Paul and Barbara Hernke, and moved to Burbank, California. From the day he moved there, he signed up with Central Casting and began booking work every week. In September, he started classes at the New York Film Academy. He loved the school very much and he recommends to everyone who is starting out in the field to attend one of their intensive workshops. One of his best films he directed at the New York Film Academy was "A Blessing," a story about the September 11th attacks and how some people were blessed not to be on the planes that were hijacked. He was moved to see how the audience reacted to his film at the screenings. After finishing school, he continued to book work and search for an agent to represent him. Hans has a heart and passion for his craft, he loves to see production happen and is always staying on top of things, seeing they get done professionally, properly and having a good time on the set. Hans would like to thank God, his parents, his close friends, and his close industry friends, for the support they have shown him!

Hans Hernke

Resume

SAG

THEATRE
The Invisible Man
Harvey
MK Christmas Special
Judgment Houses

FEATURE FILMS
Held For Ransom
Freaky Friday
Florida City
Characters
Virgins
The Bros
The Haunting of Misty Creek
I am Vengeance
American Wedding
Neo Ned
Love Hollywood Style
In Enemy Hands

MUSIC AUDIO
Creed (Higher)

MODELING
Parisian Hair and Nail Salon Promo (Live)
The Masters Academy Brochure Promo
    /Drama Dept. (Print)
Shand's Medical Hospital, Gainesville,
    Florida (Print)

TRAINING
Drama/Improv -- The Master's Academy
Lou Diamond Phillips Master class -- AIA Studios
The Acting Class -- Henry Polic II
The Commercial Class -- Mr. Ken Grant – KVG Studios
The Monologue Class -- Mr. Ken Grant – KVG Studios
Marketing Seminar -- Michael Cairns

SKILLS
Rollerblading, Roller Skating, Street Hockey, Ice Skating, Swimming, Soccer, Basketball, Volleyball, Baseball, Fishing, Football, Green Screen Experience, 2nd Unit Experience (Sheena, The Italian Job)

TELEVISION/COMMERCIAL
AT&T Mexico commercial
Liquid Golf.com commercial
Islands of Adventure commercial
Grinchmas
Jurassic Park III Promo
Sheena (5)
Noah Knows Best (4)
Taina (1)
Judging Amy (1)
Birds of Prey (2)
Family Affair (1)
The West Wing (1)
Do Over (1)
FireFly (1)
Frasier
The Division
Las Vegas
Oliver Beene
Phil of the Future
American Dreams
Astonishing News

SHORT FILMS
Food for Thought
Sports Worship
Mormon Beer
The Cop and The Pedestrian
Frosted Mini Wheats
Madame Tussauds New York City

148

HOLLYWOOD
PRODUCTION
DIRECTOR
CAMERA
DATE   SCENE   REEL

Hans Hernke Contact:

Website: http://hometown.aol.com/actorhans223/

William Windom

Favorite Quote:

"From Evil Comes Good."

William Windom

Profile

Born in New York City, William spent his childhood in Boston, Washington, D.C., Majorca, Virginia, England and France. After WWII he successfully hit the New York stage, then Hollywood. An illustrious career in film (To Kill a Mockingbird-Somersby) and television (Farmer's Daughter, Emmy winning My World And Welcome To It, Murder She Wrote, playing Dr. Seth Hazlitt) led to many years of audience thrilling one-man performances of (James) Thurber and (Ernie) Pyle. Other television efforts, and they are legion, of more than routine interest include "They're Tearing Down Tim Riley's Bar" on Rod Serling's "Night Gallery," which got an Emmy nomination and Commodore Decker of "Star Trek's Doomsday Machine." He is credited with over 90 films. His fifteen years in New York include Shakespeare, 20 Broadway plays, 6 Off Broadway, stock, road shows, live TV, radio and a glorious 3 months as a grip on Candide. Upcoming credits include over 30 shows with the California Actors Radio Theatre, several commercials and audio performances of a number of books including Abuse Of Power, The New Nixon Tapes, Sudden Mischief by Robert B. Parker, Poetry Of Walt Whitman, Collected Stories of Paul Theroux and California Fault by Thurston Clarke. His love of sailing, chess and tennis, along with a wife and four children, take up his non-working time. His favorite accolade? His name in *The New York Times* crossword puzzle.

William Windom

Resume

FEATURE FILMS

EARLY BIRD SPECIAL
TRUE CRIME (w/CLINT EASTWOOD)
THE ATTACK OF THE 50 FT. WOMAN
SOMERSBY
PLANES, TRAINS & AUTOMOBILES
NOW YOU SEE HIM, NOW YOU DON'T
GRANDVIEW, USA
ESCAPE FROM THE PLANET OF THE APES
FOOLS PARADE
MEPHISTO WALTZ
THE GYPSY MOTHS
BREWSTER MCCLOUD
THE ANGRY BREED
THE DETECTIVE
FOR LOVE OR MONEY
THE AMERICANIZATION OF EMILY
SHE'S HAVING A BABY

CHILDREN OF THE CORN IV
MIRACLE ON 34TH STREET
DEAD AIM
FUNLAND
STREET JUSTICE
SPACE RANGE
TO KILL A MOCKINGBIRD
PRINCE JACK
SEPARATE WAYS
GOODBYE FRANKLIN HIGH
MEAN DOG BLUES
ECHOES OF A SUMMER
THE MAN
HOUR OF THE GUN
CATTLE KING
ONE MAN'S WAY
PINOCCHIO AND THE
EMPEROR OF THE NIGHT

TELEVISION-SERIES REGULAR

PARENTHOOD	NBC 1990
MURDER, SHE WROTE	CBS 1985-1993
BROTHERS AND SISTERS	NBC 1979
THE GIRL WITH SOMETHING EXTRA	NBC 1973-74
MY WORLD AND WELCOME TO IT	NBC 1969-1970
(Emmy Award Winner)	
THE FARMER'S DAUGHTER	ABC 1963-1966

TELEVISION

Over 250 guest appearances, including:

JAG	Dir: Brad May
THE DISTRICT	Dir: Rick Rosenthal
PROVIDENCE	Dir: Greg Beeman
ALLY MCBEAL	Dir: Billy Dickson
JUDGING AMY	Dir: Ken Olin

BROADWAY

Appeared in 20 Broadway productions and 6 Off-Broadway productions

ROAD

Over 700 one-man performances on the works of James Thurber and Ernie Pyle.

William Windom Contact:

House of Representatives
400 S. Beverly Dr., Suite 101
Beverly Hills, CA 90212
Phone: 310-772-0772

Aaron Fiore

Favorite Quote:

"The one who says it can't be done is generally passed up by someone doing it."

Aaron Fiore

Profile

Born and raised in New Jersey, outside New York City, Aaron Thomas Fiore grew up with an over disciplining father. Movies had become an escape from his everyday life. He would attend all the films playing in the local theatre the first day they were released. When he had finished watching them all, he would see them again. The fine character detail portrayed in these films captivated Aaron. It wasn't uncommon for him to attend the same movie 20 or more times. The fact a person could become a completely unique human being, other than one's self, opened his eyes to this whole new world.

Upon graduation from college, after witnessing how fellow NYC film professionals struggled, Aaron decided to begin in a smaller film market... Wilmington, North Carolina. There he developed his craft and learned all the skills necessary for a successful film career. After years of continuous acting training, film projects, and just plain trial and error, he felt he was ready to compete in a tougher northeast market. NYC became the next big step to a professional career in California.

Friends, family, and peers have always been impressed with Aaron's determination, drive, and willingness to do anything. These traits will no doubt return greatness to his acting career and personal life. The fact Aaron is profoundly effecting people in a positive way, through his work and his example, is the most satisfying accomplishment of his career. He didn't choose this vehicle; the acting profession chose him. Like his favorite quote says, "The one who says it can't be done is generally passed up by someone doing it."

154

Aaron Fiore

Resume

SAG

FILM (Full List upon Request)

Courage & Stupidity (Short)	Young George Lucas (Lead)	Spotlight Video Productions, Inc.
Ladder 49 (Feature)	Tim Guinee's Stand In	Buena Vista/Disney
Back to Manhattan (Feature)	Jersey Man in Queen's Park (Supporting)	Cinemook Film Productions
The Date (Short)	Kip (Lead)	AMVF Productions
Assassin Nation (Feature)	Chris Tyler (Lead)	Sheldon Entertainment, Inc.
Murray & Marie (Feature)	Young Murray (Supporting)	Over the Edge Productions
Misdirected (Feature)	Bar Guy (Supporting)	Super-Nerve Entertainment
The Vampire Kids (Feature)	JT (Supporting)	Blue Rock Studios
Townies (Feature)	Intern Tom (Supporting)	Neo-Pangea Productions
The Pink House (Feature)	Young Pritchard's Crony (Supporting)	Asset Pictures, Inc.
The Movie (Working Title) (Feature)	Richard (Supporting)	T-Productions
Steam Cloud Rising (Feature)	Player C (Supporting)	Eric Pictures
Moral Arithmetic (Feature)	Officer Ted (Supporting)	Sideshow Cinema
Fearsome (Feature)	Security Guard #2 (Supporting)	Six Lower Entertainment
Youth of a Nation (Feature)	Juvenile Inmate: Jake (Supporting)	Alabama Productions, Inc.
The Lives & Deaths of Clowns (Short)	The Man (Lead)	U.N.C.W. Productions
The College Guy (Feature)	Ralph (Supporting)	Keystone Pictures
Two Soldiers (Short)	Corporal (Principal)	Shoe Clerk Picture Co., Inc.
Intermission (Feature)	Evan (Supporting)	Swan Pictures, Inc.
Ya Ya Sisterhood (Feature)	The Ballroom Photographer (Featured)	Warner Brothers

TELEVISION

The New Detectives (Episode #1592)	Mark Bosom (Lead)	Discovery Channel
The FBI Files (Episode #1663)	FBI Agent #1 (Supporting)	Discovery Channel
Maury "Medical Miracles" (Dramatization)	Highway Worker (Principal)	Universal Television
Life-N-General-The Series	J.M. Morehead III (Lead)	Kearns Ent. AMVF Prod.
Life-N-General (Test Pilot) Summertime	B.J. McFadden (Lead)	Kearns Entertainment
Karmic 8 (Music Video)	The New Guy (Principal)	Infinity Productions
Sopranos (Series)	Stand In	HBO Pictures

THEATRE

Death of a Salesman	Happy	Keystone Theatre
Off To the Races	Randy	7AM Productions
You're a Good Man, Charlie Brown	Schroeder	Dinner Playhouse
Egad! What a Cad!	Augustus	Stage Works
The Sisters Rosensweig	Tom	Scranton Players
Boys' Life	Phil	Keystone Theatre
Mystery Dinner Theatre	Multiple Roles	Pocono's Troupe
The Lunch Time Theatre	Multiple Roles	Guild Improv Troupe

COMMERCIAL/INDUSTRIAL   List Available upon Request

VOICE-OVER/VOICE ACTING   List Available upon Request

TRAINING
Academic:

AA, Communications	Television/Theatre Emphasis	Keystone College
Delta Psi Omega	Dramatic Honor Society	National Society

Professional:

Acting for the Camera	Tammy Arnold	T.A.P. Studio
Commercial Technique	Gene Terinoni	Philadelphia, PA
Military Ceremony/Technique	Ed Ruggero	NYC
Teleprompter/Ear prompter	Pat McDade/Diane Heery	Mike Lemon Casting, C.S.A.
Cue Card Acting	Gene Terinoni	Philadelphia, PA
Acting Technique	Gregory Bach	American Studio of Acting
Acting for the Theatre	Dr. Sherry Strain	Theatre at Brooks Studio
Voice & Speech	Susan S. Stewart	Kernersville, NC
Voice & Diction	Dr. Sherry Strain	Theatre at Brooks Studio
Improvisational Acting	Susan Stacy	T.A.P. Studio
Scene Study	Tammy Arnold	T.A.P. Studio
Auditioning Techniques	Marilyn Allen	Kernersville, NC

SPECIAL SKILLS

KICKBOXING (NOVICE); SNOW SKIING (NOVICE); BASEBALL; SWIMMING; SNOW MOBILE OPERATION; SAFETY & USAGE OF FIREARMS; CAMPING; HORSEBACK RIDING; STUNT EXPERIENCE; BLUE SCREEN ACTING EXPERIENCE; ACCENTS: STANDARD AMERICAN, SOUTHERN, NEW YORK; SING NATURALLY BAD; BURP, WHISTLE, & WIGGLE EARS ON COMMAND; BLOWING BUBBLE GUM BUBBLES; WEAR CONTACTS/GLASSES; SUIT & TUX AVAILABLE; LICENSED DRIVER, STANDARD; VEHICLE TRAILER OPERATION; AIRCRAFT TUG OPERATION; AIRCRAFT FUELING EXPERIENCE; LANDSCAPE DESIGN; HOTEL EXPERIENCE; CPR CERTIFIED.

Aaron Fiore Contact:

Toni Cusumano Talent
Phone: 212-712-7184
Website: www.actoraaron.com

156

David Naughton

David Naughton

Profile

David made his first national appearance as the lead singer-dancer in a series of Dr. Pepper commercials, which became some of the most popular ads in television history. He was also seen in Los Angeles with Cybil Shepard as a pitchman for Mercedes Benz.

He starred in the TV series "Makin' It" and received a gold record for his hit single, which was the title song from the show.

Mr. Naughton's screen debut came in "Midnight Madness" from Buena Vista Pictures with Michael J. Fox. David is best remembered for his leading role in John Landis's classic horror film "An American Werewolf in London" from Universal. Mr. Naughton also starred in the sequel, "Amityville, The New Generation," "Hot Dog, the Movie," "The Boy in Blue," "The Sleeping Car," "Urban Safari," and "Separate Vacations."

His television roles include "My Sister Sam" on CBS with Pam Dawber and "At Ease" for Aaron Spelling.

A multi-talented performer, Mr. Naughton's career includes roles on the American stage in such classics as Joseph Papp's production of "Hamlet," "Da," "Much Ado About Nothing," "Poor Little Lambs," and the musical revues "Both Barrels" and "A Good Swift Kick."

Born in West Hartford, CT, David graduated from The University of Pennsylvania with a degree in English Literature. He went on to study at The London Academy of Music and Dramatic Art. He is an avid golfer and cyclist and is the father of two terrific kids, David and Kendal.

David Naughton

Resume

FEATURES

AN AMERICAN WEREWOLF IN LONDON	John Landis
BODY BAGS	John Carpenter
URBAN SAFARI	Reto Salimbeni
AMITYVILLE – A NEW GENERATION	John Malowski
BEANSTALK	Michael Paul Davis
HOTDOG, THE MOVIE	Peter Markle
NOT FOR PUBLICATION	Paul Bartel
SEPARATE VACATIONS	Michael Anderson
THE BOY IN BLUE	Charles Jarrot
MIDNIGHT MADNESS	David Wechter
THE FLYING VIRUS	Jeff Hare

TV SERIES

MY SISTER SAM	Warner Bros.
MAKIN' IT	Paramount
AT EASE	Warner Bros.
TEMPORARY INSANITY	Chris Thompson - Pilot
THOSE TWO	Bob Randall - Pilot
THE BELLES OF BLEEKER STREET	Stephen Cannell - Pilot

MOW'S/EPISODICS

CHANCE OF A LIFETIME	CBS MOW
KATE BRASHER	CBS
ER	NBC
JAG	CBS
CHICKEN SOUP FOR THE SOUL	PAX
VIP	UPN
THE YOUNG AND THE RESTLESS	CBS
DIAGNOSIS MURDER	CBS
TOUCHED BY AN ANGEL	CBS
CYBILL	CBS
SILK STALKINGS	USA
MELROSE PLACE	FOX

THEATRE

BOTH BARRELS	Luna Park
A GOOD SWIFT KICK	Variety Arts
JOHN BROWN'S BODY	Lobero Theatre
HAPPY HOLIDAYS	Pasadena Playhouse
ALL I REALLY NEED TO KNOW	Tiffany Theatre
HAIR	Starlight Theatre
THE FANTASTICKS	Lobero Theatre

POOR LITTLE LAMBS   St. Peter's Church
TIN PAN MAN   La Mirada Theatre
HAMLET   Vivian Beaumont Theatre

David and the cast of *My Sister Sam*

David Naughton Contact:

The Marshak/Zachary Co.
8840 Wilshire Blvd.
Beverly Hills, CA 90211
Phone: 310-358-3191

160

Michael Rosenbaum

Michael Rosenbaum

Profile

Michael Rosenbaum's quick wit, creativity and personable demeanor have garnered him roles that are quickly skyrocketing him to the highest ranks of Hollywood stardom. Rosenbaum, voted one of *People Magazine*'s Most Eligible Bachelors of 2002, stars on the hit television series, "Smallville" on the WB. Rosenbaum plays, "Lex Luthor" and co-stars with Tom Welling in the Sci-Fi drama.

Rosenbaum can be seen in 2003's "Bringing Down The House," and in the Buena Vista feature "Sorority Boys" with co-stars Barry Watson and Harland Williams about three rowdy college students who are kicked out of their fraternity after being falsely accused of embezzling funds and dress up in drag to join a sorority and incriminate their old fraternity. "Sorority Boys" came out in Fall 2002.

Additionally, Rosenbaum starred in the TriStar feature "Urban Legend," opposite Jared Leto, Alicia Witt, Josh Jackson and Rebecca Gayheart. Rosenbaum portrayed 'Parker' – the eternal 'Frat' brother who ultimately provided the comic relief in this ensemble thriller. Rosenbaum also starred in the television sitcom "Zoe, Duncan, Jack & Jane" opposite Selma Blair on the WB.

Growing up in Indiana, but born in New York, Rosenbaum has always considered himself a New Yorker. He found that he was able to express his creativity in the cultural diversity of the Big Apple. Rosenbaum put his creativity to use, when he decided, on a bet, to audition for a high school play in which he subsequently landed a role. From there, he was hooked. Rosenbaum took on lead roles while pursuing a Theatre Degree at Western Kentucky University and doing summer stock in North Carolina.

Upon graduation, Rosenbaum instantaneously packed up his Toyota Tercel and moved to New York to pursue acting. He quickly landed roles in off-Broadway productions and small independent films. Rosenbaum then segued into guest starring appearances on several sitcoms and a recurring role in the 'Amsterdam Kid' skit on "The Conan O'Brien Show."

Rosenbaum's "big break" happened when, in the same month, he landed both the series regular role of 'Jonathan' on the WB show "Tom" and the role of 'George Tucker' in the Warner Bros. feature "Midnight in the Garden of Good and Evil" directed by Clint Eastwood and starring John Cusack and Kevin Spacey. While shooting "Tom" on the Universal lot, Rosenbaum explains, "The biggest perk about working at Universal was getting to ride the Jurassic Park ride every day during lunch." When asked the difference between working with Tom Arnold and Clint Eastwood, "Both are great, but Clint's a bit more low key and sexier!"

Rosenbaum currently resides in the Hollywood Hills. Despite his busy acting schedule, he tries to find time to play in an ice hockey league, watch movies and play with his full-size Galaga video game.

Michael Rosenbaum Contact:

Baker/Winokur/Ryder
9100 Wilshire Blvd., Floor 6, West
Beverly Hills, CA 90212
Phone: 310-550-7776
Website: www.michaelrosenbaum.com

Elizabeth Ashley

Elizabeth Ashley

Profile

Elizabeth Ashley made her Broadway debut in 1959. Broadway credits include "Take Her, She's Mine," (Tony and Theatre World Awards), "Barefoot in the Park" (Tony Nomination), "Legend," "Hide and Seek," "The Skin of our Teeth," "Caesar and Cleopatra," "Agnes of God," Gore Vidal's "The Best Man," "Suddenly Last Summer," "Enchanted April," "Cat on a Hot Tin Roof," (Tony Nomination)."

Off-Broadway: "The Red Devil Battery Sign," "The Milk Train Doesn't Stop Here Anymore," "When She Danced," and "If Memory Serves." Regional: "The Glass Menagerie," "Sweet Bird of Youth" (Millennium Recognition Award) and "The Little Foxes" (both for the Shakespeare Theatre, D.C.), "Vanities," "A Coupla White Chicks," "Who's Afraid of Virginia Woolf?," "Full Gallop," "Master Class," "The Enchanted," "The Perfect Party." Film: "The Carpetbaggers," "Ship of Fools," "Rancho Deluxe," "92 in the Shade," "Golden Needles," "Stagecoach," "The Great Scout and Cathouse Thursday," "Coma," "Paternity," "Split Image," "Dragnet," "Vampire Kiss," "Happiness." TV appearances include "Evening Shade" (Emmy nomination), A&E's "The Rope" (ACE Award nomination), "The Two Mrs. Grenvilles," "The War Between the Tates," "Sandburg's Lincoln," "Law & Order," "Law and Order: SVU," "The Larry Sanders Show," "Homicide: Life on the Street," "Miami Vice," Edith Wharton's "The Buccaneers" and many appearances on "The Tonight Show" with Johnny Carson. Ms. Ashley was appointed to the first National Council on the Arts under Presidents Kennedy and Johnson. She is the author of the best-selling book *Actress: Postcards from the Road* and can be heard on Lou Reed's CD *The Raven*.

Elizabeth Ashley Contact:

Writers & Artists
19 West 44th St., Suite 1410
New York, NY 10036
Phone: 212-391-1112

Deborah Spielman

Favorite Quote:

"I believe with perfect faith that my friends/co-workers and I will make each other shine as we work towards Enlightenment, Truth and honoring this craft which we call The Arts."

Deborah Spielman

Profile

Deborah is an actress and singer because she knew from day one that she was filled with passion that she had to release. There was a direct link between opening her mouth, moving her body and filling the room with sound which "creative energy" represents in her life.

Deborah did 13 plays/musicals at Framingham High School and completed 3 years of conservatory (Stella Adler) in 1997. On April 1, 2001, Deborah and her cast won a NY MAC award for the pre-post WW2 Berlin themed musical "Indigo Rat" (written by John-Richard Thompson who just published his first book with Anne Ford). The show exuded the dark, yet sexy world of Berlin cabaret music and moods with the score of Kurt Weill and Friedrich Hollaender. The First 2003 NY Nightlife Award winning satirical musical, Rick Crom's "What in the World?!" marked her second collaborative award winning show in the NYC cabaret theatre scene which she only discovered after performing in union work for 5 years. "WITW" is a fast paced 18 number show, which deals with everything from too much Botox injections to the now less recent Enron fallings and poor Mrs. Kenneth Lay. "WITW" was proud to present a whole slew of new numbers when it opened Off-Broadway late Fall of 2003.

Deborah's NYC credits include, playing Inez in "No Exit" (Present Company), touring with Theatreworks USA, other inventive and exhausting musicals such as "The Medicine Shows," "Mr. Shakespeare & Mr. Porter," and various films and voice-over work. Her favorite stock roles include Judy/Ginger in "Ruthless!" (Maryland Theatre on the Hill), Storyteller in "The Beautiful Children Of Eden" (Weathervane) and of course Deborah's first stunning Off-Off Broadway (years ago) role as the vivacious Queen of the Vampires Martina Rain in Wing's Theatre's production of "Vampires in Da House" (a hip pop musical), directed by Shela Xoregos.

Deborah is officially bi-coastal now, but will never consider herself Bi-polar. She finds balance by paying as much attention to becoming a Yogi as she is inspired to continue her craft of acting and singing.

Her website www.debspielman.biz will serve as a great reminder to herself and to others that all is so very good, and that all is moving forward as the universe has promised.

166

Deborah Spielman

Resume

AEA

TELEVISION

True Stories (Cable Series)	Featured Storyteller	Zilo Prod's –Dir. Michaline Babich/LA
Guiding Light	Featured	Dir. Joe Cotugno
Public Affairs TV	Guest Star	WHSH TV 66, (MA)
www.MyOnLineDemo.Com	Voice-Over Artist	Depaul Productions

FILM

Crosseyed (Feature)	Lead	Adam Jones Prod/Dir/NY
Campaigner (Ind. Film)	Principal	Askari Prod's –Dir. Adam Moore/NYC
Game Over (NYU Film)	Principal	Dir. Jeffrey Abrahams
Report For Duty	Principal	Dir. Travis Graalman

THEATRE

Rick Crom's "What In the World?!"	Company	Rose's Turn/Off-Bway *Winner 2003 Nightlife Award
Indigo Rat	Rosa Blum	Rose's Turn **Winner 2001 MAC & Bistro Awards
No Exit	Inez	Present Company
Mr. Shakespeare & Mr. Porter	Lady Macbeth/Hermia	Medicine Show
Children of Eden	Storyteller	Weathervane Theatre
Black Beauty	Lady Lovely	Theatre Works USA
Vampires in Da House	Martina Rain	Wings Theatre
Mystery at Cafe Noir	Sheila "Femme Fatale"	NY Dinner Theatre
The Cretaceous Cabaret	MC	Open Eye Theatre
Ruthless	Judy/Ginger	Theatre On the Hill
Music Man	Marian	S.T.A.G.E. Productions
The Mystery of Edwin Drood	Rosa Bud	S.T.A.G.E. Productions
Judy and The Maccabees	Judy	Merkin Hall / Lucy Moses School
Pinocchio	Cricket	Silligilligus Prod's /Singatell Players
James and the Giant Peach	Narrator / Old Woman	Weathervane Theatre
The Princess and the Pea	Queen	Theatre On the Hill
Fefu and Her Friends	Paula	Stella Adler-Dir. Daniela Varon
The Maids	Madame	Stella Adler- Dir. Milton Justice
A Midsummer Night's Dream	Bottom	Stella Adler- Dir. Jed Diamond
Project D.E.P.T.H	Educational Tour	United Way (MA)

VOICE-OVER

Upon request

EDUCATION

Tisch School of the Arts, New York University / BFA
Stella Adler Conservatory of Acting – 3 Years

TRAINING
Singing - Jeff Halpurn, NYC; Lynn Starling, NYC; Dr. George Perrone, MA (Theory & Opera)
Acting - James Tripp; Milton Justice; Alice Winston; Deborah Kampmeir
Voice - Robert Perillo; Tommy Adler
Voice-Over / Commercial and Narrative - David Goldberg / Edge Studio, NYC
Commercial Course - David Cady (NY); Terry Burland (LA)
Soap Opera Course - Scott Powers

SPECIAL ABILITIES
Dialects: British (Proper & Cockney)/Southern/NY Yenta/Yiddish/Boston/Puerto Rican; Speaks Spanish and some Hebrew; Creative Characters/Facial Expressions & Comic Timing; Modern dance and Movement / Choreography; Yoga, Kickboxing, Bicycling, Swimming; License (Driving and Bartending)

Deborah Spielman Contact:

Signature Artists
Phone: 323-651-0600
Website: www.debspielman.biz

168

Shelley Malil

Favorite Quote:

*"Almost everything we do in life is of no importance, but
it is of the utmost importance that we do it."*
Mahatma Gandhi

Shelley Malil

Profile

Actor Shelley Malil caught national attention as "*Chad*," one of the Budweiser "*What are you doing*?!" guys in Anheuser-Busch's inspired "*Whassup*?!" commercial spin-off. After the clever send-up was voted best Super Bowl commercial by a number of trades, magazines and entertainment commentators, Shelley resurrects "*Chad*" in another two TV spots. The spotlight helped Shelly score a lead role in FX's dark comedy pilot, "Bad News, Mr. Swanson," in which he plays "*Ashid*," best friend to Frank Whaley's "*Mr. Swanson*."

Shelley first came to Hollywood eight years ago, after a two-year stint at New York's famed American Academy of Dramatic Arts. With $600 to his name and a phone number of a friend of a friend in his pocket, Shelley drove his van West. He had dreams of becoming a comedic actor like his idol Bob Hope, whom he first saw on a neighbor's TV set, the only one in the fishing village on the southern tip of India where he was raised. Within three weeks of his arrival, he had landed a manager, a guest star role on FOX's "Briscoe County Jr." and his SAG card.

Since that time, Shelley has worked steadily, appearing in such television shows as "ER" (*in the Emmy-winning episode "Love Labor Lost"*), "Seinfeld," two seasons on "NYPD Blue," "Sabrina The Teenage Witch," "Party Of Five," "The West Wing" and "The Jamie Foxx Show" just to mention a few.

In addition, he has worked with director Tommy Schlamme and the incomparable Tracey Ullman in her award-winning HBO series "Tracey Takes On," with James Earl Jones in the feature film "Second Civil War" and with Jeff Daniels and Elizabeth Hurley in the big screen version of "My Favorite Martian" directed by Donald Petire. He also recently starred in Regent's "Just Can't Get Enough: The Chippendale's Story," which premiered at the American Film Market, in which he gained 35 pounds to play the role of "*Steve Banerjee*" the owner of the Chippendale's Clubs, then Shelley followed that with work on both "Collateral Damage" with Arnold Schwarzenegger and "Holes" with Henry Winkler under the direction of Andrew Davis.

Shelley began pursuing his dream of entertaining people on the high school stage, where his leading turns often earned awards in district competitions in Texas, where his family settled after emigrating to the U.S. in 1974. "*Chili*," his teenage nickname, got a taste of the entertainment spotlight during his work in theatre and as a disc jockey at a local radio station.

After high school, he spent a few seasons performing classic musicals like "Annie, Get Your Gun," "Carnival" and "Showboat" on the Dallas dinner theatre circuit until he auditioned for the American Academy of Dramatic Arts and moved to New York City. Shelley longs to return to the stage. His portrayal as Bottom in "A Midsummer Night's Dream" at Hollywood's Stella Adler Theatre garnered him a Best Featured Actor nomination at the Los Angeles Ovation Awards. Shelley's most recent turn was in "Chaos Theory" at the ArtWallah Festival in Los Angeles where he played both a 63 year old and then a 24-year-old (in a flashback scene) "*Mukesh Singh*," a professor of English literature. His performance left most of the sold out audience members wondering who the younger actor was.

Shelley is proud to be from the Indian state of Kerala and a Malayalee, a people known for their comedic take on life. In his spare time, Shelley takes a Zen-like approach to golf, goes to approximately five films a week, devours motivational books and recently joined the Big Brother Program. A plaque on his office wall bears Shelley's motto for living "*Almost everything we do in life is of no importance, but it is of the utmost importance that we do it*" – Mahatma Gandhi

Shelley Malil Contact:

Agent: Mark Measures
Phone: 310-859-1417, Ext. 126
Website: www.malil.com

170

Annie Potts

Annie Potts

Profile

Annie Potts has long been considered one of Hollywood's most popular and versatile actresses.

She recently was in a Lifetime telepic, and a television reunion of epic proportions. She starred in "Defending Our Kids: The Julie Posey Story." It told of Julie Posey, a stay at home wife and mother who began a crusade to help the police catch sexual predators after a pedophile approached her teenage daughter in an online chat room.

Most recently, Potts starred in the much-anticipated reunion of one of television's most beloved sitcoms, "Designing Women." The telecast marked the first time in 12 years that the show's original cast had reunited to share their memories and experiences.

The "Designing Women Reunion" aired on Lifetime Network. Potts finished a very successful four-year run in Lifetime's one-hour drama, "Any Day Now," which became the network's signature series upon their entrance into primetime television.

The show followed the special relationship between two women – a white homemaker with children (Potts) and a highly successful African American attorney (Lorraine Toussaint) – who shared a friendship that dated back to their childhood in the 1960's South, where the civil rights movement is seen through their young eyes via flashbacks.

Howard Rosenberg of *The Los Angeles Times* proclaimed, "No one on TV is doing better work than Potts." *USA Today* declared, "'Any Day Now' is graced by a perfectly pitched performance from Annie Potts." For her efforts, Potts received a Screen Actors Guild nomination for "Best Actress in a Television Series" for the last two consecutive years. A 1998 Viewers For Quality Television (VQT) survey found "Any Day Now" the highest quality rated new drama series of the season.

Audiences may be seeing Potts again in NBC's "Stuck in the Middle With You." The comedy revolves around a suburban family that struggles to stay a part of the middle class. Potts will play "Dori," wife of co-star Timothy Busfield and mother of three unruly kids. "Dori" is a wry, sarcastic woman who loves her family, yet feels she is struggling to balance her career and home life.

On the big screen, Potts lent her voice to the hit of the 1999-2000 holiday season, Disney's TOY STORY II, in which she reprised her role of a Little Bo Peep lamp who is the light of Woody's (Tom Hanks) life. In April of 2000, Potts made her New York stage debut with a two-week stint in Eve Ensler's award-winning play, "The Vagina Monologues."

This came after Potts successful "V-Day 2000" performance of the play in Los Angeles, where she shared the stage with Gillian Anderson, Kirstie Alley, Roseanne, Winona Ryder and Rita Wilson amongst others.

Potts was born in Franklin, Kentucky and received a BFA in Theatre from Stephens College in Columbia, Missouri. She began acting in summer stock theatre before coming to Los Angeles to further her education in graduate school at Cal Arts. Once in Los Angeles, she continued to work on the stage where she caught the attention of both critics and casting directors. Soon after, she landed her feature film debut role in the comedy "Corvette Summer," in which she starred opposite Mark Hamill. Her disarming performance as a quirky would-be prostitute earned her a Golden Globe nomination and immediately established her as one of the most promising talents in the industry.

Potts soon lived up to that promise with her starring role in the comedy "Heartaches," for which she was honored with Canada's Genie Award. Critical and audience raves followed for her standout performance as the droll Brooklyn-accented receptionist in Ivan Reitman's smash hit comedy "Ghostbusters."

Ironically, her performance was so convincing that the Southern-born actress was almost typecast as "too urban." In 1986, Potts turned that impression on its ear when she debuted in a new CBS series called "Designing Women." Potts starred as one of four women running an interior design firm in Atlanta. "It was groundbreaking. It was one of the first series to star an all-woman cast and to portray women as smart and funny," Potts attests. The show was an immediate hit and went on to enjoy a successful seven-year run, enduring cast evolutions and time slot changes. Through it all, Potts remained an audience favorite for her multi-layered portrayal of 'Mary Jo,' a divorced single mother who tried to juggle career and family.

Following "Designing Women," Potts did a two-year stint on CBS' "Love and War." She received an Emmy Award nomination for "Best Actress in a Comedy" for her performance as gourmet chef 'Dana Palladino.' She also received critical acclaim starring as 'Louanne Johnson' on the ABC drama "Dangerous Minds." Her gutsy portrayal of the tough Marine-turned-inner city teacher garnered her considerable praise, with Newsday proclaiming, "Potts is a powerhouse at the center of it all, a dynamo of spirit and determination!"

In addition to her television success, Potts has continued to appear in a variety of feature films. She received critical acclaim for her work as Jeff Bridges' wife in "Texasville," Peter Bogdanovich's follow up to "The Last Picture Show," and she has also appeared in "Crimes Of Passion," "Pretty In Pink," "Who's Harry Crumb?," 'Pass The Ammo," and "Breaking The Rules."

Annie's "Bad Girl" Image

Annie Potts Contact:

Jay D. Schwartz & Associates
3255 Cahuenga Blvd.
West, Suite 205
Los Angeles, CA 90068
Phone: 323-512-9100

173

Nicolas Read

Favorite Quote:

"Paul Rudd was born in the 60's and is all about peace, love and flowers and I'm a product of the 70's! So I'm all about Disco, Polyester and platform shoes!"

Nicolas Read

Profile

Nicolas was born in London, England and moved to the United States when he was six. He lived in Canada for a short time, Wyoming, Washington State, Walnut Creek, California and Santa Barbara before arriving in Los Angeles. He studied at the Lee Strasberg Institute in Los Angeles under the tutelage of Marc Marno. He was an improv player at the Up Front Comedy Improv in Santa Monica, California. Nicolas has enjoyed playing numerous parts in film and television as well as playing many complex characters in theatre.

Nicolas at the Balls of Fire Celebrity Bowling Tournament

Nicolas Read

Resume

SAG/AFTRA

<u>Demo Reel Available</u>

FEATURE FILMS

Deadly Stingers	Starring	Dir. J. R. Bookwalter
The Rose Technique (*with Jobeth Williams*)	Starring	Dir. Jon Scheidie
Slaughter Studios	Starring	Dir. Brian Katkin (*Roger Corman Producer*)
Redemption	Supporting	Dir. Kaylene Peoples
If Tomorrow Comes (*with James Franco*)	Supporting	Dir. Gerritt Steenhagen
Papers, Rocks, Scissors	Starring	Dir. Tim Rosenow
Zombie Ninja Gangbangers	Starring	Dir. Jeff Centauri
Midnight Witness	Starring	Dir. Peter Foldy
Dead Silence	Supporting	Dir. Peter O'Fallon

TELEVISION (*Sample Credits*)

MTV's Undressed	Recurring	Dir. David Fickas, MTV
The Amanda Show	Co-Star	Dir. Ken Whittingham, Nickelodeon
S Club Seven in LA	Guest Star	Dir. Andy Margetson, BBC/FOX
Sunset Beach	Guest Star	Dir. Grant Johnson, NBC
Beverly Hills 90210	Guest Star	Dir. Michael Uno, FOX
Days of Our Lives	Recurring	Dir. (Various), NBC
What Happened	Guest Star	Dir. Bob Jaffe, NBC
Palm Beach (*Pilot*)	Series Regular	Dir. Ivan Reitman, Universal

SHORT FILMS & INDUSTRIALS

Shattered (*DreamWorks/Disney Short*)	Starring	Dir. Angela French
The Right Choice	Supporting	Dir. Jack Shea
My Life	Starring	Dir. Warren Shumway
Jaime's Secret (*With Paul Rudd*)	Starring	Dir. Peter Foldy

THEATRE

The White Liars	Tom	The Rose Alley Theatre
Call Me By My Rightful Name	Elliot	Lee Strasberg Theatre
Split Second	Willis	Studio Stras
Crazed Victimless Victims	Improv Comedy Regular	Up Front Comedy, Santa Monica
Detective Story	Arthur	Marilyn Monroe Theatre
The Zoo Story	Jerry	Lee Strasberg Theatre
Death Of A Salesman	Biff	Lobero Theatre, Santa Barbara
True West	Lee	Santa Monica College

TRAINING
Lee Strasberg Theatre Institute-Marc Marno
Stella Adler Institute-Arthur Mendoza
Up Front Comedy Improv-Jeff Michalski

SPECIAL SKILLS & INTERESTS
Accents: Excellent British, Cockney, *Yorkshire*, New York, Southern, East Indian, Scottish, Irish and others.
Impressionist: Do a great Jack Nicholson, Don Knotts, Woody Allen, Eric Roberts, Nick Nolte, Elvis, and others.
Martial Arts, Trained Clown, Can Make Balloon Animals, Swimming, Rollerblading, Bowling, Team Sports, and Surfing.
Is a dual citizen of England and the U..S. and has a valid British passport

Nicolas Read Contact:

Website: www.nicolasread.com

Robert Arevalo

Favorite Quote:

"…and talk of peace! I hate the word as I hate hell, all Montagues ,and thee."
From Romeo and Juliet by William Shakespeare

Robert Arevalo

Profile

Hailing from the culturally rich border town of El Paso, Texas, Robert moved to Los Angeles to pursue a career in film. He landed at HBO where he started as an intern. He eventually moved to the 20th Century Fox lot where he met director Robert Rodriquez who was prepping for his film the 1995 blockbuster "Desperado." Arevalo auditioned and won the role of the "*Opponent.*" He then took on a supporting role in Andy Tennant's "Fools Rush In," and guest starred in various TV shows among them: FOX's "Space Above and Beyond," and HBO's "Arliss." He also played Ernest Borgnine's nephew on NBC's "The Single Guy," as well as co-starred in ABC's MOW "The Runaway Virus."

As an actor/filmmaker Arevalo plans to create what he calls Neo-Latin cinema, as a result of the mix of influences that shaped his vision, from MTV, Bruce Lee to Japanimation, comics and cartoons. He believes young Latinos are much more savvy and ready for something new and cutting edge because they have been exposed to a new world through technology and pop culture like never before.

Arevalo's next project is the feature film "Kinky." A comedy about a struggling actor pondering the path he's chosen while searching for his place in life. A mix of "Fast Times at Ridgemont High," "Swingers" and "Y Tu Mama Tambien."

Robert Arevalo Contact:

Heidi Rotbart Management
Phone: 310-470-8339

Defining Artists
Agent: Kim Dorr
Phone: 818-506-8188

Lee Garlington

Favorite Quote:

"Happiness is wanting what you have, not having what you want."

Lee Garlington

Profile

Lee Garlington started out as a sound and radio engineer in Washington, D.C., ending that career with the best "straight" job she ever had: working for National Public Radio. She moved to Los Angeles in 1980 to pursue an acting career, having no agent, credits, contacts, union memberships, or experience! She was one of the very, very blessed and fortunate ones. In 1982 she was cast in two plays by the same playwright, back to back, that allowed her to be on a small stage 4 nights a week for 22 months. That was how her career began. She got her first agent and movie part from that run. Since then she has appeared in 26 films, 32 movies of the week, 10 pilots and 5 series, and probably in the neighborhood of 50 to 75 guest shots on various television series. She is most grateful to director Phil Alden Robinson, who has cast her in all of his movies: "In the Mood," "Field of Dreams," "Sneakers," and "Sum of All Fears."

Her passion is the stage, and she has also performed in thirty plays during her 22 years in Los Angeles, and is most honored to have won the Ovation Award (L.A.'s answer to the Tonys) in 1999 for Best Supporting Actress.

She is currently writing a screenplay (isn't everyone??) and for the last seven years has done the Orientation for New Members to the Screen Actors Guild. She uses herself as an example that it is possible to have a career somewhere between fame and ignominy, as Lee is a working, bread and butter actress, who has made a very nice living for a long time in her chosen career. She is happily married for 12 years, the mother of two dogs and a cat, and the aunt to many.

Lee at the premiere of *The Hot Chick*

Lee Garlington

Resume

FEATURES

GUARDING EDDY	Dir.: Scott McKinsey	Freedom Films
JOHNSON FAMILY VACATION	Dir.: Christopher Erskin	Fox Searchlight
THE HOT CHICK	Dir.: Tom Brady	Disney Features
AMERICAN PIE 2	Dir.: James B. Rogers	Universal
SUM OF ALL FEARS	Dir.: Phil Robinson	Paramount
LOVELY AND AMAZING	Dir.: Nicole Holofcener	Big Truck, Inc.
ONE HOUR PHOTO	Dir. Mark Romanek.	Fox Searchlight
LIFE WITHOUT DICK	Dir.: Bix Skahill	Independent
EVOLUTION	Dir.: Ivan Reitman	Universal Pictures
LOVING LULU	Dir.: John Kaye	Millennium Films
BOYS AND GIRLS	Dir.: Robert Iscove	Dimension Films
STRANGER INSIDE	Dir.: Cheryl Dunye	Stranger Inside Prod's.
DANTE'S PEAK	Dir.: Roger Donaldson	Universal Pictures
DRIVEN	Dir.: Michael Shoob	Trianon Prod's.
THE BABYSITTER	Dir.: Guy Furland	Aaron Spelling Prod's.
REFLECTIONS IN THE DARK	Dir.: Jon Purdy	Concorde
MY LIFE	Dir.: Bruce Joel Rubin	Columbia
SNEAKERS	Dir.: Phil Robinson	Universal
JACK THE BEAR	Dir.: Marshall Herskovitz	20th Century Fox
MEET THE APPLEGATES	Dir.: Michael Lehman	New World
FIELD OF DREAMS	Dir.: Phil Robinson	Universal
THREE FUGITIVES	Dir.: Francis Verber	Disney
THE SEVENTH SIGN	Dir.: Carl Schultz	TriStar
IN THE MOOD	Dir.: Phil Robinson	Lorimar
SOME KIND OF WONDERFUL	Dir.: John Hughes	Paramount
COBRA	Dir.: George Casmotos	Cannon
PSYCHO III	Dir.: Anthony Perkins	Universal Pictures
PSYCHO II	Dir.: Richard Franklin	Universal Pictures

MINISERIES and MOWs

MURDER SHE WROTE: THE LAST FREE MAN	Dir.: Anthony Shaw	CBS/mow
IF THESE WALLS COULD TALK II	Dir's.: Jane Anderson, Martha Coolidge and Anne Heche	HBO
PRODIGAL SON	Dir.: Aaron Lipstadt	Showtime
CAN OF WORMS	Dir.: Paul Schneider	Disney/mow
VIRTUAL OBSESSION	Dir.: Mick Garris	mow
BALLOON FARM	Dir.: William Dear	ABC/mow
SUMMER OF FEAR	Dir.: Mike Robe	CBS/mow
WHOSE DAUGHTER IS SHE?	Dir.: Frank Arnold	CBS/mow
TAKE ME HOME AGAIN	Dir.: Tom McLoughlin	NBC/mow
THE CONVICTION OF KITTY DODDS	Dir.: Michael Tuchner	CBS/mow
WHEN NO ONE WOULD LISTEN	Dir.: Armand Mastroianni	CBS/mow

SHAME	Dir.: Dan Lerner	Lifetime/mow
POINT OF MURDER	Dir.: Larry Elikann	ABC/mow
WHEN YOU REMEMBER ME	Dir.: Harry Winer	ABC/mow
THE WHEREABOUTS OF JENNY	Dir.: Gene Reynolds	ABC/mow
A KILLING IN A SMALL TOWN	Dir.: Stephen Gyllenhaal	CBS/mow
LAST FLIGHT OUT	Dir.: Larry Elikann	NBC/mow
COLD SASSY TREE	Dir.: Joan Tewkesbury	TNT/mow
WINNIE	Dir.: John Korty	NBC/mow
MURDER ORDAINED	Dir.: Mike Robe	CBS-miniseries
THE YARN PRINCESS	Dir.: Tom McLoughlin	ABC/mow
LOVE MATTERS	Dir.: Eb Lottimer	Showtime/mow
LOVE KILLS	Dir.: Brian Grant	CBS/miniseries
JUDITH KRANTZ'S TORCH SONG	Dir.: Michael Miller	ABC/mow

EPISODICS AND SERIES

ABBY NEWTON	Guest Star	UPN
EVERWOOD	Recurring	WBN/pilot
ONCE AND AGAIN	Guest Star	ABC
THE DISTRICT	Guest Star	CBS
BUFFY THE VAMPIRE SLAYER	Guest Star	WB
SIX FEET UNDER	Guest Star	HBO
TOUCHED BY AN ANGEL	Guest Star	CBS
OTHER PEOPLE	Guest Star	NBC/pilot
TITUS	Guest Star	FOX
GIDEON'S CROSSING	Guest Star	ABC
JUDGING AMY	Guest Star	CBS
NYPD BLUE	Recurring Guest Star	ABC
E.R.	Guest Star	NBC
THE PRACTICE	Guest Star	ABC
CHICAGO HOPE	Guest Star	CBS
TOWNIES	Series Regular	ABC
GRACE UNDER FIRE	Recurring Guest Star	ABC
BLAME IT ON ERNIE	Series Lead	UPN/Universal
FRIENDS	Guest Star	NBC
HOME IMPROVEMENT	Guest Star	ABC
FLYING COLORS	Series Lead	ABC/pilot
ARRESTING BEHAVIOR	Series Regular	ABC
LENNY	Series Regular	CBS
ROSEANNE	Multiple Episodes	ABC
SEINFELD	Guest Star	NBC/pilot

THEATRE

SIDE MAN	Pasadena Playhouse
CRASHING HEAVEN	Court Theatre
RISK EVERYTHING*	Zephyr Theatre
BOB FUNK	The Tamarind Theatre
SWEET DELIVERANCE	Hudson Theatre (Cora)
WALKING THE BLONDE	Theatre Geo
POT MOM	The Cast Theatre (Patty)

THE MUSIC FROM DOWN THE HILL	Odyssey Theatre/Los Angeles (Margot)
NIGHT CLASS	Powerhouse Theatre/Los Angeles (Mrs. Hettry)
RUBY, RUBY, SAM, SAM	Cast Theatre/Los Angeles (Ruby)
THE TIME OF YOUR LIFE	Al's Bar/Los Angeles (Kitty)
GULLS	Powerhouse Theatre/Los Angeles (Frances)
LIARS POKER	Cast Theatre/Los Angeles (Becky)
SIBLINGS	Callboard Theatre/Los Angeles (Jennifer)
LAST SUMMER AT BLUEFISH COVE	Theatre On The Square/San Francisco (Li'l Kitty)
LAST SUMMER AT BLUEFISH COVE	Fountain Theatre/Los Angeles (Rae)
A LATE SNOW	On The Fridge Theatre/Los Angeles (Ellie)

*Winner of Ovation Award – Best Supporting Actress – 1999

SPECIAL SKILLS
Comedy improvisation, emceeing, dialects, motorcycle riding and dancing
DIRECTING CREDITS
Available upon request

Lee Garlington Contact:

Paul Kohner, Inc.
9300 Wilshire Blvd., Suite 555
Beverly Hill, CA 90212
Phone: 310-550-1060

Andras Jones

Andras Jones

Profile

      Andras Jones is probably best known for his performance as Rick in "Nightmare on Elm Street, Part 4." Other highlights include his brutal romancing of the pubescent Drew Barrymore in "Far From Home," and the lead role of Trevor Blackburn in the psychedelic horror film "The Attic Expeditions" with Seth Green and Jeffrey Combs. Andras is also an acclaimed singer/songwriter, having released 10 CD's on his own label, The City Limits, and toured the US and Canada extensively as a solo act and with his band The Previous.

Andras Jones

Resume

SAG
FILMS

The Attic Expeditions (w/Seth Green)	LEAD	dir: Jeremy Kasten
Hurricane Festival	LEAD	dir: Chi Y. Lee
The Demolitionist	SUPPORTING	dir: Robert Kurtzman
Averill's Arrival	LEAD	dir: Michel Shottenberg
The Prom (w/Jennifer Jason-Leigh)	LEAD	dir: Steven Shainberg
Tripwire (w/Viggo Mortensen)	SUPPORTING	dir: James Lemmo
Far From Home (w/Drew Barrymore)	SUPPORTING	dir: Miert Avis
Nightmare on Elm St. 4	LEAD	dir: Renny Harlin
Night Trap (w/Dana Plato)	LEAD	
Sorority Babes In the Slimeball Bowl-A-Rama	LEAD	dir: Dave DeCouteau

TELEVISION

Alien Nation	Guest Lead	FOX
Saved By The Bell	Guest Lead	DISNEY
The New Leave It To Beaver	Guest	WARNER BROS.

Andras Jones Contact:

Website: www.olywa.net/previous/

Camille Winbush

Camille Winbush

Profile

Ever ride a camel in a snowstorm? "Not yet," said Camille Winbush. However, this fifteen year old is continuously storming her way through Hollywood, and appears as a series regular on FOX's Emmy Award winning sitcom, "The Bernie Mac Show."

As Vanessa, the oldest of the three children on the show, the "girl" proves she can hold her own against tough-love parental Bernie Mac. Beating out hundreds of hopefuls for the role, Camille shines as the tough teenager every parent must endure. Being an only child herself, Camille feels she has gained a second family, and now innately inherited a younger brother and sister in her TV siblings. Possessing warmth, electricity, confidence and maturity well beyond her years, Bernie Mac likes to refer to Camille as "the quiet storm…"

At the age of two her first television appearance was a recurring role on NBC's "Viper," soon followed by a series regular role on NBC's "Minor Adjustments," and a recurring role on the hit WB family drama, "7th Heaven." Camille also co-stared on CBS' "That's Life," Lifetime's "Any Day Now," ABC's "The Norm Show" and "Hanging with Mr. Cooper," to name a few.

Camille's burgeoning list of credits also include a lead role in the Artisan Entertainment film "Ghost Dog" with Forrest Whitaker, as well as roles in "Eraser" with Arnold Schwarzenegger and "Dangerous Minds" alongside Michelle Pfeiffer. She also lent her voice to the Disney soundtrack of "Geppetto."

Rounding out this young star's talent, Camille can be heard singing the timeless holiday Christmas classics, "The Night Before Christmas" and "One Small Voice," on the teen celebrity holiday CD, "School's Out! Christmas," released October 29, 2002 and distributed by Universal Music. Camille joined some of the hottest teens on television to give their rendition of some of today's most cherished holiday songs.

Displaying a rainbow of talent, Camille also performs as a dancer, pianist and is an accomplished gymnast, currently competing at level 6.

Camille Winbush Contact:

Shannon Barr Public Relations
3619½ Crest Dr.
Manhattan Beach, CA 90266
Phone: 310-546-5069

Dennis Franz

Dennis Franz

Profile

Four time Emmy winner Dennis Franz was born on October 28th in Maywood, Illinois. He is first generation German American, and has two older sisters.

The eight-time Emmy nominee has also received two SAG awards for Best Actor in a Drama, and two for Best Ensemble Acting, five Best Actor awards from Viewers for Quality Television and a 1994 Golden Globe. Dennis plays the role of detective Andy Sipowicz on "NYPD Blue" on ABC-TV. He was presented with his star on the Hollywood Walk of Fame on February 19, 1999.

Dennis teamed up with the Dixie Chicks, playing 'Earl' in the video of their hit song, "Goodbye Earl." He is also a part of a very select VIP Group chosen to read selections from Pope John II's private prayer/poem books for a CD, which was released in early 2002.

In his junior year of high school, he landed his first part in 'The Crucible.' As Dennis's interest in acting grew, he gave up sports. He attended Wright Junior College and Southern Illinois University graduating with a Bachelor's Degree in Speech and Theatre.

Following his 1968 graduation, a notice from the local draft board arrived. Realizing that Vietnam or Vietnam, were his choices, he thought he could outsmart the service by enlisting in officer's school one day before the draft took effect. He admits to having been curious about the service, a curiosity he regretted two weeks after enlisting. Not really wishing to become an officer and stay in the military, Dennis requested a transfer. And, transferred he was...an eleven month tour of duty in Vietnam with a reconnaissance unit.

Upon his discharge, Dennis got together with some college buddies and organized several theatre companies in Chicago. Eventually, he joined the 'Organic Theatre Company,' which proved to be the turning point in his theatrical career. The company also wrote much of their own material, and "Bleacher Bums" authored by Dennis and Joe Mantegna won a local Emmy Award for its PBS presentation.

Chicago was on the verge of becoming a thriving film community. Dennis appeared in Robert Altman's "A Wedding" and Brian De Palma's "The Fury." Once in Los Angeles, he continued to perform in plays, but ended up right back in Chicago for his first television series, "Chicago Story."

His film credits include; "City of Angels," with Meg Ryan and Nicolas Cage, David Mamet's "American Buffalo," with Dustin Hoffman, "Die Hard 2, Die Harder," "The Package," with Gene Hackman, "Dressed to Kill," "Popeye," "Blow Out," "Body Double" and "Psycho II."

Dennis guest-starred on numerous television series including "Hill Street Blues," as the notorious 'Sal Benedetto.' Steven Bochco created "Bay City Blues," and asked Dennis to take a starring role. He rejoined "Hill Street Blues" as 'Lt. Norman Buntz.' Dennis starred in NBC TV's "Moment of Truth; Caught in the Crossfire," the ABC miniseries "Texas Justice," Steven Bochco's series "Civil Wars" and NBC's Movie of the Week, "In the Line of Duty: Stand-Off at Marion."

In his spare time, Dennis loves to spend time with his wife, Joanie and daughters, Tricia and Krista. He enjoys golf and snow skiing.

Dennis Franz Contact:

Cynthia Snyder Public Relations
5739 Colfax Ave.
North Hollywood, CA 91601
Phone: 818-769-0100

Terrance Camilleri

Favorite Quote:

"The commitment to the exploration into the creative process is the purist journey into an expanded consciousness."

Terrance Camilleri

Profile

Terrance Camilleri was born in Gozo, Malta to parents Joseph Camilleri a bricklayer and builder and Carmel Camilleri a housewife. He is the middle child with elder brother Frank and younger sister Mary. They are both married with families. Terrance's parents immigrated to Australia when he was four years old. At the age of eight his father would take him to the drive-in movies. Terrance was totally captivated, but what struck him most was seeing the same actors playing different roles in different movies. "That's it" he turned to his father and said, "That is what I am going to do when I grow up," and that was it. He worked as an apprentice motor mechanic, up until his twenties, at which time he quit to become a lead guitarist in a band called "The Aches 'n' Pains." At twenty-one he quit the band and started his acting career in amateur musicals. He went professional the next year in Peter Pan and hasn't looked back since.

Terrance Camilleri made his feature film debut in 1973 after touring Europe, England and Brazil with "Disney on Parade." His first feature was also Peter Weir's first feature called "The Cars That Ate Paris." "Cars" and Terrance received critical acclaim in Australia, England and Europe. He has also earned a well deserved reputation working with such directors as Bruce Beresford, Phillip Noyce, Richard Lester, Phil Alden Robinson, Paul Schrader, Martin Brest and Stephen Herek, who directed Bill & Ted's Excellent Adventure in which Terrance was highly applauded for his performance as Napoleon.

He can also be seen in: Gigli, Hey DJ, Henry X and 7 Songs.

Terrance Camilleri

Resume

SAG/Australian and British Equity

FEATURE FILMS

Hey DJ	Miguel Delgado	Full Circle Pictures
Henry The Tenth	Daniel MacCannell	Mears & Bosko Prod.
Gigli	Martin Brest	Revolution Films
7 Songs	Noah Stern	Soft Serve Pictures
Pizza Wars: The Movie	Babak Sarrafan	Elvis Anti Dead Prod.
Here Lies Lonely	Bart Dorsa	Black Dog Films
Invisibles	Noah Stern	Zero Films
The Truman Show	Peter Weir	Paramount
Spilt Milk	Gregor von Bismark	B Smart Prod.
Evicted	Michael Tierney	Evicted Prod.
Bill & Ted's Excellent Adventure	Steven Herek	Nelsen Ent.
In The Mood	Phil Alden Robinson	Kings Rd. Ent.
The Cars That Ate Paris	Peter Weir	Salt Pan Films
Backroads	Phillip Noyce	Backroads Prod.
Money Movers	Bruce Beresford	S. Aust Film Co.
Cass	Chris Noonan	Film Australia
Let's Get Harry	Stuart Rosenberg	TriStar Films
Out Of It	Ken Cameron	Cameron Prod.
Dutch Treat	Boaz Davidson	Cannon Films
Kitty and the Bagman	Donald Crombie	Adams Packe
The Night, The Prowler	Jim Sharman	NSW Film Co.
Encounter At Ravens Gate	Rolf de Heer	S. Aust Film Co.
Midnight Spares	Quenton Masters	Filmco Ltd.

TELEVISION

The District	Oz Scott	CBS
JAG	Jeannot Swarc	Paramount
Pacific Blue	Terence Winkless	North Hall Prod.
Inferno	Ian Barry	UPN
NYPD Blue	Michael M. Robin	Steven Bochco Prod.
Renegade	Recurring	Stu Segall Prod.
Love And War	Guest Star	Love & War Prod.
Witch Hunt	Paul Schrader	HBO
Hill St. Blues	Guest Star	Steven Bochco Prod.
George Burns Comedy Week	Phil Alden Robinson	Universal

STAGE (Partial List)

The Tempest	Gonzalo	Bedford Thompson Players
The Shewing Up Of Blanco Posnet	Strapper	Bedford Thompson Players
Iphigenia	Arcas	Theatre in the Park
The Diary Of A Scoundrel	Krutitsky	Theatre in the Park
The Trial	Franz, Bertold, Chief Clerk	The Company Of Angeles
Drums In The Night	Five parts	Cast Theatre
The Unreasonable Are Dying Out		Wallenboyd Theatre

194

TRAINING

Drama	Stephen Book, Ivana Chubbuck, Stella Adler, Bob Carnegie (Meisner)
Dialects	American (most), British (most), Australian, French, Italian, Spanish, Greek
Skills	Guitar, Singing, Percussion, Horse Back Riding, Water Skiing, Boxing, Yoga, T'ai Chi

Terrance Camilleri Contact:

PTI Talent Agency
9000 Sunset Blvd. Suite 506
West Hollywood, CA 90069
Phone: 310-274-7716

Gloria O'Brien-Fontenot

Favorite Quote:

"Just Do It."
Nike

Gloria O'Brien-Fontenot

Profile

Raised in Hollywood, doing commercials and movies as a child actress and singer, Gloria did her first commercial at the age of 6 and continued non-stop performing in movies, television, and commercials until she was a teenager. A competitive gymnast and a dancer she then began expanding her horizons. In the past 10 years, Gloria has become a consistent and reputable actress, singer and stuntwoman. You can see her acting on the screen, performing as a singer, as well as doing the stunts for other actresses. You can see her as the motorcycle policewoman who hooks up with Handsome Rob in "The Italian Job," a concerned shopper in "Hollywood Homicide," as a special guest performer on the BBC series "Call The Shots," or doing stunts in the motorcycle sequence for Drew Barrymore in "Charlie's Angels: Full Throttle." Her past credits include: "Cradle To The Grave," "The Hot Chick," "The Animal," "Planet of the Apes," "Deuce Bigalow, Male Gigolo," "Scream 3," "What Planet are you From," "Buffy the Vampire Slayer," "Sheena, Queen of the Jungle," "Roswell," "The Young and the Restless," and many more.

Gloria is currently working on an R&B/Pop CD on RRAAAH Records and writes and co-produces her own material. She regularly performs live and sings the National Anthem at race events.

She is one of the founding members of V10-Women Stunt Professionals, an exclusive association of the most accomplished and promising stuntwomen currently working in Hollywood. She is a member of the Academy of Television Arts and Sciences and the Taurus World Stunt Academy.

With a booming career, Gloria has also managed to raise a family and is a mother of two, a nine and ten year old, who have also done their first films. Her daughter, Megan can be seen in "Hulk" and her son in "Bad Santa." Gloria is married to Clay Donahue Fontenot who can be seen acting in "Romeo Must Die," "Spiderman II," "Firetrap" and "Dragon Fury II." Clay is also a well known stunt performer and member of Brand X Action Specialists. Clay won the "Best Fight" category in the 2003 Taurus World Stunt Awards for his work doing stunts for Wesley Snipes in Blade II.

Gloria O'Brien-Fontenot

Resume

FILM AND TELEVISION CREDITS

THE ITALIAN JOB
THE CAT IN THE HAT
CHARLIE'S ANGELS: FULL THROTTLE
SLOW BURN
PLANET OF THE APES
DEUCE BIGOLOW, MALE GIGOLO
SCREAM 3
WHAT PLANET ARE YOU FROM
I KNOW WHAT YOU SCREAMED...
44 MINUTES
PRIMETIME GLICK
FIREFLY
BUFFY THE VAMPIRE SLAYER (4 seasons)
NATIONAL LAMPOON AMER. ADVENT.
18 WHEELS OF JUSTICE
ROSWELL
THE YOUNG AND THE RESTLESS
SHEENA, QUEEN OF THE JUNGLE
THE LOVE BOAT NEXT WAVE
AMERICA'S FUNNIEST HOME VIDEOS
TOPPERS CLUBHOUSE

HOLLYWOOD HOMICIDE
THE HOT CHICK
CRADLE TO THE GRAVE
100 MILE RULE
THE ANIMAL
GHOSTS OF MARS
GROUND ZERO "QUAKE"
AGENT OF DEATH
RESURRECTION
CALL THE SHOTS
FASTLANE
ANGEL
I SPIKE
GET REAL
ACTION
BRIMSTONE
V.I.P.
SPACE WARRIOR
CRACKER
CONTROL

VIDEOS AND COMMERCIALS

NO DOUBT – EX-GIRLFRIEND, PROPAGANDA, MISSY ELLIOT – B.I.T.C.H., NISSAN CUBE, LEE JEANS – MUD FOOTBALL.

SKILLS

GYMNASTICS, MARTIAL ARTS: Kickboxing, Karate, Kung Fu, Acrobatics, Film Fighting, Wire work, TRAMPOLINE, HIGH FALLS, MOTORCYCLES (Street and Dirt), STUNT CAR DRIVING, (Motion Picture Driving Clinic Super Level II), HORSE WORK, RAPELLING: Aussie, Swiss, Hand, Zip Line. AIR RAM, RUSSIAN SWING, WATERSPORTS, SCUBA DIVEMASTER/RESCUE DIVER, Free Diving, Sea Kayaking, Small Motorcraft, Waverunner, Wakeboarding. SWIMMING: Breast stroke, Backstroke, Butterfly, In-line Skating, Bungee Trapeze, Climbing, Acting & Dance

LACC Theatre Department, Dan Desmond
Ivana Chubbuck Studios Advanced Class.

Gloria O'Brien-Fontenot Contact:

Culbertson/Argazzi
8430 Santa Monica Blvd., Suite 210
West Hollywood, CA 90069
Phone: 323-650-9454

198

Brad Greenquist

Brad Greenquist

Profile

Mr. Greenquist was born October 8, 1959 in Fort Meade, Maryland, and grew up in Falls Church, Virginia. At age 18 he wrote and directed an award-winning film, "Run For Your Love" (1979 EVOL International Film Society's Grand Prize and Best Acting Awards). He attended Virginia Commonwealth University 1979-1983, earning a BFA in Theatre. He subsequently moved to New York City where he continued private study and began working as an actor, first in off-off-Broadway productions, then off-Broadway and then in feature films and television. In 1993 he moved to Los Angeles where he continues to work in film, television and on stage, and where he also teaches acting. Stage credits include "The Night of the Iguana," "The Glass Menagerie," "Orpheus Descending," "Abundance," "The White Rose" and "Fool for Love." In addition to many television guest star appearances, notable film and television movie credits include "The Bedroom Window" (1987), "Pet Sematary" (1989), "The Yearling" (1994), "Crime of the Century" (1996), "In Cold Blood" (1996), "Gang Related" (1997), "Inherit the Wind" (1999), "Crime and Punishment in Suburbia" (2000), "Lost Souls" (2000), "Ali" (2001), "The Pennsylvania Miners' Story" (2002), and "The Diary of Ellen Rimbauer" (2003).

Brad Greenquist

Resume

TELEVISION

THREAT MATRIX (2003) TV Pilot, role of Marc Radenmacher (Guest Star). ABC.

THE DIARY OF ELLEN RIMBAUER (2003) TV Movie, role of Doug Posey (Lead). Craig Baxley, director, ABC.

STAR TREK: ENTERPRISE (2003) TV Episode *Dawn,* role of Khata'n Zshaar (Guest Star). UPN

THE PENNSYLVANIA MINERS' STORY (2002) TV Movie, role of Hound-Dog (Lead). David Frankel, director. Touchstone/ABC.

THE AGENCY (2002) TV Episode *The Prisoner,* role of Jean Pret (Guest Star). CBS.

SIX FEET UNDER (2002) TV Episode *The Invisible Woman,* role of Building Manager (Co-Star). HBO.

THAT'S MY BUSH! (2001) TV Episode *SDI—Aye Aye,!* role of Austrian Soldier (Co-Star). Comedy Central.

DIAGNOSIS: MURDER (2001) TV Episode *Dance of Danger,* role of Natwa (Co-Star). CBS.

GETTING AWAY WITH MURDER: THE JON BENET RAMSEY STORY (2000) TV Movie, role of Detective Guilty (Lead). Ed Lucas, director. FOX.

THE PRACTICE (2000) TV Episode *Mr. Hinks Goes to Town,* role of Eric Slauson (Guest Star). ABC.

WALKER, TEXAS RANGER (2000) TV Episode *The Day of Cleansing,* role of Lomax (Guest Star). CBS.

INHERIT THE WIND (1999) TV Movie, role of Davenport (Lead). Dan Petrie, Sr., director. Showtime/CBS.

HARSH REALM (1999) TV Episode *Kein Ausgang,* role of Wolff (Guest Star). FOX.

NASH BRIDGES (1999) TV Episode *Boom Town,* role of Calvin Reddick (Guest Star). CBS.

THE MAGNIFICENT SEVEN (1999) TV Episode *The Trial,* role of James Lightfoot (Guest Star). CBS.

V.I.P. (1999) TV Episode *Val Under Siege with a Vengeance,* role of Heinrich (Guest Star). Syndicated.

THE D.R.E.A.M. TEAM (1999) TV Episode *Loose Nukes,* role of Schmidt (Guest Star). Syndicated.

THE RANSOM OF RED CHIEF (1998) TV Movie, role of Strange Pierre (Supporting). Bob Clark, director. ABC.

CHARMED (1998) TV Episode *The Truth is Out There...and it Hurts,* role of Gavin (Guest Star). WB.

THE PRETENDER (1998) TV Episode *Gigolo Jarod,* role of Frank Linden (Guest Star). NBC.

STAR TREK: DEEP SPACE NINE (1998) TV Episode *Who Mourns for Morn?,* role of Kritt (Guest Star). UPN.

VENGEANCE UNLIMITED (1998) TV Episode *Eden,* role of Deputy Webster (Co-Star). ABC.

DEAD BY MIDNIGHT (1997) TV Movie, role of Hendricks (Lead). Jim McBride, director. ABC.

HIGH INCIDENT (1997) TV Episode *Remote Control,* role of McDonnell (Guest Star). ABC.

CONAN THE ADVENTURER (1997) TV Episode *Lair of the Beast-Men,* role of Kiord (Guest Star). Syndicated.

IN COLD BLOOD (1996) TV Miniseries, role of Floyd Wells (Supporting). Jonathan Kaplan, director. CBS.

CRIME OF THE CENTURY (1996) TV Movie, role of Isador Fisch (Supporting). Mark Rydell, director. HBO.

DEAD MAN'S WALK (1996) TV Miniseries, role of John Kirker (Supporting). Yves Simoneau, director. ABC.

LIVING SINGLE (1996) TV Episode *I've Got You Under My Skin,* role of Edwin (Guest Star). FOX.

STAR TREK: VOYAGER (1996) TV Episode *Warlord,* role of Demmas (Guest Star). UPN.

THE FACULTY (1996) TV Episode *Carlos Garcia,* role of Ed Collins (Guest Star). ABC.

IN THE SHADOW OF EVIL (1995) TV Movie, Role of Willy Sommers (Supporting). Daniel Sackheim, director. CBS.

THE YEARLING (1994) TV Movie, role of Lem Forrester (Lead). Rod Hardy, director. CBS.

ASSAULT AT WEST POINT: THE COURT MARTIAL OF JOHNSON WHITTAKER (1994) TV Movie, role of Dr. Beard (Supporting). Harry Moses, director. Showtime.

STEPHEN KING'S GOLDEN YEARS (1991) TV Episode #3, role of Steve Dent (Co-Star). CBS.

LAW AND ORDER (1990) TV Episode *Prisoner of Love,* role of Bartender (Featured). NBC.

H.E.L.P. (1990) TV Episode, role of Mover (Featured). CBS.

MONSTERS (1989) TV Episode *The Gift,* role of Kirby (Guest Star). Syndicated.

GIDEON OLIVER: SLEEP WELL, PROFESSOR OLIVER (1988) TV Movie, role of Clerk (Featured). John Patterson, director. Universal.

ALONE IN THE NEON JUNGLE (1988) TV Movie, role of Genilli (Supporting). Georg Stanford Brown, director. ABC.

IN THE LION'S DEN" (1987) TV Pilot *Dana in the Lion's Den*, role of Forrest (Series Regular). CBS.

FILM

18 FINGERS OF DEATH! (2004) Feature Film, role of Arthur Armenian (Featured). James Lew, director.

MOMENTUM (2002) Feature Film, role of Elias (Supporting). James Seale, director. Independent.

OUTSIDE THE LAW (2002) Feature Film, role of McKenzie (Lead). Jorge Montesi, director. Columbia/TriStar.

ALI (2001) Feature Film, role of Marlon Thomas (Supporting). Michael Mann, director. Columbia/TriStar.

LOST SOULS (2000) Feature Film, role of George Viznick (Supporting). Janusz Kaminski, director. New Line Cinema.

CRIME AND PUNISHMENT IN SUBURBIA (2000) Feature Film, role of Calvin Berry (Supporting). Rob Schmidt, director. MGM/UA.

SQUINT (2000) Short Film, role of Stitch (Supporting). Tony Griffin, director.

THE PUZZLE IN THE AIR (1998) Feature Film, role of Jeff Swerdling (Lead). Gino Cabanas, director. TRLT Inc.

GANG RELATED (1997) Feature Film, role of Richard Stein (Lead). Jim Kouf, director. Orion.

WING COMMANDER: PROPHECY CD Rom Interactive Feature Film, role of Major Karl 'Spyder' Bowen (Supporting). Origin.

BLACK OUT (1996) Feature film, role of Opponent (Featured). Alan Goldstein, director. USA.

GABRIEL KNIGHT II: THE BEAST WITHIN (1996) CD Rom Interactive Feature Film, role of Georg Immerding (Supporting). Sierra On-Line.

WHISPERS OF WHITE (1989) Feature Film, role of Bluddon's Lieutenant (Featured). Ron Gordon, Sr., director. Universal.

PET SEMATARY (1989) Feature Film, role of Victor Pascow (Lead). Mary Lambert, director. Paramount.

LOOSE CANNONS (1989) Feature Film, role of German Official (Featured). Bob Clark, director. TriStar.
THE CHAIR (1989) Feature Film, role of Mushmouth (Lead). Waldemar Korzeniowsky, director. Angelika Films.
THE BEDROOM WINDOW (1987) Feature Film, role of Chris Henderson (Lead). Curtis Hanson, director. Delaurentis.
HOSTAGE AND TERRORISM CRISIS MANAGEMENT (1987) Industrial Film, role of Terrorist (Lead). U.S. Army.
MUTANTS IN PARADISE (1984) Feature film, role of Steve Awesome (Lead). Scott Apostolou, director. USA.
RUN FOR YOUR LOVE (1979) Short film, role of The Boy (Lead). Brad Greenquist, director. Carderock Films. (Best Film and Best Acting awards, EVOL '79 Film Festival, Washington, D.C.).

THEATRE
AGENCY by Christie Dowda and Andy Ellis (1996) Theatre, Equity Waiver, role of Peter. Craig Tapscott, director. Coast Playhouse, LA.
LYDIE BREEZE by John Guarre (1993) Theatre, Off-Off-Broadway, role of Jeremiah Grady. Jim Williams, director. Lightning Strikes Theatre Co., NYC.
THE GRAND INQUISITOR by Fyodor Dostoevsky (1992) Theatre, Off-Broadway, One-Person Show, role of Ivan Karamazov. Roger Mrazek, director; adaptation by Brad Greenquist. Primary Stages, NYC.
AWOKE ONE by Jack Agueros (1992) Theatre, Off-Off-Broadway, ensemble. Curt Dempster, director. Ensemble Studio Theatre, NYC.
ABUNDANCE by Beth Henley (1990) Theatre, Off-Broadway, role of Prof. Elmore Crome. Ron Lagomarsino, director. Manhattan Theatre Club, NYC.
THE LAST TEMPTATION OF JOE HILL (1988) Theatre, Off-Off-Broadway, role of Joe Hill. Bob Scott, director. The Working Theatre, NYC.
THE GLASS MENAGERIE by Tennessee Williams (1986) Theatre, Off-Off-Broadway, role of The Gentleman Caller. Peter Von Berg, director. Players' Acting Corp., NYC.
RICHARD III by William Shakespeare (1986) Theatre, Off-Off-Broadway, role of Richard III. Samuel Becket Theatre, NYC.
FOOL FOR LOVE by Sam Sheppard (1986) Theatre, LORT, role of Eddie. Mary Best, director. Virginia Rose Theatre, Richmond, VA.
NIGHT OF THE IGUANA by Tennessee Williams (1985) Theatre, Broadway, role of Wolfgang. Arthur Sherman, director.
CAN WE TALK? (1984) Theatre, Touring Industrial Show. Patrik Williams, director. Pepsico.
TELEMACHUS CLAY by Luis Jon Carlino (1984) Theatre, Off-Off-Broadway, role of The Prophet. George Stevenson, director. NYC.
THE BRICK AND THE ROSE by Luis Jon Carlino (1984) Theatre, Off-Off-Broadway, role of Tony. George Stevenson, director. NYC.
GILGAMESH (1983) Theatre (Opera, concert performance), role of The Storyteller. Gary Hopper, director. Virginia Commonwealth University Symphony Orchestra, Richmond, VA.
HUGS AND KISSES, THE JAMESTOWN STORY, SANTA'S ENCHANTED WORKSHOP (1983) Theatre, Children's Touring Company, ensemble. Theatre IV, Richmond, VA.
AND TO YOU, MABEL NORMAND, GOOD NIGHT by Brad Greenquist and Lucinda McDermott (1983) Theatre, Regional, role of Mack Sennett. Brad Greenquist, director. Shafer Street Playhouse, Richmond, VA.
THE SOLDIER'S TALE by Igor Stravinski (1982) Theatre (dance), Regional, role of The Soldier. Hyrum Conrad, director. Richmond Symphony, Richmond, VA.
STREET MIME (1977-1979) Street Theatre, Georgetown, Washington, D.C.

COMMERCIALS
Honda, Toyota, Microsoft, Jim Beam, Colorado Lottery.

TRAINING
Michael Moriarty, Ian Tucker, John DeLancie
BFA, Theatre, Virginia Commonwealth University

ABILITIES
Any and all accents and dialects, usual and not-so.
Foreign Languages: German

Brad Greenquist Contact:

Agents:
Martin Gage, Kitty McMillan, Gerry Koch, Peter Kaiser
The Gage Group
14724 Ventura Blvd., Suite 505
Sherman Oaks, CA 91403
Phone: 818-905-3800

Managers:
Maryellen Mulcahee, Cornelia Frame
Framework Entertainment
9057 Nemo Street, Suite C
West Hollywood, CA 90069
Phone: 310-858-0333

Tony Devon

Tony Devon

Profile

Tony was born Anthony Armand Acchione, December 5, 1951, in Philadelphia, PA, to a show business family. His dad had a brief period as a road manager and also owned a music publishing company, but it was Tony's Uncle Bernie Rothbard a theatrical agent who represented Joey Bishop, that was his big influence. Tony always knew he wanted to be an actor and his parents Tony and Lee would take him to see shows as a youngster. At the age of nineteen Tony began performing in nightclubs as a singer and impressionist and after a stint in the U.S. Army won "The Best Singer in the Army Award" entertaining troops throughout the orient.

In the late 70's Tony became an opening act for Rodney Dangerfield in New York City, which later led to theatre such as "The Fantasticks," "A Hatful of Rain" and "Death of a Salesman." In 1980 he landed a role in "Blow Out" with John Travolta and "The King of Comedy" with Robert De Niro. "The more you work, and if it's good, the more recognition you get," says Tony whose career has spanned over 50 film and television roles. Tony says, "It's nice once in awhile to have a director send you a script and say 'this is what we'd love for you to do if you're interested.' That makes my agent Dorothy Palmer's job a little bit easier. It also helps a lot to get an excellent agent like Dorothy Palmer, representing me since 1986." Tony also advises those who are starry-eyed, to be in love with acting, not in love with being an actor. Performing is not just something actors want to do but need to do. At present Tony can be seen in the "25th Hour," "Molly Gunn" and "Navy Seals."

***Note: Dorothy Palmer has been a Talent and Literary Agent for 35 years. She also packages independent films and welcomes investors to contact her for excellent scripts and attachments. She can be reached at 212-765-4280 in New York.

Tony Devon

Resume

SAG/AFTRA/AEA/AGVA

FILM		DIRECTORS
Murder Below the Line	Co-Starring	Norman Macera
The Black Hand	Co-Starring	Alan DeHerrera
The Family Dog	Co-Starring	Patrick Rodio
They Walk Among Us	Co-Starring	Eric Jeitner
Driftwood	Co-Starring	Patrick Rodio
The Life & Times of Charlie Putz	Co-Starring	Robert Rothbard
The Disintegration of a Boy Band	Co-Starring	Patrick Rodio
Telling Lies in America	Supporting	Guy Ferland
Recipe for Disaster	Supporting	Greg Olliver
As Long As You're Alive	Supporting	Alan Reed
The Adventures of the Devil's Pulpit	Supporting	Brendon Faulkner
Sudden Change	Supporting	Suk Kee Lee
Fighting Back	Supporting	Lewis Teague
Cookie	Supporting	Susan Seidelman
The Lottery	Supporting	Joe Calabrese
The Demo Crew	Supporting	John Vitali
Stain	Supporting	Patrick Rodio
The Reappearance of Homer Pitts	Supporting	Patrick Rodio
The Strike Zone	Supporting	Norman Macera
The Father, The Son	Supporting	Anthony Caldarella
Better Days	Supporting	Patrick Rodio
The Sterling Chase	Principal	Tanya Fenmore
Blow Out	Principal	Brian De Palma
The King of Comedy	Principal	Martin Scorsese
Without A Trace	Principal	Stanley Jaffe
The Lemon Sisters	Principal	Joyce Chopra

TELEVISION		
One Life to Live	Guest Star	Judge Franklin
Navy Seals	Lead	Joe Wiecha
The F.B.I. Files	Lead	Jeff Fine
U.S. Customs Classified	Lead	Paul Chitlik
Law and Order	Guest Star (Recurring)	Constantine Makris
One Life To Live	Principal	Bruce Cooperman
Found Money	Principal	Bill Persky
America's Most Wanted	Principal	Tom Shelly
Unsolved Mysteries	Principal	Mike Mathis

THEATRE

The Fantasticks	Matt	Williamstown Theatre, NJ
Death of a Salesman	Happy	Manhattan Theatre Club, NYC
O.J. Law	Various Roles	Complex Theatre, LA
A Hatful of Rain	Polo	Williamstown Theatre, NJ

Tony Devon Contact:

Dorothy Palmer Talent Agency
235 W. 56th St., Suite 24K
New York, NY 10019
Phone: 212-765-4280

Tami Anderson

Tami Anderson

Profile

Known to devotees around the world from her stint as a "Real World" housemate, Tami Anderson has gone on to become a viable presence in the entertainment industry as a rising TV and film personality. She was a host of the nationally syndicated version of the classic game show, "Card Sharks."

Originally from White Plains, New York, in her early teens Tami moved with her mother to Los Angeles to pursue a better life than the one they had left behind. A series of misfortunes resulted in her mother's return to the east coast leaving Tami, armed with her billion-watt smile and irresistible personality, to make her own way. Mother and daughter reunited shortly thereafter to begin a new life in the heart of downtown Los Angeles. Tami worked at numerous odd jobs before landing her much-loved job at an HIV healthcare center where she was sent by a friend to meet the producer of "The Real World."

After her unforgettable year as a notably belligerent housemate, she moved to New York, where "feisty" pays off, and into hosting MTV's "Beach MTV," "MTV Jams," and "Rude Awakening." Things looked promising but fate had another surprise up its sleeve.

During her Manhattan odyssey, Tami married NBA star Kenny Anderson, with whom she had two beautiful daughters and a luxurious life, but at whose hands she also suffered spousal abuse. She divorced him and found herself scrambling to find a new home for herself and her young children.

Starting over in Los Angeles and needing to provide a life for her daughters, Tami returned to the career she had abandoned at her ex-husband's insistence. She landed guest starring roles on television shows such as "The Steve Harvey Show," "The Parkers," "Married With Children," and "Silk Stalkings." Her feature film credits include, "Sacred Is the Flesh" (with Elise Neal), "Tara" (with Ice-T) and "MacArthur Park." She is also developing film and television projects through her own production company.

With an endless supply of energy and determination, Tami rules a roost that includes her daughters, Lyric Chanel and Kenni Lauren, and her mother, Nadine. She makes time to express her gratitude for her own good fortune in a significant way by supporting Best Buddies, an organization geared towards helping mentally challenged children and the Morristown Center, which helps battered children find shelter.

Tami Anderson Contact:

Lisa Sorensen Public Relations
12522 Moorpark St.
Studio City, CA 91614
Phone: 818-761-0430

Andy Schofield

Favorite Quote:

"Follow your heart and may all your dreams become realities."

Andy Schofield

Profile

Andy Schofield was born in Medina, Ohio. As far back as he can remember he always had a hidden passion and desire to act. He has been involved in several excellent projects including a TV movie called "Brotherly Love" and a documentary for the History Channel called "Silent Service." He was the associate producer and first assistant director for "We Have Your Daughter," which was submitted to Sundance. In addition he played the lead, was co-producer and assistant director in the feature "Judge and Jury." He is a First Gup Red Belt in Moo Duk Kwan Tae Kwon Do. He believes anyone who has the drive, passion and determination will succeed in this business.

Andy Schofield

Resume

FILM

Scene: Homecoming	Shepard	Video Verite Productions
Without Warning	Paul (Paralegal)	StoneKap Productions Ltd.
Natural Bridges	Captain Heat	Natural Bridges LLC
Common Sense: Self Defense for Women 1-3	Stunts/Male Trainer	Guerilla Productions
Brotherly Love	Doug Armstrong	Dreambuilder Celebration Inc.
Silent Service	World War II Re-enactor	Greystone Communications
Psyclone	Technician # 1	Cinevid Production
Mythological Nocturne	John-Lead	Infectious Art Films
Back Office	Mr. Mann-Lead	Sonnyboo Productions
Little Girl	Manny-Lead	Prelude Productions
Sultana	Civil War Re-enactor	Koba Productions
Night Owls of Coventry	Coventry Friend	Night Owl Productions
Blood Kiss	Pale Kid	Prelude Productions
I Dare You to Kill Her	Mr. Shine	Prelude Productions
Puppet Love	Harold-Lead	Combined Efforts
Lips of Crimson	Red Man-Lead	Combined Efforts
The Vigilante	Cop/Stunts	MDI Productions
The Calling	Cop # 1	Rico Films
Look for the Women	Stunt Double for Lead	Plato's Cave Production
One	Student/Stunts	Oracle Films
White Flight	Graveman	Clear Window Productions
Let's Just be Friends	Bartender	Highway Pictures

TELEVISION/COMMERCIALS/INDUSTRIAL/VIDEOS

McDonald's: Training Video	Stable Hand	Quantas Pictures
First One Bank	Insurance Salesman	Cinecraft Productions
Conflict	Paramedic-Andy	Avatar Communications
Mowing Rules: Safety Rocks	Dan	BFL Communications
Without Warning	Paul	Stone Kap Productions
Grass Roots	Host	CRG Media
Greyhound	Passenger # 2	Avatar Communications
DSW Shoe Warehouse	Associate # 2	SOS Productions

THEATRE
Available upon request

TRAINING
Getting Your Big Break: On Camera Auditions/Sue Johnson
Tricks of the Trade: Survival Skills for the Aspiring Actor/Sue Johnson
D.P. Lighting Workshop/David Litz with Robert Banks
Audition Technique/Alex Michaels
Playhouse Square Center: Education Department Presents: Elton John/Tim Rice/Broadway
Backstage Master Class
Playhouse Square Center: Education Department Presents: Gary Sandy//Broadway Backstage
Master Class
The Playhouse: Introduction to Acting//Tim Perfect
Seven Years Vocal Training
Independent Film Festival//Volunteer
First Gup Red Belt Moo Duk Kwan Tae Kwon Do
Hollywood Screen Actors Workshop/Mark Archer

SKILLS
Acting, Stunts, Impersonations, Improvisation, Grip, Editing, Voice-Over, Singer, Swimmer, Tae
Kwon Do, Cooking, Limited Pyrotechnics, Drivers License, First Aid, CPR, OSHA Certified, Local
#38, Inside Wireman, Photographer

Andy Schofield Contact:

Website: www.moviemanandy.com

Jan Eddy

Jan Eddy

Profile

When it comes to screen time you are most likely to find 6'4", 295 pound Jan Eddy playing tough guy roles as bikers, security guards and thugs. Though he is tough, Eddy is a brown belt in Taekwondo. Born in Marshalltown, Iowa, September 23, 1951, he actually began his acting days performing light opera at the Martha Ellen Tye Playhouse in Marshalltown in such plays as "Kiss Me Kate," "Fiddler On The Roof," "My Fair Lady" and many others. At the age of 22, Eddy headed to Arizona to work construction and ended up acting professionally at the Arizona Theatre Company. It was there that he was spotted by an agent who helped him audition for his first film role as a store clerk in the Academy award winning film, "Alice Doesn't Live Here Anymore." In 1984, Eddy headed to Hollywood where his first TV guest appearance was "Dukes of Hazzard." He has since been in over 75 Television, Film and Stage productions some of which are "Quantum Leap," "Seinfeld," "Ellen," "Murphy Brown," "Walker, Texas Ranger," "Charmed," "Fire Down Below" "The Villain" and many more. His most recent Stage performance was in the concert version of the hit Broadway play, "City of Angels." Continue to look for Jan Eddy in any one of the different venues doing what he does best, Acting!

Jan Eddy

Resume

SAG/AFTRA/EQUITY (AEA)
FILMS (Partial List)

SHUT INS	SUPPORTING	BELAVICTOR FILMS
THE ONE	SUPPORTING	EVOLUTION PRODUCTIONS
FIRE DOWN BELOW	SUPPORTING	WARNER BROTHERS
MR. PAYBACK	SUPPORTING	SONY PICTURES
HOUSEGUEST	SUPPORTING	CARAVAN PICTURES
ORGAZMO	SUPPORTING	TREY PARKER PRODUCTION
DIE TRYING	SUPPORTING	CONCORDE PICTURES
CHASING THE DREAM	SUPPORTING	PLATINUM DUNES PRODUCTIONS
THE VILLIAN	CAMEO	COLUMBIA
ALICE DOESN'T LIVE HERE ANYMORE	SUPPORTING	WARNER BROTHERS
EVICTION	SUPPORTING	BAY FILMS
BLACK BELT UNDERCOVER	SUPPORTING	COMET ENTERTAINMENT
THE MAJIC KID	SUPPORTING	PM PRODUCTIONS

TELEVISION (Partial List)

DAYS OF OUR LIVES	CO-STAR	NBC
MARTIAL LAW	GUEST STAR	CBS PRODUCTIONS
CHARMED	CO-STAR	SPELLING TELEVISION
JAG	GUEST STAR	BELISARIUS PRODUCTIONS
WALKER, TEXAS RANGER	GUEST STAR	AMADEA FILM PRODUCTIONS
HIGH INCIDENT	CO-STAR	DREAMWORKS TELEVISION
QUANTUM LEAP (2 episodes)	GUEST STAR	BELISARIUS/UNIVERSAL
SEINFELD	CO-STAR	CASTLE ROCK ENTERTAINMENT
MIKE HAMMER	CO-STAR	MIKE HAMMER PRODUCTIONS
MURPHY BROWN	CO-STAR	WARNER BROTHERS
ROSE CITY CAFÉ	RECURRING	ROSE CITY PRODUCTION (PILOT)
THE VANISHING SON	GUEST STAR	STU SEGALL PRODUCTIONS
THE WONDER YEARS	GUEST STAR	NEW WORLD ENTERTAINMENT
BEVERLY HILLS 90210	CO-STAR	SPELLING TELEVISION
ELLEN	CO-STAR	TOUCHSTONE PRODUCTIONS
RENEGADE (2 episodes)	CO-STAR	STU SEGALL PRODUCTIONS
FBI THE UNTOLD STORY	GUEST STAR	THE ARTHUR COMPANY
JUST THE TEN OF US	GUEST STAR	WARNER/GSM PRODUCTIONS
ANYTHING BUT LOVE	CO-STAR	20TH CENTURY FOX
HOOPERMAN	CO-STAR	20TH CENTURY FOX
HEART OF THE CITY	CO-STAR	20TH CENTURY FOX
DUKES OF HAZZARD	CO-STAR	WARNER BROTHERS
SANTA BARBARA	RECURRING	NEW WORLD TELEVISION
GENERAL HOSPITAL (3 episodes)	GUEST STAR	ABC
FALCON CREST	CO-STAR	LORIMAR

THE AMAZING LIVE SEA MONKEYS	GUEST STAR	ARTEMIA NYOS PRODUCTIONS
CALIFORNIA DREAMS	CO-STAR	NBC
ONE SATURDAY MORNING	CO-STAR	DISNEY

THEATRE (Partial List)

CITY OF ANGELS (CONCERT PREMEIRE)	BIG SIX/PASCO	JOE LEONARDO
OF MICE AND MEN	LENNY	NORMAN SWARTZ
THE VISIT	BURGERMEISTER	DONNA LESLIE
FIDDLER ON THE ROOF	TEVYE	BILL MOORE
DARK OF THE MOON	PREACHER HAGGLER	DONNA LESLIE
FORTY CARATS	EDDIE EDWARDS	SANDY SCHLESINGER
ALL MY SONS	CHRIS	SAM KENNEDY
A CHRISTMAS CAROL	FEZZIWIG	SANDY ROSENTHAL
KISS ME KATE	FATHER	STAN DOOR

SKILLS
HORSE BACK RIDING (WESTERN), MARTIAL ARTS, SINGING (BARITONE/BASS), LARGE BIKES, DIRT BIKES, STOCK CARS, FARMING, CONSTRUCTION WORK, HEAVY EQUIPMENT, ELECTRICIAN, WEIGHT LIFTING, FOOTBALL, WRESTLING, COOKING, FIRE ARMS (EXPERT), CROWD CONTROL (BOUNCER/BODY GUARD), FIGHTS, FALLS. VOICE-OVER, ADR WORK, AND BILLIARDS.

TRAINING
CHARLES CONRAD, FILM INDUSTRY WORKSHOPS, COMMERCIAL WORKSHOPS WITH SHANCY PIERCE AND HOLLY (HIRE) COLLIER, VOICE WORKSHOPS WITH DAVE MADDEN AND TOM WILLIAMS.

Jan Eddy Contact:

The Morgan Agency
Phone: 323-469-7100

Jack Plotnick

Favorite Quote:

"I feel so happy here. This place makes me feel flooded with love. The important thing is to have lots of love about. I was very stingy with it back home. I used to measure and count it out. I had this obsession with justice you see. I wouldn't love anyone unless they loved me back exactly as much. And, as they didn't, neither did I. The emptiness of it all."
From: "Enchanted April"

Jack Plotnick

Profile

Jack Plotnick grew up in Columbus, Ohio, and got a BFA in Drama from Carnegie Mellon University. He went to New York with dreams of performing on Broadway, but soon found his true passion was creating and performing comedy shows. He got his big break on "Late Night With Conan O'Brien," when they were looking for somebody "freaky" to play Slim Organbody, the manic depressive children's entertainer.

In a March 1999, *Interview Magazine* feature, "The Big Screen Best Bits: Titans In Tiny Parts," Jack Plotnick was singled out for his performance as the smarmy interviewer in "Gods and Monsters," whose bluff is nearly called in Ian McKellen's game of strip poker.

Jack Plotnick can be seen in the 2003 release of "Down With Love" starring Renee Zellweger and Ewan McGregor.

Jack acted opposite Sally Field, as her son, Leon, in the Farrelly Brothers produced film "Say It Isn't So." On television, Jack was a series regular on the critically acclaimed Hollywood film industry satire, "Action," executive produced by Joel Silver for the FOX network. Jack worked opposite Jay Mohr, and played Stuart, the Machiavellian head of film production at Dragonfire Films.

More recently, Jack starred in the FOX pilot "Hey Neighbor" from the creators of MTV's "The State" and Comedy Central's "Viva Variety" in which he played an assortment of uniquely strange small town characters. Plotnick wrote and performed on the MTV sketch comedy series, "The Jenny McCarthy Show," playing a wide range of irreverent characters, from a talking pimple to a serial killer.

His numerous recurring television roles include playing the Deputy Mayor of Sunnydale on the popular one-hour drama, "Buffy The Vampire Slayer," the fastidious assistant to *Joely Fisher* on "Ellen," and a quirky self help addict on Showtime's, "Rude Awakenings." His dramatic roles include "NYPD Blue" and "Dawson's Creek,"Jack and Dennis Hensley's short film, "Evie Harris: Shining Star," played many festivals and was a finalist in the PlanetOut Short Film Competition.

Jack Executive Produced and starred in the feature film "Girls Will Be Girls," which was chosen for Sundance and was released in theatres October '03 by IFC Films.

Jack recently appeared in George Meyer's (Exec. Prod. of "The Simpsons") live comedy show "Up Your Giggy" at The Court Theatre in LA. With Seth Rudetsky, he wrote and performed "An Evening With Joyce Dewitt" (without Joyce Dewitt), the awkwardly titled "Plotnick and Rudetsky" (which ran for a year at New York City's Caroline's Comedy Club) and "Mortification Theatre" at The HBO Workspace.

He recently enjoyed a successful run of his play "Space Station 79" at the HBO Workspace and Comedy Central Stage, and it is currently being adapted into a TV show for Comedy Central.

Jack attended the 2001 Aspen Comedy Festival with Jennifer Elise Cox and their show "It's Our Time To Shine." In 2003 he returned with his film, "Girls Will Be Girls" and along with his two co-stars, was awarded The Aspen Comedy Festival's Best Actress Award. Jack also wrote the screenplay, "The Three Faces of Evie," with plans toward production.

Jack Plotnick

Resume

FILM

MEET THE FOCKERS	Universal	Dir: Jay Roach
DOWN WITH LOVE	FOX 2000	Dir: Peyton Reed
GIRLS WILL BE GIRLS – (also executive produced)	IFC Films	Dir: Richard Day
TACO BENDER	Coppos Films	Dir: Richard Sears
SAY IT ISN'T SO	20th Century Fox	Dir: JB Rogers
		Prod: Peter & Bobby Farrelly
MYSTERY MEN	Universal	Dir: Kinka Usher
GODS AND MONSTERS	Lions Gate	Dir: Bill Condon
CHAIRMAN OF THE BOARD	Trimark	
STRAIGHT JACKET	Independent	Dir: Richard Day

TELEVISION

HEY NEIGHBOR (Pilot)	FOX/Greenblatt Janollari	Series Regular
ACTION	Columbia TriStar/FOX	Series Regular
THE JENNY McCARTHY SHOW	MTV	Series Regular
LIFE ON MARS	HBO Pilot	Series Regular
		Dir: Michael Lehmann
NYPD BLUE	ABC	Guest Star
DAWSON'S CREEK	WB	Guest Star – Dir: Robert McNeil
BUFFY THE VAMPIRE SLAYER		Recurring Role
DEAD LAST	WB	Guest Star Dir: Tim Hunter
FOR YOUR LOVE	WB	Recurring Role
RUDE AWAKENINGS	Mandalay TV/Showtime	Recurring
ELLEN	ABC	Recurring Role
CLERKS	Disney/WBN Pilot	Recurring Role
SEINFELD	NBC	Guest Star
LATE NIGHT WITH CONAN O'BRIAN	NBC	Recurring Role
RENO 911	Comedy Central	Recurring

THEATRE

UP YOUR GIGGY– by George Meyer	The Court Theatre	Prod: Maria Semple

ORIGINAL WORKS

SPACE STATION '79	HBO Workspace/Arcade
IT'S OUR TIME TO SHINE	2000 Aspen Comedy Festival
PLOTNICK & RUDETSKY	Caroline's NYC

BROADWAY

SHEIK OF AVENUE B	Town Hall

OFF BROADWAY
THE NEW SIN REVUE   Del's Down Under
PAGEANT   The Blue Angel
CLASS CLOWN   Theatreworks USA/Promenade

TRAINING:
Carnegie Mellon University,
B.F.A. in Drama

Jack Plotnick Contact:

Lighthouse Entertainment
Steven Siebert
Phone: 310-246-0499

222

Adriana Millan

Adriana Millan

Profile

Adriana Millan is a Los Angeles born actress whose gorgeous demure looks and impeccable talent have distinguished her in a wide variety of roles. Her ability to transform her Betty Page looks into Judi Dench type characters can be seen in films such as "El Padrino" opposite Jennifer Tilly, "The Hunt for J-Man," "Tauromaquia" and "Hoodrats." She has been brilliant in over 20 theatre productions including "Real Women Have Curves" directed by Josefina Lopez, Grupo de Teatro Sinergia's "In the Name of God," "Salome" and "Danny and the Deep Blue Sea." Several of her performances received critical acclaim. She has also proven her ability in film and commercial voice-over.

Adriana has two Bachelor's degrees: one in psychology and one in criminal justice. She has also been studying acting since she was eight years old, but has managed to work as an investigator for the Public Defender's office, work as a counselor for abused and neglected children, own and operate her own café for five years and travel the world over: all of which have greatly contributed to her character studies. To further increase her knowledge of the film industry she has worked on commercial and television production teams and as a casting assistant for numerous films. She also interned for the National Hispanic Media Coalition, an organization dedicated to improving the image of Latinos in the media. Adriana enjoys sharing her love of theatre and is currently employed as a drama, improvisation and playwriting teacher for East Los Angeles Classic Theatre.

In her free time, Adriana enjoys boxing at the local gym, going to art museums, painting, taking dance and martial arts classes and learning web design. She is a proud member of the Screen Actors Guild, American Federation of Television and Radio Artists, Independent Feature Project/West (IFP), National Association of Latino Independent Producers (NALIP), Nosotros, Premiere Weekend Club and the American Film Institute (AFI).

Adriana Millan

Resume

SAG/AFTRA

FILM

Baby's Momma Drama	Douglas T. Green Prod.	Dir. Douglas T. Green
El Padrino	Rosebud Pictures	Dir. Damian Chapa
The Replacement Killers	Sony Pictures	Dir. Antoine Fuqua
Diary of a Serial Killer	King Productions	Dir. Joshua Wallace
Tauromaquia	Muddy Creek Pictures	Dir. Christopher J. Barry
Hoodrats	Hoodrats Productions	Dir. Edgar Arellano
The Hunt for J-Man	Boricua 3 Productions	Dir. Tino Rodriguez
Jessie	Galindo Productions	Dir. Jesus Galindo
Dykestars	ACK Productions	Dir. Knudson/Choi
Today	Loyola Marymount University	Dir. Angela Breene
Bon Appetit	Univ. of Southern California	Dir. Tijerina/Hall
Faces	Univ. of Southern California	Dir. Lissy-Maria Sturz
Paper Anniversary	Univ. of Southern California	Dir. Liron Reitner

TELEVISION

Johnny X – Pilot	Co-Star	Touchstone Television
Quien Tiene La Razon?	Guest Star	Auckland Productions
The Bold and the Beautiful	Day Player	CBS
The DA	Day Player	Warner Bros.

COMMERCIAL & VOICE-OVER

List available upon request

THEATRE *(partial list)*

Real Women Have Curves	Pancha (Ensemble)	Casa 0101 / Dir. Josefina Lopez
In The Name of God	Isabel de Carvajal (Lead)	Frida Kahlo Theatre
Creative Playground	Ensemble	Touring Company
Safari	Orue (Ensemble)	Grupo de Teatro Sinergia
Salome by Oscar Wilde	Queen Herodias (Lead)	The Raven Theatre thru Cal Arts
Ghosts and Legends	Doris Venkeisen / Show Guide	R.M.S. Queen Mary
Danny and the Deep Blue Sea	Roberta (Lead)	Friends and Artists Theatre
Careless Love	Julia (Lead)	Friends and Artists Theatre
La Boda	Angelina (Lead)	CVS Productions
Our Town	Mrs. Gibbs (Lead)	La Mirada Theatre Troupe
Play On	Polly Benish (Lead)	La Mirada Theatre Troupe
The Crucible	Elizabeth Proctor (Lead)	La Mirada Theatre Troupe
Under Milkwood	Ms. Beynon / Narrator	Pilgrim Players
The Anniversary	Merchutkina (Lead)	La Verne Theatre Festival, CA

IMPROV

The Berubians	Improv Player	The Comedy Store & Irvine Improv

TRAINING *(partial list)*

Larry Moss Studios – Advanced Acting

Stacey Martino – Scene Study

Catherine Worth (2nd City) – Improv

Stephen Carnovsky – Characterization

Carolyne Barry – Comm. Technique

Ebba-Marie Gendron – Grotowski

South Coast Repertory – Scene Study

Cindera Che (The Edge) – Movement

Sal Romeo – Camera & Aud. Tech.

Camille Ameen – Voice & Movement

CSU, Fullerton – Character Analysis

CSU, Fullerton – Script Analysis

SPECIAL SKILLS

B.A. (Psych. and Criminal Justice)

Drama & Improv Teacher

Horseback Rider (Western)

Private Investigator

Bilingual (Spanish)

Boxer (Professionally Trained)

Fencer

Kickboxer (Muay Thai)

Tae Kwon Do (Beginning)

Intermediate French

Dancer (Jazz, Latin & Go-Go)

Firearms Experience (Intermediate)

Mountain Biker

Voice-Over (ADR, Char. & Comm.)

Dialects (Most Latin, British & French)

Adriana Millan Contact:

Jaime Ferrar Agency
Phone: 818-506-8311
Website: www.geocities.com/adrianacmillan

Joyce DeWitt

Favorite Quote:

*"You are here to enable the divine purpose of the universe to unfold.
That is how important you are."*
Eckhart Tolle

Joyce DeWitt

Profile

Miss DeWitt is most widely known to audiences for her starring role as "Janet Wood" in the ABC Television hit series "Three's Company." She also has an extensive background in the Theatre. Her career as an Actress and Director provided a strong foundation for Miss DeWitt to co-produce the NBC television movie, "Behind the Camera: The Unauthorized Story of Three's Company." She also serves as the on-camera narrator for the project.

In her extensive Stage career, which spans forty years, Miss DeWitt, has starred in numerous theatrical productions including the Canadian premieres of the 2000 Pulitzer Prize-winning play "Dinner With Friends" and Alfred Uhry's Tony Award-winning play "The Last Night of Ballyhoo." Other stage performances include the North American premiere of the Australian comedy "Daylight Savings," the British farce "Noises Off," the revival of Cole Porter's "Anything Goes,' and the Broadway musical "Olympus on My Mind," for which she completed the cast recording – her first record album.

Miss DeWitt's other Theatre credits include starring roles in "Chapter Two," "Sweet Charity," "Damn Yankees," "Middle of the Night," "Star Spangled Girl," "The Crucible," "Medea," 'Tartuffe," "A Hatful of Rain," 'Desire Under the Elms," "Macbeth," "The Mikado," "Lil' Abner," "South Pacific," "The Man Who Came To Dinner," "Peter Pan," "Brigadoon," "All the Way Home," "A Month in the Country," "The Tempest," "The Impossible Years," "Dracula: An Original Rock Musical," "Stop the World, I Want To Get Off," and "Same Time, Next Year."

Her other television credits include singing and dancing in numerous specials having had the pleasure of appearing with such wonderful talents as Greer Garson, Ann Miller, Perry Como, Bill Cosby, Anne Murray, Tony Randall, Rich Little, Cheryl Ladd, John Ritter and Steve Martin. She has also made numerous guest-starring appearances on popular television programs including "The Loveboat," "The Osmonds," "Hope Island," "Cybill," "Twitch City," and 'Living Single," as well as starring in the television movies "With This Ring" and "Spring Fling."

Miss DeWitt holds a Bachelor of Arts Degree from Ball State University and a Master of Fine Arts Degree from UCLA where she was awarded the Master of Fine Arts Fellowship as well as the Clifton Webb Scholarship.

Born in Wheeling, West Virginia, on April 23rd, Miss DeWitt is one of four children. Her childhood years were divided between West Virginia and Indiana.

Having had the good fortune to work with such wonderful human beings as Valerie Harper and Dennis Weaver, whose dedication to ending hunger and homelessness in our world and support of environmental issues is boundless, Miss DeWitt participated with members of the House and Senate at the Capitol Hill Forum on Hunger and Homelessness and has hosted presentations for the Family Assistance Program of Hollywood. She is most grateful for having been allowed the privilege of hosting the International Awards Ceremony at the White House for the Presidential End Hunger Awards, as well as co-hosting, with Jeff Bridges, the World Food Day Gala at the Kennedy Center.

Joyce DeWitt Contact:

JG Business Management
P.O Box 7309
Santa Monica, CA 90406
Phone: 310-576-1584

Sheryl Matthys

Favorite Quote:

"Take the Chance – Live Life"

Sheryl Matthys

Profile

Sheryl Matthys is a professional TV, film, and theatre performer with more than 10 years of National experience. She always "delivers quality in every take" in her range of projects in television, film and theatre as she has been a principal character in more than 150 industrials, commercials, and theatre showcases/one-acts. Her experience includes work as a TV and Radio news reporter, independent film actress, show host, national commercials, infomercials, and industrials, "live" trade shows, voice-over and hand modeling.

Sheryl's national commercials include: Viagra, Toys R Us, Ovaltine, A & E History Channel, A & E Phil Collins Special, The Daily Show, The Movie Channel, Quicken Loans, Body by Jake, and McCalls. Regional spots include: Philly Tourism, Aamco, and I Love NY!

Corporate Industrials are a big part of Sheryl's expertise. Large crowds have seen her perform "live" at international trade shows where she's memorized copy and used ear prompter. Clients include: Fisher Price, SONY, Xerox, Canon, and Audi. On tape, Sheryl has portrayed numerous roles from a pharmaceutical sales rep to a mom to a spokesperson. Sheryl has the know how to make difficult copy sound smooth. She's tackled medical jargon, and different characters for clients such as Aventis, Novartis, BMW, Eli Lily, Blue Cross, Blue Shield, Playtex Bottles, Party Time, Ethan Allen, and SONY.

A natural as a host, Sheryl did "Education Showcase" a national cable show sponsored by the Discovery Channel, which highlighted educational issues in public schools. She also hosted a half-hour infomercial for the shoe company, Cloudwalkers.

Sheryl first thrived as a news reporter for three network affiliates. She was a TV news reporter for WLFI in Lafayette, Indiana and covered stories from agriculture to riding with the police. In Louisville at WLKY, she anchored news cut-ins every half hour and reported on weekends. While in Louisville, Sheryl also co-hosted a half-hour Syndicated TV show for Churchill Downs on Horse Racing called, "In Season." Then in South Bend, Indiana at WNDU, Sheryl encompassed many roles. Sheryl reported "Live" everyday for the Morning TV show from all over town and called in the story to the number one rated Radio Show on U93. Then, on the 5 o'clock news, Sheryl created, produced, and anchored her own segments called, "Inside the Net" which featured internet sites.

Sheryl's professional experience and work ethic are based on work hard/play hard. With a strong educational foundation, Sheryl attained a master's degree in Radio/TV from Butler University and worked as an adjunct professor of public speaking at the University of Notre Dame, St. Mary's College and Indiana University-South Bend. But, fun and physicality were always in the mix too as Sheryl has performed as a Professional Cheerleader for the Indiana Pacers.

Her newest adventure is as the "Greyhound Gal." Sheryl is in the works of pitching TV shows with other hosts and her co-stars Shiraz and Buffett, her greyhounds. The TV shows feature dogs and their owners and their unusual antics and lifestyles via her web dog site called *www.GreyhoundGal.com*. They're set on "making a dog lover out of everyone." Sheryl is also pitching a documentary on the island dogs of St. Maarten. And, Shiraz, Buffett and Sheryl are turning the camera on themselves with their own Dogumentary, "Is Life Greyt?"

Many of Sheryl's clients are so satisfied with her work that they request repeat performances inviting her to lend her talent and professionalism to additional projects. If you're looking for talent for your next project, think of Sheryl Matthys.

Sheryl Matthys

Resume

AFTRA/SAG Eligible

TELEVISION

Education Showcase	Host	National Cable
Dream Travel	Reporter	Japan
In Season Churchill Downs	Co-Host	ABC-TV
Biography of Malcolm X	Co-Star	The Learning Channel
Home Design	Co-Host	Syndicated
TV Reporter/Anchor	WLKY	CBS
TV Live Shot Reporter, Internet Reporter	WNDU	NBC
TV Reporter	WLFI	CBS

THEATRE

Carnage (Samuel French Festival Finalist)	Rebecca (Lead)	Churnuchian Theatre, NY
Joined at the Head (Butterfield)	Maggie Mulroney (Lead)	El Bodegon Theatre, NJ
Mixed Doubles (Feydeau)	Philomiele (Supporting)	Creative Place Theatre, NY
The Rehearsal at Versailles (Moliere)	Mille Du Croisy (Supporting)	Creative Place Theatre, NY
The Abortion (O'Neill)	Lucy (Lead)	Creative Place Theatre, NY
At Sea (Simon)	Edie (Lead)	The Acting Studio, NY
Helen is a Heterosexual (Wilhelm)	Jane (Lead)	Producers Club, NY
The Power and the Glory (Wilhelm)	Inez (Lead)	Actor's Loft, NY
Cabaret	Kit Kat Girl	Battel Center, IN

FILM

Champagne from a Coffee Can	Lead	Cary Woodworth, Director
Change of Heart	Lead	Stacey Kattman, Director
First Kiss (Sundance Entry)	Supporting	Antonio Campos/Joe Parlagreco
The Fix	Supporting	Brett Caruso, Director
I'm Comin' For You	Supporting	NYU Graduate
Hansel & Gretel	Supporting	NYU Student

INDUSTRIALS (Partial List)

Canon (2 videos & Live Narrator)	Intel	Weight Watchers
SONY (9 videos & Live Narrator)	Eli Lilly	Retail Bakeries (2 videos)
Audi (Live Narrator)	Novartis (8 videos)	Ethan Allen
Vtech (Live Narrator)	Aventis	Optimum Online
Knex (Live Narrator)	Bayer (2 videos)	American Banking (2 videos)
Fisher Price (Live Narrator)	US Surgical Corp.	Ricoh & Mita copiers
	Blue Cross Blue Shield	Symbol Technologies

COMMERCIALS

Upon request

TRAINING

Meisner Intensive Program	Wendy Ward	The Ward Studio
Monologue	Loretta Greco, Charles Gerber	TVI Actors Studio, Private
Soap Technique	Penny Templeton, Eli Tray	Templeton Studio, TVI
Commercial Technique	Arista Baltronis, S. DeAngelis, Joan See	TVI, School for Film & TV
TV/Film Scene Study	Olivia Harris, DiMatteo & Long	TVI Actors Studio
Voice	Vicki Shaghoian	Private
Education	B.A. Psych., Master's Radio/TV	Butler University
	Alliance Francaise	Paris, France
	Univ. of Notre Dame, St. Mary's, IU-SB	Adjunct Professor

SKILLS

Ear Prompter, Teleprompter, USTA Rated Tennis Player, Golf, Jog, Jazz, Aerobics, Yoga, Tap, Tae Kwon Do, Pilates, Swim, Operate Power Boat & Car (Stick), Horseback (Western), Figure Skate, Former Indiana Pacer Cheerleader, Hand Model

Sheryl Matthys Contact:

www.lightscameratalent.com
Email: nygalnow@aol.com
Phone: 917-771-5586

Gene Costa

Gene Costa

Profile

Gene was born in Taunton, Massachusetts to a very poor family. His first job paid 50 cents per *week* collecting garbage and he turned all of that over to his parents. He later was promoted to paperboy at around age 7. His customers were always amazed at how well he could count change. Some would try to take advantage of him but he was never fooled because he was born with a proclivity for numbers.

After serving in the Navy during the Korean conflict he used the GI Bill to go to College. He graduated with honors and later went to graduate school and received his Masters degree. He then went on to work on his Ph.D. in applied statistics and worked for many years as a Corporate Statistician.

While working at the Research Center, he gave a sterling performance as George Patton in a farewell party for his boss, which brought the house down. Many were literally rolling in the aisles in raucous laughter. The organizer of the farewell party moonlighted as a producer of a local community theatre and suggested to Gene that he should get involved in theatre.

After transferring to Memphis, Gene tried out for the musical "The Sound of Music" and landed a speaking part as Admiral Von Schrieber. This in itself was quite an accomplishment because Theatre Memphis is one of the biggest community theatres in the country. Over 250 people auditioned for a part and Gene, with no experience, landed a speaking part and the rest is history. Gene thanks Theatre Memphis' Executive Producer/Director Sherwood Lowry for giving him that chance.

Gene Costa

Resume

FILM

The Firm	Mr. Morolto MAFIA	Feature	Sidney Pollak, Paramount Pictures
The Black Wedding	Dr. Carl Von Cosel	Lead	Chad Eidschun, Atomic Age Films
Live, Cry, Shampoo & Die	Doc (Psychologist)	Principal	Daryn Murphy, Yitibit Films
Course of Action	Chief Nichols	Principal	Joseph Cupicha, Full Sail Student Film
The Zombie Project	General Scott	Principal	Brian Scott, U. of Miami Student Film
Memphis Beat	Wes Chambers	Principal	Molli Benson, Molli Benson Productions
Cattle Car Complex	Limo Driver	Principal	Scott Berchman, Penn State U. Student Film
The Eyes Have It	Sgt. Lyle Crawford	Principal	Molli Benson, Molli Benson Productions

INDUSTRIALS

Decisions by the Numbers	Principal	International Paper
Internal Auditing	Lead	International Paper
Implementing SPC	Lead	International Paper
Statistics For Managers	Principal	International Paper
Statistics For Operations	Principal	International Paper

COMMERCIALS

List Upon Request	POC, MOS

THEATRE

The Wedding From Hell	Jackie Fitzhugh		Playhouse 19
A Pack of Lies	Bob Jackson	Lead Role	Germantown Community Theatre
Guys and Dolls	Arvide Abernathy		Bartlett Community Theatre
Tina n Tony's Wedding	Nunzio MAFIA		The Itinerate Theatre Company
The Gift of the Magi	The Narrator (O'Henry)		Harrell Theatre of the Performing Arts
Rumpelstiltskin	The Miller		Harrell Theatre of the Performing Arts
Mame	Claude Upson		Bartlett Community Theatre

The Good, The Dead & the Ugly	Max Shepherd MAFIA	Mysteries on Beale
Guys and Dolls	Big Jule	Memphis Jewish Community Center
The Sound of Music	Admiral Von Schrieber	Theatre Memphis

AWARDS

1999 Telly Award	Decision By the Number
2001 Crystal Award – Nomination for Best Supporting Actor	The Wedding From Hell
2002 Crystal Award – Best Short Film	Course of Action

TRAINING

Terry Berland	Audition to Win Workshop	Los Angeles Based
Linda Fionte Zerne	Auditioning for Comm's & Next Step	Miami
Patti Robinson	Film Acting Workshop	Orlando
Jean Hammonds	Acting and Singing Workshop	New York City Based
Molli Benson	Film Acting Workshop	Los Angeles Based
Allen Dysert	Acting for the Camera	Chicago Based
Cary Spears	Acting Workshop	Washington, DC Based

SPECIAL SKILLS

Music: Vocalist (Baritone), Pianist, Music Theory
Dialects: British, French; Accents: New England, New York
Tennis, Golf, Softball, Baseball, Football, Swimming, Diving, Chess, Sketch & Paint Artist, Photography, Showing Dogs, First Aid

Gene Costa Contacts:

Alexa Model and Talent Inc.
4100 West Kennedy Blvd.,
Suite 228
Tampa, FL 33609
Phone: 813-289-8020

Arthur Arthur
6542 U.S. Hwy. 41 North, Suite 205A
Apollo Beach, FL 33572
Phone: 813-645-9700

Azuree Talent Group
140 N. Orlando Ave., Suite 120
Winter Park, FL 32789-3679
Phone: 407-629-5025

Brevard Talent Group
906 Pinetree Dr.
Indian Harbour Beach, FL 32937
Phone: 321-773-1355

The Chistensen Group
235 Coastline Road
Sanford, FL 32771
Phone: 407-302-2272

The Diamond Agency
The Historic District
204 W. Bay Ave.
Longwood, FL 32750
Phone: 407-830-4040

Famous Faces
3780 South West 30th Ave.
Fort Lauderdale, FL 33312
Phone: 954-922-0700

Florida Stars
225 A W. University Ave.
Gainesville, FL 34104
Phone: 239-353-0044

Peter Speach

Favorite Quote:

"One thing that cannot be taught is self-knowledge."

Peter Speach

Profile

For as long as Peter can remember he has been an artist. He has been intrigued and inspired by the "art...and craft of acting," first working in theatre productions and later learning the unique qualities of film acting. "To act is to live, and in order to live completely, one has to embrace life experiences with vigor," he says. He has learned some important wisdom from a casting director that once stated: "One cannot find an acting job, much less carve out a career in this business without a clear understanding of who he or she is, both inside and out. Sometimes this happens at a very tender age, sometimes later in life and sometimes never.

Acting cannot be learned from a class, or a book, it comes from self-knowledge. When self-knowledge happens something "clicks" and all of the elements seem to fall into place. It's at this point that an actor may start to really work. Until that happens all he can do is study, make contacts, perfect his or her product and persevere. Most of all it is important to keep active and constantly working whether it be paid or non-paid." These are the words he has embraced and these are the words that have changed his approach to working in the business.

Peter can be seen in the films "Illegal Witness," "Garden of the Gods" and "All the Marbles," to name a few. Plus he stays busy with television, commercials, and theatre work.

Peter Speach

Resume

FILM

Illegal Witness (2002)	John McNamara (Lead)	DV24 Productions
All the Marbles (2002)	Rich (Lead)	Manness Productions
Final Draft (2002)	Paul (Lead)	Point Break Pictures
Garden of the Gods (2002)	Sam (Lead)	Point Break Pictures
Precious Time (2002)	Dad (Lead)	Hong Film Works
All American Fairy Tale (2001)	Duke Murdock (Lead)	Digital Dream Pictures

TELEVISION

American Water Works	Host	Clubhouse Production
Unexplained Mysteries	Roman Senator	PAX Television
Unexplained Mysteries	John Parker	PAX Television
Unexplained Mysteries	Jimmy Hoffa	PAX Television
Busted	Judge Fitzgerald	Animal Planet
Busted	FBI Agent	Animal Planet
Busted	Texas Ranger	Animal Planet
Days of Our Lives	Detective (Recurring)	NBC – TV
LA Law	Bailiff (Feature)	NBC – TV
Princess & the Cabbie	Guy on the Street	ABC/MOW

THEATRE

The Wager	Mark	Theatre Artaud, SF
Rosancrantz/Gilderstern	Rosancrantz	Theatre Artaud, SF
Death of a Salesman	Biff	SOMO Theatre Project, SF

COMMERCIALS

KOOL Lights (South America)	Sax Player	Foot Cone Belding, SF

TRAINING

Advanced Master Acting	Bruce Glover	Los Angeles, CA
Scene Study/Cold Reading	Bonnie Richardson	Studio City, CA
Staniszlavsky Technique	Johnathan Stutz	San Francisco, CA
Acting & Improv	Jeff Geller	San Francisco, CA

SPECIAL SKILLS

Directable, versatile, willing to travel, horseback riding (western), snow skiing (advanced), Motocross, surfing, graphic artist, extensive travel, cooking, motivational speaker, driver's license, stage combat, handle firearms.

Peter Speach Contact:

Manager: Jeff Martin
Phone: 212-947-2854

Nick Pellegrino

Favorite Quote:

"With misery or without, I am still the king."

240

Nick Pellegrino

Profile

Nick was born in Boston, Massachusetts, where he participated in Equity Children's Theatre, attended several summer Performing Arts Youth Camps sponsored by The Boston Symphony Orchestra Foundation and later, studied arts/sciences at Boston University and Harvard. He completed a Master of Science Degree in Communications (Film-TV Production/Advertising) at the University of Illinois in Champaign-Urbana. In the mid-70's, he moved to Los Angeles seeking film/TV acting work. He received his first TV role in the final episodes of the popular, "Adam-12."

Other notable work followed on "Kojac," "Bionic Woman," "The Incredible Hulk," "CHIPS," "Columbo," "The Seekers" (miniseries), "The Remarkable Margaret Sanger" (CBS MOW), "Hunter," "The Greatest American Hero" and a 3-month run in the ABC (NY) soap, "One Life To Live."

Later, he did "Dream On," "Arrest & Trial," Malcolm in the Middle" and the "Girls Club" (pilot). His first recognizable film role came, after many smaller ones, in "The Enforcer" ("Dirty Harry III") starring Clint Eastwood. Next came the zany, teenage, Beatle's comedy, "I Wanna Hold Your Hand" (Robert Zemeckis's first film, produced by Steven Spielberg), followed by the well-received "The China Syndrome" starring the late, great Jack Lemmon, Jane Fonda and Michael Douglas and directed by the late James Bridges. The 90's brought "Steal Big, Steal Little" starring Andy Garcia and Alan Arkin.

In addition he's also in "Crossroads," "John Q," Anger Management," starring Adam Sandler/Jack Nicholson and Steven Spielberg's, "Catch Me If You Can." The 80's industry strikes financially forced him out of Los Angeles. In 1988, he used his Master's Degree to accept a sales/promotions position with the new Florida Lottery in Miami. He returned to Los Angeles in 1994-95 to continue his acting career and won The Los Angeles Drama Critics Circle Award (Best Ensemble Cast) for the extended, successful run of Odet's "Awake And Sing" at the Odyssey Theatre. He still does theatre in Los Angeles for pay or no pay. Since his return, he has patiently accepted all camera acting to selectively update his "demo reel" with his current look and present a marketable variety of characters. With this reel, soliciting for better representation, he signed with Ray Cavaleri & Associates. Acting in quality film and television again with the best directors, writers and actors is his goal-in progress.

241

Nick Pellegrino

Resume

FILM

CATCH ME IF YOU CAN	S. SPIELBERG/DREAMWORKS
CROSSROADS	T. DAVIS/PARAMOUNT
FAST LANE TO VEGAS	J. QUINN/INDIGO
HOT CLUB CALIFORNIA	J. QUINN/INDIGO
STEAL BIG, STEAL LITTLE	A. DAVIS/SAVOY
INSIDE MOVES	R. DONNER/ITC
THE CHINA SYNDROME	J. BRIDGES/COLUMBIA
I WANNA HOLD YOUR HAND	R. ZEMECKIS/UNIVERSAL
THE ENFORCER (DIRTY HARRY)	J. FARGO/WARNER BROTHERS
THE BIG BUS	J. FRAWLEY/PARAMOUNT

TELEVISION

ARREST & TRAIL: "BEACHSIDE ATTACKER"	Co-Star
SEXY URBAN LEGENDS: "NO SMOKING PLEASE"	Guest Star
DREAM ON: FINALE	Co-Star
GREATEST AMERICAN HERO: "DREAMS"	Guest Star
CHIPS: "OVERLOAD" AND "VINTAGE '54"	Guest Star
INCREDIBLE HULK: "THE PSYCHIC"	Co-Star
KOJAK: "I WANT OT KILL MY WIFE'S LAWYER"	Co-Star
ONE LIFE TO LIVE (DAYTIME SERIES)	Recurring
GENTLEMAN BANDIT (CBS MOW)	Co-Star
COLUMBO: "A CASE OF IMMUNITY"	Co-Star
REMARKABLE MARGARET SANGER (CBS MOW)	Co-Star

COMMERCIALS

SKOL BEER	RAGU SPAGHETTI SAUCE	DUTY FREE STORES INT'L (LA)
ARCTIC CIRCLE RESTAURANT	VICEROY CIGARETTES	LUCENT TECHNOLOGIES
PRUDENTIAL INSURANCE	1-800-CALL ATT	

THEATRE & EDUCATION

MASSACHUSETTS: COMPANY THEATRE (BOSTON)	CHARLES PLAYHOUSE (BOSTON)	LOEB THEATRE (CAMBRIDGE)
ILLINOIS: KRANNERT CENTER (URBANA)	GOODMAN THEATRE (CHICAGO)	
CALIFORNIA: ODYSSEY THEATRE ENSEMBLE (LA)	1994 LA DRAMA CRITICS AWARD	(ODETS, "AWAKE AND SING")
LAMAMA HOLLYWOOD	LOBERO THEATRE (SANTA BARBARA)	OAKLAND REPERTORY
EVERGREEN THEATRE		
THEATRE EXCHANGE/LA	EUREKA (SAN FRANCISCO)	

UNIVERSITY OF ILLINOIS: BA THEATRE; MS FILM/TV

SPECIAL SKILLS
CYCLING, FENCING, SAILING, SWIMMING, TRACK & FIELD, DANCER, FIREARMS, ITALIAN ACCENT, MID-EAST ACCENT, NEW ENGLAND ACCENT, NEW YORK ACCENT, RUSSIAN ACCENT, SPANISH ACCENT

Nick Pellegrino Contact:

Cavaleri & Associates
178 S. Victory Blvd., Suite 205
Burbank, CA 91502
Phone: 818-955-9300

Maggie Moline

Maggie Moline

Profile

Maggie is an actress and stunt performer who has a very impressive sports background. She has excelled in basketball, volleyball, softball and baseball and has won awards. The *Chicago Tribune* voted her Athlete of the Week, and she won the award of being Athlete of the Year by *North Shore Magazine*.

Maggie is also a talented singer with a magnificent voice. Her CD, "As Long As There Is Love," is a timeless collection of romantic love songs composed by Giovanni Decarlo and written exclusively for Maggie...with echoes of the past and the voice of the present.

She has played Wonder Woman for Warner Brothers/DC Comics and The Super Heroes Live Action Show. She is also available as Wonder Woman at events. She has appeared in "Running Mates," "Independence Day" and "Washington Slept Here." She has had various TV roles and has done theatre.

Maggie Moline

Resume

SAG
SPORTS HISTORY

Basketball
4 years high school / 3 years on Varsity (played all positions) made All-state

Volleyball
4 years high school / 3 years on Varsity (played all positions made All-state…USVBA: "A" division-2 years…CBVA: "A" ranking-(beach volleyball)

Softball
4 years high school / 3 years on Varsity (can play all positions) made All-state (Specialized in pitching, 1st base, & 3rd base) University of North Carolina-Chapel Hill: Softball scholarship Bachelors Degree, ACC Honor roll

Baseball
Women's professional league – "Lady Ace" – pitcher, 1st base, 3rd base

AWARDS

Chicago Tribune
Athlete of the Week

North Shore Magazine
Athlete of the Year

OTHER ABILITIES
Stage Combat/Fighting, Pyro, Tumbling, Weapons (Lasso & Bracelets), Rollerblading, Ice Skating, Swimming (breast-stroke, freestyle, backstroke), Running, Biking, Road Biking, Aerobics, Weightlifting, Kick-boxing, Singing & Dancing

FILM
Starship Troopers – Stunt work/Special Ability
The Animal – Police Woman
Pre-High Jumper
James Dean Story – Casting Director
Independence Day – Mother
Washington Slept Here – Secret Service Agent
Fire Down Below – Feature
HOLES – Stand-In
Running Mates – Secret Service Agent

246

SINGING
As Long as There is Love – Musical CD

TELEVISION
Pacific Blue – Volleyball player
Bay Watch – Beach and Bar scenes
Ned & Stacey – Feature-restaurant
NYPD Blue – Police Woman

THEATRE
Warner Brothers/DC Comics – Wonder Woman
Super Heroes Live Action Show
Fools For Love – Supporting (Julie)

OTHER TRAINING
Method Acting Techniques -- Ned Manderino
Private Coaching – Jeanne Hartman, Diana Nadeau
Stage combat/Stunts – Todd Lester
Scene Video/Cold Reading – Actors Edge
Commercial Workshop – SAG Conservatory
Cold Reading/Scene Study – Van Mar Academy of Motion Picture & TV
Scene Study – Crossroads-private class
Commercial Workshop – Westside Academy
Cold Reading Technique – Film Industry Workshop (FIWI)

Maggie Moline Contact:

Website: www.wonderpowers.com

Colleen Camp

Colleen Camp

Profile

From her feature film debut playing a human in Twentieth Century Fox's blockbuster "Battle for the Planet of the Apes," Colleen Camp has starred in over fifty films and television productions, with standout roles in "Funny Lady," starring Barbra Streisand, and as the USO dancer in Francis Ford Coppola's "Apocalypse Now." While her performance as Connie Thompson in Michael Ritchie's "Smile" earned her kudos as a gifted comedienne – in fact the film was re-released in August 2001 with previously unreleased scenes featuring Colleen – her breakthrough performance came in Peter Bogdanovich's comedy "They All Laughed," in which she played opposite Audrey Hepburn, Ben Gazzara, and John Ritter. An accomplished singer, Colleen also garnered rave reviews singing the hit country western singles "One Day Since Yesterday" and "Kentucky Nights" by Eric Kaz. According to Bogdanovich, Colleen is a "brilliant actress, a gifted comedienne, and has the rare ability to see the big picture. She is also a great human being and a joy to work with."

Most recently, Colleen can be seen in "L.A. Twister," directed by Sven Pape. Other recent films include: "Someone Like You," directed by Tony Goldwyn, starring Ashley Judd, "24 Hours" directed by Luis Mandoki with Charlize Theron and Courtney Love, and "Rat Race" directed by Jerry Zucker and starring Cuba Gooding Jr., Amy Smart and Whoopi Goldberg. She also co-starred in Andy Fickman's comedy "Who's Your Daddy?" and "Joshua" directed by Jon Purdy, starring Tony Goldwyn, F. Murray Abraham and Giancarlo Giannini. Colleen appeared in "Election" for Paramount, directed by Alexander Payne, in which she wooed audiences with her chilling yet funny performance as Reese Witherspoon's controlling mother, Barbara Fick, and "Love Stinks," directed by Jeff Franklin, as French Stewart's officious attorney. Colleen starred opposite Beverly D'Angelo in "Jazz Night," from producer and first-time director Wallis Nicita, and "Barhopping" for John Travolta's JTP Films starring opposite Kelly Preston, Kevin Nealon, and Tom Arnold, which aired on Showtime. She was the lead in "Second To Die," directed by Brad Marlowe, appeared in "Goosed" with Jennifer Tilly, and made a cameo in Amy Heckerling's recent film "Loser."

Colleen returned to acting after a four year hiatus following the birth of her daughter in 1989 to appear in the feature films "Speed II: Cruise Control" with Sandra Bullock, "Sliver" starring Sharon Stone, and "Greedy" with Michael J. Fox. In addition she was featured in "The Associate" directed by Daniel Petrie Jr., "Last Action Hero" with Arnold Schwarzenegger, "Coneheads" with Dan Aykroyd, "Wayne's World" with Dana Carvey and Mike Myers, and Martin Scorsese's "Naked in New York." Other film credits include "Track 29" directed by Nicolas Roeg with Gary Oldman and Theresa Russell; "House Arrest;" "Police Academy II and V;" "The Joy of Sex" and the box office smash "Valley Girl," both directed by Martha Coolidge; Peter Bogdanovich's "Illegally Yours," with Rob Lowe; "D.A.R.Y.L.," directed by Simon Wincer; "My Blue Heaven," starring Steve Martin and directed by Herbert Ross; "Babysitter's Club," directed by Melanie Mayron; as well as being the female lead opposite Bette Davis in her last film, "Wicked Stepmother," with Richard Moll and David Rasche. Ms. Davis personally requested that Colleen play her antagonistic daughter-in-law. Whether she is Yvette, the French maid in "Clue," as directed by Jonathan Lynn, or New York detective Connie Kowalski in "Die Hard With A Vengeance," directed by John McTiernan, Colleen has always surprised audiences with her diverse character portrayals and fearless risk taking.

Colleen's television credits include a series regular role on "Tom" for CBS, recurring roles on "Roseanne" and "Thirtysomething," several episodes of "Dallas" and "Murder She Wrote," and a critically acclaimed turn on HBO's anthology series "Tales From The Crypt." As a frequent star of television movies of the week, she appeared in the ABC acclaimed telefilm "Suddenly" with Kirstie Alley, the miniseries "Rich Man, Poor Man Book II," and Jordan Kerner and Jon Avnet's television movies "For Their Own Good" and "Backfield in Motion."

Along with her passion for acting, Colleen has also spent the past seven years actively fulfilling her goal as a producer. She has a first look production deal at Fireworks Entertainment, as well as a consulting arrangement at Crusader Entertainment, and has numerous projects set up at Columbia, Universal, Paramount, New Line and Miramax. Colleen has produced "Creature Features," a series of five HBO movies re-making classic 1950's monster movies, with Lou Arkoff and Stan Winston, the creator of the creatures in "Terminator," "Predator" and "Jurassic Park." The movies aired Halloween 2001 on HBO. "Creature Features" includes "The Day The World Ended," directed by Terry Gross, starring Nastassja Kinski and Randy Quaid; "War of the Colossal Beast," directed by Sebastian Gutierrez, staring Rufus Sewell, Carla Gugino and Gil Bellows; "Earth Vs. The Spider" starring Dan Aykroyd, Theresa Russell, Amelia Heinle and Devon Gummersol; and "How To Make A Monster," starring Steven Culp, Colleen Camp and Clea DuVall.

Colleen also produced the documentary on singer Sophie B. Hawkins "The Cream Will Rise" with Bryan Bantry which was directed by Gigi Gaston and which can be seen on the Sundance Channel, and "An American Rhapsody," starring Nastassja Kinski, Tony Goldwyn and Scarlett Johansson, written and directed by Eva Gardos, a period film set in Budapest Hungary which was released in November 2001 by Paramount Classics. In addition, Colleen was a producer with Barbet Schroeder and Seven Arts Pictures on "Shattered Image," the English language debut of acclaimed Chilean director Raul Ruiz, starring Billy Baldwin and Anne Parillaud. Before her move to Fireworks Entertainment and Crusader Entertainment, Colleen was involved in a myriad of projects as a producing partner at Seven Arts Pictures, which co-financed a series of films from "Rules of Engagement" starring Tommy Lee Jones and Samuel Jackson to Jerry Zucker's "Rat Race."

With Howard and Karen Baldwin at Crusader Entertainment, Colleen is producing "Pre-school: The Movie" currently being written by Cannes award-winning writer John Richards, and "The Pre-Nup" written by Jonathan Lynn who is also attached to direct. Colleen is also producing a number of other projects, including "Betsy and the Emperor," starring Al Pacino with Patrice Chereau attached to direct; "Time and Chance," for Intermedia with Ron Bass attached to write; "Lady Gold" with Icon Productions, and Mel Gibson directing; "Karma," which she is producing with Terence Chang and John Woo; and "The War Magician" with Cruise/Wagner for Tom Cruise. Colleen also co-controls the books of prolific, celebrated writer Robert Nathan with Jeffrey Byron.

Colleen and Natassaja Kinski at the premiere of *The Others*

Colleen Camp Contact:

Colleen Camp Productions
132 B Lasky Dr.
Beverly Hills, CA 90212
Phone: 310-248-6228

Robert De Niro

Robert De Niro

Profile

Robert De Niro launched his prolific motion picture career in Brian De Palma's "The Wedding Party" in 1969. By 1973 De Niro twice won the New York Film Critics' Award for Best Supporting Actor in recognition of his critically acclaimed performances in "Bang the Drum Slowly" and Martin Scorsese's "Mean Streets."

In 1974 De Niro received the Academy Award for Best Supporting Actor for his portrayal of the young Vito Corleone in "The Godfather, Part II." In 1980 he won his second Oscar, as Best Actor, for his extraordinary portrayal of Jake La Motta in Scorsese's "Raging Bull." De Niro has earned Academy Award nominations for his work in four additional films: for his role as Travis Bickle in Scorsese's acclaimed "Taxi Driver," as a Vietnam vet in Michael Cimino's "The Deer Hunter," as a catatonic patient brought to life in Penny Marshall's "Awakenings," and in 1992 for his role as Max Cady, an ex-con looking for revenge, in Scorsese's remake of the 1962 classic "Cape Fear."

De Niro's distinguished body of work also includes performances in Elia Kazan's "The Last Tycoon," Bernardo Bertolucci's "1900," Ulu Grosbard's "True Confessions" and "Falling in Love," Sergio Leone's "Once Upon a Time in America," Scorsese's "King of Comedy," "New York, New York," "Goodfellas," and "Casino," Terry Gilliam's "Brazil," Roland Joffe's "The Mission," Brian De Palma's "The Untouchables," Alan Parker's "Angel Heart," Martin Brest's "Midnight Run," David Jones' "Jackknife," Martin Ritt's "Stanley and Iris," Neil Jordan's "We're No Angels, Ron Howard's "Backdraft," Michael Caton-Jones' "This Boy's Life," John McNaughton's "Mad Dog and Glory," "Bronx Tale," Kenneth Branagh's "Mary Shelley's Frankenstein," Michael Mann's "Heat," Barry Levinson's "Sleepers" and "Wag the Dog," Jerry Zaks' "Marvin's Room," Tony Scott's "The Fan," James Mangold's "Copland," Alfonso Cuarón's "Great Expectations" and Quentin Tarantino's "Jackie Brown," John Frankenheimer's "Ronin," Harold Ramis' "Analyze This," Joel Schumacher's "Flawless," Des McNuff's "Rocky and Bullwinkle," Jay Roach's, "Meet The Parents," and "Meet The Fockers," George Tillman's "Men of Honor" and John Herzfeld's "Fifteen Minutes," Frank Oz's "The Score," Tom Dey's "Showtime" and Michael Caton-Jones' "City By The Sea." He can be seen in Harold Ramis' "Analyze That," a sequel to "Analyze This," and Nick Hamm's "Godsend."

De Niro takes pride in the development of his production company, Tribeca Productions, and the Tribeca Film Center, which he founded with Jane Rosenthal in 1988. Through Tribeca, he develops projects on which he serves in a combination of capacities, including producer, director and actor.

Tribeca's "A Bronx Tale" marked De Niro's directorial debut. Other Tribeca features include "Thunderheart," "Cape Fear," "Mistress," "Night and the City," "The Night We Never Met," "Faithful," "Panther," "Marvin's Room," "Wag the Dog," "Analyze This," "Flawless," "Rocky and Bullwinkle" and "Meet The Parents."

In 1992, Tribeca TV was launched with the critically acclaimed series "Tribeca." De Niro served as one of the series executive producers.

In 1998, Tribeca produced a miniseries for NBC, based on the life of "Sammy 'The Bull' Gravano."

252

Tribeca Productions is headquartered at De Niro's Tribeca Film Center, in the Tribeca District of New York. The Film Center is a state-of-the-art office building designed for the film and television industry. The eight-story facility features office space, a screening room, banquet hall and restaurant, in addition to a full range of services for entertainment industry professionals.

Robert in front of one of his late father's paintings being shown in a French exhibition

Robert De Niro Contact:

Stan Rosenfield & Associates LTD
Public Relations
2029 Century Park East, Suite 1190
Los Angeles, CA 90067
Phone: 310-286-7474

Larry Romano

Larry Romano

Profile

Despite the fact that actor Larry Romano occupied a somewhat special position in television – starring in two sitcoms at the same time for two networks – he will still inform you:
"I love acting, but I'm a songwriter trapped in an actors life."

Romano who starred in the NBC series "Kristin," co-starring Tony-Award winning Kristin Chenoweth, and the long running CBS hit comedy, "The King Of Queens," who has also seen two of his plays staged Off Broadway and in Los Angeles local theatre, is half serious.

A major part of his life, and passion, is devoted to Romano's music, his playing (drums), singing, songwriting, and his groups. Yes, groups. Another plural for Romano, a musical double threat with two bands – Deficit and Eljay Are. Both have released CD's on the market and both run the bases musically between Roots Rock and Urban Folk/R&B, all powerfully delivered with an aggressive New York attitude. An attitude much like Romano himself – New York-born and retaining all of the elements of his roots to date.

This attitude is reflected in his song, "The House That Ruth Built," separately released. It is a track that will win no fans in high places (specifically corporate sky boxes or New York Yankees boss, George Steinbrenner). Romano calls it "a 'love song' for the memories of days at the grand old ballpark in the Bronx." It is a fan's scream against tearing down venerable old baseball stadiums, replete with history and memory. Under a repetitive groove of "Nobody rocks like we rock the Bronx," Romano warns "And Steingrabber [sic] wants to take a 75-year tradition and move it to a swamp in New Jersey." Not your typical rock lyric!

But then, Larry Romano is not your typical musician - or actor. About "Kristin," Romano notes "I'm thankful to have done this show where I'm playing an Italian-American who's intelligent and not a criminal, because that might be a first!"

Romano sees a parallel here with his own family: "My father was a successful, hardworking guy in the garment business in New York, oldest of his brothers, all born from humble beginnings and all ended up being very successful. And none of them went to jail. Being grounded in the Italian-American stereotype, that's the part that America doesn't see."

To accommodate his work on the "Kristin" series, Romano's third season of "The King Of Queens" (he played fireman Richie Iannuci) saw him appearing as his popular character in a slightly modified role during the season (even though his character's love life heats up with the addition of Rikki Lake on the show). This allowed him to move between CBS and the Paramount lot where "Kristin" was taped. "I'm very fortunate," he says, "and well aware of the difficulties that other actors face."

For Romano, preparation for this existence has included working in his father's garment factory in Mt. Vernon, NY, moonlighting as a delivery boy at Pat's Pizzeria in Tappan, NY, before heading to Manhattan to obtain a degree in Mixology from the American Bartending School of Madison Avenue, driving a gypsy cab, working as a telephone salesman for American Business Products, a copy machine company and ("apart from acting, the most dangerous," he says) a bicycle messenger.

"That's fairly typical of an actor waiting around, trying to get a foot in the business," he reflects. But music came first – and early – for Romano. He was playing his first drum set at age six. He spent time in a variety of teenage rock bands, including one with boyhood friend, Danny Spitz, who went on to found heavy metal hit makers, Anthrax, and his high school orchestra, (not marching band) he points out where he played a full set of tympani.

He observes: "My teen years were a time of just trolling around trying to start my own band, going to these rehearsal rooms in Manhattan, playing drums and sitting in with anybody, anywhere. Acting was not on my mind."

Acting, however, entered Romano's life during his time as a salesman in his father's showroom. "I did it for about three months, in a suit, on the train everyday, out at night to Chinatown to pick up the merchandise because business wasn't good and we had to resort to non-union work." It also included some unpleasant encounters ("I saw some mighty large and feisty rodents") that turned Romano's attentions elsewhere.

By chance, he wandered into Manhattan's The Learning Annex in search of piano lessons but, instead, ended up in a TV commercials class. He says: "The teacher told me I could be a John Travolta-type. I'd seen 'Saturday Night Fever' years before and had thought, yeah, I could do that. Now, here's this lady saying the same thing."

Next step was more serious – the venerable Lee Strasberg Theatrical Institute where he resisted some attempts to make him change his distinctive, NY-grown, ethnic voice patterns.

Romano discovered another talent within himself when he attended the Strasberg writer's workshop. The Institute presented his first play, "We Ain't Kids No More," where Romano discovered he could translate the scenes and characters from his life to the printed page and eventually to the stage. "I learned to write about things closest to me," he says.

An Off Broadway production of "Suitcase of Memories" followed and, from this, a casting director signed him for the role of the character First Base in the Sylvester Stallone movie, "Lock Up."

Romano's filmography grew. He landed roles in such movies as "Black Rain," "Out For Justice," "City Hall," "Sleepers" and more. He played Al Pacino's drug addicted son in "Donnie Brasco" and seemed all set for stardom in Terence Malick's highly regarded, "The Thin Red Line," which involved location work in Australia. "I was there for five months filming and then, back in New York, I got a phone call from Malick apologizing that most of my scenes had been cut," he says. "I ended up with one scene and a hell of a vacation reel."

Television came calling. Romano played a mob killer in early "NYPD Blue" episodes, a pizza guy on "Mad About You," a sex-crazed boxer on "L.A. Law" and then landed his "The King Of Queens" role.

Now relocated in Los Angeles, Romano finds time – in a very crowded schedule – to concentrate on his two bands, the hard rocking Deficit and Eljay Are, which is popular on college radio. It is a serious part of Romano's life and he resists criticism that he should focus on one band and one musical form to the exclusion of all else. "Why can't a music guy do all the different kinds of music – actors do it all the time, playing different roles. The point is the music I play and write is all part of me. I grew up listening to everything rock, the Motown grooves, R&B/pop, rap," he comments.

Another reason for the Romano attitude towards music is that he can afford to do this now. His TV work and film roles support his bands. "I support these groups – pay recording expenses, etc., because it's the only way I can remain independent and thrive," he says. "Most importantly, I want to work with the people that I want to work with, write the songs that I want to write, and wear the clothes that I want to wear. The TV money helps me do that just fine."

The talented Romano has just finished producing his first feature film "Little Athens" for Legaci Pictures. In addition, Romano and "Little Athens" cast members Michael Pena and John Patrick Amedori are now writing music together -- Romano on drums, Pena on bass and Amedori on guitar.

Larry Romano

Resume

FILM	PART	DIRECTOR
SPANISH FLY	John	Will Wallace
FINAL BREAKDOWN	Danny La Trenta	Jeff W. Byrd
THE THIN RED LINE	Mazzi	Terrence Malick
DONNIE BRASCO	Tommy Ruggerio	Mike Newell
SLEEPERS	Slugger	Barry Levinson
A HARD PLACE	Bobby	Buddy Giovinazzo
CITY HALL	Tino Zappati	Harold Becker
BULLET	Frankie Eyelashes	Julian Temple
LOCK UP	First Base	John Flynn
OUT FOR JUSTICE	Dog Food	John Flynn
OH NO, NOT HER	Pig Knuckles	Joe Bologna
BLACK RAIN	Joe Zeppi	Ridley Scott
SHE'S BACK	Da Wolf	Tim Kincaid
SPITTING IMAGE	Drag Queen	NYU Film
ON TIME	Clocker	NYU Film
DR. WHIPLASH	The Doctor	NYU Film

TELEVISION		
KRISTIN	Aldo Bonnadonna	Series Regular/NBC
THE KING OF QUEENS	Richie	Series Regular/CBS
GUY ISLAND (pilot)	Walt	Series Regular/NBC
PUBLIC MORALS	Richie Biondi	Series Regular/CBS
NYPD BLUE	Richie Cantenna	Recurring/ABC
L.A. LAW	Bobby Falcone	Guest Star/NBC
CIVIL WARS	Jimmy Bellacosa	Guest Star/CBS
MAD ABOUT YOU	Vinnie	Guest Star/NBC

THEATRE		
WE AIN'T KIDS NO MORE	Playwright/Lead	Lee Strasberg
SUITCASE OF MEMORIES	Playwright/Lead	Billy Redfield, NY
SATURDAY IN THE PARK	Playwright/Lead	The Burbage, LA

COMMERCIALS – List available upon request

TRAINING	
Lee Strasberg Theatre Institute	Charlie Laughton
HB Studios	Carol Rosenfeld
Jack Waltzer	Method & Meisner
Fred Fuster	On Camera
Tony Greco	On Camera
Richard Walter	UCLA Screenwriting
Ron Peterson	Screenwriting
Stuart Brown	Playwright Workshop

SKILLS
Collegiate Baseball, Racecars, Football, Karate, Boxing, Swimming, Billiards, Drummer, Bandleader, Live Rock Band.

Larry on the 2004 Summer Televison Preview Tour

Larry Romano Contact:

Brown Wolf Public Relations
6464 Sunset Blvd., Suite 803
Los Angeles, CA 90028
Phone: 323-466-0499
Website: www.larryromano.com

Brande Roderick

Brande Roderick

Profile

In a city where beautiful women are a dime a dozen, Brande Roderick stands out as a star among the masses. She shot a co-starring role in the much anticipated feature film "Starsky and Hutch" opposite Ben Stiller and Owen Wilson. The movie was released by Warner Brothers Pictures in April of 2004 and was a remake of the famous 1970's television series. She can also be seen in an independent movie, "Out of Control" which was released in May of 2003. In addition she completed a starring role in "Dracula II: Ascension" released in June 2003 by Dimension Films.

Within her first year in Tinsel Town, Brande landed a co-starring role in the hugely popular Aaron Spelling drama, "Beverly Hills 90210." She followed that with a string of guest starring roles on shows like "Just Shoot Me," "Jesse," "Love Boat: The Next Wave," as well as being cast in a string of national commercials for products such as *Snickers, Mentos and Dr. Pepper.* Brande's big break came in 2000 when she was asked to audition for "Baywatch Hawaii." During Brande's screen test, executive producer/writer Frank South felt she "hit it out of the park," and gave her the starring role of Leigh Dyer in the enormously popular show, which is syndicated to countries all around the world.

Brande followed Baywatch by taking a bite out of reality, as one of the stars in "The Surreal Life" for The WB network that aired in January 2003. She also reprised her starring role as Leigh Dyer in the Baywatch reunion movie, "Baywatch: Hawaiian Wedding," which also aired as a ratings bonanza for FOX in February.

Not one to rest on her laurels, Brande also played Susan in the independent feature "Out of Control," filmed in Switzerland. The film is a coming of age story about a young man following his dreams and having to choose between those dreams and his family. Brande's character is the driving force that helps him realize what's really important in life.

Since arriving in Los Angeles, Brande has trained under famed theatrical coach, Ivana Chubbuck, as well as Howard Fine and Jim Crenna. Her outside interests include playing softball in her local league where she lives in Los Angeles, hiking in the canyons with her cocker spaniel and bowling.

Brande Roderick Contact:

Shannon Barr Public Relations
3619½ Crest Dr.
Manhattan Beach, CA 90266
Phone: 310-546-5069

Linda Suarez

Favorite Quote:

"When love and skill work together, expect a masterpiece."

Linda Suarez

Profile

Linda was born in Madrid, Spain and traveled extensively throughout Europe as a child. She has lived in Madrid and London, England. She has a Master's Degree in Secondary Education from Seton Hall University and is a former English as a Second Language teacher. She has taught all grade levels from preschool to college. While taking a writing seminar, Linda was encouraged to take an acting class. Acting opened up a new and wonderful form of expression, which Linda chose to pursue professionally at The Atlantic Theatre Company Acting School in New York City. Walking away from a successful teaching career to pursue acting was a giant step into the unknown, but one she felt she needed to take. Since taking that step, Linda has performed an original one-act for the WTC Maintenance Worker's Relief Benefit at the Caymichael Patten Studio in NYC and co-produced and starred in "Do Over" by Frederick Stroppel. Linda has also performed in Shirin Neshat's "Logic of the Birds" at the Lincoln Center Festival and she was featured in "Love Letters" a TV drama for Nippon TV, Tokyo, Japan.

The quote she finds appropriate to her life is one by John Ruskin she first used in her high school yearbook: "When love and skill work together, expect a masterpiece."

Linda Suarez

Resume

NEW YORK THEATRE

LOGIC OF THE BIRDS	Ensemble	Lincoln Center Festival Shirin Neshat
DO OVER	Lisa	Raw Space
ENCOUNTER AT PENN STATION	Woman	Caymichael Patten Studio WTC Benefit
FOOL FOR LOVE	May	Atlantic Theatre Co. Acting School
CLOSER	Anna	Atlantic Theatre Co. Acting School
BOYS' LIFE	Lisa	Atlantic Theatre Co. Acting School
DIMLY, IN FLASHES	Stewardess/Miss Doolan	TSI/Playtime Series
OVER THE PHONE	Velma	TSI/Playtime Series
THE FATHER	Bertha	TSI/Playtime Series

FILM & TELEVISION

THE EARRING	Linda	Indie Short
LOVE LETTERS	Doctor	Nippon TV (Japan)
THE SOPRANOS	Friend of Bride & Groom	HBO
TWO WEEKS NOTICE	Award Banquet Guest	Castle Rock Production
CRADLE TO CRADLE	Doctor	NYU Student Film
THE TEA PARTY	Principal	New School Student Film

TRAINING

Atlantic Theatre Company Acting School

Advanced Scene Study	Robert Bella, Hilary Hinckle
Monologue Workshop	Karen Kohlhaas
Improvisation	Paul Urcioli
On Camera	Robert Bella

Atlantic Theatre Company Summer Intensive

Acting Seminar	David Mamet, F. Murray Abraham
Script Analysis	Robert Bella, Scott Zigler
Performance Technique	Paul Urcioli, Ron Butler
Repetition	Anya Saffir
Voice	Xan Garcia
Speech	Susan Finch
Movement	Renee Redding-Jones
Suzuki	Kelly Maurer

SPECIAL INTERESTS & SKILLS

Former ESL certified teacher, ballet, ballroom dancing, yoga, swimming, kickboxing, pilates, tai chi, computer skills, writer, own car, great day and evening wardrobe

Michael Taylor Gray

Favorite Quote:

"Everyone counts, but not everyone makes a difference."

Michael Taylor Gray

Profile

Michael Taylor Gray was born in Montana, raised in Ohio and currently lives in Los Angeles, CA. He knew from the early age of 6 years old that he wanted to live the life of an actor and singer. He was watching an episode of "Emergency" with his family and his father noted that young Michael – sitting inches away from the TV screen and entranced by the action of the scene – was quite possibly going to give birth along with the character in labor on the show!

He was the original "Benny/Miss Iona Traylor" from the multi-award winning original L.A. run of "Southern Baptist Sissies," and brought his hit cabaret with Amanda Abel (granddaughter of Hollywood Screen legend, Eddie Cantor) to the Zephyr Theatre in L.A. and The Wilde Goose in Palm Springs. It was the second and third stops for the "Switched At Birth Tour" – the first of which was a STANDING ROOM ONLY performance at The Gardenia in Hollywood!

A review in *Variety* of Michael's performance in "Southern Baptist Sissies" stated that, "(Michael Taylor) Gray turns in the most refreshing performance of the evening as the outrageous, thoroughly unapologetic queen-from-birth Benny, who was practicing drag routines by the time he was 12."

Michael is a graduate of Bowling Green State University (BGSU) – a B.S. in Secondary Education/Communications Comprehensive – cum laude and California Institute of the Arts (CalArts) – MFA in Acting – with Honors.

"I act, I sing, I move well! I'm so completely involved with my life's work as an actor/singer, that I don't have time for hobbies. But I do enjoy my quiet time, reading a great biography or just listening to the waves lapping against the shoreline along the California coast."

"My favorite personal quote and mantra is: 'Everyone counts, but not everyone makes a *difference*.' It's my goal in life to make a positive and profound *difference* in people's lives – either through my life's work or just plain ole daily living. I am most thankful for my best friend Ted, my unconditionally loving Aunt Josie and Uncle Eugene (Mom & Dad), my amazing and talented nephew Christopher and my bevy of supportive, loving and trusted friends...Amanda, Bert, Terri, Glenn, Ken, Frank and more!"

Michael Taylor Gray

Resume

SAG/AFTRA/AEA

FILM

Strange & Charmed	Max	Shari Frilot
Such a Night	Featured	Leslie Iwerks
Feverish	Lead	CSULB
Kenneth Patchen	Henry Miller	T.R. Koba

TELEVISION

Without A Trace (CBS)	Featured	
Maybe It's Me (WB)	Co-Star	Michael Katleman
Will & Grace (NBC)	Co-Star	James Burrows

STAGE

L.A. Theatre

Neo A La Carte	Franklin	Theatre Neo
Bed, Boys & Beyond	Michael	Hudson Theatre
Del Shores' Southern Baptist Sissies	Benny/Iona Traylor	Zephyr Theatre
Resa Fantastiskt Mystisk	The Cat	The Actor's Gang
SPIDERS	Alex	Bitter Truth Playhouse
Poe!	Larry	Theatre Geo
The Imaginary Invalid	Beline	L.A. Co. Courthouse
Comrades	Gaga	2nd Stage Theatre
Dancing at Lughnasa	Michael	Coffeehouse Theatre
The Scarlet Letter	Governor Bellingham	Luna Park

CABARET

Switched At Birth! Tour	Michael Taylor Gray &	The Gardenia, The Zephyr
When Good Divas Go Bad...	Amanda Abel	Wilde Goose (Palm Springs)

COMMERCIALS

Demo Reel available upon request and online at www.nowcasting.com/mtg

TRAINING

California Institute of the Arts (CalArts), MFA in Acting-1993
Theatre Neo Company Member - Current

SPECIAL SKILLS

Singing (Tenor), Fencing, Ping Pong, Tai Chi, Bowling, Hair/Make-Up, Flute/Piccolo, Dialects: Southern, Irish, British

Michael Taylor Gray Contact:

CLinc. Talent Agency
Phone: 323-461-3971
Website: www.nowcasting.com/mtg

Ellie Weingardt

Favorite Quote:

"Prepare, Promote, Pray."

Ellie Weingardt

Profile

Ellie Weingardt was born and raised on the south side of Chicago. As a child, she studied with Jack and Jill Players, appearing in several roles for the theatre company and the famed opera singer, Rosa Raisa, for voice as her youngest pupil. "I remember singing, 'In My Sweet Little Alice Blue Gown' for my third grade class, and as a senior in high school I did a monolog in a drama class from 'Joan of Arc' and when the bell rang everyone stayed frozen in their seats. I always believed entertaining was my God-given pursuit – my singular contribution."

Upon graduation from high school, Ellie studied dance and acting for a year in New York with a private coach nights and worked days. After a few months, she landed a part in an off-Broadway production of "Beauty and the Beast." The play was a combination of "Beauty and the Beast" and "Cinderella." Ellie started in the role of one of the "Wicked Step-Sisters" and later did the leading role of "Beauty." Upon her return to Chicago, Ellie went to work at CBS in television. While there, she was on the "Music Wagon" radio show and later on "Ted Mack" singing "Got A Lot of Living to Do."

"During her time in Chicago she was married and had a child on the way. Four kids later, Ellie did some local community theatre where a fellow "thespian" asked her to go to the Big City with her for acting classes. Ellie studied with W. C. Macy (Fargo) and learned the art of The Method. From there, she went to Second City to learn the art of improv. She studied television commercial and film acting from the best, and now teaches voice-over at Columbia College in Chicago.

After the method acting class, Ellie decided to try her luck at the profession. She acquired headshots, a resume, and a voice-over demo and has been fortunate to work with the tops in the business over the years both on stage, in film and in "the booth."

Recently, Ellie had the privilege of working with Jean Reno in "Just Visiting," a hugely entertaining romp through Chicago by a Medieval Knight. She also appeared in "Save the Last Dance." Ellie is probably best known for her role as "The Charm School Teacher" in "A League of Their Own" for which she was featured in *Entertainment Weekly* and *Northshore Magazine*. "The funniest thing is seeing yourself on screen speaking in a different language," remarks Ellie.

Ellie has played barflies to Queens in her career on stage and in film. She appeared in the long running hit, "Shear Madness" on stage as Mrs. Shubert and, more recently, as Phyllis in "Follies" by Steven Sondheim.

Ellie has also performed as an improv-impressionist for corporate and social events. "Joan Rivers on the red carpet, and Lucy are my most sought after doubles," Ellie says. She also won two trips to Hollywood. One was to the Academy Awards where she walked down the real red carpet. The other was for a Joan Rivers look-alike contest from FOX Television where she ended up on Joan's "Late Show." Ellie also went to Hollywood for the "Lucy-Desi Search" and was featured in *Star Magazine* as a Lucy-look-alike.

Voice-overs have been Ellie's mainstay in show business. After winning the highly coveted "Windy Award" for best Chicago voice-actress, she discovered that her imagination is best served in the quiet confines of a glass booth where she can be a talking bear or a daredevil. Ellie still has a client of almost twenty years for which she has done thousands of voice-over commercials.

Ellie's clients have been a who's who of companies, like Coca Cola, Sears, Kelloggs, Allstate, AT&T, and McDonald's to name a few. Her on-camera commercial work has led her all the way to Europe for Camel Cigarettes in an unforgettable spot where she is squashed by a falling camel!

Ellie remarks, "My husband finds it hard to believe that I still have time to be a wife, mother, grandmother, and homemaker---and still do good work as a Rotarian along with serving on the Cultural Arts Commission of my hometown."

Ellie can be seen in: "Bad Meat," "The Evil One" and "Unaware."

Ellie Weingardt Contact:

Shirley Hamilton, Inc.
333 East Ontario
Chicago, IL 60611
Phone: 312-787-4700

Kelly Bishop

Kelly Bishop

Profile

Veteran actress Kelly Bishop has portrayed many memorable roles in film, television and the theatre since her breakout performance as one of the original cast members of the hit Broadway musical "A Chorus Line."

The Colorado Springs native grew up in Denver, CO, where she trained to be a ballet dancer. At 18, she headed to New York and landed her first job dancing in a year-round ballet company at Radio City Music Hall. Bishop danced in Las Vegas, summer stock and on television until she was cast in 1967 in "Golden Rainbow," her first Broadway role.

Her big break came when she was cast as the sexy, hard-edged Sheila in "A Chorus Line." She won Tony and Drama Desk Awards for her performance, giving her the confidence she needed to eventually leave the acclaimed original ensemble to pursue a dramatic acting career.

It wasn't long before she was cast opposite Jill Clayburgh in Paul Mazursky's big-screen drama "An Unmarried Woman." She went on to play "mom" to several high-profile stars in numerous features: Jennifer Grey's mother in the box-office hit "Dirty Dancing," Howard Stern's mother in the Betty Thomas-directed comedy "Private Parts" and Tobey Maguire's mom in "Wonder Boys." Her additional feature credits include "Blue Moon," "Café Society," "Miami Rhapsody," "Queens Logic," "Me and Him" and "A Guy's Guide to Marrying Money."

On television, Bishop is currently starring on the WB series "Gilmore Girls" as "Emily Gilmore." Bishop also starred in the Mike Nichols' series "The Thorns" and played Lisa Ann Walter's mother on "My Wildest Dreams." She has guest-starred on "Law & Order," "Law & Order: Special Victims Unit" and "Murphy Brown."

Bishop's extensive theatre credits include the lead in the Broadway production of "Six Degrees of Separation," as well as Broadway productions of Neil Simon's "Proposals," the Tony Award-winning "The Last Night of Ballyhoo" and "Bus Stop." She also has starred in numerous regional theatre and off-Broadway productions.

When she's not working, Bishop practices pilates and aerobics, loves animals, and enjoys gardening and hiking near her home in New Jersey, where she lives with her husband, TV talk show host Lee Leonard.

Kelly Bishop

Resume

SAG/AFTRA/AEA

BROADWAY

THE LAST NIGHT OF BALLYHOO	BOO LEVY	HELEN HAYES THEATRE
PROPOSALS	ANNIE	
BUS STOP	GRACE	CIRCLE IN THE SQUARE
SIX DEGREES OF SEPARATION	OUISA	LINCOLN CENTER
PRECIOUS SONS		
A CHORUS LINE	SHEILA- **WINNER OF TONY AND DRAMA DESK AWARDS**	

OFF BROADWAY

LAST GIRL SINGER	IVA	KAMPO CENTER
DEATH DEFYING ACTS	PHYLISS	VARIETY ARTS
PTERODACTYLS	GRACE DUNCAN	VINEYARD THEATRE
THE BLESSING	NAN	AMERICAN PLACE THEATRE
PIANO BAR		CHELSEA WESTSIDE

REGIONAL THEATRE

INSPECTING CAROL	ZORAH	GEORGE STREET PLAYHOUSE
THE SUBSTANCE OF FIRE	MARGE HACKETT	WESTPORT PLAYHOUSE
THE FOURTH WALL (A.R. GURNEY)	JULIA	WESTPORT PLAYHOUSE
THREE PENNY OPERA	JENNY	GREAT LAKES THEATRE FESTIVAL
A LITTLE NIGHT MUSIC	COUNTESS	BERKSHIRE THEATRE FESTIVAL
THE NIGHT OF THE IGUANA	MAXINE	MCCARTER, PRINCETON & VA STAGE
VOICE OF THE TURTLE	OLIVE LASHBROOK	AMERICAN THEATRE COMPANY
VANITIES	MARY	DRURY LANE, CHICAGO

FILM

WONDER BOYS	AMANDA LEER
GUY'S GUIDE TO MARRYING MONEY	MRS. COHEN
PRIVATE PARTS	RAE STERN
CAFÉ SOCIETY	MRS. JELKE
MIAMI RHAPSODY	ZELDA
QUEENS LOGIC	MARIA
ME AND HIM	MRS. KARAMIS
DIRTY DANCING	MARGE HOUSEMAN
AN UNMARRIED WOMAN	ELAINE

TELEVISION

GILMORE GIRLS	SERIES REGULAR/EMILY	WB
TALK TO ME	GUEST LEAD	ABC-TV
ONE LIFE TO LIVE	DR. MARCIA ROBBINS	ABC-TV
MY WILDEST DREAMS	GLORIA (SERIES REGULAR)	FBC-PILOT '95
MURPHY BROWN	GUEST STAR	
LAW AND ORDER	GUEST STAR	NBC
RUTH HARPER	CO-STAR	CBS PILOT '91
THE THORNS	GINGER THORN	ABC SERIES
RECOVERY ROOM	KAY-CO-STAR	CBS PILOT
KATE AND ALLIE	GUEST STAR	
THE NEW ODD COUPLE	GUEST STAR	

HAWAII FIVE-0	GUEST STAR	
ADVICE TO THE LOVELORN	CO-STAR	NBC/MOW
A YEAR AT THE TOP	CO-STAR	NORMAN LEAR
ALL MY CHILDREN	FREIDA LANDAU	ABC
ANOTHER WORLD	DR. FOSTER	NBC
AS THE WORLD TURNS	GRACE	CBS

Kelly at the 100th episode party for *Gilmore Girls*

Kelly Bishop Contact:

Abrams Artists Agency
275 Seventh Avenue, 26th Floor
New York, NY 10001
Phone: 646-486-4600

273

Andre Roger

Favorite Quote:

"The way you think and feel, is the way you live."

Andre Roger

Profile

Born and raised in Switzerland, Andre Roger spent his childhood in the French-speaking region of his native country. His early acting career started in school plays. As a teenager he moved to the German-speaking region of Switzerland where he graduated as an electro mechanical engineer and sales coordinator. The duties of his country soon called him to military service, where after a couple of years, Andre graduated from the Officer School.

In his later teens, Andre worked as a runway and print model and he won the title Mister Switzerland in 1994. The win of this pageant gave him instant fame, new opportunities and ideas, especially since it was the first time that such an event took place in his country. He had the advantage to be the first one and will always be remembered as such. Andre had a busy time hosting shows, working on movie productions, photo shoots, and interviews. He made the headlines in national papers, and TV and radio news on a regular basis.

In his spare time, Andre loved to take off on his motorcycle together with his buddies and he would spend the wintertime on his snowboard. Soon he met his future wife who was living in Los Angeles at that time. Andre always had the vision to go to the entertainment capital of the world, learn the ropes and "make things happen." He enrolled at Playhouse West in North Hollywood, worked regularly on movie sets as an actor, stand in and body double, which enabled him to join the Screen Actors Guild.

During time off, he and his wife would travel the countryside, camp out in the desert, ride motorcycles and sail their yacht to Catalina Island. An interesting business opportunity caused them to move to Miami, Florida where they bought a house and settled down in 1999. Andre signed up with the local talent agents and soon worked as an actor in SAG commercials and did extensive print work. His most exciting print job was a one-week photo shoot in Honduras. He has appeared in many films and TV series, including the film "Lemonade," a dark comedy in which he played the eccentric character of Mr. Flanagan, the funeral director, in a starring role. Director/Teacher Marc Durso, with whom he studies the Uta Hagen Technique and Linklater Voice Technique, coaches Andre.

Andre Roger

Resume

SAG/AFTRA

FILM

BIRTHDAY	CO-STAR	SOJI KUDAKA
RUM WITH A TWIST	PRINCIPAL	WILLIAMS/WELLS PRODUCTION
BLOODY MEAL	PRINCIPAL	SOJI KUDAKA
THE FOUR HORSEMEN	PRINCIPAL	MERIDIAN ENTERTAINMENT
HARRY DICK AND MARY	PRINCIPAL	BRAD PRESLAR
LEMONADE	STARRING	CAPITOL PICTURES, W. PALM BEACH
HURLY BURLY	FEATURED	FOOLS IN LOVE PROD., INC.
AMISTAD	DAY PLAYER	DREAMWORKS
BLADE	FEATURED	WESLEY SNIPES
JACKIE BROWN	FEATURED	MIGHTY MIGHTY AFRODITE PROD.
HIGH VOLTAGE	DAY PLAYER	VOLTAGE PRODUCTION

TV SERIES

LOVE BOAT	DAY PLAYER	WINDMILL LANE PRODUCTION
BEVERLY HILLS 90210	DAY PLAYER	90210 PROD., INC. SPELLING
ER	DAY PLAYER	DAVID E. KELLY PRODUCTIONS
WORKING	DAY PLAYER	SITCOM NBC STUDIOS
JENNY	FEATURED	PARAMOUNT PICTURES / NBC
NEWSRADIO	FEATURED	BRILLSTEIN-GREY PROD. HBO

TV HOST/ANCHOR

VIP LOUNGE MIAMI	HOST/ANCHOR	VIP-TV, BIE PROD., MIAMI, FL

TV COMMERCIALS   LIST AVAILABLE UPON REQUEST

PRINT WORK   LIST AND PORTFOLIO AVAILABLE UPON REQUEST

TRAINING

LINDA ZERNE	AUDITION/CAMERA/COLD READING	FT. LAUDERDALE, FL
MARC DURSO	ACTING COACH/HAGEN TECH.	FT. LAUDERDALE, FL
PAT BATISTINI	COMMERCIAL, IMPROVISATION	LOS ANGELES, CA/MIAMI, FL
TOM LOGAN	TV, SOAPS, COMMERCIAL	LOS ANGELES, CA/MIAMI, FL
BARBARA DIPRIMA	COMMERCIAL, AUDITION	MIAMI, FL
POLARIS PROCUREMENT SPEC.	WEAPONS & TACTICS	MIAMI, FL
PRO VOICE/BETH COHEN	SINGING/VOCAL	PLANTATION, FL
PLAYHOUSE WEST	ACTING/MEISNER	NORTH HOLLYWOOD, CA
VAN MAR ACADEMY	ACTING/COLD READING	HOLLYWOOD, CA

STAND IN   LIST AVAILABLE UPON REQUEST

ABILITIES
SAILING & POWERBOATING, SNOW BOARDING AND SKIING, ROLLER BLADING, TENNIS, SWIMMING, SNORKELING, MOUNTAIN BIKING, MOTORCYCLING, FISHING, BALLROOM DANCING, HANDGUNS & RIFLES (SEMI AND FULL AUTOMATIC WEAPONS), SOCCER, GARDENING, MECHANIC, HANDYMAN

LANGUAGES (FLUENT)
ENGLISH, FRENCH, GERMAN & SWISS GERMAN

Andre Roger Contact

Wilhelmina Miami
Phone: 305-674-7206

Bridget Barone

Favorite Quote:

"All things come to those who go after them!"
Rob Estes

Bridget Barone

Profile

Born and raised in Zurich, Switzerland, Bridget Barone, a graduated law student, was sent to Los Angeles by an international modeling agency in 1992 with which she signed a 3-year modeling contract. Having worked as a model in Los Angeles, the entertainment capitol of the world, Bridget very quickly found huge interest in the craft of acting. She enrolled at the Playhouse West in North Hollywood, owned by actor Jeff Goldblum, and soon earned her SAG card. She kept modeling until her acting career started taking off fulltime in 1995.

Today she resides in Miami, FL, with her husband, Andre Roger, who is also a professional actor, whom she met in LA in 1994. Bridget has her own personal acting coach, Marc Durso. His students star in NBC and FOX TV shows and international films. He has coached super models and Latin singing stars for Film/TV in LA and Miami. The acting in Miami keeps Bridget busy at this time, by booking national and international TV-Commercials and also working on TV-Shows and Featured Films. She has also founded her own production company in 2002. She has finished a script about a comedy that takes place in Rio de Janeiro, Brazil. It is her first full-length independent feature film. Her goal is to turn it into a hit TV show or motion picture.

Bridget Barone

Resume

SAG/AFTRA

FEATURE FILMS

HURLY BURLY	DAY PLAYER, Cashier	STORM ENTERTAINMENT
A LIFE IN THE DAY	STARRING	SOARING LOW PRODUCTIONS, MIAMI
JACKIE BROWN	DAY PLAYER, FBI Agent	MIGHTY MIGHTY AFRODITE
MAGNOLIA	DAY PLAYER, Receptionist	EB PRODUCTIONS
IN THE LINE OF FIRE	DAY PLAYER, Reporter	CASTLE ROCK
THE LAST ACTION HERO	GUEST STARRING, Nun	COLUMBIA PICTURES
SHADOW FORCE	DAY PLAYER, Gambler	SYNTETIC FILM WORK

TV SERIES

BORN FREE	GUEST STARRING, Explorer	ELEMENT PRODUCTIONS
THE BREAST MEN	DAY PLAYER, Nurse	HBO PRODUCTIONS
SLEEPING WITH THE DEVIL	DAY PLAYER, Doctor	NBC PRODUCTIONS
BEVERLY HILLS 90210	DAY PLAYER, Waitress	SPELLING PRODUCTIONS
MELROSE PLACE	DAY PLAYER, Police Woman	SPELLING PRODUCTIONS

TV COMMERCIALS

EAGLE RIDER	PRINCIPAL	DEUTSCHE WELLE PRODUCTION
CHEVROLET	PRINCIPAL	VAN DYKE PRODUCTION
DELPHI INTERNATIONAL	PRINCIPAL	WEITZ PRODUCTION

STAND-IN & BODY DOUBLE

LIST AVAILABLE UPON REQUEST

RUNWAY/PRINTWORK

LIST AND PORTFOLIO AVAILABLE UPON REQUEST

TRAINING

LARRY MOSS ACTING	DIALECT/DICTION COACH	LOS ANGELES, CA
DELIA SALVI	ACTING/DIRECTING	SANTA MONICA, CA
VAN MAR ACADEMY	ACTING/COMMERCIAL	HOLLYWOOD, CA
PLAYHOUSE WEST	ACTING, SANFORD MEISNER	NORTH HOLLYWOOD, CA
SAG/AFTRA CONSERVATORY	ACTING/COMMERCIAL	MIAMI, FL

| MARC DURSO | ACTING COACH/HAGEN TECHN. | MIAMI, FL |
| TOM LOGAN | TV/SOAPS/COMMERCIAL | MIAMI, FL & LOS ANGELES, CA |

ABILITIES
FIGURE SKATING (5 yrs professional), ROLLER BLADING, HORSEBACK RIDING, TENNIS, WEIGHT TRAINING, BASKETBALL, SWIMMING, CYCLING, WINDSURFING, SKIING – WATER & SNOW (Certified Ski Instructor), GOLFING, SAILING (Certified USCG), SNORKELING, VOLLEYBALL, AEROBICS, DANCING (Jazz, Modern, Salsa, Lambada, Standard), MODELING, HANDGUNS AND RIFLES (Semi and Full Automatic)

LANGUAGES (FLUENT)
ENGLISH, GERMAN, FRENCH, ITALIAN, SWISS GERMAN

Bridget Barone Contact:

Alliance Talent Group
Phone: 954-727-9500

Pete Leal

Favorite Quote:

"There is more time than life."
His Mom

Pete Leal

Profile

Pete Leal was born in San Juan, Texas on August 18, 1938. In 1959 immediately after graduating from high school, he enlisted in the Navy and served four years. After knocking around in several jobs for the next five years he enrolled at El Centro Community College in Dallas, Texas. There the acting bug bit him. The play that hooked him was "A Marriage Proposal" by Anton Chekhov. He began his studies for his Masters Degree in Theatre at the Dallas Theatre Center in January of 1971, completing his studies in July of 1972. A month prior, he had auditioned and landed a starring role in a bilingual children's show for PBS at UT, Austin. The show was titled "Carrascolenda." Between 1972 and 1976, he performed in 187 episodes as the character "Caracoles."

Returning to Dallas he worked as an extra in several movies and appeared in a few commercials and eventually decided to relocate to Los Angeles. To survive during this time he worked constantly as a temp, and was able to land a few sit-com jobs and some commercials. In 1985 he decided to stop temping and concentrate on his acting career. It was "sink or swim" for him at that point in his career. After nine years of some success and struggling to survive, the need to go back to work was obvious. His ship was sinking. He worked for a law firm for five years. He then was cast in a sit-com in Spanish in 1999 and was on the show for one season.

In 2001, he was cast in the PBS family show "American Family" starring Edward James Olmos. Since that time he has had a successful career in films, television and theatre. He has been in many short films written and directed by students and up and coming directors and writers. One was "Hotel Oasis," written and directed by an AFI ex-student from Spain named Juan Calvo. This project won several prizes in European Film Festivals. Another was "El Artista" written and directed by his very good friend Ruben Romo, which also won several awards at different film festivals in California. In fact, it aired on network TV twice. Pete has performed in over 125 TV commercials both in Spanish and English and he has done numerous radio commercials. Pete has never longed to be a big star. His goal has been to be a working character actor. He has accomplished that goal and is happy with his life as it is.

Pete Leal

Resume

SAG/AFTRA/AEA

FILM (Partial List)

REAL WOMEN HAVE CURVES	GUEST STAR	REAL WOMEN HAVE CURVES PRODS.
100 WOMEN	GUEST STAR	100 WOMEN, INC.
ROAD DOGZ	GUEST STAR	SHOOTING STAR PICTURES
MI FAMILIA	FEATURED	EAST LA PRODS./GREGORY NAVA-DIR.
GENERATIONS	FEATURED	EMBASSY TELEVISION
HOUSE OF CARDS	FEATURED	BLINN/THORPE/NBC
SWALLOWS COME BACK	FEATURED	HBO

TELEVISON (Partial List)

FAMILY AFFAIR	GUEST STAR	CBS
PORT CHARLES	GUEST STAR	ABC
AMERICAN FAMILY	SERIES REGULAR	EL NORTE PRODUCTIONS
LIZZIE McGUIRE	GUEST STAR	DISNEY PRODUCTIONS
THE WEST WING	STEWARD	NBC
LOS BELTRAN	SERIES REGULAR	TELEMUNDO/SONY/COLUMBIA/TRISTAR
BEVERLY HILLS 90210	FEATURED	SPELLING PRODUCTIONS
FOUR CORNERS	FEATURED	CBS
A QUESTION OF CITIZENSHIP	STARRING	PBS/LAUSD
TKR	FEATURED	STERLING PACIFIC FILMS
SUNSET BEACH	GUEST STAR	AARON SPELLING / NBC
EL ARTISTA	STARRING	UNIVERSAL STUDIOS
MANGAS (RECEIVED ALMA AWARD)	STARRING	PBS / ECHO PRODS.
THE NANNY	FEATURED	MONTROSE PRODS.
CARRASCOLENDAS (187 EPISODES)	SERIES REGULAR	PBS

THEATRE (Partial List)

IN THE NAME OF GOD	FRIDA KAHLO THEATRE
TOO MANY TAMALES	BILINGUAL FOUNDATION
BLOOD WEDDING	VENTURA COURT THEATRE
FEATHER IN THE SNOW	VICTORY COURT THEATRE
LIFE ON THE LINE	VICTORY THEATRE
BERNABE	GEO THEATRE
ZAPATA	GOODSPEED OPERA HOUSE

TRAINING
BA, SPEECH & DRAMA, UNIVERSITY OF NORTH TEXAS
MA, THEATRE, TRINITY UNIVERSITY AT THE DALLAS THEATRE CENTER
MICHAEL SHURTLEFTS'S HOW TO AUDITION WORKSHOP, LOS ANGELES, CA
CHIRS & CHARLIE'S VOICE ANIMATION WORKSHOP, BURBANK, CA
MILTON KATSELAS ACTING WORKSHOP, BEVERLY HILLS, CA

Pete Leal Contact:

Alvarado Rey Agency
8455 Beverly Blvd., Suite 410
Los Angeles, CA 90048
Phone: 323-655-7978

Jack Amos

Favorite Quote:

"Live your Dreams."

Jack Amos

Profile

Jack is originally from South Carolina and is now living in the Tampa Bay area of Florida. He has been an athletic trainer and has worked three summer camps with the Atlanta Falcons. He's a professional scuba diver and a florist. He is now a fulltime actor in the Florida market.

Film credits for Jack include: "The House on Haunted Hill," "Any Given Sunday," "The Waterboy" and "Outer Twilight."

Jack Amos

Resume

FILM

We're Coming to Help	John Norton-Lead	JDcasey Productions
The Penny Game	Adult Sam-Lead *	Penny Production
Bum Luck	Conroy-Lead	Panhandler Productions
Time and Again	Clarence-Supporting	Stars North Productions
Chill Out	Cousin Ernie-Supporting	Top Line Cinema
Sweet Joe	Boris-Supporting *	Sweet Joe Productions
Outer Twilight	Mueller-Supporting	Rosal Films
The Last Case	Patrick-Supporting	LBD Productions
The Profit	Sr. Naval Officer-Principal	Totally Fun Inc.
The Last Black Klansman	Grand Dragon of KKK-Principal	Monumental Films
Six More Miles	Pastor Greed-Principal	Catalyst Films
Essence of Irwin	Mayor Rhett Rhimes-Lead	Downright Funny Films
Judy Garland Slept Here	Vernon Parsons-Principal	White Wolf Productions
The House on Haunted Hill	Steve Freed, Reporter	Warner Bros. Productions
Any Given Sunday	Officer Binder	Warner Bros. Productions
The Waterboy	Security Guard	Touchstone Productions

COMMERCIALS (Last 12 months only, conflicts on request)

K-Mart	Confused neighbor-Principal	Jay Thomas Productions
Direct TV-Season's Pass	The Big Cheese-Principal	NFL Films
Tampa Bay Devil Rays (x4)	Baseball Scout-Lead***	CB&Reid Productions
Tyndall Federal Credit Union	Retiree-Lead	Lampher Productions
Remington Steakhouse	Jesse James-Lead**	Time Warner Productions
Ft. Myers News-Press	Irate Neighbor-Supporting**	National Media Services
Ron Jon Surf Shop	Upscale Beach Bum-Supporting	Convergence TV
Audi-4 Project	Newspaper Vendor-Principal	Will Vanderylugt Productions
Gourmet Gardens	Farmer-Spokesman	Time Warner Productions
Merlins Bookstore	Merlin-Spokesman	Time Warner Productions
BC Truck, Van, SUV Dealership	BC-Spokesman	Time Warner Productions
Titleist Golf	Fan	HSI Productions

TELEVISION

Angel of Death-Aileen Woumos	Peter Seims-Principal	United Film and TV Productions
Tampa Bay Bucs/Shania Twain	Asst Ms. Twain	NFL Films
Jack Harris-Live	Unruly Viewer-Principal/Stunts *	WFLA/NBC
Wonderful World of Disney	Singer	Disney/ABC Productions

INDUSTRIALS

Identifying Impaired Practitioners	Angry Doctor-Principal	Roskins/Taylor
$20,000 Countdown (x2)	Car Shopper-Principal	BigGross.com
Medical Hair Replacement	Patient-Supporting	HMS Productions
NAPA	NAPA Joe-Principal	Disney I.D.E.A.S.
Florida Hotel Association	Businessman-Principal	Florida Educational Productions
T-Net	Ralph-Principal	Black Coffee Productions

Publix-Corporate Strength Volcano Spectacular	Competitor Manager-Principal Prof. Geophani-Spokesman	Publix Video Department Hollywood-Orlando Productions
Publix Manager Training-Gross Profit	Eli-Spokesman	Publix Video Dept.
Paradigm Learning-Countdown Video	Team Member	CB&Reid Productions

MODELING

Museum of Science and Industry	Spokesman	Bright House Productions
Bay Pharmaceutical	Spokesman	Bright House Productions
Disney Animal Kingdom	Park Guest	Convergence Promotions
Universal Escape	Spiderman/Businessman-Print	Universal Promotions
Busch Gardens-Williamsburg	Irish Musician-Print	Busch Gardens Promotions
Griffith-Cline Funeral Home	Father of Teenage Girl-Print	Clark Advertising
BC Truck, Van, SUV Dealership	BC-Print	The Flyer
Dr. Richard Merritt	Construction Worker-Print	Lakeland Ledger

VOICE-OVER

Winn Dixie	Pit Crew, Steak Guy	Oasis Films
Worms Way Garden Center	Wormy	Time Warner Productions
Smooze and the Holiday Adventures	Smooze, Capt. Redbeard, Squeeze, Ratso	Holiday Family Productions
Prairie Town	Various Characters	Prairie Adventures
Annual Talent Show Promo	Mariachi Man, Crooner Man	WTTO/FOX

AWARDS FMPTA *Crystal Reel, **Silver Award, ***Bronze Award

TRAINING

On Camera Film Acting Workshop Series	Patrick Cherry, Instructor
Television and Film Auditioning	Ellen Jacoby, Instructor
Television and Film Auditioning	Lori Wyman, Instructor
Animation-Voice-Over Workshop Series	Lew Car, Instructor
On Camera Precision/Extreme Driving Workshop	Grady Bishop, Instructor

SPECIAL SKILLS/INTERESTS
Stunt Fighting (Certified), Precision/Extreme Driving (Certified), Scuba Diving (Certified-PADI/Advanced), Teleprompter, Boating (to 35 ft.), Firearms (pistol, rifle, shotgun), Archery, Golf, and Tennis. DIALECTS: Spanish, Scottish, Irish, Cockney, British, Southern, Yiddish, Italian, West Indian, French, Swedish, German, Greek, Canadian

Jack Amos Contact:

Email: jackamos@mindspring.com

Paula Philip

Favorite Quote:

"Let go of your fears and embrace your dreams."

Paula Philip

Profile

After attending college, in which she earned a fashion merchandising degree, Paula decided to take the risk of pursuing her lifelong dream to become an actress. Paula has studied theatre at the Lee Strasberg Theatre Institute in NYC. Acting credits include ED/NBC, five independent films, six Off-Off Broadway theatre productions, six NYU grad films, re-enactment video for The Maury Povich show and voice-over, film projects for the American Sign Language Institute. Her hobbies include dancing, traveling, international cuisines, museums, art, and fashion. Paula has also assisted in makeup artistry and wardrobe.

Paula Philip

Resume

FILM AND TELEVISION

A Good Day	Evelyn (unfit mother)	Black Feet Productions
Race	Georgey (snob)	Race Productions
Running With Scissors	Hair Stylist	Indie Film
The Audition	Nora (rude actress)	Dir-Chicita Cook
Peace Be Still	Rory (controlling sister)	NYU Grad/Dir-M. Brazier
Untitled	Ama (slave)	NYU Grad/Dir-Jenna Feldman
Three Arms	Fran (manipulative girlfriend)	NYU Dir-Kattie Stern
Mustard	Sandy (deli clerk)	NYU/Dir-Chaiki Yoshimine
Spider	Annie	NYU/Dir-Abbey Erickson
No News Is Good News	Tammy (anchor woman)	NYU/Dir-Ian Urghart
The Confrontation	Jennifer (call girl)	NYU/Dir-Jeff Chow
On Guard	Beverly (secretary)	Dir-Kevin Lee

THEATRE AND STAGE

Lysistrata	Ismenia (goddess)	The Lysistrata Project
Congregation	Sister Gertrude (church diva)	Afrikaan Women Repertory
Queen Lillian	Mother (abused wife)	SUNY Purchase
The Heiress	Maria (parlour maid)	The PaperMoon Players Inc.
Waiting For Lefty	Edna (housewife)	Lee Strasberg Theatre
Imagining Brad	Brad's Wife	Lee Strasberg Theatre
Manhattan Towers	Laresse (snob)	Bonner B Productions

VIDEO

Re-enactment Video	Sharon (gunshot victim)	The Maury Povich Show
Salon True Confessions	Michelle (jealous lover)	Dramatics NYC/Dir-Yanni Stamos

TRAINING

Lee Strasberg Theatre Inst.	Scene Study	Hope Arthur
	Movement/Speech	Michael Ryan
	Audition Technique	G. VanDeckter
Broadway Dance Center	Modern Jazz	Sue Samuels
Space Dance Center	Street Jazz	Lillian Manasala

EDUCATION

Laboratory Institute of Merchandising, New York, New York, Associate Fashion Merchandising

SKILLS AND INTERESTS

West Indian Accent-Barbados Passport, Valid Drivers License, Club Promos, Fashion Styling, Propsmaster
International: Traveling and Cuisines, Museums, Art, Cultural History, Music, Theatre

Commercial/Print/Promotional – Lists available upon request

Paula Philip Contact:

Phone: 917-319-7587

Tom Bower

Tom Bower

Profile

Tom's motion picture credits include: "Below the Belt," (New Deal Pictures), directed by Robert M. Young and produced by Tom Bower," In The Land Of Milk And Money," directed by Susan Emshwiller; "How's My Driving," directed by Jason Eric Perlman; "Tulse Luper Suitcases," directed by Peter Greenaway; "The Laramie Project," (HBO/Good Machine), directed by Moises Kaufman; "The Badge," with Billy Bob Thornton (Lions Gate), directed by Robby Henson; "High Crimes" (20th Century Fox), starring Ashley Judd and Morgan Freeman and directed by Carl Franklin; "Hearts in Atlantis" (Castle Rock), starring Anthony Hopkins, Hope Davis and David Morse and directed by Scott Hicks; "Bill's Gun Shop," starring John Ashton, directed by Dean Hyers and produced by Tom Bower; "Pollock" (Sony Classics), starring and directed by Ed Harris; "Million Dollar Hotel," starring Mel Gibson, directed by Wim Wenders; "A Slipping-Down Life" (DVC Productions, Tony Kalem, Director); "Shadrach" (Nu Image, Susanna Styron, Director) which premiered and opened in 1998 at The Los Angeles Independent Film Festival; "The Negotiator" (New Regency, F. Gary Grey, Director); "Poodle Springs" (Mirage, Citadel, Bob Rafelson, Director); "The Buffalo Soldiers" (Citadel, Charles Haid, Director); "The Postman" (Warner Bros., Kevin Costner, Director); "Nixon" (Disney, Oliver Stone, Director); "Georgia" (Mirimax, Ulu Grosbard, Director); "White Man's Burden" (Rysher Entertainment, Desmond Nakano, Director); "Clear and Present Danger" (Paramount, Philip Noyce, Director); "Die Hard II" (20th Century Fox, Renny Harlin, Director); "Far From Home the Adventures of Yellowdog" (20th Century Fox, Philip Borsos, Director); "River's Edge" (Island, Tim Hunter, Director); "Wildrose" (Troma, John Hanson, Director); "The Ballad of Gregorio Cortez" (Embassy, Robert M. Young, Director); "Shadows" (John Cassavettes, Director) and others.

Tom has also appeared on numerous television programs and MOW's, including, "The Practice," "Law & Order," "West Wing," "The Beast," "The X-Files," "Roswell," "NYPD Blue," "The Philadelphia Miners' Story" (ABC MOW); "Monday After the Miracle" (MOW, CBS, Dan Petrie, Sr., Director), "Riders of the Purple Sage" for TNT; "Attica Against the Wall" for HBO; and, "Arliss" for HBO.

Also, a veteran of the stage, Tom has appeared in more than 80 theatrical productions across the United States, including a recent production of Harold Pinter's "The Caretaker," for which the production received the "Best Revival" award from *L A Weekly*. He is one of the founding members and is on the Board of Directors of The Loretta Theatre.

In 1981, Tom was invited by Robert Redford to be a resource actor at the Sundance Institute for film and television. He has remained active in the Institute since that time, and has served as a member of the Nominating Committee.

Tom serves on the various committees at The Screen Actors' Guild and is a Co-Chair of the Rule One Committee and Co-Chair of the Indie Outreach Program at Screen Actors Guild.

Tom is also on the Advisory Board of the Minnesota Film Board and Chief Creative Officer for New Deal Pictures in Denver, Colorado.

Tom Bower Contact:

Lasher/McManus/Robinson/Kipperman
1964 Westwood Blvd., Suite 400
Los Angeles, CA 90025
Phone: 310-446-1466

Tommy Lee Jones

Tommy Lee Jones

Profile

Academy Award winner Tommy Lee Jones was awarded the Best Supporting Oscar for his uncompromising portrayal of U.S. Marshal Sam Gerard in the box office hit "The Fugitive" in 1994. For this performance, he also received a Golden Globe Award as Best Supporting Actor. Three years previous, Jones had received his first Oscar® nomination for his portrayal of Clay Shaw in Oliver Stone's "JFK."

Audiences saw Jones re-team with Will Smith and director Barry Sonnenfeld in the box office hit "Men in Black 2," and also "The Hunted" for director William Friedkin opposite Benicio Del Toro.

Jones starred in "Space Cowboys" with James Garner and Donald Sutherland for director/actor Clint Eastwood. Before that he starred in "Rules of Engagement" with Samuel L. Jackson.

Jones starred with Ashley Judd in the box-office hit "Double Jeopardy." In 1998 he reprised his role as U.S. Marshal Sam Gerard in "U.S. Marshals," the follow-up to "The Fugitive," and in 1997 he starred with Will Smith in the No. 1 box office hit of the year, "Men In Black," which grossed over $500 million worldwide.

Jones made his feature film debut in "Love Story" and, in a career spanning three decades, has starred in such films as "Eyes of Laura Mars," "Coal Miner's Daughter" – for which he received his first Golden Globe nomination – "Stormy Monday," "The Package," "Under Siege," "Heaven and Earth," "The Client," "Natural Born Killers," "Blue Sky," "Batman Forever," "Cobb" and "Volcano."

In 1995, Jones made his directorial debut with the critically acclaimed telefilm adaptation of the Elmer Kelton Book "The Good Old Boys" for TNT. Jones also starred in the telefilm with Sissy Spacek, Sam Shepard, Frances McDormand and Matt Damon. For his portrayal of Hewey Calloway, he received nominations for both a Screen Actors Guild Award and a Cable ACE Award.

Jones had previous success on the small screen. In 1983, he won an Emmy Award for Best Actor for his performance as Gary Gilmore in "The Executioner's Song" and, in 1989, was nominated for an Emmy Award and a Golden Globe Award for Best Actor for the miniseries "Lonesome Dove."

His numerous network and cable credits include the title role in "The Amazing Howard Hughes," the American Playhouse production of "Cat on a Hot Tin Roof," "The Rainmaker" for HBO, the HBO/BBC production of "Yuri Noshenko, KGB" and "April Morning."

In 1969, Jones made his Broadway debut in John Osborne's "A Patriot for Me." His other Broadway appearances include "Four on a Garden" with Carol Channing and Sid Caesar, and "Ulysses in Nighttown" with the late Zero Mostel.

Born in San Saba, Texas, he worked briefly with his father in the oil fields before leaving for Harvard University, where he graduated cum laude with a degree in English.

Tommy Lee Jones Contact:

PMK/HBH
8500 Wilshire Blvd., Suite 700
Beverly Hills, CA 90211
Phone: 310-289-6200

Diane Matson

Diane Matson

Profile

Diane Matson is an exceptionally, talented actress who lives in the state of Washington. She has been performing since the age of three and started acting classes at the age of six. She has a four-year drama scholarship from Seattle Pacific University. She's a musician that can play flute, guitar, accordion and piano. In film and television she has appeared in "The Lotus Eaters," "Executive Beats," "Pendemonium," "Dougie's Room," and "Ray of Darkness," to name a few, plus she was in the music videos, "Yesterday Is Gone" and "Remember." Diane also has done voice-over, commercials and theatre. She's a bundle of energy with a sense of humor that can work as a clown and a mime artist. This bright, artistic actress is shooting for stardom and with her talent she will get there fast!

Diane in the "Madonna" period

Diane Matson

Resume

SAG

FILM/TELEVISION

Merv's Tavern	Supporting/Sally	Three Blind Artists
B.U.S.H. League	Principal/Edith/Mindblower	Chromazone
The Waiting Room	Principal/Mary Turner	Second Glance
Captain's Log	Segment Host/Diane	Foregger Films/Inc-TV
The Lotus Eaters	Principal/Cindy	Flybynight Productions
Dogonit	Principal/Blind Woman	Strikes Twice Films
Executive Beats	Principal/Business Woman	Barn Doors Productions
Alone?	Principal/Helen	Ed 'N Dave Productions
Dougie's Room	Principal/Dr. Amanda Campbell	Fat Dragon Productions
Ray of Darkness	Principal/Dawn	Realms Entertainment
Pendemonium	Principal/Waitress	BAMF Productions
Fishing Frenzy – TV Pilot	Principal/Co-host	White Lightning Productions
Yudit's Choice – Documentary	Principal/Voice-Over	Mary Peterson Productions
Yesterday Is Gone – Music Video	Principal	Backstage Management
Remember – Music Video	Principal	Backstage Management

COMMERCIALS & CORPORATE VIDEOS & GAMES *Full list available upon request*

The Suffering	Screams, Moans, Whispers	Surreal Software
BPH Diary Training – Corp.	Principal/Trainer	Media Arts, Inc.
How to Perform Pastoral Care – Corp.	Principal/Spokesperson	White Lightning Productions
COSTCO – Point of Purchase – Corp.	Principal/Voice-Over	Counterbalance Productions
US West "Airtouch Powerband" – Corp.	Principal	US West Productions

THEATRE

The Way To Bethlehem	Lead/The Traveler	St. Madeleine Sophie Church
Child Abuse Conference	6 Year Old	Harborview Center
Medieval Minstrel	Female Leads	Camlann Medieval Village
Dr. Seuss Stories	One Woman Show	Various Performances
The Importance of Being Earnest	Lead/Cecily	Seattle Performing Arts Fellowship
The Art of Dining	Supporting/Nessa Vox	Seattle Pacific University
Our Town	Supporting/Mrs. Soames	King's Productions

TRAINING

Improvisational – Theatre Sports	Various	The Actor's Studio
B.A. in Theatre *Magna Cum Laude*	4 Year Drama Scholarship	Seattle Pacific University

On-Camera & Voice-Over: John Jacobsen (On-going), Mark Malis, Joey Paul, Steven
                                 Black, Jodi Rothfield, Patti Kalles, Jay Hopper, Pat French,
                                 Tony Barr, John Vreeke, Susan Conners, Gary Austin

SPECIAL SKILLS/INTERESTS:

Greenscreen & teleprompter; Juggler; Clowning; Mime artist; ASL; roller blader; flautist; skier
(water & snow); pianist; scuba diver; horseback rider; massage; hand model; computer literate;
WIF; Short Fiction Writer, CPR; handgun trained; weight lifter; nutrition; volleyball player; dialects;
can shoot baskets with either hand.

Diane Matson Contact:

Wink Talent
Phone: 917-816-0743
Email: wink-inc@verizon.net
Website: http://www.dianematson.com

Matt Damon

Matt Damon

Profile

Matt Damon has become one of Hollywood's most sought-after talents. Audiences have seen Damon star as Jason Bourne in "The Bourne Identity" and "The Bourne Supremacy," for Universal Pictures. Additionally Damon starred as Linus Caldwell in "Ocean's 11" and "Ocean's 12" with George Clooney, Brad Pitt and Julia Roberts for director Steven Soderbergh. Matt also starred in "Gerry" with Casey Affleck, for director Gus Van Sant. "Gerry" premiered at the Sundance Film Festival and was released in February 2003. In addition, Damon starred in the comedy "Stuck on You" for the Farrelly Bros. The film also stars Greg Kinnear. Damon's next films "The Brother's Grimm," and "Syriana" are due to be released in 2005.

In 2000 alone, audiences saw Damon star in "The Legend of Bagger Vance," for director Robert Redford and in the film version of the Cormick McCarthy book "All the Pretty Horses" for director Billy Bob Thornton.

In 1999, Damon starred in Anthony Minghella's "The Talented Mr. Ripley" for which he received a Golden Globe nomination for Best Actor. That same year he rejoined "Chasing Amy" director Kevin Smith and pal Ben Affleck in "Dogma," a film about a pair of outcast angels.

In 1998, he won an Academy Award for Best Original Screenplay with longtime friend Ben Affleck for the critically-acclaimed drama "Good Will Hunting" a coming-of-age story about a young mathematical genius who, due to his upbringing in inner-city Boston, can't live up to his potential. Damon also earned an Academy Award nomination for Best Actor for his work in the title role. In addition, both he and Affleck received a Golden Globe Award for their screenplay, and Damon also garnered a Golden Globe nomination for his performance. The film, directed by Gus Van Sant, received seven additional Oscar nominations, including one for Best Picture and a win for Robin Williams for Best Supporting Actor.

In the same year, Damon starred in the title role of the World War II drama "Saving Private Ryan" for Academy Award-winning director Steven Spielberg and in John Dahl's "Rounders" about a reformed gambler who is drawn back into New York's underground poker world to help a recently paroled friend pay off loan sharks.

In 1997, Damon made a cameo appearance in Kevin Smith's "Chasing Amy." In the same year, he starred as an idealistic young attorney in Francis Ford Coppola's "The Rainmaker," based on the best-selling novel by John Grisham.

But Matt Damon is no overnight sensation. He first gained the public's eye in 1996, when he gave a vivid performance in FOX's "Courage Under Fire," in which he portrayed a guilt-ridden Persian Gulf War soldier tormented by an incident, which happened in the heat of battle.

The versatile young actor made his feature film debut in 1988 in a small role in the critically well-received "Mystic Pizza." He went on to play Brian Dennehy's medical school dropout in the TV movie "Rising Son" (TNT, 1990) and gained further attention when he returned to the big screen as a fascist preppy in Paramount's "School Ties" (1992).

For director Walter Hill, Damon enjoyed a sizeable supporting role as the green second lieutenant new to the West who narrates "Geronimo: An American Legend" (1993). In 1995, he appeared in "The Good Old Boys," directed by Tommy Lee Jones for TNT. Set in turn of the century Texas, Damon portrayed a forward thinking and mechanically inclined young man who leaves his family behind to follow his heart and pursue his passion for automobiles.

In 1998, Damon and Affleck partnered with "Good Will Hunting" Associate Producer and longtime friend Chris Moore to form Pearl Street Productions, now known as LivePlanet. This unique company created integrated media, a new kind of entertainment experience that combines traditional media, new media and the physical world. LivePlanet created and oversees, Project Greenlight, where filmmaking hopefuls submitted their original scripts to Affleck, Damon and Moore via an internet competition. A 13-episode documentary series chronicling the making of an independent feature film, debuted on HBO in December 2001 and the film, "Stolen Summer," was released in March 2002.

Damon, who attended Harvard University, first gained acting experience at the American Repertory Theatre as well as other Boston-based theatre venues.

Matt with Charlize Theron and Will Smith at the premiere of *The Legend of Bagger Vance*

Matt Damon Contact:

PMK/HBH
8500 Wilshire Blvd., Suite 700
Beverly Hills, CA 90211
Phone: 310-289-6200

Bonnie Somerville

Bonnie Somerville

Profile

Bonnie Somerville with her natural beauty was seen as "Mona," Ross' latest girlfriend, on "Friends" last season. She also recently starred in the NBC sitcom "The In-Laws" opposite Jean Smart and Dennis Farina.

Born and raised in Brooklyn, New York, Bonnie grew up in a large and close-knit Irish Catholic family. Passionate about performing at a young age, she sang and acted in school and community theatre productions since she was a child. She studied theatre at Boston College then moved to New York City to study at the Lee Strasberg Theatre Institute. While in New York, she formed her own rock and blues band, which performed all over the city.

Television audiences will remember her for her starring role which showcased both her singing and acting talents, portraying 'Lyne Danner,' a singer/songwriter during the 1950's in the CBS miniseries "Shake, Rattle and Roll." In addition, she starred in the WB series "Grosse Point." She is currently playing the role of Det. Laura Murphy on NYPD Blue.

Bonnie has also been busy with feature films, working with Steven Weber and Swoosie Kurtz in the independent black comedy "Sleep Easy, Hutch Rimes" and with Brendan Fraser and Elizabeth Hurley in Harold Ramis' romantic comedy "Bedazzled."

Bonnie at the 2005 Hollywood Style Awards

Bonnie Somerville

Resume

FILM		**Director**
BEDAZZLED		Harold Ramis
SLEEP EASY, HUTCH RIMES		Matthew Irmas
CRIME AND PUNISHMENT IN SUBURBIA		Rob Schmidt

TELEVISION		
NYPD Blue	Series Lead	ABC
JACK'S HOUSE (Pilot)	Series Lead	FOX
INLAWS	Series Lead	NBC
FRIENDS	Recurring	NBC
TIKIVILLE (Pilot)	Series Lead	NBC/James Burrows
THIS COULD WORK (Pilot)	Series Lead	NBC/Jonathan Groff
GROSSE POINTE	Series Lead	WB
TECHNO 3 (Pilot)	Series Lead	HBO
SHAKE RATTLE AND ROLL (Miniseries)	Lead	CBS

THEATRE		
CABARET	Sally Bowles	Boston College
TRAGEDY OF OTHELLO	Desdemona	B.U. SFA
OUR TOWN		THE HEIGHTS PLAYERS, NYC

TRAINING
Sandy Marshall (Currently), Los Angeles, CA
Lee Strasberg Theatre Institute, New York, NY

SKILLS
Singing, songwriting, volleyball, swimming, diving, dance, many dialects

Bonnie Somerville Contact:

McKeon Valeo Management
9150 Wilshire Blvd., Suite 102
Beverly Hills, CA 90212
Phone: 310-288-5888

Krista Grotte

Favorite Quote:
"There are no shortcuts to anyplace worth going."

Krista Grotte

Profile

Krista Grotte was born in Minneapolis, MN, and she will tell you, "I am an aspiring actress who loves nothing more than what I do." One of three children raised by a single mother, she wanted to pursue acting as a child but due to her mother's limitations, it was far too impossible. She moved to Florida at the age of 17, and after a couple of years of struggling she started taking acting classes for fun. She enrolled in college studying psychology and soon discovered the two subjects had much in common, in addition to being symbiotic. After 3 months working in a rundown schizophrenic unit, as the only staff member on duty with a clientele of 16 patients, all with a criminal record, they learned that someone truly loved them and she bonded with them. In those 3 months she learned what she felt to be everything else she needed to know about life, in addition to the fact, if she could handle this, she could handle anything.

It was time to pursue her acting career, and she found an agent and started going to auditions. Her first audition was for a schizophrenic character, and yes, she got the part. She loves acting more than anything. Krista says, "I will treat each and every character I play as my patient focusing on the sociological aspects of how she is and who she is. If I can just deliver a message through my work, make a sad person laugh, an ignorant person change a view, a tough guy shed a tear, then I have achieved my ultimate goal in the field of psychology. I have a lot of work to do and thankfully I have film projects lined up." Look for Krista playing Alyssa in "Hardscrabble," a film written by Linda Campbell.

Krista Grotte

Resume

EDUCATION

Venue Theatre	Acting and Commercials	St. Petersburg, FL
St. Petersburg College	Improvisation	St. Petersburg, FL

FILM

2002 Filthy (Horror)*	Feature	Metropol Productions
2002 Live, Cry, Shampoo, Die	Feature	Yitibit Productions
2002 Hardscrabble	Lead	Hardscrabble Productions
2002 Valley of the Shadow (T.Tr.)	Feature	Genxsis Productions
2003 Nightmare Collection	Lead	Enigma Films

TELEVISION

2002 Tomas Tan/Infomercial	Feature	Healthcare Networks
2002 KI Pills/Testimonial	Feature	Reliant Media Corp.
2003 The Spot/T.V. Show	Feature	NBC/WFLA T.V.

COMMERCIAL

2001 Recreational Factory Warehouse	Extra	National

PRINT

2002 E. Walter Lewis Galleries	Gallery Portrait Model	Photographer: Ed Walter Lewis
2002 Miami Night Out.Com	Feature Model	
2002 Genxsis Calendar Shoot	Feature Model	

PROMOTIONS

2002 Captain Morgan Promotions	Morganette
2003 Saints and Sinners III Film Fest	Necro Nancy

SPECIAL SKILLS AND INTERESTS

Driver, Track and Field, Aerobics, Weight Trainer, Tennis, Baseball, Bicycler, Horseback Rider, Cheerleader, Dancer, Kickboxer, Vocalist, Lyricist, Painter, Model, College Student – GPA 3.8

*Nominated Best Supporting Actress at the Crystal Reel Awards for "Filthy" 2003

Krista Grotte Contact:

Website: www.kristas.biz

Stuart Pankin

Favorite Quote:

"I put my talents into my work, and my genius into my life."
Oscar Wilde

Stuart Pankin

Profile

Stuart Pankin is a five time nominated, *CableAce Award* winner for HBO's national and international award winning series "Not Necessarily The News." He received his Master's Degree in Theatre from Columbia University, and went on to perform with the New York Shakespeare Festival, The Brooklyn Academy of Music Repertory Company, The American Place Theatre, The Repertory Company of Lincoln Center, and The Folger Shakespeare Theatre, with "The Winter's Tale," "The Inspector General," "Bartholomew Fair," and "The Three Sisters" among his favorites. He created the roles of Reuben and Queen Victoria in the New York premiere of Andrew Lloyd Weber's "Joseph and the Amazing Technicolor Dreamcoat."

Mr. Pankin starred in over thirty-five Off Broadway, summer, and regional theatre productions ("Lend Me A Tenor," "Tartuffe," "Joe Egg," "Sly Fox," "Chapter Two," "Carnival," "Born Yesterday," "Talley's Folly," "Wait Until Dark," etc.), and more recently in "Strike Up The Band" and "1776" for Reprise!" "LA," and "Happy Days: The Musical for Gary Marshall."

In films, he has starred in "Honey We Shrunk Ourselves" (the first live action made-for-video feature), "The Hollywood Knights," "Mannequin On The Move," "The Dirt Bike Kid," "Second Sight," "Encounter in The Third Dimension," (an IMAX 3-D movie, as the live Professor, and voice of the adorable animated robot), as well as a number of MOW's ("Babylon 5," "Down, Out and Dangerous," "Like Father Like Santa," etc.). Stuart has been featured in "Fatal Attraction," "Arachnophobia," "Life Stinks," "Congo," "An Eye For An Eye," "Irreconcilable Differences," "Squanto: A Warrior's Tale," (directed by Academy Award winner Xavier Kohler), and "Striptease."

Mr. Pankin was a series regular on nine prime time television productions and pilots. His over fifty guest starring television appearances include "Ally McBeal," "Walker, Texas Ranger," "Veronica's Closet," "Sisters," "Action," "Mad About You," "Family Ties;" multiple appearances on "Hooperman," "Dharma and Greg," "Night Court," "It's Gary Shandling's Show," "Matt Houston," "Barney Miller," and "Mike Hammer;" recurring roles on "Falcon Crest," "Zenon Girl of the 20th Century" and "Zenon, the Zequel," "Trapper John M.D.," "For Your Love," and "Knot's Landing. In addition he has performed many cartoon voices (including the title characters in "Uncle Gus," and "Super Dog and Mr. Monkey;" "Animaniacs," "Batman" and "Batman Beyond," "Superman," and "Aladdin"). Stuart was the voice of Earl Sinclair, the blustery father, on the award winning show Dinosaurs. He also sang and composed two songs for the Disney Album "DINOSAURS: THE BIG SONGS," and performed Earl on the "Dinosaurs: Classic Tales" tape release.

He starred in, co-wrote, and co-executive produced the Stuart Pankin Cinemax Comedy Experiment ("HUMP!"), the musical comedy version of Richard III), in which he played five roles, and sang his own original music. Stuart is blessed with Joy and Andy.

Stuart Pankin Contact:

Abrams Artists Agency
9200 Sunset Blvd., 11th Floor
Los Angeles, CA 90069
Phone: 310-859-0625

Anthony Turk

Favorite Quote:

"Every success in my life has come from taking advantage of the opportunities that people have given me rather than taking advantage of the people who have given me the opportunities."

Anthony Turk

Profile

Anthony Turk's film credits include "YMI," "The Marriage Undone," the cable film "Cyberdorm" and "2 Degrees," now available on video. Perhaps most recognized for his commercial campaign work, he has been seen in TV ads for "Mop-n-Glo," "Kelloggs," "Hardees," "Jack In The Box," "PNC Financial," "Volvo" and "M&M's" among others.

A veteran of over 35 stage plays, Turk, a Minnesota native received critical praise in San Diego for a performance of "Norman, Is That You?" and again in Los Angeles for a production of "Beautiful Thing."

Turk sits on the Board of Directors of Public Interest Productions, a non-profit organization producing PSA's for television and he is in the process of acquiring an entertainment public relations firm. Anthony Turk lives in both Los Angeles and Palm Springs, California.

Anthony Turk

Resume

SAG

FILM

THE MARRIAGE UNDONE	Starring	Bokken Films	Dir: Sarah N. Bruce **
YMI	Starring	Temple IV Films	Dir: Marek Probosz
2 DEGREES	Supporting	Bandwagon Films	Dir: Anthony Spires
TOWN & COUNTRY	Supporting	New Line/Avery Pix	Dir: Peter Chelsom
DODGE ALLEY	Starring	Dodge Alley Productions	Dir: Duncan McLeod
CRAZY WORLD	Starring	Crazy World Productions	Dir: Michael Franzini
CYBERDORM	Supporting	The Movie Secter	Dir: David Secter
RENDEZ-VOUS	Supporting	Hardkore Pictures	Dir: Matt Grone
ROUTE 260	Supporting	Freeway Films	Dir: David Smythe
LENNON IS DEAD	Starring	San Diego Productions	Dir: Craig Stokle

TELEVISION

MARTIAL LAW	Co-Star	CBS/Carlton Cuse Prod.	Dir: Stanley Tong
KEENEN IVORY WAYANS	Co-Star	Disney/Buena Vista	Dir: John Landis
CORPSE HAD A FAMILIAR FACE	Co-Star	CBS/Lakeside Productions	Dir: Joyce Chopra
HALF LIFE	Co-Star	PBS/Film in the Cities	Dir: Various

VOICE-OVER

"Murder at Woodside Village"	Announcer/Bad Leroy	Museum of Radio and Television

COMMERCIALS

Conflicts available upon request.

THEATRE

BEAUTIFUL THING	Lead	St. Genesius Theatre, W. Hollywood
SHATTERDAY	One Man Show	Gardner Stages, L.A.
ROSENBAUM'S LEMMA	Lead	Mythos Gallery, L.A.
THERE IS NO HAPPY MEDIUM	Supporting	Limelight Theatre, L.A.
"NORMAN, IS THAT YOU?"	Lead	On Stage, San Diego
THE LADY FROM DUBUQUE	Supporting	Grove Playhouse, San Diego
MARVIN'S ROOM	Supporting	Hahn Cosmo, San Diego

314

JOSEPH & THE AMAZING TECH.	Supporting	ACT, San Diego
10 LITTLE INDIANS	Supporting	TLG Theatre, Mpls.
AUDITION	Supporting	TLG Theatre, Mpls.
SINBAD THE SAILOR	Lead	E. Bushe Theatre, St. Paul
12 DAYS OF CHRISTMAS	Lead	Jacob's Well Theatre, St. Paul
ON GOLDEN POND	Supporting	Lakeshore Players, St. Paul
SOUND OF MUSIC	Supporting	Lakeshore Players, St. Paul
OLIVER	Supporting	Jacob's Well Theatre, St. Paul

DRAMATIC TRAINING

Alan Feinstein	Bitter Truth	Los Angeles
Lawrence Folgo	Gardner Stages	Los Angeles
Paul Tuerpe	The Complex	Los Angeles
Monologue Workshop	Actor's Lab	Los Angeles
Actor's Alliance of San Diego	Member 1992-94	San Diego
Restoration Period Method	University of Minnesota	Minneapolis
Cold Reading	Guthrie Theatre	Minneapolis
Colleen Kelly	Chimera Theatre	St. Paul

Official Selection of the 2002 Los Angeles International Short Film Festival, 2003 Dallas Video Festival, 2003 Pacific Palisades Film Festival

Anthony Turk Contact:

Axiom Management
10701 Wilshire Blvd., Suite 1202
Los Angeles, CA 90024
Phone: 310-446-4498

Richard Azurdia

Favorite Quote:

"I would rather die standing than to live on my knees."
Emiliano Zapata

Richard Azurdia

Profile

Richard Azurdia is a Los Angeles born actor who has been described as an eccentrically charismatic character actor. His passion for acting came at an early age when he first saw the film "Westside Story," which coincidentally was the first play he ever did. His inherent ability to portray a wide range of characters has led to his involvement in over 30 theatre productions, including East L.A. Classic Theatre's "Cyrano de Bergerac" (directed by Tony Plana), Collage Dance Theatre's award winning "After Eden," Grupo de Teatro Sinergia's "Frida Kahlo" and "In The Name of God," a national tour of "How To Love A Black Man," "Yerma," "Short Eyes" and "Don Juan." His film and television credits include lead, supporting, guest star and co-star roles in "Killers II," "Demon's Kiss," the cult hit "Space Banda," "Hunting of Man" (directed by Joe Menendez), "The Disappeared," "Hoodrats," "Surviving Paradise," "Stereotypes," PBS's "On Common Ground," PBS's "English for All" in a recurring role and FOX's "America's Most Wanted." Other work includes voice-over and commercials.

He has organized and promoted events such as the Screen Actors Guild's "Big Screen, Small Screen: Latinos Are Watching, Are You Reaching Them?" symposium (as the SAG Latino/Hispanic Sub-committee assistant chair), the 1st Annual Latino USC Film Festival and the CINE SIN FIN: East Los Angeles Chicano/a Film Festival. He is the founder of LovingStar Casting and has found talent for countless independent films including "Forgotten Voices," "Angelo," "Pan Dulce Y Chocolate," the award winning films "No Turning Back" and "Espiritu."

Aside from all this, he works along with his mother in the family business: Azurdia's Legal Services. In this business they handle all legal matters including performing civil matrimonies. He is a Justice of the Peace and at his young age he has married over 500 couples. Everyone he has married has contributed so much to his character studies.

He is a proud member of the Screen Actors Guild (SAG), Actor's Equity Association (AEA), American Film Institute (AFI), Premiere Weekend Club and Nosotros.

Richard Azurdia

Resume

SAG/AFTRA/AEA

FILM

HARD-BITTEN	Lead	Dir.: Marc-Andre Samson
THE DISAPPEARED	Lead	Bonar-Arguello Films/Jefferson Bonar
SPACE BANDA (*2002 San Diego Latino Film Fest.*)	Lead	Estrada Bros./Kieron Estrada
MUSTANG	Lead	Dinero Films/Andres Nieves
YESTERDAY, TODAY, & TOMORROW	Co-Lead	Starving Artists Pictures/Paul Stamat
KILLERS 2	Supporting	The Asylum/David M. Latt
HUNTING OF MAN	Supporting	Narrow Bridge Films/Joe Menendez
DEMON'S KISS	Supporting	Sterling Ent./Brad Sykes
STEREOTYPES	Supporting	Stereotypes Prods./Michael Regalbuto
THE VAMPS	Supporting	Leo Films/Steve Lustgarten
NOW EAT	Supporting	Wonderland Ent./Kerry Williams
CASTRO'S DAY IN L.A. (*2000 ch. Islands Film Fest.*)	Supporting	Curious Joel Prods./Joel Sadilek
SURVIVING PARADISE (*1999 Cairo Intl. Film Fest.*)	Supporting	New Light/Kamshad Kooshan
THE LIBERATION OF FILIBERTO GARCIA	Supporting	Estrada Bros./John Estrada
BLASPHEMY THE MOVIE	Supporting	Mendoza Ent./John Mendoza

TELEVISION

ALMA	Series Regular	Telemundo Pilot/Jojo Henrickson
GENERAL HOSPITAL	Guest Star	ABC
ON COMMON GROUND	Guest Star	PBS/Quinton Peeples
PLACAS (*2 episodes*)	Guest Star	Telemundo/Joe Menendez
ENGLISH FOR ALL	Recurring	PBS/Roberto Donati
AMERICA'S MOST WANTED	Co-Star	FOX/STF
GREAT IMPOSTERS	Co-Star	Discovery/Jay Miracle
SUENOS VERITE	Co-Star	KJLA/Jr. Ocampo
JOBCENTRO.COM	Co-Host	Pilot/Benjamin Torres
DOS MAS DOS	Series Regular	Pilot/Prietos Prods.

COMMERCIAL & VOICE-OVER-List available upon request.

THEATRE (Over 30 productions)

SATISFACTION GUARANTEED	Veterano/Akbar	Century City Playhouse/John Walter
MUCH ADO ABOUT NOTHING	Verges	East L.A. Classic Theatre/Tony Plana
IN THE NAME OF GOD	Felipe (*Lead*)	Frida Kahlo Theatre/Ruben Amavizca

AFTER EDEN (*4 Lester Horton Awards, 2002*)	Xavier	Collage Dance Theatre/Heidi Duckler
FRIDA KAHLO	Diego (*Lead*)	Grupo de Teatro Sinergia
CYRANO DE BERGERAC	Light Fingers Luis	East L.A. Classic Theatre
MACBATO	Miko	Frida Kahlo Theatre
HOW TO LOVE A BLACK WOMAN	Austin	Stella Adler Theatre
THREE QUEENS	Randy/Coco (*Lead*)	Frida Kahlo Theatre
CASTRO & THE PITCHER	Pepe (*Lead*)	Bitter Truth Playhouse
HOW TO LOVE A BLACK MAN	Luis	LATC/W. Las Vegas Theatre, NV
YERMA	Juan (*Lead*)	Divarious Theatre Co.
SHORT EYES	Juan (*Lead*)	Divarious Theatre Co.
STATE OF SIEGE	Diego (*Lead*)	Westside Artists Ensemble
WESTSIDE STORY	Chino	Flying Sparrow Theatre Co.

IMPROV/SKETCH COMEDY

FUNERAL PARLOR	Marcus/Ensemble	Actors Anonymous, Novel Café
THE LINE THAT'S PICKED UP 1000 BABES	Charlie/Ensemble	Actors Anonymous, The Un-urban
LITTLE SISSY MAN & HIS AMAZING WONDER WOMAN	Voice of Director	Luna Park

TRAINING

Acting: Dr. William Zucchero, John Sparrow

Movement (Commedia dell'arte, Pantomime): Perviz Shetty

Voice, speech, body training: Kathleen Dunn

Scene study, make-up for stage: Terrin Adair-Lynch

Classical (Greek, Shakespeare, Farce, Brecht, Absurd): Dr. Adrianne Harrop

Directing for stage, Musical theatre: Dr. Janie Jones

SPECIAL SKILLS

Fully bilingual: Spanish/English. Accents: All Latin (Cuban, Mexican, etc.) Voice-Over (Character/Cartoon), ADR. Read teleprompter. Improv, Physical comedy, Tongue tricks. Harmonica, Bongos. Dancing (Disco, Hip-Hop). Baseball, Bicycling, Billiards, Tennis.

Richard Azurdia Contact:

Website: www.geocities.com/rrazurdia

Amy Brassette

Amy Brassette

Profile

There is no easy way to sum up Amy Brassette, one of the stars of FOX's Peoples Choice Awards nominated half-hour, fast-paced, laugh-out-loud comedy, "Cedric the Entertainer Presents." Amy is <u>much</u> more than just a beautiful 22-year-old comedic actress. Her vast array of crazy characters flows seamlessly in a totally relaxed stream of comedy thanks to her lithe body, incredible facial expressions, vivid imagination, and versatile voice. She spoofs everything from nasty old truck drivers to the ghetto fabulous Tanisha, the girl from "around the way" who is set on injecting drama into Cedric's life. This multitalented actress has stunned audiences as she portrays a variety of multi-ethnic characters, each one more memorable than the last.

Originally from Lake Charles, Louisiana, a town of 80,000 people, Amy Brassette is the middle of three daughters born to Duane and Angie Brassette. Amy credits her parents for her creative flair and vivid imagination…traits that she saw in them while growing up. "I love my parents so much, they're both so talented. My dad can build anything, fix anything, and do anything. The sky is the limit. He's unbelievably creative. My mom has always been my heart and soul. She's amazing! My parents' maxim has always been, 'Trust your instincts and follow your passion.' I've always tried to do just that." Her parents own several small businesses, with her mother running the office.

"A lot of the inspiration for what I do stems from the assortment of interesting personalities I observed while growing up in Louisiana. I could talk for hours about the characters right in our neighborhood. It's easy to develop a love for creating characters when you are practically swimming in material everyday."

Around the age of 8, Amy started collecting wigs, eyeglasses, costumes and props to aid in the development of her growing cache of impersonations. "I have created characters for as long as I can remember and have always been fascinated by transformation." When she was ten she got hold of the family video camera and never let go. "It was my favorite toy," she explains. To her family, it did not seem unusual for this precocious child to write and direct her own homemade plays, music videos, skits and commercials. "I would draw my cast from the available talent pool which included everyone from the family cat (in full costume), to my little sister, the neighborhood kids, and my Barbie® dolls." Even the family parakeet did not escape Amy, always on the lookout for the newest star to perform in her early documentaries.

At the age of 14 Amy developed, her character, *Francis*, who lives in a trailer park with her doormat of a husband Harold. *Francis* is a proud chain-smoker who appreciates the refined tastes of Virginia Slims and 'TV Dinners.' She is very opinionated and can't understand why she always accidentally burns her carpet and everything around her. She also breaks up cigarettes to make potpourri to freshen the air inside her home. "Francis lives in my sub-conscious as do all my characters," she explains, making it all sound so easy.

When Amy was a sophomore in high school, she took her characters and creativity and traded in her well-worn video camera for the stage by joining her high school speech team. Her first performance was "Serious Biziness," by David Babcock, a play where Amy performed thirteen characters. She won first place, so for the next few years she toured the state and the country performing in Humorous Interpretation and Duet Acting, winning over two dozen awards. "I preferred pieces that allowed me to do as many characters as possible. When I performed 'America Hurrah' I played 24 characters in 10 minutes."

By the time she was a freshman on a theatre scholarship at Northwestern State University in Natchitoches, Louisiana, Amy was performing in school productions and in a locally owned improv comedy troupe. After one year she transferred to McNeese State University back in her hometown and performed weekly at a local bistro as a member of a new comedy troupe, *Dysfunction Junction*. Amy and the rest of the cast wrote a new show every week. "Lake Charles had never had a comedy troupe. They loved it. We poked fun at local absurdities and celebrities as well as national ones. We packed the house with a few hundred every Wednesday. Sometimes there wasn't even enough room if you didn't get there early." The following year she performed with *Fun Dip*, a troupe with a few of the same members and characters as *Dysfunction Junction*. "We had a great fan base. We had quite a local following and everyone had a blast!"

Drawing from her experience on stage, Amy knew she had to move to Los Angeles to take her career to the next level. At the age of 19, after four semesters in college, she entered the lion's den of Hollywood armed with 40 copies of her self-produced VHS entitled "One Face, Many People," which showcased her talent.

Upon arriving in Los Angeles, Amy signed almost immediately with a modeling agency and started booking print work, music videos and commercials. One thing led to another and while starring in an independent film, Amy's performance caught the eye of Marv Dauer, who became her manager.

She began landing roles as the principle in several national and European commercials. Some of her commercials include Apple iBook, Apple iPhoto, McVities Cookies, and SBC.

Within a few months Amy was cast as a regular on a FOX pilot "Reno 911," working with Beth McCarthy-Miller, director of "Saturday Night Live." FOX offered Amy a two-year holding deal and she was under contract with FOX Television until June 30, 2003. During this time, she was a series regular on "Cedric the Entertainer Presents" and it began airing in the fall of 2002. After 22 episodes, FOX stopped production of the series but six new episodes aired in the Fall of 2003.

When Amy isn't working directly in her field, this dynamic young actress spends her time writing, singing, and playing the guitar. She also makes the best gumbo west of the Mississippi.

Amy Brassette

Resume

TELEVISION

Cedric the Entertainer Presents	Series Regular	FOX Television Dir.: Stan Lathan
Reno 911	Series Regular	FOX Television/Jersey Films Dir.: Beth McCarthy-Miller
Reno 911	Guest Star	Comedy Central/Jersey Films Dir.: Ben Garrant

FILM

Pretty Cool	Lead	Hope Street Entertainment Dir.: Rolfe Kanefsky

COMEDY COMPANIES

Roustabouts	Improv	Natchitoches, LA
Dysfunction Junction	Improv and Sketch	Lake Charles, LA
Fun Dip	Improv and Sketch	Lake Charles, LA

THEATRE AND AWARDS

Dark of the Moon	Mrs. Jenkins	Northwestern State University
Evening w/John Barrymore	Joan	McNeese State University
America Hurrah	24 characters	CFL Tourn. Topeka, KS-National Finalist
Serious Bizness	13 characters	New Orleans Classic Champion
The Kathy and Mo Show	6 characters	Regional Champion
The Magenta Shift	2 characters	LA State Dramatics Champion

COMMERCIALS: List available upon request

TRAINING

Acting	Steven Anderson	Actorswork
Acting	John Homa	Private coaching
Improv	Christen Nelson	The Groundlings
Scene Study	Christina Hart	Hollywood Court Theatre and private coaching
Acting technique	James Stacy	Northwestern State University
Script Analysis	Charles McNeely	McNeese State University
Improv Training	Robin Armstrong	Natchitoches Fine Arts Center
Commercial VO	Cynthia Songe	Blupka Productions
Animation	Cynthia Songe	Blupka Productions

DIALECTS: Texan, Cajun, Old Southern, Swedish, Midwestern, French, New York, Chicago, Hispanic and more…

SPECIAL SKILLS: singer, songwriter, guitar player, improv skills, various impressions and original characters, certified lifeguard, fluent in signed language, dancing, swimming, golf, ice skating, snow skiing, bowling, fishing, firearms, and she makes a mean gumbo.

Amy Brassette Contact:

Marv Dauer Management
11661 San Vicente Blvd., #104
Los Angeles, CA 90049
Phone: 310-207-6884

Barbie Orr

Favorite Quote:

"If you are not living on the edge…you are taking up too much space."

Barbie Orr

Profile

Barbie is a paid regular at the L.A. Comedy Store, and has been a stand-up comedian all over the nation. Her hosting highlights include the GEAR TV magazine show, Motor Mouth, and BID.com with fellow comedian Lewis Black. Barbie was a series regular on Slick Danger, Orbital Broadcast, and VIDeITS. She has guest starred in numerous television shows, including The 70's, Café DuArt, Arrest & Trial, and Lyricist Lounge. Barbie has extensive music, video, stage, and commercial experience as well. She has acted and performed in New York, Florida and LA. Barbie and her dog Diva, are the new faces of Petco's national campaign. Diva also performs comedy on stage with Barbie.

Barbie Orr

Resume

FILM/TELEVISION

Motor Mouth (Host/Interviewer)	STARRING	Manny
Orbital Broadcast One	SERIES REGULAR	Samaniego/Sergio
Slick Danger (1/2 animated pilot)	SERIES REGULAR	AJ Wedding
VIDeITS	SERIES REGULAR	Eric Kiertaner
Femme Cop	STARRING	Avatar Ent.
BID.com with Lewis Black	CO-HOST live	William Hewitt
The Drive Network (co-host)	unscripted	Mark Lucas-Dir.
Lyricist Lounge (2 episodes)	STARRING	Bruce Martin-Dir.
Café DuArt (5 episodes)	GUEST STAR	Paul Casey-Dir.
Arrest & Trial (Linda Sobek)	GUEST STAR	Rick Locke-Dir.
The 70's Bellbottoms to…(Stand up)	GUEST STAR	Studios USA/Andrew Solt Productions
Tales of A Fly on The Wall (Darva)	CO-STAR	Brian Tochi-Dir.
MTV Awards Promo	Madonna-Stand in	MTV

THEATRE

Murdered By The Mob	Benson-Killer	MMI Productions
Skullduggery Pirate Adventure	Anita Mann	Wizard Works

Many more credits…

STAND UP COMEDY

The Comedy Store CA (Paid Regular), Toyota Comedy Festival NY, Fun Kruz FL, Sidesplitters FL, Improv CA, Ice House CA, HaHa Café CA, Coconut's FL, Dangerfield's NY, Stand Up NY, New York Comedy Club NY, TV Appearances, Comic Strip NY, Comedyworks FL, Gator Nationals FL and LOTS more!

TRAINING

University Stony Brook, Liberal Arts, Voice, Tom Butler
Cold Reading, Mel Johnson, Voice-Over, Marla Kirban, etc.

SPECIAL SKILLS

Teleprompter, Earpiece, Drummer, Precision Driver, Tennis, Yoga, Racquetball, Basketball, Soccer, Volleyball, Sing, Belly Dance, Drums, Dance, Swimming, Horseback Riding, Viola, Hula Hoop, Bowling, Discus, Improv, Running, Stand Up Comedy, Puppeteer, Darts, Hurdles, and more…

RADIO, INDUSTRIALS, INFOMERCIALS AND COMMERCIALS

List available upon request.

Barbie Orr Contact:

Website: barbieorr.com

Keith Szarabajka

Keith Szarabajka

Profile

Keith Szarabajka (sarah-bike-ah) spent most of the WB's "Angel" 2001-2002 season playing the 18th Century English vampire hunter, Capt. Daniel Holtz, who comes to the 21st century to seek justice (or is it revenge?) from Angel. Prior to that, he played Mickey Kostmayer on CBS' "The Equalizer," starring Edward Woodward, from 1985 to 1989. Keith endured six hours of make-up each day in order to become seventy-year old janitor Harlan Williams, who grew younger in Stephen King's "The Golden Years" on CBS (1991), his Chaz Gracen mentored Adrian Pasdar's Jim Profit in the short-lived, highly praised "Profit" on FOX (1996). Other TV work includes "ER," "Crossing Jordan," "Star Trek Voyager," "Enterprise," "Roswell," "X-Files" and "Law and Order."

Film work includes: Randall Wallace's "We Were Soldiers" (2002), Tim McCanlies' "Dancer, Texas, Pop. 81" (1998), George M. Miller's "Andre" (1994), Clint Eastwood's "A Perfect World" (1993), Costa-Gavras' "Missing" (1982), Alex Cox's "Walker" (1987), Roger Donaldson's "Marie: A True Story" (1986), Herbert Ross' "Protocol" (1984), John Gray's "Billy Galvin" (1985), Lee Grant's "Staying Together" (1987) and Marshall Brickman's "Simon" (1979). Keith appeared on Broadway as Kim Feston in Howard Korder's "Search and Destroy" (1992). Keith also worked on Broadway as B.D. in Garry Trudeau's "Doonesbury" (1983) and made his Broadway debut in Stuart Gordon and Bury St. Edmund's sci-fi epic adventure play "Warp!" (1973).

Off-Broadway work includes Hollywood Confidential in Peter Parnell's "Hyde and Hollywood" (1989), Joseph Dougherty's "Digby" (1985) and John Patrick Shanley's "Women of Manhattan" (1986) at Manhattan Theatre Club, Nigel Williams' "Class Enemy" (1980) at The Players' Theatre, Stephen Willem's "A Perfect Act of Contrition" (1987) at Manhattan Class Company and "Bleacher Bums" (1978) (which he also co-wrote) with The Organic Theatre Company of Chicago.

Keith was a member of The Organic Theatre of Chicago for six years (1972-1978), whose members included Joe Mantegna, Meshach Taylor, John Heard, Andre De Shields and Dennis Franz under the artistic direction of Stuart Gordon. He also worked at The Eugene O'Neill Theatre Center, Yale Repertory Theatre, The Goodman Theatre, Williamstown Theatre Festival, and The Mickery in Amsterdam, New York's Second Stage, Cucaracha Theatre of New York's "Underground Soap" and New York Stage and Film at The Powerhouse Theatre/Vassar. He greatly enjoys reading short stories for National Public Radio's "Selected Shorts" program, taped before live audiences at New York's Symphony Space and at the Getty in LA.

Books read on tape include: Tom Robbins' *Fierce Invalids Home From Hot Climates* (Audie award for Best Unabridged Fiction—2001), William Least Heat-Moon's *Blue Highways*, Michael Crichton's *Rising Sun*, Lawrence Sanders' *The Sixth Deadly Sin*, Bruce J. Fierstein's *Real Men Don't Bond*, and Harry Stein's *Magic Bullet*.

Keith attended the University of Chicago in Chicago, Illinois (his hometown) and Trinity University in San Antonio, Texas. Keith currently resides with his eight year old son, Jack, and four year old son, Caleb, in Los Angeles. Other interests besides show business include scuba diving (advanced open water certified), softball, hiking, mountain biking, cooking, kickboxing and writing.

Keith Szarabajka

Resume

AEA/SAG/AFTRA/DRAMATISTS' GUILD

FILM

MISSING	David Holloway	Costa-Gavras, dir.
ANDRE	Billy Baker	George M. Miller, dir.
A PERFECT WORLD	Terry Pugh	Clint Eastwood, dir.
STAYING TOGETHER	Kevin Burley	Lee Grant, dir.
WALKER	Timothy Crocker	Alex Cox, dir.
BILLY GALVIN	Donny Burke	John Gray, dir.
MARIE: A TRUE STORY	Kevin McCormack	Roger Donaldson, dir.
PROTOCOL	Earl Crowe	Herbert Ross, dir.
SIMON	Josh	Marshall Brickman, dir.
DANCER TEXAS, POP. 81	Squirrel's Dad	Tim McCanlies, dir.
A MOTHER'S TESTIMONY	Warren Stubbs	Julian Chojnacki, dir.
WE WERE SOLDIERS	Diplomatic Spook	Randall Wallace, dir.

TELEVISION SERIES (Regular or Recurring)

24	Four Episodes, Robert Morrison	FOX
ANGEL	3rd Season, Daniel Holtz	WB-David Greenwalt/Josh Whedon, e.p.
PROFIT	Regular, Chaz Gracen	FOX-John MacNamara/David Greenwalt, e.p.
STEPHEN KING'S THE GOLDEN YEARS	Lead, Harlan Williams	CBS-Richard Rubinstein/Stephen King, e.p.
THE EQUALIZER	Co-star, Mickey Kostmayer	CBS-Jim McAdams, e.p.
THANKS	Recurring, Rev. Goodacre	CBS-Phoef Sutton/Mark Legan, e.p.
LAW AND ORDER	Three episodes, Neal Gorton	NBC-Ed Sherin, e.p./dir.
SPY GAME	Recurring character, Shank	ABC-John MacNamara/Sam Raimi, e.p.
BLEACHER BUMS	Co-author, The Cheerleader	PBS-Stuart Gordon, dir.

BROADWAY

SEARCH AND DESTROY	Kim Feston	David Chambers, dir.
DOONESBURY	B.D.	Jacques Levy, dir.
WARP!	David Carson	

OFF-BROADWAY

HYDE IN HOLLYWOOD	Hollywood Confidential	Gerald Gutierrez, Dir.
A PERFECT ACT OF CONTRITION	Thomas	Brian Mertes, Dir.
DIGBY	Harry	Ron Lago Marsino, Dir.
CLASS ENEMY	Iron	Tony Tanner, Dir.
BLEACHER BUMS	Cheerleader	Stuart Gordon, Dir.

Keith Szarabajka Contact:

Website: www.darktale.tv

Alanna Ubach

Alanna Ubach

Profile

Alanna Ubach has amassed a wealth of experience in the areas of film, television and theatre. She has worked with well-known directors such as Penny Marshall and Betty Thomas, and acted alongside film veterans such as Danny Devito, Whoopi Goldberg, Rita Moreno, and Ben Gazarra. Ubach, who is Latina, and from Downey, California, was described as "an actress to keep your eye on" by the *NY Times* and "one to watch," by *USA Today*. Alanna recently played the role of Isabel in the hit movie "Meet The Fockers" with Robert De Niro and Ben Stiller. "Legally Blonde II," in which she reprises her role as Serena, best friend and sorority sister to Reese Witherspoon premiered in July 2003. She also stars in the film "Wasabi Tuna," with Tim Meadows and Barney Cheng. "A Mi Amor Mi Dulce," a short film in which she stars with Guillermo Diaz and Devon Odessa, which she also wrote and directed, premiered at LA's Outfest in July 2003. She also appears in two independent films, "Hard Scrambled" (with Kurtwood Smith), and "Philadelphia Freedom" (with Molly Shannon and George Wendt).

Ubach re-teamed with "Freeway" co-star Reese Witherspoon in "Legally Blonde." She also teamed with Chris Eigeman and Jenny McCarthy in Matt Miller's independent comedy "The Perfect You." On the small screen, Ubach can be heard in the Disney and ABC animated series, "Teamo Supremo," voicing two of the three title superheroes, the new WB animated series "Ozzie and Drix," and Disney's "Brandy and Mr. Whiskers."

Ubach was also seen on the big screen in "Blue Moon." Ubach portrayed Peggy, one half of a troubled couple who learn to sort out their differences after spending one long night with an older couple played by Rita Moreno and Ben Gazarra. She also did a turn as an intern accusing Rob Lowe of sexual harassment in "West Wing." Other completed projects include a starring role in Tanya Fenmore's debut film "Graduation Day" starring with Sean Patrick Thomas and Nicholle Tom, and "Nobody Knows Anything" with cameos by Mike Meyers, Ben Stiller and Janeane Garofalo.

Past film credits include the title role in "Denise Calls Up," (a sequel is in pre-production) which won a special mention at the 1995 Cannes Film Festival. She played the ringleader in a women's juvenile prison alongside Reese Witherspoon in Matthew Bright's darkly comic debut film "Freeway," a temp looking for something better in "Clockwatchers" alongside Lisa Kudrow and Parker Posey, and the only female lead alongside David Arquette and Lukas Haas in Scott Silver's "Johns," all of which played at Sundance. She also co-starred with Vince Vaughn in "Just Your Luck" and opposite Jeremy Piven and Edie Falco in "Layin' Low." In "Pink as the Day She Was Born," Ubach starred as a young rock and roll singer who works in a domination parlor to support herself. One of the producers of the film was *Four Non Blondes* lead singer Linda Perry, who wrote several songs for Ubach to sing in the film. Other projects include "Sister Act 2," "Airborne," and playing Danny DeVito's daughter in Penny Marshall's "Renaissance Man."

Ubach has also done extensive television and theatre work. On television she created the role of "Josie" on the Cable Ace Award winning educational children's science series "Beakman's World." Some of her guest-starring roles include Dominic Purcell's Mensa buddy on FOX's "John Doe," Will's (Scott Grimes) gregarious girlfriend Gina on "Party of Five," a homeless teen on "ER," a crack addict who is born again on "Touched By An Angel," and a hand transplant recipient on "Chicago Hope" as well as an ambitious publicist on the critically acclaimed ABC series, "Sports Night." She has also starred in several television movies including "All of It" in which she and Leslie Ann Warren played a warring mother and daughter. On the New York stage, Ubach, who is described by *Village Voice* as "a marvelously affecting and unaffected young actress," received critical acclaim for her performance in "Kindertransport" at the Manhattan Theatre Club and "Club Soda" at the WPA Theatre. She has starred in the Chicago production of Eve Ensler's "The Vagina Monologues." Last summer at Stages Theatre and the Hudson Theatre, she did her critically acclaimed one-woman show, "Patriotic Bitch," which will have its New York debut in the summer of 2005.

Alanna Ubach

Resume

FILM

MEET THE FOCKERS	Universal	Dir. Jay Roach
A MI AMOR MI DULCE (Short)	Independent	Dir. Alanna Ubach
RED, WHITE AND BLONDE	MGM	Dir. Charles
(LEGALLY BLONDE 2)		Herman-Wurmfeld
LEGALLY BLONDE	MGM	Dir. Robert Luketic
THE PERFECT YOU	Independent	Dir. Mathew Miller
BLUE MOON	Paradise Pictures	Dir. John Gallagher
GRADUATION WEEK	Redwood	Dir. Tanya Fenmore
ALL OF IT	Lifetime	Dir. Jody Podolsky
CLOCKWATCHERS (SUNDANCE 1997) BMG		Dir. Jill Sprecher
THE BIG DAY	Independent	Dir. Ian McCrudden
DO ME A FAVOR	Independent	Dir. Sondra Locke
ENOUGH ALREADY	Independent	Dir. Tom Keenan
PINK AS THE DAY SHE WAS BORN	Global Ent.	Dir. Steve Hall
FREEWAY (SUNDANCE 1996)	Kushner/Locke	Dir. Matthew Bright
JOHNS (SUNDANCE 1996)	First Look	Dir. Scott Silver
JUST YOUR LUCK	Polygram	Dir. Gary Auerbach
LAYIN' LOW (BERLIN FILM FEST, 1997)	Shooting Gallery	
		Dir. Danny Leiner
DENISE CALLS UP (CANNES 1995)	Sony Classics	Dir. Hal Selwen
VIRTUOSITY	Paramount	Dir. Brett Leonard
THE BRADY BUNCH	Paramount	Dir. Betty Thomas
HITS	Symphony Pic.	Dir. William Greenblatt
SISTER ACT II	Touchstone	Dir. Bill Duke
RENAISSANCE MAN	Touchstone	Dir. Penny Marshall
AIRBORNE	Warner Bros.	Dir. Rob Bowman

TELEVISION

JOHN DOE	TOUCHED BY AN ANGEL
THE WEST WING	PARTY OF FIVE (Recurring)
TWO GUYS AND A GIRL	TRACY TAKES ON
OZZIE AND DRIX (Voice-Over)	ER
TEAMO SUPREMO (Voice-Over)	MURDEROUS PASSION (NBC/MOW)
GARY & MIKE (Voice-Over)	WHY MY DAUGHTER (ABC/MOW)
SPORTS NIGHT	APT. 2F (Recurring)
THE HUNTRESS (Recurring)	ROCK THE VOTE (MTV)
CHICAGO HOPE	BEAKMAN'S WORLD (series regular)
PROVIDENCE	

THEATRE

PATRIOTIC BITCH	Stages Theatre, LA
VAGINA MONOLOGUES	Apollo Theatre, Chicago
KINDERTRANSPORT	Manhattan Theatre Club, NY
CLUB SODA	WPA Theatre, NY

Alanna Ubach Contact:

Margrit Polak Management, Inc.
1411 Carroll Ave.
Los Angeles, CA 90026
Phone: 213-482-0777

John Mahoney

John Mahoney

Profile

Mr. Mahoney's recent theatre credits include a production of "The Drawer Boy" at Steppenwolf, Dublin, and Galway, Ireland as well as the Geffen Theatre's production of "The Weir," in Los Angeles. Prior to that he appeared in "Long Days Journey Into Night" at the Irish Repertory Company in Chicago and Galway. Other Steppenwolf credits include "The Man Who Came To Dinner," (also in London), "No Man's Land," Wrong Turn At Lungfish, "Orphans" (also New York – Theatre World Award), "The Collection," "Supple In Combat," "Arms and the Man," and "Death and the Maiden." For Steppenwolf he directed "Talking Heads." Other Chicago productions include "Uncle Vanya" (Goodman Theatre), "After the Fall" (National Jewish Theatre) and "The Price" (Northlight Theatre). John made his Broadway debut in "The House of Blue Leaves" (Tony Award, Clarence Derwent Award).

On screen John has appeared in many films including "Say Anything," "Moonstruck," "Tin Men," "Betrayed," "In the Line of Fire," "The American President," "Primal Fear," "Reality Bites," "She's the One" and "Broken Hearts Club." He voiced major roles in the animated films "Antz," "The Iron Giant," and "Atlantis." John played the role of Martin Crane for eleven years on NBC's "Frasier" and has twice been nominated for Golden Globe and Emmy Awards.

The Emmy Award-winning cast of *Frasier*

John Mahoney

Resume

FILM

FATHERS AND SONS	Rodrigo Garcia, Jared Rappaport, & Rob Spera, Directors
ALMOST SALINAS	Terry Green, Dir.
ATLANTIS: THE LOST EMPIRE (Voice-Over)	Preston Whitmore, Dir.
THE BROKEN HEARTS CLUB	Greg Berlanti, Dir.
THE IRON GIANT (Voice-Over)	Brad Bird, Dir.
ANTZ (Voice-Over)	E. Darnell et al., Dirs.
SHE'S THE ONE	Ed Burns, Dir.
PRIMAL FEAR	Gregory Hoblit, Dir.
MARIETTE IN ECSTASY	John Bailey, Dir.
AMERICAN PRESIDENT	Rob Reiner, Dir.
REALITY BITES	Ben Stiller, Dir.
HUDSUCKER PROXY	Joel Coen, Dir.
IN THE LINE OF FIRE	Wolfgang Peterson, Dir.
STRIKING DISTANCE	Rowdy Herrington, Dir.
ARTICLE 99	Howard Deutsch, Dir.
BARTON FINK	Joel Coen, Dir.
THE RUSSIA HOUSE	Fred Schepisi, Dir.
THE IMAGE	HBO Film
LOVE HURTS	Bud Yorkin, Dir.
SAY ANYTHING	Cameron Crowe, Dir.
EIGHT MEN OUT	John Sayles, Dir.
SUNDOWN	Costa-Gravas, Dir.
FRANTIC	Roman Polanski, Dir.
SUSPECT	Peter Yates, Dir.
MOONSTRUCK	Norman Jewison, Dir.
TIN MEN	Barry Levinson, Dir.
STREETS OF GOLD	Joe Roth, Dir.
MANHATTAN PROJECT	Marshall Brickman, Dir.
CODE OF SILENCE	Bill Davis, Dir.

TELEVISION

FRASIER	NBC
THE HIDDEN HISTORY OF CHICAGO	A&E
NOTHING SACRED	ABC
THE MEDICINE SHOW	CPTV
BUYING A LANDSLIDE	BBC
WITH TWO LUMPS OF ICE	BBC
MARITAL PRIVILEGE	USA
THE WATER ENGINE	TNT
HUMAN FACTOR	CBS Series – Lead
TEN MILLION DOLLAR GETAWAY	USA
DINNER AT EIGHT	TNT/MOW
H.E.L.P.	ABC Series
FAVORITE SON	NBC Miniseries

PRISONER OF SILENCE	CBS
LADY BLUE	NBC
FIRST STEP	CBS
THE KILLING FLOOR	PBS
CHICAGO STORY	NBC

BROADWAY
| HOUSE OF BLUE LEAVES | Jerry Zaks, Dir. |

(Tony & Clarence Derwent Award, Drama Desk nomination)

OFF-BROADWAY
THE WEIR	Randall Arney, Dir.
THE SUBJECT WAS ROSES	Jack Hofsiss, Dir.
ORPHANS	Gary Sinise, Dir.

(Orphans was a Theatre World Award; Drama Desk nomination)

STEPPENWOLF THEATRE (CHICAGO)
THE DRAWER BOY	Anna D. Shapiro, Dir.
THE MAN WHO CAME TO DINNER	James Burrows, Dir.
SUPPLE IN COMBAT	Max Mayer, Dir.
DEATH AND THE MAIDEN	
THE SONG OF JACOB ZULU	Eric Simonson, Dir.
WRONG TURN AT LUNGFISH	Garry Marshall, Dir.
BORN YESTERDAY	
YOU CAN'T TAKE IT WITH YOU	Frank Galati, Dir.
STAGE STRUCK	Tom Irwin, Dir.
THE HOTHOUSE	Jeff Perry, Dir.
AND A NIGHTINGALE SANG	Terry Kinney, Dir.
A PRAYER FOR MY DAUGHTER	John Malcovich, Dir.
THE HOUSE	John Malcovich, Dir.
LOOSE ENDS	Austin Pendleton, Dir.
OF MICE AND MEN	Terry Kinney, Dir.
BALM IN GILEAD	John Malcovich, Dir.
NO MAN'S LAND	John Malcovich, Dir.
ARMS AND THE MAN	Sheldon Patinkin, Dir.
SAVAGES	John Malcovich, Dir.
ABSENT FRIENDS	John Malcovich, Dir.
DEATH OF A SALESMAN	Sheldon Patinkin, Dir.
TAKING STEPS	Pauline Brailsford, Dir.

John Mahoney Contact:

ICM
40 West 57th St.
New York, NY 10019
Phone: 212-556-5600

Rena Owen

Favorite Quote:

"Do what you love, and do it to the best of your ability."

Rena Owen

Profile

Rena Owen is one of New Zealand's most successful actresses, and it's most recognizable star on the international film platform following her performance as Beth Heke in "Once Were Warriors," New Zealand's most successful film to date. Her performance earned her Best Actress Awards at the Montreal, Oporto, Seattle, and San Diego Film Festivals. She received the Cannes Film Festival's Spirit Award and while in New Zealand she received the Benny Award for Excellence and Contribution to the Industry, and the Toast Master's Communicator of the Year Award.

She began her acting career in London in the mid 80s, trained at the Actors Institute, and worked in British Theatre. Credits include: "Voices from Prison" for the Royal Shakespeare Company, "Co-Existences" for the Elephant Theatre, and "Outside In," which debuted at the Edinburgh Festival and toured London. She worked for two years with a London based Theatre Company, Clean Break, who produced the first play written by Rena: "The River that Ran Away." Directed by Ann Mitchell, and starring Rena in the lead, it enjoyed a successful London tour. Playmarket later published the play.

Rena returned to NZ in 1989 and continued to work extensively in theatre and television. Her theatrical credits include Stephen Berkoff's "West" and "Kvetch" for Ocean Productions, "The Hungry City," which opened the Watershed Theatre, "Whatungarongaro" which toured NZ and played at the Adelaide Festival in Australia and "Iwitaia" and "Te Hokina," amongst others, for the Depot Theatre. "Daddy's Girl" written by, and starring Rena and Wi Kuki Kaa, enjoyed a critically acclaimed Wellington season. During this period she also directed stage plays, worked as a Dramaturgy for Playmarket, and read short stories for radio NZ. Her theatrical credits include starring in a classic NZ Play: "Haruru Mai," directed by Colin McColl for the 2000 International Festival of the Arts, and directed Toa Fraser's, "Bare" for the AATC in San Francisco 2001.

Television credits include NZ series: "Shark in the Park," "Betty's Bunch" and "Coverstory" which earned her a TVNZ Best Actress Nomination. One-hour dramas for television include: "The Call Up," "The Visitation" and, "Savage Play," a BBC/TVNZ miniseries. Rena was principal cast of an Australian Medical TV series, Medivac, for two seasons. In 2000 she guest starred in a British TV series, "Dark Knight," and in 2001, guest starred in David Kelley's TV series, "Gideon's Crossing." She also completed a lead role in the NZ Aroha Series, "Mataora." Rena has also done voice-over work, and presented documentaries for television.

Rena's first feature film was a supporting role in the Kevin Costner/Kevin Reynolds, "Rapa Nui" in 1993, followed by the lead in "Once Were Warriors," voted one of *Time Magazine*'s top 10 films in 1995. Her other NZ feature films include: "Roimata," "I'll Make You Happy," "What Becomes of the Brokenhearted" and "When Love Comes." NZ short films include: "Her Iliard," "Nine Across," and "Hinekaro." Australian feature film credits are: "Vaudeville House" and "Dance Me to My Song," which was in competition at the 1998 Cannes Film Festival and earned Rena a Best Supporting Actress Nomination at the Australian Film Awards.

The year 2002, found Rena based in Los Angeles. She was seen in Cinemas as Taun We in George Lucas's Star Wars Episode 2: "Attack of the Clones." In addition she was seen in Steven Spielberg's, "A.I.," and in an American Independent Action Feature, "Soul Assassin," shot in Holland. She was also seen on television in a supporting role in a USA Network Movie of the Week, "An All American Girl," and was seen in WB's "Angel," playing a Demi-Goddess called Dinza.

In 2003 Rena completed the following roles: a pre-colonial Warrior Woman in an Indie film shot in Fiji, "Fire in the Womb;" a Hit Woman in a Los Angeles short film, "Sidney;" a Tibetan Nun gone wrong, in a Martial Arts film for Sunset Studios USA.; a Psycho Killer in a Lions Gate feature, "Paper, Scissors, Stone," set and shot in Toronto; a supporting role as Crazy Norma in "The Water Giant," a Canadian family film; and a cameo role as Maria MacIntyre in a USA Independent feature, "Pledge of Allegiance."

Finally, during the last 7 years, Rena has extensively toured the International Film Festival circuit to promote various films, and also to serve on the Jury of the Montreal, Manila, Hawaii, Santa Barbara and the USA Film Festivals. She has also served as a consultant for the Sundance Screenwriters Lab and been on the Sundance Selection Panel. When time allows, Rena does public speaking, lectures at universities, and teaches drama.

Rena at the Third Annual Celebration of New Zealand Filmmaking

Rena Owen

Resume

FEATURE FILMS	ROLE	DIRECTOR	PRODUCTION COMPANY
STAR WARS EPISODE III	TBA	George Lucas	Jak Productions USA
THE CROW: WICKED PRAYER	Mary	Lance Mungia	Wicked Prayer Prod. USA
PLEDGE OF ALLEGIANCE	Maria MacIntyre	Lee Madsen	POA Partners USA
PAPER, SCISSORS, STONE	Emily Grey	Jessie Warne	Method Films CANADA
WATER GIANT	Crazy Norma	John Henderson	Ogopogo Prod. UK
STAR WARS EPISODE II	Taun We	George Lucas	Jak Productions USA
ARTIFICIAL INTELLIGENCE	Ticket	Steven Spielberg	Warner Brothers USA
FIRE IN THE WOMB	Maka	Vilsoni Hereniko	Te Maka/Netpac USA
SOUL ASSASSIN	Karina	Lawrence Malkin	Clock Filmworks USA
AN ALL AMERICAN GIRL	Soona	Lloyd Kramer	Grosso Jacobson Com. USA
DANCE ME TO MY SONG	Rix	Rolf de Heer	Vertigo Prod. AUS
VAUDEVILLE HOUSE	Nadine	Marianne Rischert	Rischert Prod. AUS
BROKENHEARTED	Beth Heke	Ian Mune	South Pacific Pictures NZ
WHEN LOVE COMES	Katie Keen	Garth Maxwell	MF Films NZ
I'LL MAKE YOU HAPPY	Mickie	Athina Tsoulis	Ample Films NZ
RAPA NUI	Hitirenga	Kevin Reynolds	Windmill Films USA
ONCE WERE WARRIORS	Beth Heke	Lee Tamahori	Communicado NZ

SHORT FILMS			
FAMILY TREE	Nurse/Nun	Luke Mayes	Family Tree Prods. NZ
SIDNEY	Clarissa	Malik Booth	Dakota Films USA
NINE ACROSS	Joey	Jessie Warne	Method Films NZ
HINEKARO	Hinekaro	Christine Parker	L'Arte Ltd NZ
VARIATIONS OF A THEME	Nancy	Don Selwyn	Te Manuka Film Trust NZ
ROIMATA	Girlie	Riwia Brown	Te Manuka Film Trust NZ
HER ILIARD	Lena	Jessie Warne	Method Films NZ

TELEVISION	ROLE	FORMAT	PRODUCTION COMPANY
ANGEL	Dinza	Series	Warner Brothers Television USA
LIVING FACE	Wai	Drama	Aroha Productions NZ
GIDEON'S CROSSING	Tara	Series	Touchstone Television USA
DARK KNIGHT	Rock Witch	Series	Palama Productions UK
SAVAGE PLAY	Takiora	Miniseries	Pony Productions UK
NIGHTMARE TO A DREAM	Cindy	Drama	ITV UK

MEDIVAC	Macy	Series	Liberty & Beyond AUS
COVERSTORY	Mairanga	Drama	Gibson Group NZ
CALL UP	Emily	Drama	James Wallace Ltd NZ
THE VISITATION	Cheryl	Drama	He Taonga Films NZ
BETTY'S BUNCH	Shirley	Series	South Pacific Features NZ
SHARK IN THE PARK	Ngaire	Series	Gibson Group NZ

AWARDS

Once Were Warriors	1994 Best Actress, Montreal, Seattle, San Diego, Oporto Film Festivals
	1995 Benny Award for Excellence in Film, New Zealand
	1995 Toast Masters Communicator of the Year Award, New Zealand
	1995 Best Actress Independent Spirit Awards Cannes Film Festival France
Coverstory	1997 Best Actress in a Television Drama Nomination, New Zealand
Dance Me To My Song	1998 Best Supporting Actress Nomination, Australia Film Institute Awards

STAGE	**ROLE**	**DIRECTOR**	**PRODUCTION COMPANY**
VOICES FROM PRISON	CB	Ann Mitchell	Royal Shakespeare Co. UK
CO-EXISTENCES	Susie	H Nunn	Elephant Theatre Co. UK
THE RIVER THAT RAN AWAY	Toni	Ann Mitchell	Clean Break/London Tour
OUTSIDE IN	Sandy	Hilary Beaton	Edinburgh Festival/London UK
FINE DANCING	Hina	Vilsoni Hereniko	Netpac Productions USA
HARURU MAI	Pearl	Colin McColl	NZ Int. Festival of the Arts
WEST	Sylvia	Roger Morton	Ocean Productions NZ
THE HUNGRY CITY	Riria	Michael Hurst	Watershed Theatre NZ
WHATUNGARONGARO	Ruby	J Anderson/R Potiki	Depot Theatre NZ
OUTSIDE IN	Di	Bernie Harfleet	Theatre Workshop NZ
THE FEDS	Various	Simon Marler	Bandana Theatre Co. NZ
KVETCH	Donna	Roger Morton	Ocean Productions NZ
TE HOKINA	Girlie	Apirana Taylor	Te Ohu Whakaari NZ
DADDY'S GIRL	Rose	Riwia Brown	Te Ohu Whakaari NZ
LAND OF TRASH	Rahui	Jenny Wake	Calico Touring Co. NZ
NO ORDINARY SUN	Various	Jim Moriarty	Te Rakau Hua Co. NZ

PRODUCTION

BARE		Director	AATC San Francisco USA
THE RIVER THAT RAN AWAY		Writer	Produced & Published UK

TE HARA	Director	Theatre Marae Season NZ
IN THE WILDERNESS	Director	Te Rakau Hua Co. NZ
TE WHANAU A TUANUI JONES	Director	National Tour NZ
DADDY'S GIRL	Writer	Produced & Published NZ

INTERNATIONAL

2001 Jury Santa Barbara Film Festival USA. 2000 Chairman of the Jury Manila Film Festival Philippines. 2000 Jury Montreal Film Festival Canada. 2000 Judge New Zealand Film Awards. 1999 Sundance Screenwriters Summer Lab, Consultant. Sundance Selection Panel for Native Screenplays USA. 1998 Jury USA Film Festival, Dallas Texas. 1998 Cannes Film Festival Competition, Dance Me to my Song. 1995 Jury Hawaii International Film Festival. 1993 Transatlantic Playwrights Conference Australia. 1992 South Pacific Arts Festival Writer/Actor. 1991 Playmarkets National Playwright Conference.

SPECIAL SKILLS

Singing- Mezzo Soprano, Voice-Over, Dramaturgy, Script Editor, Photographic Modeling, Horse Riding,
Most Sports, Yoga, Accents, Radio Drama, State Registered Nurse

Rena Owen Contact:

Greene & Associates
Phone: 323-960-1333

Peter Fraser Dunlop
Phone: 44-171-352-7270 (England)

KR Actors Agency
Phone: 64-9-378-9016 (New Zealand)

Eddie Sicoli

Eddie Sicoli

Profile

What really drove Eddie Sicoli to become an actor? Eddie says, "Although I always had an interest in entertaining people, what really clinched it was that my mother's friend knew the 2nd AD of "The Godfather" and in the 70's long hair was in and I had it. So my mom's friend asked me, 'would you want to be an extra in the wedding scene of the movie?' I said, "Sure, what do I have to do?" She replied, "CUT YOUR HAIR!" "I did and the rest is history. I loved being in the movie even if it was only as an extra at 16 years of age. It was a great experience."

Eddie has always been around some aspect of the entertainment business since he was young. His dad was a well-known musician and singer in the tri-state area. In addition, he was also a recording engineer at a well-known recording studio in West Orange, New Jersey. Many of his dad's friends would go on to become famous, Frankie Valli, Joe Pesci, and Frank Vincent among others. Growing up around this, Eddie's interest was music and then he discovered his passion for acting. You can see Eddie in "Back to Manhattan," "It's a Miracle" and "Cleaners of Broadway." He's also a musician, singer and songwriter.

Eddie Sicoli

Resume

SAG/AFTRA

THEATRE

In Cold Blood	William Paterson College	2nd Lead

COMMERCIALS/VOICE-OVER

Opening Theme for Steve Gordon Radio Show in Las Vegas, using voice characterizations; e.g., Cartoon character "Popeye"

TV/FILM

It's a Miracle	Peter (Husband)	PAX TV
Style Court	Plaintiff	Hurricane TV-Style Network
Saturday Night Live "2003 premiere"	Skit/Featured	NBC
NY Rocks	Guest Spot	Time Warner
Sledge (DV Short)	Supporting	Lake Films
Back to Manhattan	Frankie the Gangster (Principal)	Dir. Rob Reilly
Dickhead	Sammy Davis Jr. Impersonator	Dir. Catherine Natale
Final Exam	Police Officer	Dir. John Moulock
Cleaners of Broadway	Police Lt.	Dir. Peter Minn
Julian August	2nd Lead Private Inv.	Infocus Prod.

TRAINING

Olinda Turturro Acting Studio	Ongoing weekly classes	NYC
NY Performance Works	Acting for Camera w/ Richard Scanlon	NYC
Madelyn Burns Casting	Acting for Commercials	NYC

SPECIAL SKILLS

Various accents and voice characterizations including, cartoon characters and impersonations. Musician/Singer/Songwriter.

Eddie Sicoli Contact:

Phone: 973-366-6364
Website: www.actoreddie.com

Michele Greene

Favorite Quote:

"Life shrinks or expands in proportion to one's courage."
Anais Nin

Michele Greene

Profile

A Latina from Los Angeles, Michele Greene is an Emmy-nominated actress whose work in the television series, "L.A. Law" is now seen in seventy-nine countries. A second-generation musical performer, her mother sang and recorded for many years with a Mexican trio and appeared on some of the first televised musical variety shows, Greene has been singing and composing since she was a teenager. Her music combines elements of North American and Latin folk; drawing on the musical influences she grew up with.

"My dad was from a small town in Oklahoma and he loved the classic country and folk music of Hank Williams Sr., Johnny Cash, and Woody Guthrie. My mom is Mexican/Nicaraguan and we were always listening to the Mariachi Vargas or Tona La Negra singing Agustin Lara, and of course, Lola Beltran." As her own musical style evolved, Greene realized that there were certain elements in both styles that were so much a part of her musical foundation that she had to create a sound that encompassed all of them. "My sound is a hybrid, taking musical elements from both cultures in a way that is unique and accessible. I wanted to merge that beautiful fluidity of the acoustic guitar that you find in the great Mexican trios with a North American folk sound that has an intimate simplicity." Greene writes in both Spanish and English and her debut CD, "Ojo de Tiburon" is currently in stores across the country and in Europe on Appleseed Recordings. It was produced by acclaimed Peruvian producer/guitarist, Ciro Hurtado. Hurtado and Greene are currently preparing to record her second CD for the label, entering the studio sometime in early spring.

A classically trained actress, Greene appeared on "L.A. Law" for five years as well as numerous television and independent films. She starred in a production of Shakespeare's "As You Like It" directed by Louis Fantasia, artistic director of The Old Globe Theatre in San Diego. The indie feature "A Family Affair" in which Greene plays the narcissistic romantic foil, Reggie Abravanel, has been released on screens around the country. Greene starred in the PAX TV movie, "Floodzone," as well as appearing on the CBS series, "CSI: Crime Scene Investigation." In addition she starred in an Indie feature entitled, "Outrage," appeared on the ABC series "Miracles," as well as musical appearances at the historic Mayan Club and with folk luminary, Ellis Paul, at McCabes.

Greene has also expanded her artistic career into writing, with an indie film in development as well as a one-woman theatre piece. She opened her own production company (Requinto Productions) to service her projects and move more heavily into producing. She is a native Angeleno, an animal lover, an excellent horseback rider, a novice surfer and a would be soccer player.

Michele Greene

Resume

FILM

OUTRAGE	Lead	Movie Venture
A FAMILY AFFAIR	Lead	
DETERMINATION OF DEATH	Lead	Independent
LIGHTENING: STORM OF DESTRUCTION	Lead	Porchlight/Edgewood
THE PERFECT WIFE	Lead	Win Ventures
GRIZZLY LAKE	Lead	Porchlight Entertainment
FUGITIVE MIND	Lead	Independent
DADDY'S GIRL	Lead	Image Organization
STRANGER IN THE HOUSE	Lead	Independent
THE UNBORN 2	Lead	Roger Corman Prods.
SILENT VICTIM	Lead	Independent
SEDUCED	Supporting	Image Organization
STRANGER BY NIGHT	Supporting	Wilshire Court
THE DREAM FACTORY	Cameo	Sidewalk Productions

TELEVISION/MOW

CROSSING JORDAN	Lead	NBC
JUDGING AMY	Lead	CBS
FLASH FLOOD	Lead	Animal Planet
LA LAW: REUNION	Lead	NBC
REDEEMER	Lead	USA
LOST TREASURE OF DOS SANTOS	Lead	Family Channel
BADGE OF BETRAYAL	Lead	ABC
SHE WOKE UP PREGNANT	Lead	ABC
THE HEART OF A CHILD	Lead	NBC
NIGHTMARE ON THE 13TH FLOOR	Lead	USA
POSING	Lead	CBS
GOING TO THE CHAPEL	Lead	NBC
DOUBLE STANDARD	Lead	NBC
IN THE BEST INTEREST OF THE CHILD	Lead	CBS
PERRY MASON RETURNS: THE CASE OF THE NOTORIOUS NUN	Lead	NBC
FOR MY DAUGHTER	Co-Star	CBS

EPISODIC

MIRACLES	Guest star	ABC
CSI	Guest star	CBS
JAG	Guest star	NBC
DIAGNOSIS MURDER	Guest star	CBS
THE OUTER LIMITS	Guest star	SHOWTIME
TWICE IN A LIFETIME	Guest star	PAX TV
L.A. LAW	Series regular	NBC
STARGATE SG-1	Recurring	SHOWTIME

THEATRE (partial list)

7 YEAR ITCH	Lead	STAGE WEST THEATRES CANADA
THE SHADOW BOX		
AS YOU LIKE IT	Lead	
ANTONY AND CLEOPATRA		

TRAINING
B.F.A. Theatre Conservatory Program,
USC – James Wilson, Peggy Feury
The Loft Studio – Louis Fantasia

SKILLS
Bilingual – Spanish, Excellent Horseback
Riding, Professional Singer

Michele at the Power Up Premiere Awards

Michele Greene Contact:

Marilyn Atlas Management
8899 Beverly Blvd., Suite 704
Los Angeles, CA 90048
Phone: 310-278-5289

J.R. Stuart

J.R. Stuart

Profile

J. R. Stuart is a Theatre Performance graduate of Ball State University, and has been a professional actor since 1986. He has crossed the United States and Canada in the national tours of "Brigadoon" (Beaton), "Chicago" (Amos "Mr. Cellophane" Hart), and Gigi (Honore "Thank Heaven For Little Girls" Lachailles). He also toured five seasons with Bridgework Children's Theatre, performing in issue-oriented plays for schoolchildren.

Since 1990, Stuart has been a resident character actor at the Derby Dinner Playhouse where he has logged over a hundred productions. With Jim Hesselman and Jon Martin Kitchen, Stuart co-authored a very successful original Christian musical, "Peace in the Valley," which has enjoyed runs in seven different venues so far. He also has crafted his own one-man literary portrait "Twain: The Gospel According to Mark," which he performs as often as possible.

Stuart's Favorite roles include Estragon in "Waiting for Godot" Willie Clark in "The Sunshine Boys, President Truman in "Give 'Em Hell Harry!, Ben Franklin in "1776," Tevye in "Fiddler on the Roof," Pseudolus in "A Funny Thing Happened on the Way to the Forum," Doolittle in "My Fair Lady," Fancourt Babberly in "Charley's Aunt," Joe in "The Shadow Box," Weller Martin in "The Gin Game," Sheridan Whiteside in "The Man Who Came to Dinner," and several characters played in "Greater Tuna." His directing assignments include: "That Championship Season," Bent," The Gin Game," and "Greater Tuna."

Stuart enjoys the study of film comedy (particularly Laurel and Hardy), spending time with family, and enjoying his Jack Russell Terrier, Sweeney.

J.R. Stuart

Resume

THEATRE (Representative)

Gigi	Honore Lachailles	1996 National Tour	3DII International
Chicago	Amos Hart	1995 National Tour	3DII International
Brigadoon	Beaton	1993 National Tour	3DII International
Peace in the Valley	Old Soul/Playwright	2000	Derby Dinner Playhouse
Sunshine Boys	Willie Clark	2000	Derby Dinner Playhouse
Annie	FDR	2000	Music Theatre Louisville
Fiddler on the Roof	Tevye	1999	Derby Dinner Playhouse
You Can't Take it With You	Grandpa Vanderhof	1998	Derby Dinner Playhouse
Charley's Aunt	Fancourt Babberly	1997	Derby Dinner Playhouse
My Fair Lady	Alfred P. Doolittle	1997	Derby Dinner Playhouse
Damn Yankees	Old Joe	1996	Derby Dinner Playhouse
The Gospel According to Mark	Twain/Adapter	1995	Derby Dinner Playhouse
The Gin Game	Weller Martin	1995	Rudyard Kipling Roundtable Theatre
Give 'Em Hell Harry!	President Truman	1994	Derby Dinner Playhouse
Do Black Patent...Reflect Up?	Reilly	1993	Derby Dinner Playhouse

FILM

Eight Men Out	Bar – Extra	1987	John Sayles, dir.

VIDEO

UPS Spoof	Barney Fife Infomercial Host Crocodile Hunter	2000	Video Bread
Kentucky Tourism (Commercial)	Diner	1999	
Floyd Memorial Cancer Services (Voice-Over)	James Earl Jones	2000	Pro Video Media

RADIO

Mall Clearance Sale Spots (5)	Gruff Editor	2001	VML
McDonalds Spots (3)	Blue Collar Worker	2000	VML
Derby Dinner Playhouse Promotional Spots (numerous)	Various Characters	1991-2000	

SPECIAL SKILLS

Character voice, movement, and makeup. Can conquer most regional American dialects and standard British, Cockney and Russian. Adept at slapstick comedy.

J.R. Stuart Contact:

Visit CHARACTERMANONSTAGE! At:
http://members.tripod.com/~characterman

Marlene Sosebee

Marlene Sosebee

Profile

Marlene Sosebee was born in Stafford Spring, Connecticut on April 12, 1952. She grew up in Somers, Connecticut and then attended North Yarmouth Academy, Yarmouth, Maine in her final two years of high school. Marlene learned to play the guitar at 8 years of age and always played in a band. At the age of 17, she went to Woodstock in the summer of 1969 and partied with half a million hippies.

In the '70's, Marlene attended the University of Southern California in Los Angeles where she protested the Vietnam War and studied art, music, psychology, religion and philosophy.

After college, Marlene headed out on the road, playing in various rock bands. She lived in New Jersey, New York, Vermont, Massachusetts, Connecticut and California. In 1984, Marlene hooked up with the all-female rock band "Lipstick" and toured the East Coast and Canada. In '86 she and her lead singer, Cheri Gates, moved to Los Angeles and reformed "LYPSTIK" under a different spelling. This band got worldwide exposure in magazines, and airplay of tapes and videos.

In the '90's, Marlene joined the Screen Actors Guild and studied at Stella Adler Academy of Acting. She has done a national SAG commercial for Minolta and had a few small parts in TV and movies. She has continued to write and record music and has three albums for sale at queenboudica.com. On these albums, Marlene plays all the instruments and recorded them herself.

Marlene also has an art gallery at queenboudica.com.

Marlene Sosebee

Resume

SAG

FILM   **CHARACTER**

Drifting Schools   L.A.P.D. Cop   Shower Prod.

TELEVISION

413 Hope St.	Counselor Marilyn	20th Century Fox
If These Walls Could Talk	Officer Myers	HBO Productions
California	Prostitute	CBS Prod.
Melrose Place	L.A.P.D. Cop	Spelling Prod.
Deep Space Nine	Klingon Nemchick	Paramount
Co-Ed Call Girl (CBS MOW)	Prostitute	CBS Entertainment

THEATRE

Live Oldies Comedy Show   50's Biker Chick   Riviera Company

COMMERCIAL

1999 Minolta Mom (National commercial)

TRAINING

Stella Adler Academy of Acting – Hartford Conservatory of Music

RECORDING

Institute of America – Univ. of Southern Calif. (theatre & music)

SPECIAL SKILLS

10 years as lead guitarist for all – female rock band "LYPSTIK." Toured USA and Canada. Radio time – Studio videos – Magazines – Billboards – ESP Guitar Endorsement. Stunt abilities, bodybuilding, roller blade, horseback, swim, boating, skiing, billiards. Author of three books.)

Marlene Sosebee Contact:

www.queenboudica.com

Scott Winters

Favorite Quote:

"Strength and Faith"

Eleonora Duse

Scott Winters

Profile

Mr. Winters grew up in New Jersey. He attended Northwestern University's renowned theatre training program and then moved to New York and continued to study privately with: HB Studio, Terry Schreiber, and Fred Kareman for Meisner Technique.

He spent 20 years in New York doing a mix of classical theatre and new plays, commercials and soaps, corporate videos and plain old day jobs. He married an actress-singer-teacher and they had 2 children. After some trepidation about relocating to New England (for family reasons), he found himself busier than ever in the smaller market.

Current roles include Clint Eastwood's "Mystic River" and the independent films "Cathedral" and "The Sandpiper." His recent stage work is mostly classical: "Macbeth," "Candida," "Julius Caesar," and "The Sea Gull."

Scott during a promotional photo shoot

Scott Winters

Resume

AEA/AFTRA/SAG

FILM AND TELEVISION

Mystic River (dir. Clint Eastwood)	Detective	Day Player	Warner/Malpaso
The Sandpiper	Ted Wheelock	Principal	Sandpiper Films
Cathedral	The Man	Principal	A Small Good Thing Prods.
His Life	Michael	Day Player	Mindscape Pictures
New York Wired	Co-Host	Principal	NBC, FOX
American's Most Wanted	Robert Legare	Principal	FOX
As The World Turns	Mike Fleischer	Day Player & U5	CBS
One Life to Live	Philip Clark	Recurring U5	ABC

NEW YORK THEATRE

Trelawny of the "Wells"	Tom Wrench	Theatre-Off-Park
Jupiter Blue	Dagwood	Ensemble Studio Theatre
The Merry Wives of Windsor	Doctor Caius	Riverside Shakespeare Company
Servant of Two Masters	Florindo	Riverside Shakespeare Company
The Three Sisters	Fedotik	Equity Library Theatre
A Midsummer Night's Dream	Theseus/Oberon	Horace Mann Theatre
Orpheé	Orpheé	NADA
I Think It Would Be Correct…	Sempronio	NADA
Home Game	Belly	Manhattan Class Company
Nights in Hohokus	Lenny	West Bank Café
Macbeth	Ross	Kings County Shakespeare Co.

REGIONAL THEATRE

Candida	Rev. Morell	Island Theatre Company
The Sea Gull	Dr. Dorn	Island Theatre Company
Beauty for Ashes	Saúl Jorge	Millennium Music Center
Macbeth	Lennox & 2nd Witch	Sandra Feinstein-Gamm Theatre
The Investigation	The Judge	Jewish Theatre of New England
The Duke	Fred	Boston Theatre Marathon

362

Scam (Early Stages series)	Duane	American Stage Festival
Show and Tell	Seth	12 Miles West Theatre Company
Crossing Delancey	Sam	Forum Theatre Company
Henry VI, Part 2	Jack Cade (u/s)	New Jersey Shakespeare Festival
Richard III	Ratcliffe (u/s)	New Jersey Shakespeare Festival
As Is	Saul	Hippodrome State Theatre

COMMERCIAL/INDUSTRIAL

Over 80 industrials, including AT&T, Bayer, Citibank, Coca-Cola, Computer Associates, Deloitte & Touche, Fidelity, Hewlett-Packard, IBM, KPMG, Liberty Mutual, Merck, Mobil, Parents Magazine, Prudential, Radio Shack, Sheraton

Commercial conflicts upon request ◆ Voice-over and video clips on the Web

TRAINING

Meisner Technique -- Fred Kareman, NYC
Scene Study -- Terry Schreiber, T. Schreiber Studio
Stage Combat -- Paul Barry, NJ Shakespeare Fest.
Scene Study -- Carol Rosenfeld, HB Studio

B.S. in Theatre, Northwestern University

Scott Winters Contact:

swinters59@hotmail.com

Dustin Nguyen

Favorite Quote:

"Walk On"

Dustin Nguyen

Profile

After escaping from Vietnam with his family on the day Saigon fell in 1975, Dustin Nguyen (pronounced "gwen") has established himself as one of the few prominent Asian-American actors. Having starred on such shows as "21 Jump Street" and "Seaquest DSV," Nguyen was most recently seen co-starring opposite Pamela Anderson Lee on the number one syndicated series "V.I.P." As a result of his work on the show, Nguyen won a 2000 Ammy Award, the Asian equivalent to the Emmy, for Best Male Actor and was again nominated for 2001.

Nguyen completed shooting 20th Century Fox's one-hour drama pilot "The Break." Nguyen plays "Rusty Kealoha," the Senate-candidate husband of lead actor Dylan Bruno's sister. The pilot was executive produced by Brian Grazer and was shot in Oahu, Hawaii.

The storyline revolves around Detroit city cop "Dane Patterson" (Bruno) and his son "Alex." When "Alex" seems headed for a life of crime, "Patterson" decides to move back to his hometown of Oahu, Hawaii. The two move in with his sister "Sara" and her politician husband "Rusty" (Nguyen), and "Dane" soon gets a job with his old friend "Kawika Jones" on the HPD's Crime Reduction Unit. Nguyen also guest-starred in an episode of CBS's hit drama "JAG."

In the hit one-hour action series "V.I.P.," Nguyen played 'Johnny Loh,' an action movie star from Hong Kong who is framed for the murder of his best friend and has escaped to Los Angeles. In an attempt to clear his name, 'Loh' joins forces with V.I.P., the elite professional bodyguard agency led by Lee's character.

Nguyen's little known martial arts expertise was showcased when he starred in the Levi Jean's European "Hero" campaign, which expanded upon his ever-growing international profile. The campaign was uniquely ground-breaking in that it was the first time Levi's used an Asian lead in their popular role of the "Levi's Hero." For Nguyen, it offered the first opportunity to apply his love for the martial arts along with his dramatic training as he collaborated with the director on the fight choreography.

In recent years, Nguyen has also found success in feature films. He landed a pivotal role in Warner Bros. "Heave and Earth," directed by Oliver Stone, followed by TriStar Pictures' "3 Ninjas Kick Back." In addition, he starred in the action-drama "No Escape, No Return."

Born in South Vietnam, Nguyen enjoyed a comfortable existence where his father was one of the nation's top film and stage actors. Leaving the country behind on a moment's notice, the Nguyens became the first Vietnamese family to settle in St. Louis, Missouri. During his junior high school years, Nguyen found "personal excellence" through martial arts, which he describes as "the first awakening of my soul." Following high school, he moved to Southern California to attend Orange Coast College, and at the suggestion of a friend, he took an acting class; "the second awakening of my soul." And the rest, as he puts it, "was a series of fateful events."

After making his professional debut on a special two-hour "Magnum P.I.," where he portrayed a young Cambodian freedom fighter, Nguyen went on to enjoy enormous popularity as "Suki" on "General Hospital." His breakthrough role, however, came when he was cast as "Detective Harry Ioki" in the FOX network's flagship show "21 Jump Street," on which he starred for four seasons. It was here that Nguyen became the first primetime Asian heartthrob, and his official introduction to "that ridiculous and unnecessary, mind-warping thing called fame!"

What is more to his liking is testing his limits on his Ducati, or practicing his Muey Thai Kickboxing. "You can't make a mistake doing 100 plus on a superbike, or when your opponent is trying to take your head off," Nguyen emphasizes. "For me, if you really want to know yourself, this is it. You can talk all day about techniques this and philosophy that, and it's nothing but an intellectual and theoretical mess! You've got to go out and DO."

Though he maintains a strong connection to his Asian roots, Nguyen feels that there's danger in this "identifying process." His Buddhist background teaches that to identify is to separate. "I try not to think of myself as 'Asian.' I try to think of myself as an individual. This way there's less separation between myself from the 'Anglo-Saxons,' the 'African-Americans,' the 'Latin-Americans,' and so on, and so on. If we all practice this, I believe this planet of ours would be more cohesive."

Dustin Nguyen

Resume

FILM

ONE HUNDRED PERCENT	Indie	Dir: Eric Koyanagi
HEAVEN AND EARTH	WB	Dir: Oliver Stone
THREE NINJAS	TriStar	Dir: Charles Kanganis
NO ESCAPE, NO RETURN	HBO	Dir: Charles Kanganis

TELEVISION

THE BREAK (Pilot)	Guest Star	FOX/FBC
JAG	Guest Star	Paramount/CBS
VIP	Co-Star	FOX/TriStar
JOHNNY X (Pilot)	Lead	ABC/Touchstone
DIE GANG	Co-Star	Syndicate
VANISHING SON	Co-Star	Syndicate
THE COMMISH	Guest Star	CBS
HIGHLANDER	Guest Star	Syndicate
21 JUMP STREET`	Co-Star	FOX
GENERAL HOSPITAL	Co-Star	ABC

THEATRE

THE ZOO STORY	Jerry	Friends & Artists Theatre
MERRY WIVES OF WINDSOR	Argucheek	Friends & Artists Theatre

TRAINING
Sal Romco: Stanislavsky Techniques, Lee Strasberg Relaxation

SPECIAL SKILLS
Motorcycle Racing, Martial Arts

Dustin Nguyen Contact:

Jay D. Schwartz & Associates
3255 Cahuenga Blvd., West, Suite 205
Los Angeles, CA 90068
Phone: 323-512-9100

Jorja Fox

Jorja Fox

Profile

With a variety of memorable roles filling up her resume, it would not be clichéd for one to hum a few bars of "Jorja On My Mind." Actress Jorja Fox currently stars on the top-rated series on television, "CSI: Crime Scene Investigation" for CBS. Fox stars as a member of the autopsy team who heads-up the gritty drama series that is executive produced by Jerry Bruckheimer.

No stranger to television, Fox also starred on NBC's top-rated series "ER" as resident intern Dr. Maggie Doyle prior to her segue as Secret Service Agent Gina Toscano on Aaron Sorkin's Emmy Award-winning drama "The West Wing." Additional credits include guest turns on "Law and Order" and the historic "coming out" episode of "Ellen."

Fox has also managed to carve out some impressive film credits that include "Memento," which was a dramatic competitor at the Sundance Film Festival. She portrays the wife of lead, Guy Pearce. This marks Fox's third foray into Sundance. She has previously made the trip in conjunction with her roles as sister to Clea Duvall in the quirky comedy "How to Make the Cruelest Month" and as the town gossip in "The Kill-Off" which was based on the book by renowned author Jim Thompson ("The Grifters"). More recent feature credits include the comedy "Forever Fabulous" with Jean Smart and "Down with the Joneses" opposite Joshua Leonard ("The Blair Witch Project").

Having appeared in numerous stage productions, Fox continues to work tirelessly in conjunction with the theatre company which she co-founded, Honeypot Productions. Honeypot has put up three plays to date, two of them scribed by Fox. The fourth play, "Loving Stanley," which she also penned, offers up a comedic romp about the women's bowling circuit.

Born in New York City, Fox moved to the small coastal town of Melbourne Beach, FL with her French Canadian parents. Upon completion of high school, she moved back to New York to pursue her career in acting. Now residing in Los Angeles, Fox enjoys traveling, playing guitar, singing, and has an affinity for the ocean, which dates back to her childhood.

Jorja Fox Contact:

Pinnacle
8265 Sunset Blvd., Suite 201
Los Angeles, CA 90046
Phone: 323-654-6600

Frank Vincent

Frank Vincent

Profile

Frank Vincent is best known for his roles in such gangster classics as "Casino," "Goodfellas" and "Wiseguys." He first became recognized for his work in the unforgettable part of 'Salvi' in Martin Scorsese's "Raging Bull." Vincent can be seen in the feature films "This Thing of Ours," "Tale of Two Pizzas," "Snipes' and "Last Request." He also starred in the movie "Under Hellgate Bridge" with Vincent Pastore and Dominic Chianese. Vincent also had the lead role as Aristotle Onassis in the feature film "Isn't She Great" with Bette Midler and Nathan Lane. Prior, Vincent starred with Sylvester Stallone in Miramax's hit film "Cop Land" and played the role of Jennifer Aniston's father in the box office hit "She's The One" directed by Sundance Film Festival winner, Edward Burns.

Currently, Frank Vincent is the spokesperson for a national line of cigars called "Public Enemy" represented by Celebrity Cigar Corp. His new line of cigars was launched with the cover of the premiere issue of *New York Smoker Magazine*. Vincent has also dabbled in modeling being named the "face" for a Tommy Boy Gear national advertising campaign.

His acting experience also includes starring roles in over 30 feature films and made for television movies ("The Grind," "Gotti," "Jungle Fever," "Honeymoon in Vegas," "Do The Right Thing," "Pope of Greenwich Village," "Federal Hill," "Easy Money" and "The Devil"). Vincent currently plays the part of 'Phil Leotardo' on the hit HBO series, "The Sopranos." Vincent has also appeared in the two-part NBC miniseries "Witness To The Mob" and such television series as "NYPD Blue," "Cosby," "New York Undercover," "Swift Justice" and "Law & Order." He also hosted a month long gangster movie marathon on Turner Classic Movies.

Vincent was in the NBC miniseries, Tom Clancy's "Netforce" and also appeared in the feature film "Vig" starring Peter Falk, Lauren Holly and Timothy Hutton. He also appeared in the Hype Williams film "Belly," which stars musical artists Nas, DMX and Method Man. Vincent lives in Nutley, New Jersey with his wife Katherine.

Frank Vincent

Resume

FILM

COALITION	ALVARO	DIR: JOSEPH ARIOLA
SNIPES	JOHNNY MARANDINO	DIR: RICHARD MURRAY
THE CREW	MARTY	DIR: MICHAEL DINNER
IF YOU ONLY KNEW	GINO	DIR: DAVID SNEDEKER
ISN'T SHE GREAT	ARISTOTLE ONASSIS	DIR: ANDREW BERGMAN
REMEMBERING MARIO	JOEY BIG EARS	DIR: VAL FRANCO
UNDER HELLGATE BRIDGE	BIG SAL	DIR: MIKE SERGIO
GUNSHY	CARMINE MINETTI	DIR: ERIC BLAKENEY
ENTROPY	SAL	DIR: PHIL JOANOU
UNDERCURRENT	EDDIE TORELLI	DIR: FRANK KERR
BELLY	ROGER	DIR: HYPE WILLIAMS
THE NORTH END	DOM DI BELLA	DIR: FRANK CIOTA
MADE MEN		DIR: DON CLOSE
TEN BENNY	RAY SR.	DIR: ERIC BROSS
COP LAND	PBA PRESIDENT	DIR: JAMES MANGOLD
THE DELI	TOMMY TOMATOES	DIR: JOHN GALLAGHER
GOTTI	ROBERT DIBERNARDO	DIR: ROBERT HARMON
SHE'S THE ONE	RON	DIR: ED BURNS
NIGHT FALLS ON MANHATTAN	CAPTAIN	DIR: SIDNEY LUMET
NOTHING TO LOSE	DAD	DIR: ERIC BROSS
CASINO	FRANKIE MARINO	DIR: MARTIN SCORSESE
GRIND	NICK	DIR: CHRIS KENTIS
MEN LIE	UNCLE FRANK	DIR: JOHN GALLAGHER
FEDERAL HILL	SAL	DIR: MICHAEL CORRENTE
HANDGUN	EARL	DIR: WHITNEY RANSICK
HONEYMOON IN VEGAS	JERRY MELTON	DIR: ANDREW BERGMAN
JUNGLE FEVER	MIKE TUCCI	DIR: SPIKE LEE
MORTAL THOUGHTS	DOMINIC	DIR: ALAN RUDOLPH
STREET HUNTER	DON MARIO	DIR: JOHN GALLAGHER
GOODFELLAS	BILLY BEATS	DIR: MARTIN SCORSESE
LAST EXIT TO BROOKLYN	PRIEST	DIR: ELI EDEL
DO THE RIGHT THING	CHARLIE	DIR: SPIKE LEE
WISE GUYS	LOUIS FONTUCCI	DIR: BRIAN DE PALMA
POPE OF GREENWICH VILLAGE	CREW CHIEF	DIR: STU ROSENBERG
MADE IN ARGENTINA	MARTY	DIR: LOUIS RUIZ
LOU, PAT & JOE D.	POP	DIR: STEVEN VICTORIA
EASY MONEY	BOOKIE	DIR: JAMES SIGNORELLI
BABY IT'S YOU	VINNIE FRANKO	DIR: JOHN SAYLES
DEAR MR. WONDERFUL	LOUIS	DIR: PETER LILIANTHAL
RAGING BULL	SALVI	DIR: MARTIN SCORSESE
DEATH COLLECTOR	BERNIE FELDSHUH	DIR: RALPH DEVITO
VINNY D	VINNY D	DIR: JOHN GALLAGHER
LUCKY MAN	PAULIE	DIR: MICHAEL ORBACH
AFTERLIFE OF GRANDPA	DAD	DIR: P.J. PESCE

TELEVISION

THE SOPRANOS	PHIL LEOTARDO	HBO
NYPD BLUE	DINO FERRERA/RECUR.	ABC/STEVEN BOCHCO PROD.
THE VIG	PETE	MOW/LIONS GATE
WITNESS TO THE MOB	FRANKIE DECICCO	MOW/NBC
SWIFT JUSTICE	TONY ACCARDO	UPN
NEW YORK UNDERCOVER	RAY TERRAFINO	FOX
7TH AVENUE/PILOT		NBC
INDIANA JONES	JONNY TORRIO	PARAMOUNT
DEAD & ALIVE	JOE ZANNI	DIR: PETER MARKELE
CIVIL WARS	GUEST STAR	CBS
LAW & ORDER	GUEST STAR	NBC
AFTER DRIVE	GUEST STAR	COMEDY CENTRAL
ONE LIFE TO LIVE	GUEST STAR	ABC

THEATRE

EAST OF EVIL	WEST BANK THEATRE	DIR: JOHN GALLAGHER
NEW VAUDVILLIANS	BROADWAY	R.F.K. THEATRE

MISCELLANEOUS

BRUCE HORNSBY VIDEO
RECORDING DRUMMER FOR: DON COSTA, PAUL ANKA, STEVE LAWRENCE, EYDIE GORME, TRINI LOPEZ, THE DUPREES, DION

Frank Vincent Contact:

Melissa Prophet Management
1041 North Formosa Ave.
Formosa Bldg., Suite 200
West Hollywood, CA 90046
Phone: 323-850-2722

Kyla Pratt

Kyla Pratt

Profile

Within just ten years in the entertainment business, eighteen year old Kyla Pratt has already built an impressive resume with over 35 television appearances as well as a number of feature film credits to her name. The star of UPN's "One On One," which is currently in its fourth season and The Disney Channel's "Proud Family," also in its fourth season, Kyla is no stranger to hard work.

Kyla began her career in 1995 after being cast in the "Di Vinci, Time and Space" interactive computer game commercial and has been on a roll ever since. In 1999 Kyla was voted "Favorite Rising Star" at the *Nickelodeon Kids Choice Awards*. The term "rising" was correct, by the age of twelve, Kyla had appeared in almost twenty supporting, guest starring and recurring roles on television shows such as "Friends," "Family Matters," "Touched by an Angel," "The Smart Guy" and "Moesha." She also has a very impressive list of motion picture credits and has worked with some of the finest directors and actors in Hollywood. Her feature film credits include "One Night Stand," directed by Mike Figis, "Psalms From the Underground," directed by Eric La Salle, "Love and Basketball," directed by Spike Lee, "Dr. Dolittle" and "Dr. Dolittle 2," starring opposite Eddie Murphy. Her roles in both "Dr. Dolittle" movies earned her an NAACP Image Award nomination.

Kyla's series, "One On One," just wrapped a highly successful third season on UPN by becoming the top rated comedy in African American households (beating out the Emmy Award winning comedy "The Bernie Mac Show"). The show also rose to become the networks #1 rated comedy. In the series, Kyla plays Breanne, a young teen, who has moved in with her fun-loving ladies-man father (Flex Alexander) who wants to be his daughter's best friend. In the show, Kyla shows her amazing comedic skills and timing as well as spirit, charm and love of life. Kyla's second series is The Disney Channel's highest rated animated series, "Proud Family," in which she voices the role of "Penny Proud." In the show, Kyla stars opposite, Tommy Davidson, Paula Jai Parker and Jo Marie Patton.

When Kyla isn't working, she enjoys dancing, rollerblading, ice-skating, shopping and basketball. She also participates in many charitable events throughout the summer including Challengers Boys & Girls Club fundraisers. Kyla also has a love for school and maintains her place on the honor roll.

Kyla has recently received an award for *Best Comedic Performance* at the *2003* NAMIC Vision Awards and that same year was honored with the *Bethel Smith Positive Youth Image Award*.

Kyla Pratt Contact:

Shannon Barr Public Relations
3619½ Crest Dr.
Manhattan Beach, CA 90266
Phone: 310-546-5069

David M. Evans

David M. Evans

Profile

David M. Evans was raised in a seaside town between Los Angeles and San Diego. It was a small town of less than ten thousand people and for all those people there was one old movie theatre. On Friday nights and if the picture was particularly good, on Saturday and Sunday afternoons too, you could count on finding David there. For a quarter you could see a double feature and a cartoon. He still remembers the movies and the stars. Cooper and Gable appearing in their last films, Sean Connery in the first Bond films and Karloff and Lorre having a grand time working in the Roger Corman Poe classics. So many wonderful films, so long ago.

David goes on to say, "And I remember this, this idea that came to me in the endless stream of flickering lit Saturday afternoons. I remember looking up at those people on that big screen and thinking, 'An actor...now there's something to be.' I grew up and worked in a variety of businesses and did a variety of things, but I carried that revelation learned in that old movie theatre over the years and remembered it like I never had remembered an idea before or since because, an actor is something to be. And so now I am." David has starred in the films, "The Waiting Room," "18th Amendment" and "Till Death do us Part." His credits also include a variety of television roles and Theatre.

David M. Evans

Resume

FILM / VIDEO

The Waiting Room	Starring	C Powell / Ind
18th Amendment	Starring	A Dahlgren / Ind
'Til Death Do Us Part	Starring	F Alessandri / USC Grad
Chicken Foot	Co-Starring	A Bogna / CF Prods
Enzo's Choice	Co-Starring	R McCall / Chapman Grad
Little Girl Blue	Co-Starring	E Alymac / Chapman Grad
Teddy Bear Syndrome	Co-Starring	K DiMasi / Ind
The Cross	Principal	L Tracy / Emerald Cove
For Love Of The Game	Principal	S Raimi / Universal
Like Juice But Fizzy	Principal	J Berkowitz / USC Grad
Three Dead Rats	Principal	J Berkowitz / USC Grad
Mothers Of Angels	Principal	A Nakahara / Chapman Grad

TELEVISION

Sexy Urban Legends	Co-Starring	PB Ent
Codename Liquidator	Co-Starring	T Miller / Ind
Dawn Of Our Nation	Principal	Green Dragon Prods
Lords Of The Mafia	Principal	PBS

THEATRE

Charlotte's Web	John Arable	D Inglima / Laguna Playhouse
The Dining Room	Harvey	H Landon Jr / SCR
Three Sisters	Tchebyutykin	K Hensel / SCR PC
Rosa and Franco	Petey	S Harwood / UCI
The Old Boy	Bud	S Gomer / El Camino Real
Hands Of Its Enemy	Howard	P Fennell / Saddleback Coll

COMMERCIAL
List furnished upon request.

DRAMATIC TRAINING / EDUCATION
Karen Hensel – Intensive Stage, Film South Coast Repertory
Hal Landon Jr – Improvisation Professional Conservatory
Mark L Taylor – Television/Commercial SCR
Sharon Harwood – Film Technique and Scene Study UC Irvine
Patrick Fennell – Stage & Film Acting and Scene Study, Saddleback Coll

SPECIAL SKILLS
Sports / Athletics / Martial Arts / Weapons
Sailing, stage combat

Dialects
Wide variety of dialects and accents

Other
Voice-over, staged readings, medical actor (Standardized Patient Programs for UCI and UCSD Medical Schools) former Jeopardy champion, fine cooking, motorcycles
Active member of MENSA USA, Ltd
Associate of Inside Out (Community Outreach Program)

David M. Evans Contact:

Icon Talent Agency
1717 W. Magnolia, Suite 100
Burbank, CA 91505
Phone: 818-526-1444

Carson Grant

Favorite Quote:

"Life unfolds each day with great experiences to nurture, whether joy or tragedy; understand the importance of your feelings and be true to yourself first."
Carson Grant

Carson Grant

Profile

Carson Grant trained in acting with Lee Strasberg (1970-74) and has portrayed various characters in over 200 short films in the last four years. He was fortunate to romantically kiss Christina Ricci as the acting teacher in Woody Allen's summer project 2002. You can see him in "An American Cyborg," "Master Shot," "A Place Between Heaven & Hell," "Wasted Sunshine" and "Down That Road & Back." He has appeared on TV on the "Chris Rock Show" and "Monday Night Mayhem." His theatre credits include "Denmark," and "Who Killed Holly Hollingworth." He also does commercials and voice-overs.

Carson Grant

Resume

SAG/AFTRA/AEA/GIAA

FEATURE/INDI FILMS	Lead/Principal Roles	Director-Production
Alyssa and Sara	Prof. Bardolph	Josh Wich, Imperfect Films
An American Cyborg	Peter (Lead)	Christian Varley, Varley Films
Anything Else	Ron Keller, Act.tchr-Ricci's lover	Woody Allen, Perdido Productions
A Place Between Heaven & Hell	Peter	Craig Horowitz, Total Support Productions
Beautiful George	Director (Lead)	Juraj Szabo, Szabo Films
Beshay's: The Lost Face	Mark (Lead)	Emad Beshay, Beshay Film Productions
Broken Wing of Elijah Footfalls	Hy Wire	Gabriel Judet-Weinshel, Bluecat Pictures
Bronx Bound	Skipper	David Chung, D.S. Films
Concert Joe	Adler & Narrator	Roy Szuper, UB Productions
Dead Serious	Rev. Bob Ribington	Joe Sullivan, Moodude Films
Down That Road & Back	Doctor Gender (Lead)	Chris Sendrowski, Sendrowski Films
Eleven Monkeys & the Mailman	Drake	Rebecca Scott, Monkey Films
Garden	Doctor Lang	Dennis Conway, Banshee Wail Productions
Good Humor	Marty	Stephen T. Neave, Good People Productions
Hazard	Bruce Hack	Shiom Somo, Hazard Productions
He Outta Be Committed	Einstein	Douglas Zimmerman, Primal Productions
HH	Howard Hughes (Lead)	Alphan Eseli & Gokhan Mutlu, EM2 Productions
Loving Randy	John	Ellery Ngiam, Ngiam Films
Master Shot	Frank Falcone (Lead)	Edoardo Amati, Human Touch Communication
Nicotine Whitebread	Damien	Gavin Blake/Harvey Brooks, Influx Media Group
Paper Soldiers	Attorney Herb	David Daniel/Damon Dash, Paper Soldiers Prod.

Seduction	Face-off	Yuval Adler, South First Productions
Soliloquy	Lawrence	Jacques Zanetti, Inside & Out Films
Stir	Burt	Zhen Li, Stir Productions
Summertime Fly Child	Father Coughlin	Richard Kaplinski, Summertime Productions
Taste (adapted Roald Dahl)	Richard Pratt (Lead)	Gabriel Kahan, Kahan Productions
Wasted Sunshine	Victor (Lead)	Casey Safron, Ridgewood 13 Production
Where Broadway Ends	Detective Hawkins	Sean Ludan, Ludan Films

For Complete List of more than 200 Films, Lead & Prin. roles, check Carson's website -- www.carsongrant.com

SHORT FILMS (under 30 mins.) Title-Director-Lead Roles

Boxing Bukowski, d-James Smith, r-Max

I Heard it Did Well at Sundance, d-Matt Lipson, r-Disgrun

Charcoal, d-Roy Szuper, r-Bill

Interrogation, d-Josh Sanchez, r-Detective Dewey

Central Park Jog, d-Juan Castillo, r-Sniper

Messiah, d-Grady Feldgus, r-Rabbi Cohen

Clone, d-David Silverton, r-Dr. Z, Scientist

MoneyMatters, d-Ryan Richmond, r-Father Lewis

Duchamp's Curse, d-Paolo Marinou-Blanco, r-Duchamp

Portraits, d-Gina Abatemarco, r-Jack

Drowning Fish, d-Toshi Takatsuka, r-Mikhail

Route 11, d-Tim Estep, r-Bob, Father

Empty, d-Zac Nicholson, r-Sam Manning

Savior, d-Keith Ng, r-Captain O'Reilly, Policeman

Glengarry, Bob Ross, d- ake Hart, r-Mister Rogers

Shaheed, d-Uri Appenzeller, r-Judge Saul

Healing By Hypnosis, d-Ryan Richmond, r-Dr. Goldfield

Stripling in the Night, d-Sergio Umansky, r-Officer George

How People Do, d-Alexandre Moors, r-Marco

Wynn Albright, d-Phelphs Harmon, r-Wynn Albright

TELEVISION	Supporting Roles	Director-Production
Chris Rock Show	Policeman Jones	Scott Preston, HBO Productions
Monday Night Mayhem	Leonard Tose	Ernest Dickerson, TNT Productions
The Last Ballot	Thomas Jefferson	Donald Fouser, WNET Productions

382

COMMERCIALS   Web PC-Dell, Ames, Corona, American Airlines, Chase Bank, Mercury Mountaineer, Merrill Lynch

VOICE-OVERS   Film Narration: Concert Joe, Wildcop, Slowdown, Wasted Sunshine, Elia Ostrich
Animation: character/animal-voices & storytelling

THEATRE

Denmark	Ghost Hamlet	David Thorn, Walter Theatre, NYC
Sketched of the Damn	Dare	George Romaine, Dramatic Guild, NYC
Who Killed Holly Hollingworth	Hal	George Romaine, Dramatic Guild, NYC

TRAINING

Acting	With Lee Strasberg 1970-74, David Le Grant 1975-77
Voice	Wally Harper <u>Accents</u>: New England, Midwest, Mid-Atlantic, Mt., Southern, Russian. East Euro
Movement	Phil Black (Jazz), Finus Jhung, Bob Audy (Tap), Frank Wagner (Modern), Julia Jones (Fencing)
Skills	White/Blue collar skills: Artist, Animator/Editor, Sports, Horseman, Carpenter/Construction Equipment

Carson Grant Contact:

Website: www.carsongrant.com

Jessica Sunshine

Favorite Quote:

*"Our doubts are traitors, and make us lose the good we oft might win,
by fearing to attempt."*
William Shakespeare – Measure For Measure

Jessica Sunshine

Profile

The love for acting has always been a part of Jessica. She worked on movies that came through her hometown of Indianapolis, Indiana during her youth. She always planned on pursuing acting fulltime, and then finally did after moving to Los Angeles when she graduated college from Indiana University. When she arrived in Los Angeles she worked behind-the-scenes in various capacities, using the set of skills, which she had been working on, and learning about in college. She believed that learning all aspects of filmmaking would alter her perspective of the acting profession. She has been in a number of independent films. Her passion for acting has certainly proven itself and she looks forward to success as an actress.

Jessica Sunshine

Resume

FILM

*Masters Of The Medium	Lead	Dir: Kate Randolph
Get Some	Lead	Dir: Roberto Caudillo
Allure	Lead	Dir: Lupe Valdez
**Mockingbird	Supporting	Dir: Mel Rodriguez
Going All The Way	Featured	Dir: Mark Pellington
Forgive Me Father	Featured	Dir: Ivan Rogers
Walker, Texas Ranger	Featured	Final Episode
Graduation Day	Lead	Dir: S. Christian

Malibu Film Festival 8/02
**New York Film Festival 2002 Award Winner and Los Angeles Film Festival 8/02*

THEATRE

Grease	Lead	Santa Monica College
Henry the IV, Part I	Supporting	Santa Monica College
Naomi In The Living Room	Lead	Indiana University
The Total Meaning of Real Life	Lead	Indiana University
A Midsummer Night's Dream	Lead	Ball State University
Flowers For Algernon	Supporting	Indianapolis Civic Theatre
A Streetcar Named Desire	Lead	*Award Winning Production, 1 year run*
Vanities	Lead	*Award Winning Production, 1 year run*

TRAINING

Cunningham Conservatory	Los Angeles	Kate Randolph
Working Actors Group	Los Angeles	Pepper Jay
Larry Moss Workshop	Los Angeles	Michelle Danner
Advanced Classical Study	Los Angeles	Adrianne Harrop
Indiana University	Indiana	Theatre Studies (grad. 2000)
Ball State University	Indiana	Theatre Studies

SPECIAL SKILLS

Horseback riding (Western), Dialects (Southern, British), Rollerblading, Singing, Dancing (Ballroom), Improv, Yoga, Hiking, Swimming, Modeling, Bicycling, Aerobics, Snorkeling

Heaven Nez Cree

Favorite Quote:

"Many a struggler has given up, when he might have captured the victor's cup and he learned too late when the night went down, how close he was to the golden crown."

Heaven Nez Cree

Profile

Heaven Nez Cree is a very talented actress/singer-songwriter. After graduating from Central State University in her home state of Ohio, Heaven struggled to find a way to make her dream become a reality. She was on the move testing the ground in Chicago, LA, Cleveland, Baltimore, D.C. and Newark, N.J. She finally found her "home" in Harlem, New York.

She has appeared in the rock musical "The Misanthrope" in New York. She is working on her debut CD "7 For Love, 7 For Life," an exploration of lessons learned through music. She has appeared in Baltimore, MD in the play "True Love Waits." She also played Glinda in a production of "The Wiz." In addition she is working on an independent short film with filmmaker Shetal Shah, and has signed on to do a new urban drama – "Confessions, Lies and Secrets."

Heaven enjoys working with children, teaching dance and giving writing and fitness workshops through her partnership company Standing Ovations Because...

Heaven Nez Cree

Resume

THEATRE

No One Is Promised Tomorrow	Deb (lead)	Tellin' Tales Inc.
Angry Jellow Bubbles	Bubble 8	Eva Minemar
New Testament	Angel/Young Girl	Damian Bailey
The Misanthrope	Can-Can Girl / singer	Courtney L Wagner
This is a Test	Student	MHS Theatre
Anthology	Angel	CSU Drama Dept.
Women: A conversation	Lead #3	CSU Drama Dept.
Black is Not a Color	Lead / choreographer	CSU Drama Dept.
Our World	Writer / costumes	CSU Drama Dept.

TELEVISION

Sex and the City	Club patron	HBO
Sex and the City	Seminar attendee	HBO

COMMERCIALS

Conflicts available upon request

FILM

Two Weeks Notice	Gala event guest	Castle Rock Productions
Up to The Roof (Hunter Hicks)	Starlet	Back-House Productions
Perfection (Pete Dumas)	Bartender	Endless Films
An Accident of Faith (L. McGill)	Accident victim	Extreme Image Films
Johnny Raygun (Todd Johnson)	Secretary	Todd Johnson
Father Galileo's Last Days	Church member	Independent
Digital Dance (Madera Scrum)	Spirit dancer	School of Vies. Arts

DANCE

Tribe of Judah Dance Troupe / Newark, NJ
Pyramid / Montclair, NJ
Central State University "Fly-Girls" / Wilberforce, OH
CSU Belles-Jazz Dance Team / Wilberforce, OH
CSU Modern Dance Co. / Wilberforce, OH

EDUCATION

Central State University – Radio/TV Broadcasting – Theatre
Madelyn Burns Studio (NYC) – Scenes for Sitcoms

SPECIAL SKILLS
Singing (gospel, pop, rock, rib), song writing & jingle writing, aerobics, dance (modern, jazz, hip-hop, stepping), work well with children, work well with animals, climbing trees, Southern and Midwest dialect, character roles, improvisation, licensed driver, poetry/spoken word, roller skating, formal wardrobe, vintage wardrobe, various wigs/costumes. Able to portray Indian, Native American, Caribbean, African-American.

Heaven Nez Cree Contact:

Website: http://homepage.mac.com/heavennezcree

Brooks Utley

Brooks Utley

Profile

Brooks was born in Salt Lake City, Utah, October 16, 1973. He didn't always dream of becoming an actor. He never gave what he would end up doing much thought. His life has been a roller coaster for the most part.

At ten years old he was diagnosed with arthritis. It became so severe he missed most of his childhood. He was in and out of hospitals, had to have home schooling, and was being pumped full of all kinds of medication. By the time he reached fifteen, every doctor he had seen told him that he would never play any sports, he would have a stunted growth, and possible problems with medications.

He stopped taking all meds, and played every sport he could excel in. He's almost six foot now, has broken at least a dozen bones, and believes that your mind will and can overcome anything. In fact, he was struck by lightning one summer during his youth and walked away unharmed, changing his outlook and he started living more aggressively.

Shortly after turning twenty-one he had an unexplained event shape his life. In a matter of days he became paralyzed from the chest down. Being in a wheelchair, he had come to believe that everything happens for a reason. He would not give up on the belief that he would walk again and two months later he did.

A few years later he was living in Arizona and was managing a car lot, but felt out of place. It was three years later when he fell into acting. It felt like slipping into a favorite pair of jeans. Brooks believes you are everything you ever wanted to be, just look inside you it's there. Life is a struggle, everyday, the moment you feel that it's not you're not living. He agrees with Johnny Depp, who said "Keep trying, don't listen to what anyone says about you. Who cares what they think. You choose who you are."

Brooks will continue to pursue his dream. Give him a thousand no's, because anything worth living for doesn't come easy.

Brooks Utley

Resume

SAG/AFTRA Eligible

FILM

Stranded	Starring	Little Mischief Prod.- Dustin Riggs
Day of Defense	Starring	NuWorld Productions - Adam Lawson
Heavens Hullabaloo	Starring	4-Leaf Films - Rob Diamond
Supreme Belief In Lady Luck	Support	June Sundance Film Lab 2002
Ocean's 11	Guard/Stand In/Body Double	Warner Bros.- Steven Soderbergh
Rush Hour 2	Featured	Warner Bros.- Brett Ratner
Scorpion King	Black Turban Fighter	Universal Studios
Dead Air	Wacko	Independent - Chuck Waagon
Abby Singer	Featured	Independent - Rayan Williams
Man In The Box	Café Guy	Independent - Ben Barraell

TELEVISION

Make My Day	Support	NBC Pilot
City Beat/Cities	Show Host	Capestany Productions
Concierge.Biz		
Cover Me	Cuban Soccer Coach	Panamore Productions

COMMERCIALS

Air Force Reserve	Principle (national)	Sterling Martell
Montel Williams System 21	Principle (national)	Montel Williams
Paris Hotel, Las Vegas	Principle (national)	Directez Productions
Sprint PCS	USA Team Snowboarder	National Olympic Use
Petsmart	Principle (national)	Directez Productions
Rodizio Grill	Principle (UT)	Capestany Productions
HBO's Taxi Cab Confessions	Principle (national cable)	HBO Promo Spot
U Wynn 2 - Auto Infomercial	Principle (national)	AZ Commercials

THEATRE

Stealing Stones	Lead	Tempe Little Theatre
Man Of La Mancha	Support	Evalyn G. Durval
Diablo	Support	Steven Hill

TRAINING

Actor's Lounge	On Going Adv. Scene Study (01-02)	Rob Diamond
Auditioning Skills	6 months (2000)	Jon Lithum
Background Players L.A.	Assist. Casting-Rush Hr 2	David Anthony
Rich King Casting L.A.	Assist. Casting-Ocean's 11	Rich King

Ocean's 11 L.L.C./WB Prod.	Body Double/Stand-in/PA work	Rich King
Intense Scene Study	Intro Into Acting	Dan Merrit
Scene Study/Survey to Theatre	3 Month Course Sierra NV College	Evalyn G. Durval

SPECIAL SKILLS AND INTERESTS

Improv., Snow Ski Competitor-Instructor, Snowboarding, Water Ski, Rock Climber, Mountain Biker, Scuba Diver, Swim Instructor, Diver, River Rafting, Skateboarding, Golf, Football, Baseball, Soccer, Boxing, Rollerblading, Volleyball, Horseback Riding, Broad Sword Fighting, Archery, Dancing, Building Furniture, Motorcycle Riding

Accents: <u>Irish, English, New York, Southern</u>

Brooks Utley Contact:

McCarty Agency
1326 South Foothill Blvd.
Salt Lake City, UT 84108
Phone: 801-581-9292

Jason Beverett

Favorite Quote:

"If you don't stand for SOMETHING, you can offer proceeding generations NOTHING!!!"

Jason Beverett

Profile

Jason was born June 10, 1976 in the Bronx, NY. He never had an opportunity to appreciate the glory of New York, because at the tender age of 2 his mother moved Jason and his older brother to Detroit, Michigan. He was known as a bright but extremely timid child, that is, around strangers. When in the company of family and friends he was quite impressive. He was the life of the party, or bedroom, or living room, or kitchen, basically the home's attention getter. His mom thought he had a "spark" and thought he should showcase his talents to the world, or at least his school. After a lot of coaxing he mustered up the courage to partake in his first audition, the 3rd grade glee club.

In 1986 the family packed their bags and moved to New Jersey. During his senior year of high school he was spotted in a local mall by a talent coordinator for a small modeling company. Never thinking he had what it took to be a model, he actually enjoyed it and excelled at it. The little timid child of old was gone, and from the age of 17, he knew that lights, cameras and lots of action were in his future.

While double majoring in Criminal Justice and Psychology at Rutgers University, he continued his stock-modeling career and made enough money to live well above the means of the average college student. One day a friend, who was also a model, and Jason were enjoying a night out at a stand-up comedy club when they were asked to be background extra's in a movie starring one of the Baldwin brothers. It was his first movie. The director called them back for a second day of shooting and gave them featured extra roles as bouncers at a nightclub. That was the life for him. He landed a featured extra role in an after school special type film in which he played a baseball player.

From there he landed his first lead role in an independent horror film entitled "Mind Tours." Then he landed a role on the HBO prison series "OZ." Being a fulltime police officer his schedule does not allow him to make all auditions, but he is focused on his goal of not so much becoming a star, but landing a huge role that will enable him to grow and flourish in the entertainment world. The auditions and projects are starting to pile up and he is confident that he will be able to showcase his talents to millions of people worldwide.

Jason's hobbies are basketball, football, and he loves playing baseball. He's a great chef, and his specialty is pastry arts. He has several fish tanks with many exotic fish and he loves growing houseplants. Jason also admits, without a doubt, he's an Internet Junkie.

Jason Beverett

Resume

TV/FILMS

OZ	Emerald City Homeboy	HBO Productions
Hung Up	Police Officer/Pedestrian	Bruce Allen Films
Mind Tours	Lead Role/Craig	4 Star Productions
Going, Going, Gone	Baseball Player	Movie Guy Productions
Table One	Club Bouncer	Table One Productions

COMMERCIALS

Reebok / Alan Iverson	Spectator	TNT Casting

MUSIC VIDEO

Jay-Z feat. R. Kelly	Pedestrian	TNT Casting

OFF BROADWAY THEATRE

Rev. Billy's Church of Stop Shopping	Deacon	Rev. Billy Productions

COMMERCIAL MODELING

	Male Spokesmodel	George Mercado
Univ. of Kentucky Basketball Hall of Fame	Tony Delk Statue	Studio EIS
Univ. of Georgia Football Hall of Fame	Quarterback Statue	Studio EIS

PRINT/RUNWAY MODELING

Men At Last Runway Showcase Video	Model	Cass Mainstream Modeling Inc
Hip Hop Fashions Magazine	Model	Hip Hop Fashions Magazine Inc
Naughty Gear Menswear	Model	Naughty Gear Inc
Uptown B-Ball Gearology	Model	Uptown Sports Apparel Inc

SPECIAL SKILLS

Stock Modeling, Hip Hop Lyricist and Song Writer, Voice-Over, N.J. P.T.C. Certified Police Officer, Certified R.A.D. Self Defense Instructor, Basketball, Football, Baseball, Cooking, Tactical Driving, Tactical Firearms

Jason Beverett Contact:

Website: http://bounce.to/1tyme

Kimberly Amato

Favorite Quote:

"You are no longer a being, you are time, and my time is now."

Kimberly Amato

Profile

Kimberly was born in Plainview, New York on July 3, 1976. She says, "I think it was understood that I was meant to be a performer of some kind. My father used to play the guitar and I would dance for my family. I would always try to be the center of attention at family gatherings, either by playing a tambourine or trying to sing."

In grammar school she managed to squeeze her way into a play here and there. In high school she did some tech work for the plays. It was there that Kimberly decided she wanted to act and write. She worked so hard on the plays but missed being on stage as the star.

Eventually Kimberly went to college and attained a degree in psychology. During this time she wrote screenplays, poetry, editorials, plays and short stories. She continued to go to school and finished a Masters Degree in Forensic Psychology. Kimberly has directed and starred in an independent feature and has gone on to do theatre and has appeared in films and television.

Her hobbies are writing, softball (plays in fall and summer leagues), rollerblading, biking, web design (she created her own page) and making home video shorts.

Kimberly Amato

Resume

FILM	ROLE	PRODUCTION CO.
RECOIL	Natalie (lead)	FOUR PAWS UP PRODUCTIONS
BILLY'S CHOICE*	Rebecca Archer (lead)	NOR'EAST PRODUCTIONS
	Karen Gaines	
THE TRAP	(principal)	NOR'EAST PRODUCTIONS
	Amy Richards	
THE INTERROAGATION OF CLARK GRANT	Samantha	NOR'EAST PRODUCTIONS
RACE		RACE PRODUCTIONS
NYU SHORT	Ellie	TONY COHEN PRODUCTIONS

*Film Festival Entry

THEATRE/STAGE	ROLE	PRODUCTION CO.
GREASE	CHORUS	OYSTER BAY THEATRE
THE WIZ	CHORUS	OYSTER BAY THEATRE

TELEVISION	ROLE	PRODUCTION CO.
MARY & RHODA	PEDESTRIAN	T.V.M. PRODUCTION CO.
UPRIGHT CITIZENS BRIGADE	NURSE	MTV PRODUCTIONS
THE BEAT	MOURNER	VIACOM
NOW & AGAIN	CULT MEMBER 5/U	PICTUREMAKER PRODUCTIONS
THE BEAT	GYM MEMBER	VIACOM

COMMERCIALS AND PRINT   Available Upon Request

EDUCATION		
PSYCHOLOGY MAJOR	BA (1998)	HOFSTRA UNIVERSITY
FORENSIC PSYCHOLOGY	MA (2001)	JOHN JAY COLLEGE

SPECIAL SKILLS / HOBBIES
Voice-Over, Published Writer (poetry, screenwriter, short stories, editorials), Sports (rollerblading, softball, ice skating, hockey, mountain biking) NYS Drivers License, Dancing, Singing, Comedy, Improvisational Skills, Weight Training, Sword and Staff Training, Can play handicapped (blind, amputee, etc.) person as well as Autistic

LANGUAGES ACCENTS
Brooklyn, Italian, and British Accent

Kimberly Amato Contact:

Website: http://www.kimberlyann.net

Craig DiFrancia

Craig DiFrancia

Profile

Craig DiFrancia was born in Westchester, NY. Craig was 4 years old when he told his father he wanted to be on TV, so his father picked him up and sat him down on top of the television set. He went on to graduate from high school and at 18 started modeling and is now a very talented east coast actor.

He has appeared in "Last Night" which was shown at the Tribeca Film Festival and "Grace and the Storm," voted best film at the West Palm Beach Florida Film Festival. You can also see Craig in "The Agent," "The Right Side of the Gun" and "Scallop Pond." His theatre roles include Romeo in "Romeo & Juliet" and Gabe in "Dinner With Friends." In addition he has appeared on Dave Chappelle's "Comedy Central."

Craig likes ice-skating, horseback riding and baseball.

Craig DiFrancia

Resume

SAG/AFTRA

TELEVISION:

Love Without Borders *(soap opera)*	Ken Divetti (Principal)	NTV Telefilms
Survivor Brooklyn	Dr. Cliff (Lead)	R2K Films
Behind the Bars	MTV Documentary (Principal)	D&R Ventures
A Witness To The Mob	Gangster	NBC

FILM:

Grace and the Storm	Officer Griffin	Chappellabe Prod.
The Passionist	Private Paul Mazzeo	Dramaticus Films
The Tenement	Officer Spinelli	Light and Dark Prod.
Scallop Pond	Young Cop	CGF Films
The Agent	Agent 2	VT Videos
Last Night	Officer Battiste	NYFA
The Corruptor	Police Officer	Alex Prod.
Bam	Paul Vincente	NYU
Sphere Of The Lycanthrope	Butch Tucker	D. Anthony Prod.

THEATRE:

El Campo The Forgotten Zone	Mr. Millionaire	Lionhearted Production Company
A Christmas Carol	Bob Crachit	Marist Theatre
Beyond Therapy	Bob Lansky	Marist Theatre
Dangerous Liaisons	Le Vicomte De Valmonte	Playmakers Company
Dinner With Friends	Gabe	Artists Theatre Company
Henry V	Henry V	Playmakers Company
Romeo and Juliet	Romeo Montague	Artists Theatre Company

COMMERCIALS/PRINT:

List upon request

TRAINING:

Meisner Intensive	William Esper Studio	William Esper
Audition/Cold Reading	School For Film & Television	Margaret Burns
Acting I, II, III	School for Film & Television	Craig Wroe
Beginning & Advanced Soap	Video Associates	Judy Henderson
Scene Study	H.B. Studios	William Hickey
Bachelor of Science	Marist College	

SKILLS/INTERESTS:
Guitar, Football (2 yr. H.S. Captain), Tattoo, Boxing, NYS Drivers License, Bartender, Ice-Skating, Baseball, Rollerblading, SCUBA, Horseback Riding.

LANGUAGES:
Spanish (Conversational), Italian (Conversational), **ACCENTS:** Italian, Bronx, Southern, British

Craig DiFrancia Contact:

William Unroch
Phone: 212-496-9280

Ernesto Tomas Gritzewsky
"Ernie G"

Ernesto Tomas Gritzewsky
"Ernie G"

Profile

Ernesto Tomas Gritzewsky is first from his Mexican, American, Puerto Rican, Russian, & French family to graduate from college. In 1994, he graduated from Loyola Marymount University with his B.A. in Psychology and a Minor in Chicano Studies. The birth of "Ernie G" came in March of 1996 with his first pro gig at the "Eastside Comedy Jam" in Alhambra, CA. He became a "Latino Comedy Night" regular at the Laugh Factory in Hollywood, and appeared at his first Latino Comedy Olympics show at the World Famous Improv.

Ernie G has performed LIVE for crowds of thousands at the 2000 Democratic National Convention, MTV Rock The Vote Fest, Dia de San Juan Puerto Rican Festival, City of Pasadena Cinco de Mayo Festival, and the Latino Laugh Festival. He has opened in concert for the Godfather of Soul, James Brown, and for rap artist Coolio at his Labor Day Weekend Bash in Puerto Peñasco, Mexico. He has also toured throughout the country on the "Qué Locos! LIVE Comedy Tour," as well as his own Tour "Ernie G's Comedy Fiesta!" He is a regular performer at Hollywood's top comedy clubs, including The Laugh Factory, The Comedy Store, The Improv and The Ice House in Pasadena.

In theatre, Ernie G appeared for 3 years in Luis Avalos' holiday musical "Paquito's Christmas" at the Pasadena Civic Auditorium. The Musical traveled to the east coast as Ernie performed and sang at the world-renowned Kennedy Center, in Washington, D.C. This gave birth to "Ernie's KIDS" and the "Ernie's KIDS Holiday Comedy Gala," a comedy event which raises money to bring the magic of The Arts to economically disadvantaged children. He is host to numerous Charity Events & Award Galas, including shows for Padres Contra el Cancer, HAFIM, HPRA, Hollenbeck Youth Center, innumerable Latino Organizations, and the Leukemia Society. He was also invited to be a celebrity presenter at the National Association for Minorities in Communications (NAMIC) Vision Awards, and the Multi-Cultural PRISM Awards.

Ernie G co-starred in the comedy film "El Matador," and the film short "Broken," directed by Elle Travis, which played in festivals throughout the US, including the Telluride and N.Y. International Film Festivals, and has co-starred in FOX's "Sabrina the Teenage Witch." He has also appeared in 6 episodes of Galavision's "Que Locos!" the network's #1 rated show, and was chosen "The Best of Que Locos!" for their one-hour Special. During Latino Heritage Month Ernie G was honored by the Mayor of the City of Los Angeles, with the Mario Moreno "Cantinflas" Award. This was a huge honor for him. He is touring nationally with the "Picante Comedy Fiesta!"

Ernesto Tomas Gritzewsky
"Ernie G"
Resume

TELEVISION - ENGLISH

Ed McMahon's Next Big Star	Champion	PAX – TV
Sabrina the Teenage Witch	Co-Star	Warner Bros. TV
¡Que Locos! (6 episodes)	Comedian	Galavisión
The Best of ¡Que Locos!	Comedian	Galavisión
¡Funny is Funny!	Comedian	Galavisión SíTV
ComicView ('98 & '99)	Comedian	BET
Make Me Laugh!	Comedian	Comedy Central
Generation Tú	Guest Star	KJLA-TV
The Best of Generation Tú	Guest Star	KJLA-TV
Café California	Guest Panelist	KWHY-TV
The Best of Café California	Guest Panelist	KWHY-TV
The Dating Game	Bachelor	WB
Match Game 1999	Contestant	CBS
Bobcat's Big Ass Show	Contestant	FX
Outrageous!	Big Man	Family Channel
Outrageous!	Wrestler	Family Channel
In The House	Bouncer	UPN
Seventh Heaven	Gang Member	WB
Shopping Spree	Contestant	Family Channel
Majority Rules	Contestant	NBC
"2 Legit 2 Quit" Video	Voice	MC Hammer Video

SPANISH AND/OR "SPANGLISH"

¡Que Locos! (6 episodes)	Comedian	Galavisión
Generation Tú	Guest	KJLA-TV
Café California	Panelist	KWHY-TV
Buscando Pareja	Warm-Up	Telemundo
Los Reciencasados	Warm-Up	Telemundo
¡Funny is Funny!	Comedian	Galavisión
ROCA LIVE Starring Ernie G!	Host	Buenavisión
Entre Amigos	Friend	Telemundo
Recuerdos De Mi Pais	Comedian	Univision
Fiesta Broadway Live	Comedian	KWHY-TV
Emparejate	Bachelor	KWHY-TV

FILM

Matador	Bodyguard	Joey Medina
Broken	Ramon	Metaphor Films
Jerry Maguire	Football Player	TriStar Pictures
Poodle Springs	Stand-In	HBO Films
Solo	Voice	Triumph Film
Fear	Tino	CineTel Films
Tacolgando	Judge	Student Film
The Eyes of a Child	Ernie	Student Film

THEATRE

Paquito's Christmas '98-'00	Rapper / Ensemble	Luis Avalos & Cinestar Productions
Paquito's Christmas '99	Rapper / Ensemble	Kennedy Center, Wash D.C.

COMMERCIALS
List available upon request

ROAD WORK, CONCERTS AND OTHER VENUES   (5,000 – 10,000 Seat)

Democratic National Convention	Staples Center, LA, CA
"Que Locos!" LIVE Comedy Tour	Numerous Cities throughout US
Ernie G's Comedy Fiesta!	Numerous Cities throughout US
Latino Laugh Festival	San Antonio, TX
Dia de San Juan Puerto Rican Festival	Los Angeles, CA
City of Pasadena Cinco de Mayo Festival	Pasadena, CA
All Star Brown & Proud Tour	Several Cities throughout Texas
California Plaza Concert Series	Los Angeles, CA
MTV Rock the Vote	Los Angeles, CA
Mariachi Festival	Los Angeles Sports Arena, CA
James Brown Concert	San Dimas, CA
Coolio Concert / Labor Day Bash	Sonora, Mexico
River Center Comedy Club	San Antonio, TX
The Comic Strip	El Paso, TX
Horn Blower Cruises	Long Beach, CA
The 4th & B	San Diego, CA
S.H.P.E. National Convention	Fresno, CA
The Fox Theatre	Bakersfield, CA
Golden West Casino	Bakersfield, CA
The State Theatre	Modesto, CA
Perico Comedy Jam	Visalia, TX
The Lobster Trap	Oxnard, CA
Funnybone Comedy Jam	Seaside, Salinas, CA
Limerick's Pub	Riverside, CA
Club Congress	San Bernardino, CA
Eastside Comedy Jam	San Gabriel Valley
Comedy in the Dugout	Pasadena, CA
Non-Profit Fundraisers (Over 100)	Various Cities

COLLEGES/UNIVERSITIES

Loyola Marymount University (LMU)	Cornell University (Ithica, NY)
University of Southern California (USC)	Northwestern University (Evanston, IL)
University of CA, Los Angeles (UCLA)	Southwest Missouri State (Springfield, MO)
University of CA, Berkeley (CAL)	University of Texas, Austin (Austin, TX)
University of CA, Riverside (UCR)	Houston University (Houston, TX)
University of CA, Santa Barbara (UCSB)	University of El Paso (El Paso, TX)
Cal State, Los Angeles (CSULA)	Sam Houston State University (Huntsville, TX)

Cal State, Northridge (CSUN)
Cal State, Bakersfield (CSUB)
Cal State, Sacramento (CSUS)
Cal Poly Pomona (CSUP)

Old Dominion University (Norfolk, VA)
University of Florida (Gainesville, FL)
University of Chicago-Illinois (Chicago, IL)
Numerous others available upon request

TRAINING
Writing Yourself Onto the Stage (UCLA)
Avery Schreiber Improvisation (Beg – Adv)
Blanca Valdez Commercial Workshop
SAG / AFTRA Comedians Caucus
Danny Mora "Sit-Com Boot Camp" Writing
Class of 1994 Loyola Marymount University

Laurel Ollstein: The One Person Show II
Danny Mora Peer Group Acting Workshop
Bob Ackley Fundamentals of Acting
Gary Bates Dance, Modern & Jazz
Balloonabilities Balloon Art & Sculpture
BA: Psychology Minor: Chicano Studies

SPECIAL TALENTS
Balloon Artist, M C, Warm-Up, Improv, KIDS! Spanish; Rapping, Dancing; Motorcycles;
Very Athletic: Basketball, Baseball, Football, Swimming, Body-Board Surfing, Skydiving

Ernie G Contact:

www.ernieg.com

Lou Martini, Jr.

Lou Martini, Jr.

Profile

Lou Martini Jr. was born Louis Azzara, December 7, 1960 in New York City. His father was a well-known character actor/entertainer until his death in 1970. Lou's screen debut was in "What's So Bad About Feeling Good" with Mary Tyler Moore and George Peppard. He also appeared in a wedding scene in "The Godfather."

He graduated from the University of Houston with a B.A. in Communications He was a sportscaster, did TV and radio in the early 80's and stand-up comedy in the late 80's, early 90's.

Off-Broadway credits include the original production of "Tony n' Tina's Wedding," "Gangster Apparel," "Revenge in the Mob," "Leftovers" and "On the Waterfront" with Budd Schuler. His TV commercials include Olive Garden, Western Union, Mercedes Benz and numerous radio spots. Lou's TV credits include "Bobby Bypass" on the CBS series "Falconer," "Law and Order," "Law and Order: Special Victims Unit," "100 Center Street," "The Beat" and "America's Most Wanted." Film credits include "City by the Sea," "Teacakes or Canola," "Abracadabra," and "LBS." He was also in the HBO production of "Brooklyn" and Showtime's "Season of the Hunted." Lou still resides in New York City.

Lou Martini, Jr.

Resume

SAG/AFTRA/AEA

FILM

EVERYDAY PEOPLE	Supporting	Jim McKay
SEASON OF THE HUNTED	Co-Starring	Ron Spelling, Dir.
BROOKLYN	Ensemble	Jim McKay, Dir.
ABRACADABRA	Co-Starring	Paul Hap penny, Dir.
"LBS."	Co-Starring	Matthew Boniface, Dir.
THE PARLOR	Co-Starring	Gwen O'Donnell, Dir.
RIGOR MORTIS	Starring	Chris Spurgin, Dir.
HEARTBREAK HOSPITAL	Supporting	Rudi Gerber, Dir.
TEACAKES OR CANNOLI	Supporting	Francine Pelerine, Dir.
BLACK SHEEP	Starring	Phil Butte, Dir.
TRADE SHOW	Co-Starring	Ronald Wilkerson, Dir.
WHO KILLED BUDDY BLUE	Co-Starring	Jennifer Marches, Dir.
PLAY BACK	Supporting	Oley Sass one, Dir.
THE GODFATHER	Bit	Francis Ford Coppola, Dir

TELEVISION

AMERICA'S MOST WANTED	Re-enactor	FOX Holly Paige Joyner, Dir.
LAW & ORDER: SVU	Supporting	NBC Juan Campanella, Dir.
100 CENTRE STREET	Supporting	A&E Steven Shill, Dir.
PRINCE CHARMING	Supporting	TNT Allen Rakish, Dir.
100 CENTRE STREET	Supporting	A&E Sidney Lumen, Dir.
LAW & ORDER: SVU	Supporting	NBC Alan Metzger, Dir.
THE BEAT	Supporting	UPN Bruno Kirby, Dir.
FALCONE	Recurring	CBS Gary Fleer, Dir.
LAW & ORDER	Supporting	NBC Dave Platt, Dir.
WITNESS TO THE MOB	Supporting	NBC Thad. O'Sullivan, Dir.
LATE NITE W/CONAN O'BRIEN	Skit Player	NBC Liz Polka, Dir.
LAW & ORDER	Supporting	NBC Jim Quinn, Dir.
LAW & ORDER	Supporting	NBC Don Sardine, Dir.
LAW & ORDER	Supporting	NBC Ed Sherwin, Dir.
MTV's CRASH PARTY	Host	MTV Pilot, Lou Martini, Dir.

THEATRE

GANGSTER APPAREL	Joey	Penguin Rep. Theatre
REVENGE IN THE MOB	Joey	La Familiar Prods.
TONY N' TINA'S WEDDING	Dominick	Artificial Intelligence
LEFT-OVERS	Alfa	Producers Club
VOODOO IT	Sam	Theatre Studios
THE HEIST	Sal	Expanded Arts
SOMEWHERE IN THE CLOUDS	Jake	Coast Playhouse, LA
BIG AL	Leo	American Renegade Thru. LA
THE WATCH	Stan	The Actor's Gym, LA
ON THE WATERFRONT	Skins/Glover	Renegade Theatre Co., NJ

TRAINING

Acting:	The Actors Institute	Twill Thompson
	Julie Batas	
	HB Studios	Dorothy Doff, Richard Maw
	The Actor's Gym	Robert Moresque
On Camera	Waist Barron	Vivian Taylor
Education:	BA Radio/TV, University of Houston	

SKILLS

Stand-up Comedy, Sports Broadcast, All Major Sports, King of all Karaoke

Lou Martini, Jr. Contact:

About Artists
Phone: 212-581-1857

Abrams Artists:
Phone: 646-486-4600

Jossara Jinaro

Favorite Quote:

"It's ok to have butterflies in your stomach, just get them to fly in formation."

Jossara Jinaro

Profile

Jossara was born in Rio de Janeiro, Brazil, and raised in Columbia. At 8 years of age she decided to become an actress after starring in a school play. "I fell in love with acting for the first time; I knew it would be my life." she says.

Jossara is now an accomplished singer, dancer and actress who has appeared on stage, screen and television. She was in "Fly Boys" and appeared in "Collateral Damage" with Arnold Schwarzenegger and has guest starred in Lifetime Network's "Strong Medicine." She portrayed Virginia Bustos in the Columbia/TriStar/Telemundo sitcom "Viva Vegas."

Jossara has performed at numerous theatres, including the American Conservatory theatre in San Francisco, Chicago's Teatro Vista, The Kennedy Center, The Doolittle Theatre, LATC, and at the International Theatre Festival of Los Angeles with Teatro Sinergia. She has been featured in numerous commercials and voice-overs. A member of the Screen Actors Guild she served on the EEOC and Latino Subcommittee. She also chaired the committee responsible for the first SAG study "Missing in Action, Latinos in and out of Hollywood" in conjunction with the Thomas Rivera Institute. Although a performer, her talents are not limited to show business. She was also the Executive Administrator for the Hispanas Organized for Political Equality (HOPE) and has worked with other non-profits such as the Children's Institute, Upward Bound, and SSG (Special Service for Groups). Jossara has a Bachelor of Fine Arts, with a major in Musical Theatre Performance.

Jossara Jinaro

Resume

SAG/AFTRA/AEA

FILM

FLY BOYS	Supporting		Dir: Rocco Devilliers
COLLATERAL DAMAGE	Supporting	Warner Brothers	Dir: Andrew Davis
GHETTO RHAPSODY	Lead	DCS World Ent.	Dir: Daryll Simien
NO SALIDA	Supporting	Claymore Productions	Dir: Bill Birell
THE TAKE	Lead	Sunset Productions	Dir: Jason Weisner

TELEVISION

STRONG MEDICINE	Guest Star	Lifetime/Columbia TriStar TV
VIVA VEGAS	Series Regular	Columbia TriStar TV/Sony Pictures Ent.
REYES Y REY	Guest Star	Columbia TriStar TV/Sony Pictures Ent.
PLACAS	Guest Star	Telemundo/Sony Pictures Entertainment
MEJOR AMIGOS	Guest Star	Telemundo/Sony Pictures Entertainment
TALES-EAST SIDE	Series Regular	Digital Entertainment Network

THEATRE

Ventura Court Theatre	BLOOD WEDDING	Leonardo's Wife
Brown Hat Productions	VETERANOS	Antonia/Mexico/Victoria
Kennedy Center	PAQUITO'S CHRISTMAS	Mother
Grupo de Teatro Sinergia	TRILOQUIA	Elisa/Nadia
Grupo de Teatro Sinergia	FRIDA KAHLO	Cristina/Paula
Ivy Theatre Company	SHAME ON THE MOON	Junior
ACT/San Francisco	DIRT	Michelle
ACT/San Francisco	DARK RAPTURE	Renee
Bilingual Foundation	FOOL FOR KOOL	Bianca
Teatro Vista-Chicago	SANTOS Y SANTOS	Vicky
Columbia Mainstage	CHICAGO	Velma Kelly
Columbia Mainstage	LADY FROM MAXIM'S	The Shrimp
York Arena	RAFT OF THE MEDUSA	Felicia
Shaw Mainstage	DREAMGIRLS	Michele
York Arena	THE TRIP	Victoria
Shaw Mainstage	JOE TURNER'S	Mattie Campbell
York Arena	ROMEO AND JULIET	Juliet
Kalamazoo Civic	HOUSE OF BLUE LEAVES	Little Nun

TRAINING AND EDUCATION

B.F.A. Musical Theatre Performance, Columbia College, IL
Theatre: Henry Godinez, Sheldon Patinkin, Estelle Spector
Voice: Brad Nitschke
Dance: Blair Bybee, Joel Hall
Western Michigan University-Von Washington
Gordon Hunt Studio
Richard Seyd Studio

SPECIAL SKILLS
Fully Bilingual (Spanish), Conversational French, Singing (Mezzo)
Dance: Jazz, Tap, Ballet, Hip Hop, Ballroom (Salsa, Merengue, Cha Cha, Cumbia, Vallenato),
Choreography, clarinet (7 years), Horseback Riding (Western, English, Paso Fino)

Jossara Jinaro Contact:

Henderson/Hogan/McCabe
Phone: 310-274-7815

Noah Watts

Noah Watts

Profile

When Noah Watts was 9 years old, his uncle gave him a Crow name. I am going to name you, Bulaagawish, Old Bull. His uncle put his hand on Noah's shoulder and continued, "That's the name Chief Plenty Coups gave your grandfather. The name refers to the buffalo bull that leads the herd. That name has good things associated with it."

A member of the Crow tribe and descendent of the Blackfeet Nation, Noah Watts grew up in Bozeman, Montana. Each summer Noah goes home to the Crow Reservation to camp at Crow Fair with his extended family.

Excelling in baseball, basketball, golf, tennis, and skateboarding as a boy, Noah also learned to ride horses, fly fish, and snowboard living in the Rockies. As part of his connection to his Native culture, Noah has been a traditional Crow war dancer since he was six years old, occasionally competing in contests, but more often dancing for pleasure at Pow Wows.

Noah has been acting on stage since fifth grade when he played the scarecrow in a school production of "Oz." In high school Noah began developing and refining his acting skills in a variety of roles that culminated in the part of 'John Proctor' in "The Crucible." Noah also worked on his acting craft in the forum of high school speech and debate contests, putting the capstone on his high school acting career by representing Montana at the National Forensic League National Tournament. His performance of the dramatic monologue "Gas" by Jose Rivera in front of 1,500 people earned him fourth place in the national tournament.

While high school dramatics was a catalyst for Noah's acting career, as a senior Noah acted in two independent feature films. First, Noah was cast in "The Slaughter Rule," playing 'Waylon Walks Along,' a teenage Blackfeet youth, who is captain of a reservation high school football team. For Noah, one major challenge of the part was to speak the majority of his lines in the Blackfeet language. Just a few months later he landed a second role as 'Herbie Yellow Lodge' in the feature film "Skins" directed by Chris Eyre. Portraying the son of an alcoholic father (Graham Greene), Noah had the third lead part and shared scenes with Indian actors Greene and Eric Schweig. It was then Noah began to dream of a career in film.

Noah graduated from high school and won a scholarship to the American Academy of Dramatic Arts in Los Angeles. After one semester at AADA, Noah was offered a part in a Chris Eyre film entitled "Skin Walkers," playing a teenage gang leader and suspected murderer, a role far different from the shy, devoted son he played in "Skins." This character provided Noah an opportunity to showcase his ability to play very different roles.

The following summer in Santa Fe and Albuquerque he performed the lead in the Southwest Repertory Company's production of the play "The Indolent Boys" written by N. Scott Momaday. Noah's character is a young Native man in a boarding school in the 1800's who is being trained to be a Christian missionary. The character struggles with an internal conflict between his Native culture and the Christian religion inculcated through the boarding school system.

When Crows bestow a name, they also bestow a wish, a prayer for the name's recipient. Noah's uncle wished for Noah to lead a life of distinction that would be a credit to the Crow people. At age 20, Noah has a name to live up to and a destiny to follow. His projects include lead in a short film, "The North Star," and an appearance on Literary Stages on KCRW in Los Angeles, reading a piece by W. P. Kinsella. Noah is currently living in Los Angeles and working towards fulfilling his dream.

Noah Watts

Resume

SAG

FEATURE FILM

NORTH STAR	DANNY/LEAD	MARCOS EFRON
SKIN WALKERS	RUBEN MAZE	CHRIS EYRE
SKINS	3RD LEAD, HERBIE	CHRIS EYRE
THE SLAUGHTER RULE	WAYLON WALKS ALONG	ALEX & ANDREW SMITH

THEATRE

THE INDOLENT BOYS	LEAD/JOHN PAI	SOUTHWEST REPERTORY THEATRE
THE DINING ROOM	JIM, GRANDFATHER, ARTHUR	HAWKS THEATRE COMPANY
THE CRUCIBLE	JOHN PROCTOR	DAVID GAY
THE GOOD DOCTOR	PATIENT BOMBELLE	DAVID GAY
RING AROUND THE MOON	ROMINVILLE	DAVID GAY
ACTORS NIGHTMARE	GEORGE SPELVIN	HAWKS THEATRE COMP.

COMMERCIAL

MTV 2GETHER BOY BAND	RECORD STORE MANAGER	PARTIZAN PRODUCTIONS
MTN CONNECTIONS	TEEN INTERNET USER	RIGHT ANGLE PRODUCTIONS

EDUCATION

ATTENDED THE LOS ANGELES AMERICAN ACADEMY OF DRAMATIC ART,
          (RECEIVED A SCHOLARSHIP)
THEATRE PRODUCTION, SPEECH I & II, SPEECH AND DEBATE I & II

ACHIEVEMENTS

NATIONAL FORENSIC LEAGUE NATIONAL TOURNAMENT

JUNE 2001-4TH PLACE	IN SOLO DRAMATIC INTERPRETATION, OKLAHOMA CITY, OK
JUNE 2000-13TH PLACE	IN DUO DRAMATIC INTERPRETATION, PORTLAND, OR

SKILLS

ACTING, SPEECH AND DEBATE, MODELING, DANCING, GOLF, TENNIS, SKATEBOARDING, HORSEBACK, SNOWBOARD, SWIMMING, BASKETBALL, BASEBALL, FOOTBALL, NATIVE AMERICAN TRADITIONAL DANCING, GUITAR

Noah Watts Contact:

N.A.S.S. Talent Management
P.O. Box 3900
Bozeman, MT 59772
Phone: 406-586-7045
http://www.noahwatts.com/

April Weeden-Washington

April Weeden-Washington

Profile

Taking the stunt world by storm, April Weeden-Washington has built a resume of unparalleled accomplishments. As one of Hollywood's leading stunt women, she has doubled for numerous high-profile celebrities including Halle Berry, Jennifer Lopez and Vanessa L. Williams, to name a few. Whether it's jumping through a plate-glass window into a swimming pool, or driving through a mustard field at high speeds with a helicopter hovering overhead, there is no question that this young lady's job falls into the category of unusual occupations.

A native of Washington, D.C., April has a long list of film and television credits. Her films include "Minority Report," "Swordfish," "Rat Race," "Blade," "Lethal Weapon 4," "I Still Know What You Did Last Summer," "Anaconda," and "Eraser." Her TV work includes "Strong Medicine," "Buffy the Vampire Slayer," "JAG," "Nash Bridges," "Melrose Place," and "Beverly Hills 90210."

April recently gave birth to a beautiful daughter named Kiera. During her pregnancy, she ballooned up to 200 pounds. Determined to get back in shape and back to work, April developed a strict diet and structured her workout schedule to reach her goals quickly. Every morning she would attend Tae Bo classes, followed by walking, swimming or riding her horse Freckles. Within weeks she lost 79 pounds and shortly thereafter she was back to work. She was completing stunts in four national network commercials, behind-the-scenes footage for the DVD to "The Scorpion King," and appeared in four feature films: "Looney Tunes," "Bruce Almighty," "Biker Boyz," and a western, "Guns And Roses." And on top of all of that, this new mother also competed and won first place in the National Barrel Horse Association's 4D Division competition in barrel racing!

April has been a source of inspiration for new mothers whose weight issues have caused them emotional distress. She plans to release a workout video to share the exercise techniques that have been vital to her successful weight loss.

As a veteran stunt professional, April has mentored many women who want to enter this thrilling occupation. In fact, she is the subject of a new documentary, "Hollywood At Its Best," which profiles a handful of successful stuntwomen in the entertainment industry.

April is married to award-winning stunt coordinator/second unit director William Washington. A talented couple in their own right, they often collaborate on projects together. They reside with their daughter on a tranquil horse ranch northeast of Los Angeles.

April Weeden-Washington Contact:

Lisa Sorensen Public Relations
12522 Moorpark St.
Studio City, CA 91604
Phone: 818-761-0430

Penn Badgley

Penn Badgley

Profile

At 18, actor Penn Badgley is seemingly destined for a distinguished acting career. Rather ironic then, that in his first starring role, Badgley's character has the unique experience to travel back in time in order to alter the outcome of his destiny. As the lead of the acclaimed Warren Littlefield-produced, WB comedy series "Do Over," Badgley portrayed a 34-year-old salesman who, through a freak accident, had the opportunity to return to the early '80s to re-live his freshman year in high school and change the outcome of his thus far unsatisfying life.

Though life began for Badgley in Baltimore, he split his formative years between Richmond, VA and Seattle, WA. It was there that he became actively involved in the Seattle Children's Theatre and voice-over work that eventually led he and his mother to Los Angeles where he had secured an agent.

Upon relocating, he landed a coveted guest star role on "Will & Grace." Shortly thereafter, recurring roles on "The Young & The Restless, The Brothers Garcia" and "Daddio" followed. He most recently filmed a guest spot on WB's "What I Like About You" as well as "The Twilight Zone." Film work includes "Debating Robert Lee," and the provocative yet acclaimed indie "The Fluffer."

When not honing his acting craft, Badgley attends Santa Monica Community College, having already completed his California High School Proficiency Exam. In his spare time, he enjoys surfing, soccer, skiing, snowboarding, singing, and playing the guitar.

Penn at the premiere of *Grind*

Penn Badgley Contact:

Pinnacle
8265 Sunset Blvd., Suite 201
Los Angeles, CA 90046
Phone: 323-654-6600

Veronica Puleo

Favorite Quote:

"Get into situations in which failure isn't an option. If you love something, you'll bring so much of yourself to it that it will create your future."
Frances Ford Coppola

Veronica Puleo

Profile

When she was just three years old, her mother placed Veronica Puleo in a dance class. It's possible that Antonia Calabro somehow saw the glimmer of talent in her young daughter's eyes. Perhaps she felt that Veronica's irrepressible energy needed a creative outlet. Or maybe she just wanted to get her out of the house for a few hours of peace and quiet. Whatever the reason, ever since her first dance recital, Veronica Puleo has known that the stage is her home.

Dance led naturally to drama, and she worked in theatre all through high school, and in college...where she won a "best actress" award for her debut performance. After graduation from William Paterson College with a degree in Communication and a minor in Theatre, she moved to Florida to be a big fish in a small pond.

In Miami, Veronica worked in regional and community theatre and landed some great roles. High among her favorites was the title character in A.R. Gurney's "Sylvia" – a talking dog. She was also a member of Laughing Gas, South Florida's longest-running comedy improv. In addition to theatre work, Veronica was also a Host/VJ for Barry Diller's WAMI TV.

During her last weeks in Miami, one of Ms. Puleo's lifetime dreams came true when she met and read with her favorite actor and fellow Sicilian, Al Pacino. Finally ready for a bigger pond, Veronica Puleo now resides in Los Angeles, California...where she's studying, auditioning, and working hard everyday to make the rest of her dreams come true...

Veronica Puleo

Resume

SAG/AFTRA

TELEVISION

ACCORDING TO JIM	Guest Star/Gabriella	Andy Cadiff, ABC Television
MIAMI SANDS	Recurring/Julietta	André Zinca, Dolphin Productions
WAMI TV, MIAMI USA BROAD.	Network Host	Bruce E. Nadeau, USA Broad.
10's	Guest Appearance	John Axelson, USA Broad.
OUT LOUD	Guest Appearance	Bill Teck, USA Broad.
KENNETH'S FREQUENCY	Guest Appearance	C. Valenziano/P. Doody, USA Broad.
THE TIMES	Guest Appearance	Amy Atkins/Chris Sloan, USA Broad.

FILM/VIDEO/INDUSTRIAL

ANY GIVEN SUNDAY	Featured	Oliver Stone/Warner Bros.
ESCAPING EDEN	Lead/Paige	Bruce E. Nadeau
THE STAND-IN	Madonna Stand-in/Mngr.	Joshua Mellville
FOR A FRIEND	Call Girl	G. Bruno
COUNTRY LIVING	Isabelle	Gary Schwertzler
BIRTHDAY PARTY	Wife	Venture Productions
REPORT FROM COSTA RICA	Café Rey Spokesperson	John Rhodes-CNBC
MOB VIOLENCE IN FILM	Host	Gerardo Bruno

COMMERCIALS   List Upon Request

THEATRE

GENERATOR GIRL	Effi-Jet	American Renegade Theatre, CA
LIQUID RADIO PLAYERS	Dancer	Acme Theatre, CA
TENANTS FROM HELL	Star	Playhouse of the Foothills, CA
JOEY & MARIA'S WEDDING	Viola	Dillstar Productions, CA
HOLLYWOOD CELEBRITY WEDDING	Volcana	Dillstar Productions, CA
LAUGHING GAS IMPROV COMPANY	Improv Ensemble	The New Theatre, Miami, FL
MADE IN HEAVEN	Ellen	Broward Stage Door, Coral Springs, FL
SNOW ORCHID	Filumena	Acorn Civic Theatre, South Beach, FL
SYLVIA	Sylvia	The Edge Theatre, South Beach, FL
SOUTH BEACH	Visitor/Eve	The Edge Theatre, South Beach, FL
IS THERE A DR. IN THE HOUSE?	Mona Payne	Off Broadway Theatre, Ft. Lauderdale, FL

TOTAL ECLIPSE	Matilde	Brundage Park Playhouse, Randolph, NJ
THE SKIN OF OUR TEETH	Sabina	Brundage Park Playhouse, Randolph, NJ
HELLO FROM BERTHA	Bertha	Hunziker Theatre, Wayne, NJ
FLORENCE	Mrs. Carter	William Paterson Theatre
ARSENIC AND OLD LACE	Dr. Einstein	Hunziker Theatre

TRAINING/SPECIAL SKILLS

Cold Reading	Margie Haber
Improv	Groundlings-Karen Moruyama & David Jahn, Laughing Gas-Gerald Owens
Acting for TV	Bob Collier
Advanced Scene Study	Elizabeth Ploth
Voice (Mezzo Soprano)	Marco Schindelmann, David Coury, Fred Silver
Dance	Alfred Freidman (Swing/Lindy, Salsa/Mambo, Argentine Tango) Phil Black (NYC-Jazz), Hannah Baumgarten (Modern)
Dialects/Accents	Italian, New York, Jewish
Languages	Italian, Sicilian and basic Spanish

B.A. in Communication and Theatre: William Paterson University, Wayne, NJ
Communication concentration: TV and Film

Veronica Puleo Contact:

Circle Talent Associates
433 No. Camden Dr., Suite 400
Beverly Hills, CA 90210
Phone: 310-285-1585

Cynthia Nixon

Cynthia Nixon

Profile

Cynthia Nixon played Miranda Hobbes on HBO's celebrated series, "Sex and the City," a role that garnered her a 2002 Emmy nomination. The cast was honored with the 2001 SAG Award for Outstanding Performance by an Ensemble in a Comedy Series, for which Cynthia gave the acceptance speech on behalf of the four women. In addition, Cynthia received her second consecutive Golden Globe nomination for her role in the show. Nixon was also seen onstage in her acclaimed performance as Mary Haines in the Roundabout's revival of "The Women," which has been broadcast on PBS' "Stage to Screen" series.

Cynthia was honored with a Tony nomination for her role in the Broadway hit "Indiscretions" as Madeleine, the vivacious bohemian Parisian bookbinder who is simultaneously having affairs with a quirky inventor played by Roger Rees, and his rambunctious son played by Jude Law.

Cynthia also appeared in Eve Ensler's "The Vagina Monologues" at both the Westside Arts Theatre and in the historic V-Day Performance at Madison Square Garden.

For her performance onstage as Soos in Douglas Carter Beane's "The Country Club," Cynthia received rave notices, including one from John Heilpern of the New York Observer who declared her performance one of the two Best Comic Stage Performances by an Actress in 1999.

Nixon won a Theatre World Award at fourteen for her stage debut as Dinah Lord in Ellis Rabb's production of "The Philadelphia Story," with Blythe Danner, at Lincoln Center's Vivian Beaumont Theatre. At fifteen, she was directed by acclaimed filmmaker Louis Malle in the title role of John Guare's "Lydie Breeze." Most remarkably, at age eighteen, she appeared simultaneously in two Broadway productions, David Rabe's "Hurlyburly" and Tom Stoppard's "The Real Thing," both directed by Mike Nichols, while a freshman in her first semester at Barnard College.

She acted throughout her college career, and a few months before graduation did double-duty again by starring as Juliet in the New York Shakespeare Festival Production of "Romeo and Juliet" and as Alex Tanner in HBO's "Tanner '88," Robert Altman and Gary Trudeau's political spoof of the 1988 Presidential campaign. Cynthia next appeared on Broadway in Wendy Wasserstein's "The Heidi Chronicles." Other Broadway roles include: Harper Pitt, a young Mormon wife struggling with her husband's homosexuality in Tony Kushner's "Angels in America" (1994) and Lala Levy, a socially inept girl with Scarlett O'Hara-esque aspirations in Alfred Uhry's "The Last Night of Ballyhoo," (1997).

Classic stage roles include: Honey in "Who's Afraid of Virginia Woolf?" directed by playwright Edward Albee and co-starring Glenda Jackson and John Lithgow (which earned her a Best Featured Actress Award nomination from the Los Angeles Drama Critics and a Robby Award nomination), Emily in "Our Town" (for which she received a Robby Award nomination), Hilde in Henrik Ibson's "The Master Builder" (opposite Sam Waterston), Raina in "Arms and the Man," Melibea in Tony Kushner's adaptation of Pierre Corneilles' "The Illusion," Hester Prynne in Phyllis Nagy's adaptation of "The Scarlet Letter" and Nora in Ibsen's "A Doll House."

As one of the founding members of the theatre company, The Drama Dept., (along with J. Smith-Cameron, Nicky Silver, John Cameron Mitchel, Sarah Jessica Parker and Douglas Carter Beane), Cynthia has appeared in their productions of Beane's "The Country Club," Ring Lardner and George S. Kaufman's "June Moon," Tennessee Williams' "Kingdom of Earth," Frank Puliese's "Hope is the Thing With Feathers" and Beane's "As Bees in Honey Drown."

Cynthia's other New York stage appearances of note include: "On the Bum or, the Next Train Through" with Campbell Scott at Playwrights Horizons, "Servy-N-Bernice 4Ever" at the Provincetown Playhouse, "The Balcony Scene" at the Circle Repertory Company, "A Joke" opposite Ethan Hawke for the Malaparte Theatre Group, and "Lemon Sky" and "Moonchildren" at the Second Stage.

Nixon began her film career at age twelve with Ronald F. Maxwell's "Little Darlings" (as Sunshine, the flower child) and went on to appear in Sidney Lumet's "Prince of the City" (as a strung-out drug addict), Milos Forman's "Amadeus" (as Lorel, Mozart's maid), Robert Altman's "O.C. & Stiggs," Marshal Brickman's "The Manhattan Project," "Let it Ride," "Addams Family

Values," "The Pelican Brief," John Hughes' "Baby's Day out," "Marvin's Room," "The Out-of-Towners," "Igby Goes Down" and "Advice from a Caterpillar," based on the play by the Drama Dept.'s Douglas Carter Beane.

Cynthia's very first professional job was an ABC After School Special, "Seven Wishes of a Rich Kid," co-starring Butterfly McQueen. Cynthia went on to appear in PBS's presentation of Mark Twain's "Private History of a Campaign that Failed," Lanford Wilson's "Fifth of July" and "Women and Wallace" (the last two for American Playhouse).

She has most recently appeared on network television in the CBS telefilm "Papa's Angels." She has also starred opposite Gena Rowlands in "Face of a Stranger," Angela Lansbury in "The Love She Sought," and when they were thirteen and fourteen, Cynthia and Sarah Jessica Parker played Vanessa Redgrave's young daughters in "My Body, My Child," about a woman's right to choose.

Other favorite television roles include: a deaf crime victim in "The Equalizer," a subway vigilante in "Law and Order," a nose-ringed valley girl in "Nash Bridges," a poor Southern factory worker in "The Murder of Mary Phagan," and a woman giving birth in an elevator in "Early Edition," filmed in the eighth month of Cynthia's real-life pregnancy.

Born and raised in New York City, Cynthia attended Hunter College High School and has a degree in English Literature from Barnard College. She has been acting professionally since the age of 12, in television, theatre and film. She lives in New York City with her partner Daniel Mozes, their five year-old daughter, Samantha and son Charles.

2004 Emmy Award-winner for Best Supporting Actress in a Comedy Series

Cynthia Nixon

Resume

FILM

IGBY GOES DOWN	Dir. Burr Steers
ADVICE FROM A CATERPILLAR	Dir. Don Scardino
THE M-WORD	Dir. Brett Parker
MARVIN'S ROOM	Dir. Jerry Zaks
BABY'S DAY OUT	Dir. Patrick Johnson
THE PELICAN BRIEF	Dir. Alan Pacula
LET IT RIDE	Dir. Joe Pytka
THE MANHATTAN PROJECT	Dir. Marshall Brickman
AMADEUS	Dir. Milos Forman
O.C. AND STIGGS	Dir. Robert Altman
PRINCE OF THE CITY	Dir. Sidney Lumet
LITTLE DARLINGS	

TELEVISION

THE WOMEN	PBS – Great Performances
PAPA'S ANGEL	CBS (MOW)
SEX AND THE CITY (Series regular) + **	HBO
KISS, KISS, DARLINGS by Wendy Wasserstein	PBS
FACE OF A STRANGER	Dir. Claudia Weill (MOW)
THE LOVE SHE SOUGHT with Angela Lansbury	Dir. Joseph Sargent (MOW)
LAW & ORDER (Guest Lead)	NBC
WOMEN AND WALLACE	Dir. Don Scardino, PBS (MOW)
TANNER '88 by Gary Trudeau	Dir. Robert Altman HBO, (MOW)
THE MURDER OF MARY PHAGAN with Jack Lemmon	Dir. William Hale (MOW)
THE FIFTH OF JULY	Dir. Kirk Browning, Marshall Mason, PBS

THEATRE

THE WOMEN	Dir. Scott Elliot/Roundabout Theatre
THE VAGINA MONOLOGUES	Dir. Joe Mantello/The Westside Theatre
THE COUNTRY CLUB	Dir. Christopher Ashley/Drama Department
HOPE IS A THING WITH FEATHERS	Dir. Randolph Curtis/Drama Department
LAST NIGHT OF BALLYHOO	Dir. Ron Logamarsino/Helen Hayes Theatre
JUNE MOON	Variety Arts Theatre
AS BEES IN HONEY DROWN	Dir. Douglas Carter Beane, Lucille Lortel
INDISCRETIONS*	Dir. Sean Mathias/Ethel Barrymore Theatre
ANGELS IN AMERICA	Dir. George Wolfe/Walter Kerr Theatre
SERVY-N-BERNICE 4EVER	Dir. Terry Kinney/Provincetown Playhouse
MASTER BUILDER	Dir. Mark Lamos/Hartford Stage
OUR TOWN	Old Globe Theatre, San Diego

WHO'S AFRAID OF VIRGINIA WOOLF?	Dir. Edward Albee/Mark Taper Forum
THE HEIDI CHRONICLES	Dir. Daniel Sullivan/Broadway
ROMEO & JULIET	New York Shakespeare Festival
LEMON SKY	Second Stage
HURLYBURLY	Dir. Mike Nichols/Broadway
THE REAL THING	Dir. Mike Nichols/Broadway
LYDIE BREEZE	Dir. Louis Malle
PHILADELPHIA STORY	Dir. Ellis Rabb/Beaumont Theatre

+Emmy Award Winner 2004
+Golden Globe Award Nominations 1999, 2000, 2003
*Tony Award Nomination
**Emmy Award Nomination 2002
Nominated L.A. Drama Critics Award 1989 for Best Featured Actor
Theatre World Award, 1981

Cynthia Nixon Contact:

William Morris Agency
1325 Avenue of the Americas
New York, NY 10019
Phone: 212-586-5100

Paula Jai Parker

Paula Jai Parker

Profile

Paula Jai Parker is quickly establishing herself as one of Hollywood's busiest starlets. She co-starred in "Phone Booth" with Colin Farrell. She had her first starring role in a feature film opposite Eddie Griffin in Miramax's "My Baby's Mama" and she co-starred in "High Crimes" alongside Ashley Judd and Morgan Freeman. In addition she landed a singing role in the Jamie Foxx movie "Unchain My Heart."

If that's not enough, Parker continues her portrayal as 'Trudy Proud,' the hilarious and insightful wife/mom/pet-doctor in the incredibly smart cartoon, "The Proud Family," the Disney Channel's highest rated program to date. Also, she will take to the stage in her very own, one-woman show, "Confessions of a Ghetto Superstar," a play that she both wrote and will produce, about the benefits, struggles and even the romance of being a young black woman trying to make it in Hollywood.

Parker has been making a name for herself on both the silver and small screens since she arrived in Los Angeles seven years ago. She practically invented the term, "hoochie mama" with her role in F. Gary Gray's ghetto-classic, "Friday," bringing the urban woman to life for the first time ever. Additionally, she has been featured in such films as "Tales From the Hood," Spike Lee's "Get on the Bus," and the Frankie Lymon biopic, "Why Do Fools Fall In Love?."

Parker's television credits include regular roles on David Kelly's detective series "Snoops," "The Apollo Comedy Hour," and Robert Townsend's variety show, "Townsend Television." Perhaps most impressively, Parker received a CableACE award as Best Actress in a Dramatic Special for her role in Tang, an installment of the 1994 HBO anthology special, Cosmic Slop. In addition Parker made her first professional theatre appearance as "Adriana" in William Shakespeare's "A Comedy Of Errors" at the first ever Los Angeles Shakespeare Festival.

The dynamic Parker was born and raised in a suburb of Cleveland, Ohio. She caught the performance bug at the early age of three, at which point her mother quickly eased into the role of "stage-mom" and enlisted the young Paula in the Little Miss Cleveland Pageant. Soon after her stint as a child beauty queen, she joined Cleveland's most successful children's group, "The Singing Angels." The international touring troupe competed throughout Europe and the United States, and gave Parker the opportunity to learn about both the world, and performing. She was a member of the group from the age of six, until she was sixteen. After high school, she went on to Howard University to fulfill a childhood promise she made to her mother: to get a degree. Parker trained on the stage and received a degree in Acting. She made the expected move to New York City after college, where she joined the Apollo Theatre, and was discovered by Robert Townsend, and the rest is history!

When Parker is not busy with her successful acting career or watching late-night movie classics on TV, she spends her time volunteering at schools, senior centers, and her Baptist church. She is dedicated to giving back to the community, and even plans to open her own acting school someday. Additionally, Parker recently taught a guest lecture series at Howard University about "How to get a job in Hollywood."

Parker currently resides in Los Angeles.

Paula Jai Parker Contact:

Karen Gold
Bragman/Nyman/Cafarelli
9171 Wilshire Blvd., Suite 300
Beverly Hills, CA 90210
Phone: 310-274-7800

435

Fisher Stevens

Fisher Stevens

Profile

As an actor, producer and director, Fisher Stevens is known for wearing many hats.

He made his Broadway debut at the age of 18, in the Tony Award-winning play "Torch Song Trilogy." On stage, he went on to perform in Nicholas Hytner's revival of "Carousel," Neil Simon's "Brighton Beach Memoirs," Terence McNally's "A Perfect Ganesh," Shakespeare's "Twelfth Night" and "A Midsummer Night's Dream" at the New York Shakespeare Festival.

As an actor, Stevens made his motion picture debut at the age of sixteen in the horror film "The Burning." But it was "The Flamingo Kid" in 1984 that established Stevens as a serious young actor. Since then, Stevens has gone on to star in such films as "My Science Project," "Reversal of Fortune," "Short Circuit," "Hackers," "Only You," "Undisputed," and many others. TV credits include two years as a series regular on CBS' "Early Edition," (1996-2000) for which he also directed numerous episodes, FOX's, "Key West," and guest roles on "Friends," "Frasier," and "Columbo."

On the production front, Stevens co-founded the New York-based theatre company "Naked Angels" in 1986, which is still going strong after over eighteen years. Members include Matthew Broderick, Marisa Tomei, Rob Morrow, Kenneth Lonnergan, and Gina Gershon. Stevens has produced and directed a number of "Naked Angels" productions including "Here Lies," and one of eight one-act plays entitled "Fear: An Issues Project" starring Dominic Chianese ("The Sopranos") at the Greenwich Street Theatre. He also starred in the critically acclaimed production of "Shyster" by Bryan Goluboff with Annabella Sciorra and Phyllis Newman.

In 1995, Stevens made his short film directing debut with "Call of the Wylie," starring Amy Irving and Patrick Breen which he produced with John Penotti. The film premiered in competition at the Sundance Film Festival in 1995. It was after this successful collaboration that he and Penotti formed GreeneStreet Films in 1996. Under GreeneStreet's banner, Stevens has executive produced several films including the five-time Oscar-nominated "In the Bedroom," (released by Miramax) directed by Todd Field, starring Sissy Spacek, Marisa Tomei, and Tom Wilkinson. He also produced the three-time ALMA award winning "Piñero" (released by Miramax) by writer/director Leon Ichaso. This critically acclaimed film based on the life of poet/playwright Miguel Piñero ("Short Eyes"), starred Benjamin Bratt in the title role, Talisa Soto, Rita Moreno and Mandy Patinkin.

In addition, Stevens served as executive producer on the critically acclaimed comedies "The Chateau," (released by IFC Films) starring Paul Rudd ("The Cider House Rules," "Clueless") and directed by Jesse Peretz and "Lisa Picard is Famous," (released by First Look) directed by Griffin Dunne and produced by Mira Sorvino and Dolly Hall. The mockumentary was an official selection of the 2000 Cannes International Film Festival.

"Just A Kiss" marked Stevens directorial debut. Paramount Classics released this romantic comedy starring Taye Diggs, Ron Eldard, Kyra Sedgwick, Marley Shelton and Marisa Tomei in September of 2002.

Fisher Stevens also produced the hit romantic comedy, "Uptown Girls," starring Brittany Murphy ("Don't Say a Word," "8 Mile") and Dakota Fanning ("I am Sam"), directed by Boaz Yakin ("Fresh," "Remember the Titans").

Stevens was kept busy in 2004 as Producer and Executive Producer of "Slow Burn," a sexy thriller starring Ray Liotta, LL Cool J, Mekhi Phifer and Taye Diggs, as well as Executive Producer of "Yes" featuring three-time Oscar nominee, Joan Allen and Sam Neill.

Fisher Stevens

Resume

FILM

ANYTHING ELSE	Dir: Woody Allen	DreamWorks
UNDISPUTED	Dir: Walter Hill	Miramax
PINERO	Dir: Leon Ichaso	Miramax
SAM THE MAN	Dir: Gary Winick	Independent
THE TAXMAN	Dir: Avi Nesher	Phaedra Cinema
THE TIC CODE	Dir: Gary Winick	Avalanche Ent.
KILL THE POOR	Dir: Alan Taylor	
PRISON SONG	Dir: Darnell Martin	New Line
HACKERS	Dir: Ian Softley	MGM/UA
ONLY YOU	Dir: Norman Jewison	TriStar
COLD FEVER	Dir: Fridrik Thor-Fridriksson	Artistic License
NINA TAKES A LOVER	Dir: Alan Jacobs	Triumph
SUPER MARIO BROS.	Dirs: R. Morton & A. Jankel	Buena Vista
LIFT	Dir: Salome Breziner	
WHEN THE PARTY'S OVER	Dir: Mathew Irmas	Independent
BOB ROBERTS	Dir: Tim Robbins	Paramount
MYSTERY DATE	Dir: Jonathan Wachs	Orion
THE MARRYING MAN	Dir: Jerry Rees	Buena Vista
REVERSAL OF FORTUNE	Dir: Barbet Schroder	Warner Bros.
SHORT CIRCUIT 2	Dir: Kenneth Johnson	TriStar
BLOODHOUNDS OF BROADWAY	Dir: Howard Brookner	Columbia
SHORT CIRCUIT	Dir: John Badham	TriStar
MY SCIENCE PROJECT	Dir: Jonathan Betuel	Buena Vista
THE FLAMINGO KID	Dir: Garry Marshall	20th Century Fox
BROTHER FROM ANOTHER PLANET	Dir: John Sayles	IFC Films

TELEVISION
Series

100 CENTRE STREET	Guest Star	A&E
FRASIER	Guest Star	NBC
EARLY EDITION	Series Regular	CBS
MOTHER COUNTRY		CBS/Pilot
KEY WEST	Series Lead	FOX
FRIENDS	Guest Star	NBC

MOWs

JENIFER	Dir: Jace Alexander	CBS
3AM	Dir: Lee Davis	Showtime
THE RIGHT TO REMAIN SILENT	Dir: Hubert C. de la Bouillerie	Showtime
COLUMBO: MURDER, SMOKE & SHADOWS	Dir: James Frawley	ABC

THEATRE
Broadway

CAROUSEL	Lincoln Center
BRIGHTON BEACH MEMOIRS	Neil Simon
TORCH SONG TRILOGY	The Little Theatre

Broadway Workshop
SCANDAL   Dir: Michael Bennett

Off-Broadway
THE UNDERPANTS   Classic Stage Company
A PERFECT GANESH   Manhattan Theatre Club
TWELFTH NIGHT   NY Shakespeare Festival
HAIRY APE   Wooster Group
LITTLE MURDERS   Second Stage
A MIDSUMMER NIGHT'S DREAM   NY Shakespeare Festival
TORCH SONG TRILOGY   Actors Playhouse

CO-FOUNDER OF THE NAKED ANGELS THEATRE COMPANY

Fisher with John Penotti and Benjamin Bratt at the premiere of *Pinero*

Fisher Stevens Contact:

Innovative Artists
1505 Tenth St.
Santa Monica, CA 90401
Phone: 310-656-0400

David Paul Boehne

Favorite Quote:

"Be true to yourself."

David Paul Boehne

Profile

David Paul Boehne was born in Huntington Beach, CA. He started pursuing an acting career when he was 23 years old. He wanted to try acting when he was in high school, but chose the Surf Team instead. He has appeared in a number of commercials and is taking acting classes to pursue more serious acting roles. He is a professional surfer and loves anything creative like photography, drawing and writing music. He is a singer/guitar player in the rock band "All-Time Radio." He also loves basketball, and has 2 dogs that are a "handful!" He loves the quote "Be true to yourself," because you are not living for anyone but yourself. He says, "Listen to the thoughts in your head and the feelings in your heart. Be kind and respect others but most importantly, respect yourself and the world is yours for the taking!"

David Paul Boehne

Resume

TELEVISION

Anchor Blue Commercial	Principle Role	5th Street Studios
SpineShank Music Video	Principle Role	Palomar Pictures
Infinity Surfboards Inc. Commercial	Featured Talent	Cox Communications
Computer Hardware Commercial	Principle Role	Cox Communications
Unleashed Surf Television	Featured Talent	Cox Communications
OCN News Channel	Principle Role	Cox Communications
All-Time Radio Music Video	Featured Talent	Lipslide Productions

TRAINING

Acting/Comedy/Improv Training	Toni Attell	Future Stars Workshop
Cold Reading	Jack Turnbull	Actorsite Workshop
Acting Training	Kathy Smith	Saddleback College

HOBBIES/SKILLS

Professional Surfer, Surf-Skate-Snow Event Announcing, Snowboarding, Skateboarding, Playing Guitar/Bass guitar, Singing in my band, Basketball, Surf Competition, Writing Music, Collecting Vinyl Records, My Truck, Photography, Playing Drums, Girls, My Dog

David Paul Boehne Contact:

Abrams Artists Agency
9200 Sunset Blvd., Eleventh Floor
Los Angeles, CA 90069
Phone: 310-859-1417

Kevin A. Perry

Kevin A. Perry

Profile

Kevin Andrew Perry was born on August 8th in Cape Cod, MA. Throughout his early years, he engaged in numerous activities. He joined the Cub Scouts, took swimming lessons, sailing lessons, and even tried his hand at music. In elementary school he played the drums, trumpet and piano. As for sports, he was involved in bowling, hockey and baseball.

In 1985 while he was still in middle school, a film student who was a film major at Boston University came to his school. He doesn't recall the details of how or why the film project titled "Delete" came about, but it was the catalyst that has driven him to pursue his interest within the film industry. At the beginning of his junior year of high school he began auditioning for the local community theatres.

Since 1988 Kevin has been pursuing acting opportunities non-stop. It has been a challenging road, but of all the activities he has been involved with, the one constant in his life has been the desire to remain active within the entertainment industry.

Kevin can be seen in "22 and Living at Home," "It's Not Worth It," "Working Relationships" and "Death by Repetition" to name a few. He also has appeared in commercials and is involved in Theatre.

Kevin A. Perry

Resume

FILM/TELEVISION (partial list)

By the Sea	Massimo (featured)	Dean Barnes-Director
22 and Living at Home	Porter Williams (lead)	Ernstrom Productions
The Devil and a 9mm	Video Customer (day player)	Valiant Pictures
Dimensionless Woman	Hips Man (supporting)	OZN Media
Death by Repetition	Snitch (supporting)	Epoch Entertainment
Central Square	Jim	CCTV (Cambridge, MA)
Working Relationships	Chase (lead)	Rent-To-Own Productions
A Night Out	Chiropractor (supporting)	Effigy Films
Parting Shots	Bill (day player)	Midnight Chimes Productions
Strictly Business	The Mojo Man (day player)	Valiant Pictures
It's Not Worth It	Pete (supporting)	Group One Productions
The Art of Arson	Mr. Martin (supporting)	Women In Motion
Dirty Hari Krishna	New Cadet (day player)	Iron Fist Motion Pictures
A Voice Between Dreams	Clerk (day player)	Ruby Dog Productions

INDUSTRIALS/COMMERCIALS

Success Automation	Computer Trainee	Robert Gilmore Associates
Ramsey Carpet	Maintenance Worker	Robert Gilmore Associates

Commercial Conflicts Upon Request

THEATRE (partial list)

Play On	Billy	President Players
Dangerous Corner	Charles Stanton	Woods Hole Theatre Company
Cyrano de Bergerac	Christian	Janus Players
Working	Tim/Eric/Brett	Woods Hole Theatre Company
Antigone	Guard	Theatre On The Bay
Arsenic and Old Lace	Klein	Academy Of Performing Arts
Wonderland	Mad Hatter	Rondileau Theatre
As Is	Doctor/Pickup/Cop/ Vinnie/PWA	Janus Players

TRAINING

TV/Film:
Jason Wood-Auditioning For Primetime Television (TVI Actors Studio)
Carolyn Pickman-Audition Techniques (Collinge/Pickman Casting)
Sue Shaw-Advanced On-Camera Techniques (Collinge/Pickman Casting)
Steve Bennett-Film Acting (Film Center-Boston)
Jen Maxcy-On-Camera Techniques (Actor's Workshop/Boston)

Acting:
B.A. Theatre-Bridgewater State College
George Tuttle-Scene Study
Jim Silverman-Scene Study
Stephen Levine-Improv Acting
Suzanne Ramczyk-Movement/Dance For Actors

Acting Coach: Edna Panaggio

Voice:
Suzanne Ramczyk-Voice For The Actor
Betty Kelly

SPECIAL SKILLS Build/Repair Computers, Softball, Biking, Bowling, Rollerblade, Stick Shift Car, Baseball, Hockey, Left Handed, Some Martial Arts.

Kevin A. Perry Contact:

Website: www.kevinaperry.com

Dick Van Dyke

Dick Van Dyke

Profile

Dick Van Dyke was born in West Plains, Missouri and raised in Danville, Illinois. Brother Jerry was born five years later. His dad Loren, nicknamed "Cookie," was a traveling salesman for the Sunshine Biscuit Company, played minor league baseball on a Terre Haute team and tenor sax in a small band. He met local beauty Hazel McCord at a dance and they were married in early spring, 1925. Dick arrived the following December 13.

As a youngster Dick spent hours alone teaching himself magic and pantomime. By the time he was in high school his voice was a rich baritone, which served him well in local radio jobs and school plays. He was on the track team and was elected junior class president.

At eighteen he joined the Air Force and met Byron Paul, who recruited him for a radio show called "Flight Time." After a year in the states, he was honorably discharged and returned to Danville to work briefly for an ad agency and announce "spots" on WDAN Radio. One day in 1946 Phil Erickson, a homegrown show business professional, came looking for a new partner for his record-pantomime act, offering a solid year's bookings in Southern California. He chose Dick and they became "The Merry Mutes." While appearing in Los Angeles Dick sent for his Danville girl Marjorie Willet. They were married on "Bride and Groom," a network radio show offering great gifts and a free honeymoon.

After two years of L.A., Las Vegas, Palm Springs, San Francisco and Reno, "The Merry Mutes" moved to the south for an engagement in Atlanta, GA and other southern venues. Anxious to settle with their families, Dick and Phil decided to stay in Atlanta where they produced their own daytime television show. Sons Christian and Barry Van Dyke were born in Atlanta in 1950 and 1951, respectively. When Dick and Phil began seeing separate opportunities, they agreed to split up. Erickson opened a comedy club in Atlanta and Dick got a local TV daytime show – chatting, sketching, doing prat falls and making 'em laugh. Within months he was accepting a better offer in New Orleans where daughter Stacy was born. That year, 1955, he heard from his old Air Force friend Byron Paul, who'd become a director with CBS Television in New York. Paul arranged for Dick to fly up for an audition with the network brass, which resulted in a seven-year contract.

His first assignment was a one-year run as host of the CBS Morning Show, with Walter Cronkite reading the news and Merv Griffin supplying the music. In 1958, after trying several CBS-created formats, including kid shows, talk shows, game shows and a pilot, Dick asked for and was granted a release from CBS. He immediately went into "The Boys Against the Girls," a Broadway revue with Bert Lahr and Nancy Walker. The show closed in two weeks – after being seen by Gower Champion. The dancer-choreographer-director was seeking a funny young guy for the lead opposite Chita Rivera in "Bye Bye Birdie."

Dick auditioned, got the part, introduced the show-stopping "Put on a Happy Face," and won a 1960 Tony Award.

"Bye Bye Birdie" was in its second year when producer Sheldon Leonard and Carl Reiner brought Dick a script – and an offer – for an untitled new series about the domestic and professional adventures of a television comedy writer. Attracted to the material and anxious to find a permanent home for the family, Dick did a pilot that immediately sold. "The Dick Van Dyke Show" premiered in 1961, the year second daughter Carrie Beth arrived. In five seasons the show earned Dick three of his five Emmys.

Settled in a comfortable L.A. suburb, Dick began a non-stop work schedule, shooting the series and doing features on hiatus, one of which was the film version "Bye Bye Birdie" in 1963, followed by what is probably his most memorable role – Bert the chimney sweep opposite Julie Andrews as "Mary Poppins." Other films included "Lt. Robin Crusoe, USN" [1966], "Divorce American Style" [1967], "Chitty Chitty Bang Bang" [1968], "The Comic" [1969], "Some Kind of a Nut" [1969], "Cold Turkey" [1971] and "The Runner Stumbles" [1978].

"The Dick Van Dyke Show" left the network after five seasons while it was still on top, a decision made by Carl Reiner with Dick's blessing. It remains a world favorite in syndication.

After a year in England shooting "Chitty Chitty Bang Bang," Dick moved his family to their ranch in Carefree, Arizona, where with Carl Reiner and his original writing team he produced "The New Dick Van Dyke Show" two seasons before moving to L.A. for a third and final season. Again, it was Carl and Dick who chose to end the series after the network balked at airing a questionable episode. Dick retired to his ranch.

After a long break, he accepted the star role in "The Morning After," a dark story about a talented and successful family man whose life is destroyed by his alcoholism. With its unrelenting approach and downbeat ending, the film broke ground for television dramas and earned Dick an Emmy nomination.

Then it was back to song, dance and comedy.

He starred in thirteen "Van Dyke and Company" variety specials plus a Mystery Movie for NBC, and then went back to drama playing an accused priest in Stanley Kramer's feature, "The Runner Stumbles."

In 1979 he returned to the theatre as Professor Harold Hill in a revival of "The Music Man," which played the major cities before opening on Broadway. The following year he toured in "Damn Yankees."

Dick received his fifth Emmy for the 1982 CBS Library Special "Wrong Way Kid." Other television movies included "Drop-Out Father," "Found Money," with Sid Caesar, the PBS special "Breakfast with Les and Bess" with Cloris Leachman, the miniseries "Strong Medicine," a Showtime production of "The Country Girl" opposite Faye Dunaway, and the NBC-TV movie "Daughters of Privilege."

In addition to his Emmys and Tony, Dick has been given the Dance Legend of the Year Award from the Professional Dancers Society of America [April 1999], the 1998 Disney Legend Award, a Lifetime Achievement Award from the American Comedy Awards, and star on the Hollywood Walk of Fame [2/23/93]. "The Dick Van Dyke Show" was inducted into the Producers Guild Hall of Fame, and in 1995 Dick was inducted into the Television Academy Hall of Fame.

Mark Sloane, the crime-solving MD, was introduced in an episode of "Jake and the Fat Man" before becoming the central figure in several television movies and the series "Diagnosis Murder" which also starred son Barry Van Dyke and ran on CBS for eight seasons through the 1990's, until 2001. Two more Dr. Sloane movies, "Town Without Pity" and "Without Warning," aired on CBS in 2002 and the series is a global favorite in syndication.

Never one to need steady work to feel whole and happy, Dick lives in a world of his own creation, always ready to learn something new, such as the latest computer technology. He rises early, he brews his own coffee, downs some vitamins, checks his email, works out at a nearby gym, then goes for more coffee with local friends. He quit smoking and drinking a long time ago, but has never given up his primary "addiction" – music. A few years ago he took up vocal harmony for the fun of it, and then formed a group "The Vantastix" made up of three talented young singer/musicians and himself. The "Vantastix" made its debut at the 2001 Society of Singers benefit honoring Julie Andrews, and brought the house down.

Performing only for charity, the quartet has raised money in Southern California for P.A.T.H. [People Assisting the Homeless] the Westside Food Bank, The Wellness Community, and several educational and environmental causes.

Alone, Dick visits the Midnight Mission, a skid row rescue center in L.A. where he serves as Chairman of the Capital Campaign. His work there began twelve years ago when he went to help serve meals to homeless families on Christmas Day. He has since returned every Christmas and Thanksgiving, and many days in between.

Years ago, when he saw D. L. Coburn's Pulitzer Prize-winning play "The Gin Game," Dick visualized it as a vehicle in which he and Mary Tyler Moore might one day reunite. That vision became a reality when he and Mary taped a new production of the play at the KCET Studios in Los Angeles. Since its initial airing on PBS' "Hollywood Presents" on May 7, 2003, "The Gin Game" with Dick and Mary has had several repeat telecasts.

Dick, who was divorced in 1984, lives in Malibu with his companion Michelle Marvin. In addition to his two sons and two daughters, he has seven grandchildren and one great grandchild.

The Cast of *The Dick Van Dyke Show* accept the Legend Award from TV Land

Dick Van Dyke Contact:

Bob Palmer
1034 Las Pulgas Rd.
Pacific Palisades, CA 90272
Phone: 310-454-5118

Adam LaVorgna

Adam LaVorgna

Profile

Adam LaVorgna played Robbie, a recurring character on "Seventh Heaven" for the WB Network and Spelling Entertainment.

LaVorgna has appeared in two independent features, "Outside Providence" from Miramax, directed by Michael Corrente, where he played the role of "Tommy The Wire," a thick-headed, short-tempered, burned out kid in the seventies, and in "The Bumblebee Flies Anyway" as the role of Mike, directed by Martin Duffy. He can also be seen in the film "Blast" in the starring role of Schnetz for Zeta Entertainment as well as in the feature "I'll Be Home for Christmas."

LaVorgna has filmed in Prague for Paramount Picture's "Beautician And The Beast" directed by Ken Kwapis. "Prague was one of the most historically interesting places I've been to film," explains LaVorgna. These features are added to the other starring credits on LaVorgna's well-accomplished resume. He has completed numerous lead roles in pictures for the big screen. His credits include Paramount Picture's "Milk Money" directed by Richard Benjamin, Director Franco Amurri's "Monkey Trouble" as well as HBO's "Blood Brothers." In addition, his first big screen role was in Director George Gallo's "29th Street."

LaVorgna has also been cast in numerous starring roles for television, including starring as Nicholas Samperelli in the CBS dramatic series "Brooklyn Bridge" for which he received the *1993 Youth In Film Award* for *Best Young Actor* co-starring in a series. "Brooklyn Bridge" was a great show about an everyday family growing up in the 50's in Brooklyn," explains LaVorgna, "I had a great experience working for Gary David Goldberg on that series."

In addition to "Brooklyn Bridge," LaVorgna completed "Degree Of Guilt," a dramatic miniseries for NBC. He portrayed a young Frank Sinatra in the mini-series "Sinatra" for CBS. Furthermore, Adam has made several guest appearances on such series as "Empty Nest," "Civil Wars" and "Matlock," and has starred in numerous pilots for television.

It would seem that LaVorgna would not have any time to experience any sort of a "normal" life. "I spend a lot of my spare time playing sports," explains LaVorgna, "I was on the varsity ice hockey team with my buddies which is really big in my previous school."

LaVorgna is the youngest of three kids. He resides in New York and commutes home to Connecticut to visit his mother Sandy, a high school English teacher, and his father Joe, a high school principal. His older brother Joey works on Wall Street, and his older sister Jill is a management professional in New York City. LaVorgna got his acting start at age three when he first appeared on the daytime dramatic series "As The World Turns."

Adam LaVorgna

Resume

FEATURES

OUTSIDE PROVIDENCE	Lead	Miramax	Michael Corrente
BLAST	Starring	Independent	Martin Schenk
I'LL BE HOME FOR CHRISTMAS	Starring	Disney	Arlene Sanford
THE BUMBLEBEE FLIES ANYWAY	Co-Star	Independent	Martin Duffy
BEAUTICIAN & THE BEAST	Starring	Paramount	Ken Kwapis
MILK MONEY	Lead	Paramount	Richard Benjamin
MONKEY TROUBLE	Starring	New Line	Franco Amurri
29th STREET	Starring	FOX	George Gallo

TELEVISION

7TH HEAVEN	Recurring	WB
LAW AND ORDER	Recurring	NBC
BECK	Pilot	CBS
DEGREE OF GUILT	Lead/MOW	NBC
COSBY MYSTERY MOVIES	Recurring	NBC
AMERICAN DREAM	Pilot	CBS
CIVIL WARS	Lead/MOW	ABC
BROOKLYN BRIDGE	Series Regular	CBS
SINATRA	Lead/MOW	CBS
BLOOD BROTHERS: Joey DiPaolo	Lead/MOW	HBO

TRAINING

Dennis LaValle
Education Center for the Arts at Yale University

Adam LaVorgna Contact:

Strong/Morrone Entertainment
8522 National Blvd., Suite 101
Culver City, CA 90232
Phone: 310-558-6249

Malinda Williams

Malinda Williams

Profile

Malinda Williams is definitely on a roll, and if you ask her some of her career goals, she will tell you "I just want to portray African-American women accurately, because that is all I represent. Not necessarily positively or negatively, just correctly."

If this beautiful actress's face seems familiar, it may be because she has worked consistently in a business where many careers are short lived. Her versatile talents and distinctive beauty have led her to a list of admirable credits.

Currently, Malinda portrays Tracey "Bird" Van Adams, a beauty salon owner and struggling entrepreneur, on the hit series "Soul Food" (Showtime). She recently earned an NAACP Image Award nomination for "Outstanding Actress in a Drama Series" and in 2002 and 2003 the series received the NAACP Image Award for "Outstanding Drama Series."

Malinda's leading roles on the silver screen include: "The Wood" (MTV/Paramount), "High School High" (TriStar), and "An Invited Guest" which won the Best Show at the 1999 Acapulco Black Film Festival and the Audience Awards at the 1999 Urban World Festival in New York. She also starred in "Dancing in September" for HBO. Other film credits include: "Sunset Park" (Columbia/TriStar) and "A Thin Line Between Love and Hate" (New Line).

Malinda's television credits include ABC's "NYPD Blue" and CBS's "What About Your Friends?" Additionally, she has appeared in such sitcoms as "Nick Freno: Licensed Teacher" where she was a series regular and on several episodes of "Moesha."

Having the ability to portray characters ranging from a sophisticated beauty salon owner, to a mentally challenged teenager, has branded Malinda as one of Hollywood's well-respected actresses.

Malinda at the premiere of *Get Rich Or Die Trying*

Malinda Williams Contact:

Lisa Sorensen Public Relations
12522 Moorpark St.
Studio City, CA 91614
Phone: 818-761-0430

Shirley Knight

Favorite Quote:

"Fulfilling our destiny is the understanding that we are not separate but one."

Shirley Knight

Profile

Shirley Knight has done extensive work in the theatre, cinema, and television both in the United States and in England. She has won the Tony Award, three Emmy Awards, two Golden Globes, The Venice Film Festival Best Actress, Jury Prize at the Cannes Film Festival, The Joseph Jefferson Award, The Evening Standard Award, and others. She has been nominated for two Tony awards, two Drama Desk awards, two Academy awards, nine Emmys, three Golden Globes, the Helen Hayes Award, and others. She holds a Doctorate of Fine Arts Degree from Lake Forest College. In January 2000 Miss Knight received from her home state the KANSAN OF THE YEAR CITATION from the governor of Kansas. She was married to the writer John R. Hopkins until his death and has two daughters Kaitlin and Sophie Hopkins.

Shirley and Kiersten Warren at the premiere of *The Divine Secrets of the Ya-Ya Sisterhood*

Darcy Belsher

Darcy Belsher

Profile

Darcy Belsher was nominated for a Leo Award for his stirring performance of 'Michael Ferguson' in Martin Cummins' directorial debut "We All Fall Down."

Other notable credits include co-starring roles in the feature film "The Guilty," opposite Bill Pullman and Devon Sawa and the low budget indie "Looking for Leonard" with Molly Parker, as well as the TNT television movie "The Virginian" produced and directed by Bill Pullman, and the MOW "Shutterspeed."

Belsher's extensive theatrical background includes an award winning performance in the L.A.-based production "Far From The Tree" mounted at the Actor's Alley. He won the ADA Theatre Award for 'Best Actor' in 1997 for the role of 'Nick.' Other theatrical credits include the title role in "Cyrano de Bergerac," as well as performances in "The Grapes of Wrath," and "Midsummer Night's Dream."

Darcy was voted one of the 10 most intriguing actors to watch out for (for his performance in "We All Fall Down") at last year's Toronto International Film Festival. Darcy can also be seen in the ABC MOW's "The Wedding Dress" and "Everything That Rises."

Darcy Belsher

Resume

SAG/AFTRA/UBCP

FILM & TELEVISION	ROLE	DIRECTOR/PRODUCTION
The Colt	Lead	Yelena Lanskaya/Hallmark Ent.
U.C.: Undercover	Guest Star	Tony Bill/Jersey/Regency/20th Fox/NBC
Everything That Rises	Lead	Jeff Bleckner/ABC/Disney
The Wedding Dress	Lead	Sam Pillsbury/Sarabande Ent./CBS
Shutterspeed	Lead	Mark Sobel/TNT/Lions Gate
First Wave	Guest Star	Mike Robison/USA Network
The Virginian	Lead	Bill Pullman/TNT
*We All Fall Down	**Lead**	**Martin Cummins/Roadcone Pictures**
The Guilty	Lead	Anthony Waller/Dogwood Pictures/HBO
Sweethearts of the World	Lead	Matt Bissionette/Steven Clark/Frustrated Films
Cold Squad	Guest Star	Jane Thompson/Atlantis
Legalese	Lead	Glenn Jordan/TNT
Fallen Arches	Lead	Saraghina Film Co.
M.M.P.R.	Guest Lead	Saban Entertainment
Three Pieces of Fruit	Lead	Darcy Belsher/George Vergette/Silver Dragon
Along For the Ride	Lead	Michael Love/Lil Devl Prod.
Art of Mummification (Writer/Director/Editor)	Lead	Vancouver Pub, School Board

*2001 Leo Award nomination "Best Male Feature"

THEATRE		
**Far From the Tree	**Nick**	**Actor's Alley**
Under Milk Wood	Ensemble	The Center Theatre
The Dining Room	Actor #2	Michael Thoma Theatre
Becoming Memories	Little Michael	C. Jehlinger Theatre
Father's Day	Harold	Jeremiah Morris
What the Butler Saw	Nicholas Beckett	Diana Stevenson
Cyrano de Bergerac	Cyrano	AADA/West
Finding the Sun	Fergus	AADA/West
The Dancers	Horace	AADA/West
The Grapes of Wrath	Al	AADA/West
Midsummer Night's Dream	Puck	Charles Best Theatre

**Winner Best Actor – ADA Theatre Awards, 1997

TRAINING

Acting	Graduate – American Academy of Dramatic Arts
	Dialects, Dance, Choreography, Mime, Stage Combat
	Stuart Robinson, Harvey Solen, Madonna Young, Jeremiah Morris
Scene Study	Ivana Chubbuck Masters Class, Mel Tuck
Improv	Stan Roth
Auditioning	John Miranda, Lynn Johnson
On Camera	Stu Berg
Singing	John Peck

460

| Shakespeare | Carl Reggiardo, Jennifer Parker |
| Voice | Alan Shaterian, Antony Holland |

SKILLS/INTERESTS

Dance	Jazz, Tap, Modern, Charleston, Minuet, Waltz, Jitterbug
Sports	Skateboard, Ski, Snowboard, Mountain Bike, Volleyball, Basketball, Tennis
Dialects	South London, Cockney, Southern, Urban Hispanic, New York, Irish, Welsh

Darcy Belsher Contact:

The Characters Talent Agency
1505 West 2nd Ave., #200
Vancouver, British Columbia, Canada V6H3Y4
Phone: 604-733-9800

Frances McDormand

Frances McDormand

Profile

Academy Award winner Frances McDormand has established a worldwide cinema audience with leading roles in a variety of films including her award winning portrayal of 'Marge Gunderson' in the acclaimed Coen Brothers' film, "Fargo." She starred in Cameron Crowe's "Almost Famous" with Billy Crudup and Kate Hudson by DreamWorks for which she was nominated for a Golden Globe, BAFTA Award and Academy Award, and for which she won several Critics Awards. In 2001, she starred in "The Man Who Wasn't There," for the Coen Brothers, starring opposite Billy Bob Thornton. She also has starred in "City By The Sea" opposite Robert De Niro. McDormand was also Oscar-nominated for her supporting performance in "Mississippi Burning." McDormand starred in Caryl Churchill's "Far Away," a play directed by Stephen Daldry. She was also in the film "Laurel Canyon."

Frances starred in Curtis Hansen's "Wonder Boys," opposite Michael Douglas and Tobey Maguire. She also starred in TriStar's "Madeline," Gregory Hoblit's "Primal Fear," John Sayles's "Lone Star," and Alan Taylor's "Palookaville." Included among McDormand's other feature film credits are performances in Mick Jackson's "Chattahoochee" with Gary Oldman; Sam Raimi's "Darkman" opposite Liam Neeson; Ken Loach's "Hidden Agenda;" "The Butcher's Wife" with Demi Moore and "Passed Away" with Bob Hoskins. She also appeared in Robert Altman's "Short Cuts" John Boorman's "Beyond Rangoon" and Bruce Beresford's "Paradise Road." With the Coen Brothers, she has made two other films, "Blood Simple," and "Raising Arizona."

McDormand studied at the Yale School of Drama. Her Broadway stage successes include her Tony-nominated performance as 'Stella' in "A Streetcar Named Desire." She also starred in "The Sisters Rosenzweig" at Lincoln Center and "The Swan" at The Public Theatre. McDormond starred as 'Blanche' in "A Streetcar Named Desire" in Dublin at the Gate Theatre and then in Dare Clubb's "Oedipus" at the Blue Light Theatre Company opposite Billy Crudup. She also starred in "The Wooster Group's," production of "To You The Birdy!"

She has starred in the television movies "Crazy in Love" directed by Martha Coolidge, "The Good Ole Boys" directed by Tommy Lee Jones, and "Talking With..." directed by Kathy Bates, and was Emmy nominated for "Hidden in America," opposite Jeff Bridges.

McDormand resides in New York with her husband, Joel and son, Pedro.

Frances McDormand Contact:

PMK/HBH
8500 Wilshire Blvd., Suite 700
Beverly Hills, CA 90211
Phone: 310-289-6200

Zachary Bostrom

Favorite Quote:

"Expect nothing. Appreciate everything."

Zachary Bostrom

Profile

Zachary Bostrom was born on January 15, 1981, and is an only child raised by his mother. At the age of nine his grandma moved in with them and has been with them ever since. He is surrounded by a large maternal extended family that keeps him very well grounded. With the loss of several family members in his short life he has learned the value of family and the responsibility that comes with it.

Zach's favorite sport is soccer and he likes to go camping, skiing, snowboarding and horseback riding. He's left-handed, a good cook and loves to BBQ. He's not a picky eater and he's not afraid to try things, although the one thing he doesn't like is raw tomato. As a youngster he fought with his Auntie Carolyn over the Chinese beef and broccoli dish. She'd often ask him if he knew that children were not supposed to like broccoli. One of his favorite things to do with his mom when he was growing up was to movie hop.

Zach was home-schooled through a private school offering independent study. He thrived on it, as he loved to be able to explore new material whenever the urge came forth. Math being Zach's least favorite subject, meant spending many days at the dining room table with his great Uncle Richard tutoring him. All four years of high school Zach was honored by being included as one of America's *Who's Who Among American High School Students*. Zach was offered academic and sport scholarships to several colleges but decided he wanted to pursue his acting full time and attend college part time.

After winning a baby contest it was suggested that due to his friendliness and vocalization he would be good as a child actor. At the age of eighteen months he was signed with an agency and he started doing print work and commercials. As a toddler on one print set his mom was sure his career was over when he threw sand in the photographer's face because he wanted to take a toy away he had given Zach earlier in the shoot. Again as a preschooler his energy level was so high on a 5-day shoot for *Kodak* he was keeping his mom really busy. The directors told mom not to worry, as he was a director's dream kid. He could be used at any time of the day without worrying about his energy level; he listened and followed directions extremely well. Zach's favorite commercial is *Nestle's Toll House Cookies* because he got to eat fresh out of the oven cookies all day long.

At the age of five he landed his first television guest-starring role on the original "Fame." Zach can be seen as Kevin Brady, Greg Brady's son, in "A Very Brady Christmas," a television Christmas movie that airs every year. Much more work followed as an actor and as a voice-over artist. On the television series "Harry and the Hendersons" Zach, with his partner in crime Bruce Davison, laughed as hard as they worked. Zach wanted the role of 'Ernie Henderson' because he is a huge fan of Kevin Peter Hall who played 'Harry' and played the title role in 'The Predator,' one of Zach's favorite movies. At the young age of ten Zach won the *Best Young Actor Award in an Off-primetime Series* for his portrayal of 'Ernie.' While filming "Johnny Tsunami," Zach got to ski and see a lot of Utah and while working on the television movie, "Night of the Wolf" with Robert Urich and Anne Archer, he enjoyed riding horses, shooting guns and getting to be with wolves. This was a dream job for Zach as the wolf is Zach's favorite wild animal. On this movie Zach also got to show off some of his creative writing skills.

Zach is always striving to improve himself. He can write family stories and then turn around and write creepy, scary stories. He has been published and two years in a row he was awarded the *Editor's Choice Award for Outstanding Achievement in Poetry* presented by the *International Library of Poetry*.

Although it is hard work and at times the hours are long Zach loves acting. He likes the creative process that allows him to explore the different characters. From the crew to the stars he enjoys the people he has met. He has potential, a great work ethic, and is very well liked and respected. His dream is to be able to continue acting and writing and someday be able to make a living from what he loves to do.

Zachary Bostrom

Resume

SAG/AFTRA

MOVIES FOR TELEVISION	Role	Director
NIGHT OF THE WOLF	Starring	David Cass Sr.
JOHNNY TSUNAMI	Starring	Steve Boyum
ALIENS FOR BREAKFAST	Starring	John T. Kretchmer
ARMED AND INNOCENT	Guest Star	Jack Bender
WAITING FOR THE WIND	Starring	Don Schroeder
TIMMY'S GIFT PRECIOUS MOMENTS	Starring (animated)	Rick Reinert
A VERY BRADY CHRISTMAS	Starring	Peter Baldwin
SECRET LIFE OF KATHY McCORMICK	Featured	Robert Michael Lewis
DINOSAUR HUNTER	Starring	Doug Rogers

TELEVISION	
SO LITTLE TIME	Recurring/Guest Star
POWER RANGERS	Starring
DAYS OF OUR LIVES	Recurring/Guest Star
THE YOUNG AND THE RESTLESS	Recurring/Guest Star
BEVERLY HILLS 90210	Guest Star
HOME IMPROVEMENT	Guest Star
HARRY AND THE HENDERSONS*	Series Regular (Ernie Henderson)
DAVE THOMAS SPECIAL	Starring
WHO'S THE BOSS	Guest Star
TWILIGHT ZONE	Featured

*YOUTH IN FILM AWARD WINNER – Best Young Actor co-starring in off-prime time or cable series

FILM		
SEVEN SONGS (aka Tangerine Palm)	Ensemble	Noah Stern
THIN WALLS	Starring	Dorian Gibbs

TRAINING	
Sean Nelson – private/classes	September 2001 – on going

SPECIAL SKILLS
Dialects (hears it, can do it. Ref.: Sean Nelson, Barbara Harris & Lee French)
Guitar – Kevin Longden, private lessons 1994-1999
Fencing, boxing, soccer, football, baseball, runner (sprint and distance), mountain biking, swimming, snorkeling, scuba, boogie boarding, body surfing, windsurfing, rollerblading, bowling, karate, ice skating, roller skating, street hockey, rock climbing, golf, skiing, horseback riding, ping pong, chess, computers, video games, impersonations

Zachary Bostrom Contact:

Kazarian/Spencer & Associates
Phone: 818-755-7570

Lainie Kazan

Favorite Quote:

*"Never give in – never, never, never, never, in nothing great or small, large or petty, never give in
except to convictions of honour and good sense. Never yield to force;
never yield to the apparently overwhelming might of the enemy."*
Winston Churchill

Lainie Kazan

Profile

Lainie Kazan is the embodiment of the word entertainer – an artist who has reached the pinnacle in virtually every area of performance. She has come a long way since she was Barbra Streisand's Broadway understudy in "Funny Girl." Once she was able to display her electrifying talent in two shows, she became the "Chanteuse" of her native New York, with nightclub stints and guest appearances on virtually every top variety and talk show in network television, including an unparalleled 26 appearances on "The Dean Martin Show." She even hosted her own variety special for NBC and opened the popular "Lainie's Room" and "Lainie's Room East" at the Los Angeles and New York Playboy Clubs.

The sensual magnetism Lainie exuded in her variety shows and nightclubs attracted film directors and producers, leading her quickly into acting on both the gold and silver screens. After watching her coo through ballads and belt like a sassy blues woman at San Francisco's Fairmont Hotel, an astonished Francis Ford Coppola offered her a plum role in "One From The Heart." The rest, as they say, is history. In 1983, Lainie received a Golden Globe nomination for her performance in Richard Benjamin's "My Favorite Year," starring Peter O'Toole. Other films included "Lust in the Dust" with Tab Hunter and Divine, "Delta Force" with Chuck Norris, "Beaches" with Bette Midler and Barbara Hershey and "Harry and the Hendersons" directed by Steven Spielberg. Also, the Disney film "The Cemetery Club," "29th Street," with Danny Aiello, "The Associate," with Whoopi Goldberg, "Love is All There Is," with Renee Taylor, Angelina Jolie, and Paul Sorvino, "The Big Hit," with Mark Wahlberg, Disney's "The Crew" with Burt Reynolds, Richard Dreyfuss, and Jennifer Tilly and "What's Cooking," with Mercedes Ruehl, Julianna Margulies, Kyra Sedgwick, and Alfre Woodard. She was in the Tom Hanks production of the hit comedy "My Big Fat Greek Wedding," which received the *People's Choice Award* for *Best Comedy Picture*. In addition, she completed filming "Gigli" with Ben Affleck, Jennifer Lopez, Al Pacino and Christopher Walken.

Lainie has also stormed series television. Her CBS series "My Big Fat Greek Life" is based on the hit film. Lainie can also be seen starring in Lifetime Television's Original Movie, "Returning Lily." She received an Emmy Award nomination for "St. Elsewhere" and a Cable ACE Award nomination for "The Paper Chase." She guest starred on "Will & Grace" as Grace's Aunt Honey and has been featured on "Beverly Hills 90210" as well as recurring roles as Aunt Frieda on "The Nanny" and as Dottie, Kirstie Alley's mom, on "Veronica's Closet." Lainie also secured the starring role as Doris Bernstein in an episode of the top rated CBS show "Touched By An Angel." She starred in a children's special, "Safety Patrol" a made for television movie by "The Wonderful World of Disney" which was directed by Savage Steve Holland and produced by Doug Drazin. The special also starred Leslie Nielson and Curtis Armstrong.

Lainie, however, has never forgotten her roots as a live performer. She reprised her role in the Broadway musical version of "My Favorite Year," which won her a Tony Award Nomination for Best Featured Actress, and has also starred on Broadway in "The Government Inspector" with Tony Randall.

Some of her recent nightclub credits include sold out engagements in Los Angeles at the Cinegrill and The Catalina Bar and Grill. Lainie has also appeared at the MGM Grand, The Suncoast Hotel and Casino in Las Vegas, Harrah's Casino and Resort, Trump's Castle in Atlantic City, the hallowed stages of New York's Rainbow and Stars, Tatou, Tavern on the Green, and the famed Oak Room at the Algonquin Hotel. Throughout the years, Lainie has also performed many symphonic concerts. She has sung with such symphonies as The Boston Pops and The Cleveland Symphony to name just a few. She has toured Europe and the Orient to sold out houses and has captivated audiences wherever she goes.

Lainie is always a supporter of various charities. She received the "Woman of the Year" award from B'nai Brith and has graced the stage for many AIDS benefits, telethons and non-profit organizations throughout the United States. Her credits in this area include "Doin' What Comes Natur'lly!" an all-star Broadway tribute to Ethel Merman to benefit Gay Men's Health Crisis that Lainie both produced and starred in. It also featured Patti Lupone, Elaine Stritch, Andrea Martin,

Madeline Kahn and Bette Midler. Lainie was also named the reigning 1997 "Queen of Brooklyn" at a ceremony hosted by Brooklyn Borough President, Howard Golden. She serves on the Board for the Young Musicians Foundation, AIDS Project LA and B'nai Brith to name just a few. In 1990 she was presented "The Israeli Peace Award."

Her voice has never sounded better. Lainie admits that her voice has changed over the years, but critics and jazz lovers praise the maturity and depth of feeling that grew from years of experience.

Lainie's album, "Body and Soul" is a collection of graceful, feline sentiment that smolders with what Rex Reed called "more talent in her little finger than most singers have in their dreams."

Lainie's CD "Lainie Kazan – In The Groove," was produced by Lainie, David Benoit and Clark Germain. Lainie's daughter, Jennifer Bena, sings on the album and award-winning pianist David Benoit also performs on the CD.

Lainie and Errol Rappaport at the 2005 *Night of 100 Stars*

Lainie Kazan Contact:

Warren Cowan & Associates
8899 Beverly Blvd., Suite 919
Los Angeles, CA 90048
Phone: 310-275-0777
Website: www.lainiekazan.com/

Arlen Escarpeta

Favorite Quote:

"To give to another is truly a gift to oneself."

Arlen Escarpeta

Profile

When you first meet Arlen Escarpeta, you are drawn to an inner spirit that holds a room hostage. His poise and gentleness are just a couple of features that have turned this 25-year-old hunk into a budding star. Currently starring on NBC's new hit drama "American Dreams" it is just a matter of time before his name is on everyone's lips.

A native of Belize (formerly British Honduras) in Central America he came to the United States with his mother after his father died when he was 3. They settled in Los Angeles and Arlen began to excel in the arts, singing and dancing in the Young Saints Scholarship Foundation. At 9, Arlen was cast in the title role of his elementary school's stylized production of "Hamlet" and was won over by the applause he received at the final curtain. From there, he attended several arts magnate schools in Los Angeles until he arrived at Hollywood High, where he honed his skills in dance, technical and music theatre, and drama. Arlen attended Pasadena City College where he majored in sociology. Despite swift times of 21.8 seconds running the 200-yard dash and a personal best of 47' – 2½ " in the triple jump – he opted to concentrate on acting rather than dedicate the necessary amount of time to the junior college's track team.

Arlen's career has begun to take off with guest-starring roles on FOX's "Boston Public," and CBS' "Judging Amy." He also appeared on the first season finale of the FX drama, "The Shield," and the pilot episode of NBC's hit drama "Boomtown." His feature-film work includes *High Crimes* (starring Ashley Judd and Morgan Freeman) and the independent film "The Playaz Court."

In "American Dreams," Arlen portrays Sam Walker, a teenager – who also runs track – at a private Catholic high school during the social turmoil of the 1960s. Arlen really feels that his character embodies a lot of him, with a sense of humor and openness to speak about world events. He also likes his character because it is a history-teaching tool for many kids today that have no clue what it was like to live through segregation. He loves the fan mail he gets from kids in their teen and pre-teen years questioning events on the show and why things are happening the way they are.

In his leisure time, Arlen loves to participate in charity events for kids to help raise awareness against drugs and alcohol. He has also helped build a house for Habitat for Humanity. Arlen is a real cartoon fanatic; he enjoys drawing and watching cartoons. In addition, he enjoys reading non-fiction books, and restoring his 1964 Volkswagen Beetle sedan. He has been asked to join the NBA Entertainment Charity League and will match his skills against the likes of Justin Timberlake, Ice Cube and Ethan Hawk to name a few. He is also a Los Angeles Lakers and Dallas Cowboys fan, and remains active working for the Young Saints Scholarship Foundation.

Arlen currently resides in Los Angeles.

Arlen Escarpeta

Resume

FILM

The Court	Lead	Dir. Greg Morgan
Gonna Be The Jam	Lead	Dir. Paul Eckstein
High Crimes	Supporting	Dir. Carl Franklin

TELEVISION

American Dreams	Series Regular	NBC/David Semel
Boomtown	Guest Star (Pilot)	Dir. Jon Avnet
The Shield	Guest Star	Dir. Scott Brazil
Boston Public	Co-Star	Dir. Thomas Schlamme
Judging Amy	Co-Star	Dir. Paul Michael Glaser

TRAINING

Marnie Cooper School of Acting
Hollywood Performing Arts Magnate
Pacoima Theatre and Fine Arts
The Young Saints Scholarship Foundation

SKILLS AND HOBBIES

Basketball, Football, Track, Drummer, Rapper, Miming, Tap, Jazz, Hip Hop, Dialects, Speak 3 Different Languages including Spanish (fluent)

Arlen Escarpeta Contact:

What The Dickens Communications, Inc.
200 North Larchmont Blvd.
Los Angeles, CA 90004
Phone: 323-463-2882

Gleb Savelev

Gleb Savelev

Profile

Gleb was born in Russia into a half Jewish, half Russian family. At the age of 14 he found himself living in Israel, where he and his parents immigrated during the fall of the USSR. After graduating with MEBS, he volunteered to join the Armed Forces where he spent 2 years. In his head he was always searching for something higher than everyday life, but could not find it. Strange circumstances brought him to Los Angeles, where he started writing short stories that made him curious about the life of characters about which he wrote. How would he convey or portray them if he tried playing them. He started acting and his search for the "higher self" had ended.

Gleb feels that being an actor is to understand human psychology and the laws of nature. Now he is acting and pursuing his real goals to become a better actor each day of his life. As far as getting work as an actor, he is not worried. It will come, it always has.

474

Gleb Savelev

Resume

FILM/VIDEO /TELEVISION

The Passenger	The Passenger	Ben Soper, UCLA
LA Dream	Dante (Lead)	William Olsson, USC
Grits	Drummer	Geneva Films
The Parallel	Will	Ed Munter
Crack the Code	Beater	Ed Munter
Jesus Christ	Lawyer	Sarah Lamb
The Couch	Steve, Homeless	Saleh Ashumov
Girls Behaving Badly	Guy Getting Trashed by Cake	Oxygen Network

THEATRE

Merchant of Venice	Salerio	Knightsbridge Theatre
Illya Darling	Nicholai	24th Street Theatre
McNeely's	Paul McNeely	Lisa Dalton
The Deputy	S.S. Lt. Kurt Gerstien	Jack Colvin
Othello	Othello	EGS Prods
Aida	Guard	Italian Tour
Romantics	Alfred DeVigny	Charles Davis
Hallelu 2002	Hallelu	Jewish Event (Sheila Manning)

COMMERCIAL
List furnished upon request

DRAMATIC TRAINING/EDUCATION
Michael Chekhov Studio West – Jack Colvin, Lisa Dalton, Mala Powers, Odessa Ferris and John Hugo. Studies included Monologue, Scene, Voice, Cold Reading, Script Analysis, Dance, Improvisation and more.
Voice/Animation – Odessa Ferris and Jack Colvin

SPECIAL SKILLS
Sports / Athletics / Martial Arts / Weapons
Israeli Forces (military), martial arts, swimming, acrobatics, firearms

LANGUAGES
Hebrew, Russian

OTHER SKILLS
Voice Animation, dance

Beethoven

by Gleb Savelev

He hears the music of his heart
The thumping sound of the striking keys
Does not disturb him, he has not heard
The crying tune, the music of the bliss

Moonlight he sees and whispers to a piano,
Listens to a quiet wooden master,
His soul united and he plays
The pain and love that felt much faster

Passionately, following his addiction
He punches the keys, he strokes his passion
Could not accept the world's conviction
The envy, hate…compassion?

His music streams and dribbles
His music twines and ties
His music conquers, grabs and tumbles
Into the heart…into the soul that cries

Virtuoso of the music never heard before
The capturer of the greatest moments
The stealer of our breaths and more…
Composer who loves and complements

Hot tempered to create
Attracted to the one who left
Lonely in his room he ate
Most people him intended to forget

Beethoven, who knew?
The talent behind the walls
He couldn't bare it and so he spew
Lying in his bed, dying in his bed he falls

Oh…what a music, now we say.
His feelings, his affection and his mood
We see him and what he wanted to convey
Now appreciated and understood.

Gleb Savelev Contact:

Victor Kruglov & Associates
7461 Beverly Blvd., Ste. 303
Los Angeles, CA 90036
Phone: 323-934-7007

Tonya White

Tonya White

Profile

Tonya White, actress, model and wrestler was born October 25, 1972. She is 5'9" and a 145 lbs. She started her modeling career in 1998 as a racecar calendar model. Since then she has been modeling all over the country from Los Angeles to New York. Tonya has appeared in magazines such as *Lady Sports Magazine* and *Model Look Magazine*. She has appeared in numerous calendars and runway modeling and print ads are other samples of her modeling career. Tonya is a graduate of Élan's school for models and actors.

Tonya has enjoyed a successful career in acting. Her movie credits include "Valley of Lost Souls," Rustin's "Glory," with actor and singer Meat Loaf, "Guardian Angels," and "Beyond the Walls of Sleep." Her voice was heard in the animated feature "Video Girl" as Marsyn. Tonya's voice also appears in the song "All About the Money" from the Ooh Wee CD by Lorenza Jones.

On a job to valet for Steve Armstrong of the WCW, Tonya stumbled into the world of wrestling. Instead of being the valet, Tonya became a professional wrestler for the Southeastern Wrestling Federation. She has completed Steve Armstrong's wresting training program. Tonya's greatest wrestling achievement is Women's Heavyweight Belt Holder.

Tonya has written her autobiography called "*A Sister's Betrayal's*," and it is now available in bookstores. Because of Tonya's handicap from a burn she received as an infant, Tonya's ultimate goals is to continue her career in acting, modeling and wrestling in order to become a role model for other handicapped people. She also has plans for opening homes for abused women and children.

Tonya White

Resume

FILM

Valley of Lost Souls	Body Double/Cult Member	Scorpion Films
Rustin's Glory	Waitress	Grab a Bat Films
Pink	Mother of Child	Fluffy Puffy Productions
America's So Beautiful	Dancer	America's the Beautiful Productions
Guardian Angels	Bell Boyd	Walkala Productions
Juwanna Man	Spectator	In Drag Productions
Beyond the Walls of Sleep	Girl with the Bad Leg	
Zeno	Mother of Child	UAB Productions

TELEVISION, VIDEOS AND COMMERCIALS

Southern Pro Wrestling	Women's WHC Wrestler	Montgomery Alabama Cable Ch 3
Bobby T Show	Model/Dancer/Judge	WABM Ch 68 Birmingham, AL
Diamond Swim Wear Video	Swim Wear Model	Omni Video Pro
Santa Rosa Fair	Southeastern Pro Wrestling	Channel 3 Santa Rosa County FL
Mariah Boats	Model	Hueytown, AL
Bridal Bliss	Wedding Gown Model	Alabama Now Morning Show
R&R Dive Shop Training Video	Student Diver	Fox One Productions
Late Talk	Guest	Fox One Productions

VOICE-OVER

Recreational Factory	Voice-Over	92.5FM Birmingham, AL
Alabama Talent	Voice-Over	92.5FM Birmingham, AL
Camelot South Homes	Voice-Over	92.5FM Birmingham, AL
Southern Women's Show	Voice-Over	92.5FM Birmingham, AL
Pinson Valley Auto Sales	Voice-Over	92.5FM Birmingham, AL
Lorenza Jones Ooh Wee Album	Vocal	Miss Kitty Records Atlanta, GA
Video Girl	Voice of Marsyn	Leading Edge Films

WORKSHOPS

Michael Meguire	Commercial Workshop	Birmingham, AL
Pro Images	Magazine Workshop	Gadsden, AL
CPI Modeling Agency	Modeling Workshop	Panama City, FL
Gregory Iseminger	Acting Workshop	Hollywood, CA
Casablanca Modeling Agency	Acting/Modeling School	Birmingham, AL

SPECIAL SKILLS AND INTERESTS

Horse Back Riding	Dancing	Camping
Professional Wrestler	Boating	Fishing
Firearms	Public Speaking	Singing
Swimming	Off Road Vehicles	
Scuba Diving	Tennis	
Rollerblading	Ring Girl	

PHOTOGRAPHY EXPERIENCE

Master Works	Shoot/Workshop	Ft. Payne, AL
RCA	Shoot/Workshop	Hummeltown, PA
Beckman Photography	Shoot/Workshop	New York, NY
Studio Time	Calendar	Las Vegas, NV
Tim Helmiton	Calendar	Birmingham, AL

PRINT WORK

Toby Lee *Out of the Blue*	CD Cover Model	Nashville, TN
Wakefield's Dept Store	Fashion Model Ad	Anniston, AL
FreedomSales.com	Catalog/Web Model	Tuscaloosa, AL
Saint Claire News	Human Interest Story	Asheville, AL
Gadsden Times	Life and Times Story	Gadsden, AL
Santa Rosa Gazette	Promo Ad	Milton, FL
Model Look Magazine	Model July 2000 Edition	Charleston, IL
Bama Airport	Spokes Model	Tuscaloosa, AL
Sassy Super Model	Super Model	Sydney NSW Australia
Mary Kay	Model of the Month Aug 2000	Gadsden, AL
Lady Sports Magazine	Model	Wilkesboro, NC
Short Looks Magazine	Model	Charleston, IL
Sexxx Pirates Addicted	CD Cover Model	New Orleans, LA

RUNWAY

Southern Women's Show	Model/1st Director	Birmingham, AL
Paul Mitchell Hair Show	Model	Homewood, AL
Mungin's Apparel	Model	Birmingham, AL
Cyberstyle 2000	Model	Fairfield, AL
Urbanham.com	Model	Birmingham, AL

Tonya White Contact:

Symons, Adams & Myers
Promotion & Talent Co.
P.O. Box 308
Fostoria, OH 44830
Phone: 419-435-1301
Website: http://www.tonyawhite.net/

Jerry Scaglione

Favorite Quote:

*"Some people succeed because they are destined to,
but most people succeed because they are determined to."*

Jerry Scaglione

Profile

Jerry Scaglione was born and raised on the east coast in New Jersey. Soon after he graduated high school he started performing in rock bands. First as a lead guitar player then as lead singer and all along he was always the main songwriter penning ninety percent of the bands material.

He first was attracted to acting when he was called by a casting director to be an extra in a film after she saw his picture in an advertisement for a band he was in, in the Village Voice. After catching the acting bug he started taking it more seriously and started studying with William Hickey at the infamous H.B. Studios in NYC. He then went on to train extensively in both Method and Meisner techniques.

Jerry loves all aspects of acting including Stage, TV and Film. He has numerous stage credits and has been seen in Independent Films, Soap Operas and National commercials. As many aspiring actors he still waits for his "BIG BREAK" and is in constant pursuit of it. He now lives in N.J. with his wife and three sons.

Jerry Scaglione

Resume

AFTRA/GIAA

FILM/TV

ADVENTURES OF STEIN KRAMEE	JORGE	J. FRUEHLING/INDIE SHORT
TEENAGE MOM	ARBITRATOR	E. MORAN/INDIE SHORT
ALL MY CHILDREN	PATIENT	ABC-TV
TUESDAY NEVER COMES	BOBBY W/ERIC ESTRADA	JASON PRODUCTIONS
DOWNTOWN HUSTLE	SLIM	HUSTLIN' FILMS
THE BUST	DEALER	THE NEW FILM CO.
CLASH	JOHNNY	CLASH PICTURES
STREET WARS	ROCK	STUDENT FILM
DOWNTOWN BABIES	BACK-UP SINGER	MUSIC VIDEO

THEATRE

A HATFUL OF RAIN	POLO	CHELSEA REPERTORY CO., NYC
RIBS	ROBERT	THE ZEPHYR THEATRE, LA
LOU GEHRIG	VICTOR	THE ACTING STUDIO, NYC
THE ZOO STORY	JERRY	THE ACTING STUDIO, NYC
SAVAGE IN LIMBO	TONY	G&G PRODUCTIONS
MASS APPEAL	MARK	G&G PRODUCTIONS
THE WOOLGATHERER	CLIFF	G&G PRODUCTIONS
COME BLOW YOUR HORN	ALAN	NJ PUBLIC THEATRE
THE FIFTH OF JULY	WESTON	NJ PUBLIC THEATRE
CAT ON A HOT TIN ROOF	BRICK	NJ PUBLIC THEATRE
AMERICAN BUFFALO	BOBBY	NJ PUBLIC THEATRE
BEYOND THERAPY	ANDREW	NJ PUBLIC THEATRE

COMMERCIALS

DIRECT TV	PRINCIPAL	NATIONAL

TRAINING

JAMES PRICE	MEISNER/TECH. & SCENE STUDY	THE ACTING STUDIO, NYC
WILLIAM HICKEY	METHOD/TECH. & SCENE STUDY	H.B. STUDIOS, NYC
ROBERT DAGNY	ADLER/PRIVATE COACHING	CHAMPION STUDIOS, NYC
ROBERT DEROSA	MEISNER/TECH. & SCENE STUDY	THE ACTING STUDIO, NYC
JENNIFER RUDOLPH	AUDITION TECHNIQUE	NYC STUDIO
GEO HARTLEY	AUDITION TECHNIQUE	THE FIGTREE THEATRE, LA
WEIST-BARON	ON-CAMERA COMMERCIAL	NYC STUDIO
DAVID CHRISTOPHER	SPEECH/DICTION	THE VOICE STUDIO

SPECIAL SKILLS
MARTIAL ARTS, WEIGHT TRAINING, BIKING, RUNNING, GOLF, SPORTS,
PHOTOGRAPHY, SCREENWRITING, PLAYWRITING & GUITAR
ALSO WORK WELL WITH CHILDREN & ANIMALS AND A LICENSED DRIVER

Jerry Scaglione Contact:
Email: jerryscag@hotmail.com

George O. Gore, II

George O. Gore, II

Profile

Upon graduating from high school, George O. Gore, II was on his way to college to study finance with dreams of becoming an investment banker. But, his plans were altered and his life forever changed when he landed the coveted role of "Junior" on the hit ABC sitcom "My Wife and Kids," starring Damon Wayans.

A native of Fort Washington, Maryland, George has been acting since the age of four. He made his debut in a Burger King commercial, and soon amassed over 20 national commercials to his credit for such leading brands as Fisher-Price and IBM. His television credits include guest roles on "Law and Order" and "Touched By An Angel." He is best remembered as "G," the young son of Malik Yoba's character on the critically acclaimed drama series "New York Undercover," for which he received three NAACP Image Award nominations.

George is totally different from his character on "My Wife and Kids," which is a testament to his natural acting ability. In real life, he is a charming, handsome young man with poise, intelligence and a laid-back style. Determined to do things on his own terms, George has plans to venture behind-the-scenes to direct and produce in the near future. He cites Ron Howard, who made the successful transition from child actor to award-winning director, as one of his role models.

In his spare time, he plays basketball, rides motorcycles and practices boxing. His favorite movies include the "Austin Powers" series, "Ocean's Eleven," "Crouching Tiger, Hidden Dragon," and practically anything starring Ben Stiller. He enjoys comedy and has plans to do more work in that genre. So take note, George O. Gore, II is the next young star to take Hollywood by storm!

George O. Gore, II Contact:

Lisa Sorensen Public Relations
12522 Moorpark St.
Studio City, CA 91604
Phone: 818-761-0430

Billy Crudup

Billy Crudup

Profile

Billy Crudup had a successful run in the acclaimed off-Broadway play, "The Resistible Rise of Arturo Ui" starring opposite Al Pacino and Steve Buscemi, after which he starred in "Big Fish," a Columbia Pictures' adventure feature for director Tim Burton. He starred in "Charlotte Gray" opposite Cate Blanchett and "World Traveler" with Julianne Moore. Prior to that, he starred in the critically acclaimed "Jesus' Son" opposite Samantha Morton, Holly Hunter and Denis Leary, which earned him a Best Actor Award from the Paris Film Festival and an Independent Spirit Award nomination. He was also seen in Cameron Crowe's Academy Award winning "Almost Famous" with Frances McDormand and Kate Hudson, and in the acclaimed "Waking the Dead" with Jennifer Connelly. Billy Crudup is currently starring in "Stage Beauty," for Lions Gate Films.

He made his motion picture debut in Barry Levinson's "Sleepers," opposite Robert De Niro, Brad Pitt and Jason Patric. He was featured in Woody Allen's "Everyone Says I Love You" and starred in Pat O'Connor's "Inventing the Abbotts." He also played the leading role in the critically acclaimed "Without Limits," the story of legendary long distance runner Steven Prefontaine. For the role he won the National Board of Review Award for Breakthrough Performance of the Year.

Crudup starred in "The Elephant Man" starring opposite Rupert Graves and Kate Burton for the Royale Theatre for which he was nominated for a Tony Award for Best Performance by a Leading Actor in a Play. He made his Broadway debut as Septimus Hodge in Tom Stoppard's "Arcadia" directed by Trevor Nunn, which won him several awards, including the 1995 Outer Critics Circle Award for "Outstanding Debut of an Actor" and the 1995 Theatre World Award. He was also honored with the Clarence Derwent Award for Actors' Equity for "Outstanding Broadway Debut." He has appeared on Broadway in the Circle in the Square production of William Inge's "Bus Stop" opposite Mary Louise Parker and in the Roundabout Theatre's production of "Three Sisters" which earned him a Drama Desk nomination. Mr. Crudup appeared in Dare Clubb's Off Broadway version of "Oedipus" with Frances McDormand. He recently starred in the New York Shakespeare Festival production of "Measure for Measure" at the Delacorte Theatre in Central Park.

Mr. Crudup received his Masters of Fine Arts from New York University and also attended the University of North Carolina at Chapel Hill. He resides in New York City.

Billy Crudup Contact:

PMK/HBH
8500 Wilshire Blvd., Suite 700
Beverly Hills, CA 90211
Phone: 310-289-6200

Katharine Leis

Favorite Quote:

"Whether you think you can or you can't, you're right."

Katharine Leis

Profile

Katharine was born just outside of Toronto, Canada. Her acting debut came as the lead in a school play at age nine. She then took a brief, ten-year break from acting before appearing in the Canadian version of ER, called "Side Effects." She also appeared in an infomercial by B & W Entertainment that had a year and a half long run.

Katharine then attended college at Niagara University in Lewiston, N.Y. She transferred to Florida State University after two years, and graduated in 1998 from FSU with a Bachelor of Science Degree in Pre-med Biology.

Katharine then decided to give acting a full go, and moved to Orlando, Florida. She attended Art Sake Acting Studio for a year, then began acting in Independent and Student Films. She also scored minor roles in both a television pilot, and a show that aired on PBS.

Katharine made her directorial debut with the movie she wrote and also acted in, "There's a Caterpillar in My Bok Choy." The movie was a slapstick comedy and utilized talent and locations all over the state of Florida.

Katharine hopes to do more directing as well as acting in the future, and is quickly making a name for herself in the Independent Film Scene.

490

Katharine Leis

Resume

EDUCATION AND TRAINING

1993	Acting Technique, Niagara University
1995	Orientation to Acting, Florida State University
1997	On Camera Workshop, NY Model Contracts
2000	Meisner Technique, Art Sake Acting Studio
2000	Scene Study, Art Sake Acting Studio
2001	Working Actor, Art Sake Acting Studio

FILM AND TELEVISION

Year	Role	Title	Company
1994	Waitress	Side Effects	CBC Canadian Broadcasting Company
1994	Lisa	Nightlife	B & W Entertainment
2001	Sarah Green	Blackout	FearFilm Independent Productions
2001	Emilia	Memory	IFAC Films
2001	Cassie	008:The Job is Not Enough	Hocus Focus Productions
2001	Ashlyn	The Uninvited	Relic Films
2002	Ghost	Ghosthunters: Point of Contact	Parrot Bay Entertainment
2002	Victim	Original Sin promo trailer	Blood Cinema
2002	Claudine	Ask A Lawyer	PBS
2002	Alexa von Stratten	Stealing God	Springfield Films
2002	Pat Kerr	We are Coming to Help	JD Casey Productions
2002	Karma	The Essence of Irwin	DownRightSwell Productions
2002	Delila	There's a Caterpillar in my Bok Choy	IMEX Productions
2002	Amy	The Right Now	United Digital Films
2003	Sarah	Phobias	FearFilm Independent Productions
2003	The Jogger	Run	Kat Pictures
2003	Wife	The Hypocrite	IKO Productions

SKILLS AND HOBBIES

Horseback riding, writing, tending bar, some martial arts, pilates, very flexible, pre medical degree and proficiency in medical terminology.

Katharine Leis Contact:

Website: http://www.i-katharine.com/

Lois Smith

Lois Smith

Profile

Born in Topeka, Kansas, Lois Smith moved to Seattle with her family about age 11 and went to school there, including two-plus years at the University of Washington School of Drama. Her first job in theatre was playing a teenager in "Time Out For Ginger" on Broadway with Melvyn Douglas as her father. She started working from her first years on stage, film and television, and has continued to do so.

Her first film was "East of Eden." In 1988, she first worked with the Steppenwolf Theatre Company in "The Grapes of Wrath" in Chicago, LaJolla, London and New York. As a member of the Steppenwolf Company, some of her stage work has been in Chicago, including "Buried Child" (also on Broadway), "Mother Courage and Her Children" and "The Royal Family." Some of her more recent films include: "The Best Thief in the World," "P.S." and "Minority Report." She lives in New York City.

Lois at the premiere of _The Laramie Project_

Lois Smith

Resume

FILM

P.S.	Dir. Dylan Kidd
A Foreign Affair	Dir. Helmut Schleppi
Iron Jawed Angels	Dir. Katja Von Garnier
Minority Report	Dir. Steven Spielberg
Red Betsy	Dir. Chris Boebel
The Pledge	Dir. Sean Penn
Tumbleweeds	Dir. Gavin O'Connor
Nora	Dir. Michael Almereyda
Dead Man Walking	Dir. Tim Robbins
Twister	Dir. Jan de Bont
Larger Than Life	Dir. Howard Franklin
How to Make an American Quilt	Dir. Jocelyn Moorhouse
Holy Matrimony	Dir. Leonard Nimoy
Falling Down	Dir. Joel Schumacher
Fried Green Tomatoes	Dir. Jon Avnet
Green Card	Dir. Peter Weir
Fatal Attraction	Dir. Adrian Lynn
Black Widow	Dir. Bob Rafelson
Reckless	Dir. James Foley
Reuben, Reuben	Dir. Robert Ellis Miller
Foxes	Dir. Adrian Lynn
Four Friends	Dir. Arthur Penn
Resurrection	Dir. Daniel Petrie
Next Stop Greenwich Village	Dir. Paul Mazursky
Up the Sandbox	Dir. Irvin Kersher
*Five Easy Pieces	Dir. Bob Rafelson
East of Eden	Dir. Elia Kazan

TELEVISION

Daughters of the New World	NBC Miniseries/Dir. Karen Arthur
Frasier	NBC/Dir. Jim Burrows
Truman	HBO/Dir. Frank Pierson
Skylark	MOW/Dir. Joe Sargeant

BROADWAY

***Buried Child
**The Grapes of Wrath (also for American Playhouse/PBS)
Blues for Mr. Charlie
Orpheus Descending
The Young and the Beautiful
Time Out for Ginger

OFF BROADWAY

Vagina Monologues	Westside Arts
Give Me Your Answer, Do	Roundabout Theatre
An Impossible Marriage	The Laura Pels Theatre
Defying Gravity	American Place Theatre
Dog Logic	American Place Theatre
Beside Herself	Circle Repertory
Measure For Measure	Lincoln Center
Bodies, Rest & Motion	Lincoln Center
The Glass Menagerie	City Center
April Snow and Others	EST Marathon

REGIONAL

The Royal Family	Steppenwolf
Mother Courage and Her Children	Steppenwolf
Hot L. Baltimore	Williamstown/Dir. Joe Montello
Defying Gravity (Workshop)	NY Stage Film & Film/ Vassar
Buried Child	Steppenwolf/Dir. Gary Sinise
The Cherry Orchard	Baltimore Center Stage
The Mesmerist	Steppenwolf
Escape From Happiness	Baltimore Center Stage/Yale Rep
The Seagull	The Guthrie Theatre

Awards

*1970 Best Supporting Actress Award – National Society of Film Critics
**1990 Best Supporting Actress – Tony Award Nomination
***1996 Best Supporting Actress – Tony Award Nomination

Lois Smith Contact:

Independent Artists Agency
159 West 25th Street, Suite 1011
New York, NY 10001
Phone: 646-486-3332

Lianna Dawn Riece

Favorite Quote:

*"Be not afraid of greatness. Some are born great,
some achieve greatness, and some have greatness thrust upon 'em."*
Shakespeare

Lianna Dawn Riece

Profile

Lianna Dawn Riece was born on May 17, 1980 in Sarasota, Florida. Even, as a child she was very active in school, sports, and in entertainment. She was either singing in chorus at her Tabernacle at age five or winning awards in gymnastics as early as age eight. Lianna displayed her stage presence and her inspiration to become an actress in middle school with performances in school plays. During her high school years she was either at cheerleading practice or taking a stand in the environmental club. After the high school clichés and the Friday night football games came to an end, Lianna looked further to pursue her dreams.

Lianna moved to Orlando where she is in the midst of completing her bachelor's degree in Business. She keeps active both on campus and off, volunteering in local clubs and organizations such as the Florida Motion Picture and Television Association and Financial Management Association at UCF.

Lianna has also modeled in various print advertisements from fashion to health, including a magazine cover. Lianna has been a Fashion Model in fashion shows both locally and internationally, from Florida to New York and Italy to Egypt. But, Lianna has more to offer than just her great looks; she is a talented actress who has brought her acting ability to both film, and television.

In the film, "Spell Of Silence" Lianna plays the lead role, Miranda, who is a young woman, disturbed from her childhood, who is forced to deal with her past in order to get out of a mental hospital and to move on with her future. Lianna is in a commercial for "Brain Injury" that was aired on MTV and VH1. She has also appeared in a national VISA commercial in Orlando.

In addition to Lianna being on the big screen and television, she also enjoys her hobbies, plugging away at her computer, writing screenplays, short stories and a few heartbreaking poems. Her second published book, "Letters From The Soul," features her poem "A Beautiful Rose" symbolizing a child maturing. Her screenplay, "BitterSweet," has a twist of love, hate, suicide and murder. We all hope to see it at the top of the box office, one day in the near future.

Lianna keeps busy looking for intriguing roles in which to act, a new model layout, or a new story for her next screenplay, as well as beginning graduate school, as she looks forward to the next chapter in her life.

Lianna Dawn Riece

Resume

SAG (Eligible)

FILM

COMING ATTRACTIONS	WOMAN (PRINCIPAL)	COMING ATTRACTIONS PROD.
SPELL OF SILENCE	MIRANDA (LEAD)	4D PRODUCTION
EVERYBODY GOES HOME	MICHELLE (SUPPORTING)	LIVE OAK ENTERTAINMENT
LAUNDRY DAY	JILL (LEAD)	CASEY SAXON PRODUCTION

TELEVISION

MAKING THE GRADE	TRACY (PRINCIPAL)	BROOKLYN STAR ENTERTAINMENT
GHOST HUNTERS	BAR CUSTOMER	PARROT BAY ENTERTAINMENT

THEATRE, CONCERT

DO I MAKE YOU HORNY	CAST (FRINGE)	OOPS COMEDY TROUPE
JOHN RINGLING MUSEUM OF ART	CHORUS (MEZZO-SOPRANO)	ANNA CLARE EPISTOLA
WINTER PERCUSSION CONCERT	WOODWIND (FLUTE)	ANNA CLARE EPISTOLA
COLLEGE NIGHT	DANCER	MARIANNE GRECO

COMMERCIALS

THINK BRAIN INJURY-PSA	PRINCIPAL	BRAIN INJURY ASSOCIATION OF FL
GRAPEVINE MARTINI LOUNGE	BAR CUSTOMER	LIVE OAK ENTERTAINMENT
VISA, WALT DISNEY WORLD	EXTRA	HEADQUARTERS PRODUCTION

PRINT

EPCOT	MODEL	EPCOT PRODUCTION
PSA HEALTH	EDITORIAL MODEL	MADISON GARDENS
SUPERB MAGAZINE	COVER MODEL	DIAMOND PROMOTIONS

FASHION SHOWS, EVENTS

LACOSTE FASHION SHOW	RUNWAY MODEL	TABU PRODUCTIONS
FRATELLI POGGI	SPOKES MODEL	JD MODELS INTERNATIONAL
PINK FASHION SHOW	RUNWAY MODEL	J-ME PRODUCTIONS
MODEL OF THE UNIVERSE	RUNWAY MODEL	COLLECTIONS MODEL MGMT
FITNESS MODEL OF THE YEAR	RUNWAY MODEL	COLLECTIONS MODEL MGMT
CRYSTAL REEL AWARDS	DEPT. HEAD MODELS	DREAM LAUNCHERS STUDIOS
HAWAIIAN TROPIC	MODEL	CENTRAL FLORIDA

PROFESSIONAL TRAINING

ACT III. STUDIOS	ACTING PROFESSIONAL	KAREN J. RUGERIO
VALENCIA BLACK BOX	VOICE TECHNIQUE	GINNY KOPF
VALENCIA BLACK BOX	ACTING I	GINNY KOPF
VALENCIA DANCE STUDIO	JAZZ DANCE I	MARIANNE GRECO
VALENCIA DANCE STUDIO	JAZZ DANCE II	MARIANNE GRECO
VALENCIA DANCE STUDIO	HIP HOP	LORA COSTANTINI

SPECIAL ABILITIES

SPORTS: VOLLEYBALL, SOFTBALL, SWIMMING, WATER SKIING, WEIGHT LIFTING, TENNIS, GOLF
SPECIAL SKILLS: YOGA, CHEERLEADING, DANCE
DIALECTS: AMERICAN (NEW YORKER, RED NECK, VALLEY GIRL), AND BRITISH

Lianna Dawn Riece Contact:

Email: liannadawnriece@msn.com

Collin Fletcher

Favorite Quote:

"Life is what happens to you when you're busy making other plans."
John Lennon

Collin Fletcher

Profile

Born in Missouri but raised in Texas, Collin was interested in acting as long as he can remember. The son of a theatre teacher, he didn't have to look far for training, and it began at a very young age. He continued this training through college and earned his BFA in Acting from Southwest Texas State University. After a series of small roles in Texas stage and film, Collin has relocated to Los Angeles, where he continues his gradual ascension to the rank of steadily working actor.

Aside from acting, Collin writes screenplays. He sees his career as a work in progress and enjoys the small, mundane things just as much as the idea of rising to the top, because as John Lennon put it, "Life is what happens to you when you're busy making other plans."

Collin Fletcher

Resume

FILM

A Kiss Remembered	Capt. Walter Reed (lead)	ISM Films
The New Guy	East Highland Student	Revolution Studios
The Duo	Philip	Damage Control Prod.
Equinox Knocks	Football Player	Equinox Prod.
Green	David	Vangil Prod.

VOICE-OVER

Valentino's Pizza	San Marcos, TX
Savage Political Campaign	Austin, TX

THEATRE

Faust	Faust	Cliff Diver Theatre
Blithe Spirit	Charles	Ramsey Theatre
Harvey	Dr. Chumley	Ramsey Theatre
Romeo and Juliet	Benvolio	Ramsey Theatre
A Christmas Carol	Cratchit	Mainstage Theatre
The Emperor Toad	Robin	Touring Show
Medea	Jason	Glade Theatre
The Comedy of Errors	Antipholus of Syracuse	Glade Theatre
Tales of the Last Formicans	Jim	Mainstage Theatre
Side Man	Al	SWT Studio
Master Harold and The Boys	Hally	SWT Studio

(others available upon request)

TRAINING

B.F.A. in Acting	Southwest Texas State University	San Marcos, TX
TV/Film Acting	Larry Hovis	
Voice-Over	David Michael McGwire	
Commercial Audition	Larry Hovis	
Movement	Jay Jennings	
Fencing/Combat	Paul Schimmelman/John Moreau	
Mime	Dennis Maganza	
Dialects	Dr. Ed Simone/Dr. Charles Pascoe	
Alexander Technique	Clark Stevens	

OTHER

Well versed in numerous dialects (English, Cockney, Regional U.S., Scottish, Irish, French), Ability to learn any dialect upon request, baritone vocal range, member of touring mime troupe for two years. Extensive theatre training in both classic and contemporary performance.

Collin Fletcher Contact:

Bonnie Black Talent
Phone: 818-753-5424

Francine Wolf

Francine Wolf

Profile

Francine Wolf is a talented character actress, model, voice-over artist, improv performer and singer. Her motto is "Have talent, will travel." With agents in Ohio, Atlanta and Florida, she travels to work in film, theatre and commercials and she can do 15 perfect dialects. She studied improv with Dick Schaal (one of the original Second City members of Mary Tyler Moore Show and Rhoda fame). During the 2003 LPGA Tournament in Florida she appeared on the commercial broadcast during the tournament for "The Villages," a central Florida community.

Francine is also a guest columnist for New York City's Inverse Theatre online newsletter for actors. She also teaches improvisation at Showbiz Kidz! Development Center in Tampa, Florida. She was thrilled to sing the National Anthem for the Toronto Blue Jays in Dunedin, Florida. Her projects include performing with the Gulfcoast Transformation Authority—a new improv group and "What a Swell Party!" A Cole Porter Musical Revue.

Francine Wolf

Resume

FILM

Sanderson County	Aunt Janis	Wild Heart Films/Wayne Porter
The Profit	Features Background	Courage Productions/Peter Alexander
Traffic (starring Michael Douglas)	Airline Passenger	CompVision Prod./Steven Soderbergh
Psychic Atomic Nuclear HS Senior Prom 2000	Wife of Plant Worker	Amorphous Productions
The Suicide (starring Lothaire Bluteau)	Henrietta Stepanova	Wexner Center/Noon Pictures/Gregg Bordowitz
Launch	News Anchor	Mercury Films/Kevin Kramer
Fountain of Youth	Gypsy Fortune Teller	Upfront Films/Sheldon Gleisser

TELEVISION

Product Demonstrations and Model	Principal	Home Shopping Network
Fem Max/Male Max	Principal	Extreme Productions
What's New in the Kitchen-Flavor Wave Oven	Testimonial	Reliant Interactive Media Group
Papi-Frisko/Music Video "The Jerk"	Director of Institution	AMN Productions/Ace Michaels
Nineteen at Noon-Live TV Spokesperson/Improv Group	Guest	WCLL TV 19/Jeff Parks
Fitness Quest Infomercial on Buffalo Meat	Principal/Testimonial	

COMMERCIALS/VOICE-OVER

Broken Back PSA with James Earl Jones & Richie Havens   Principal   Warwick Advertising/Alliance International
Current Conflicts and TV List Upon Request

INDUSTRIALS

Turbo Tiger Plus	Principal	MacIntosh Productions
Full on Football/Food Network	Referee	Innova Marketing/Peter D'Alessio
Florida State Pension Plan	Leticia	Real Productions, Inc.
The Villages	Principal	DreamCastle Productions, Inc.
Eckerd's Drugs	Pharmacy Tech.	Jay Gross Studios
Ohio Casualty Homeowners' Insurance	Principal	Ohio Casualty Insurance
Nationwide Insurance Estate Planning	Principal	Nationwide Insurance

THEATRE (Complete List Upon Request)

The Odd Couple-Female Version	Renee	Angel Cabaret Theatre/Jimmy Ferraro
JerryO	Mrs. James	Tah! Productions/Dr. Maureen Militia
Business is Murder	Candy DeVine	Mystery Dinner Theatre/Gail Fabian
Howl-O-Scream	Kashadavitch	Busch Gardens/Nancy Hutson
Silverwings Anthology	Rosa Vincenzi	Senior Rep. of Ohio/Ionia Zelenka
Oh, Jackie (World Premier)	Rose Kennedy	Act Out Productions/Frank Barnhart
Fiddler on the Roof	Grandma Tzeitel	Gallery Players/Pam Hill
Joey and Maria's Comedy Wedding	Mrs. Gnocchi	Saunders Productions/B. Saunders
La Cage Aux Folles	Jacqueline	Metropolitan Theatre
No Sex Please, We're British	Susan	Senior Rep. of Ohio/Varun Kahana
Our Town	Mrs. Webb	Senior Rep. of Ohio/Charles Dodrill

Sang National Anthem – Toronto Blue Jays, Dunedin, Florida

EDUCATION/TRAINING

Acting Coaches:	Improv, Dick Schaal, FL; Sande Shurin, NYC; American Stage Theatre Actors' Workshop, John Kuhn, A.C.T. – Gail Ramsey; Carolyn Harding, Improv, sketch comedy, Jonathan Putnam, Ionia Zelenka, CATCO
Voice:	Jim Lovensheimer, Ph.D., Ohio State University Roberta Ricci, Chair of Vocal Dept., Capital University, Columbus and Kenyon College
Ballroom Dance:	Jon Devlin, Otterbein College

B.S. Education, State University College of New York at Oswego

SPECIAL SKILLS

Dialects: British, Irish, Italian, New York, Southern, Spanish, Russian, Yiddish, etc.; Bowling, Golf, Teach Improv, Swing Dance, Double Hula Hoops, Kickboxing, Knitting, Lyric Soprano

ADDITIONAL INFORMATION

Current U.S. Passport, Extensive wardrobe, Vintage clothes, Wigs

Francine Wolf Contact:

Central Florida Talent
Fern Park, Florida
Phone: 407-830-9226

Mindy K. Decker

Mindy K. Decker

Profile

Mindy K is a professional model and actress based in Philadelphia, PA. If you know the Modeling Industry online, then you know about Mindy Decker or perhaps Mindyk.com. Mindy Decker has built, maintained and networked her name online to an International audience and impressive client base.

Mindy stayed on course and pushed her career forward, backing up her strong online brand with professional assignments including: Pfizer, Aventis, MedStar Television, Invisalign, Warner Brothers, Puffs, Panasonic, Proctor and Gamble and a host of other top clients around the country. A former Ms. Internet World 2001, Mindyk.com and Mindy herself set a clear example of how modeling and promotion can be done without sacrificing personal goals and standards.

Mindy K. Decker

Resume

FILM/TELEVISION

Medical Detectives	Marcella Lulka	Medstar Television Productions
HACK	Business Person	Big Ticket Productions, CBS
10! At 10AM	Makeover	NBC Television
HACK	Mourner	Big Ticket Productions, CBS
Undefeated"	Spectator	HBO Films
See You in Seattle	Wife	Pioneer Studio Productions

COMMERCIAL

Avenue of the Arts	Patron	DEM Group
Chamonix Esotique	Testimonial	Unimed International Inc.
Classic Loves Songs	Testimonial	Time/Life Music
Ultimate Sleep System	Testimonial	Center City Film & Video
Rittenhouse Counsel Assoc.	Lawyer	TV One Productions
Elkins Chevrolet	Mother	TV One Productions

INDUSTRIAL/INFOMERCIAL

IFPA Fraud Prevention	Trooper Alexandra Preston	21st Century Pro Productions
Baxter Pharmaceuticals	Asthma Patient	Intellimedia
Advanced Nursing Skills	Assessment Patient	Fabian-Baber, Inc.

LIVE / CONVENTION / SPOKESPERSON

EDGE Fashion Extravaganza 2003	Emcee/Host
GMC Home Life Show 2003	GMC Corporation
ASH Annual Meeting 2002	Berlex Laboratories
ASN Conference 2002	Pfizer Pharmaceuticals
ICE Tradeshow 2002	Repechage Skin Care
APA Conference 2002	Pfizer Pharmaceuticals
ASIM Conference 2002	Aventis Pharmaceuticals
AEA Conference 2001	Pfizer Pharmaceuticals
PMA Summit 2001	Naturipe Growers
ADA Conference 2001	Pfizer Pharmaceuticals

SPECIAL SKILLS & INTERESTS

Graphic design, all office skills, conversational Spanish – current passport
Bartender/waitress, tongue roll, wiggle nose-ears
Universal fitness equipment, jogging, aerobics
Junior trampoline, horseback riding, fishing, swimming, rollerblading/skating
Photography, shoot pool, bowling, dancing club/disco
Formal wear, driver's license, excellent with animals and children

Mindy K. Decker Contact:

Website: http://mywebpages,Comcast.net/mindyk17/index.htm

Corbin Bernsen

Corbin Bernsen

Profile

The eldest of three children, Corbin Bernsen was born in North Hollywood to a producer father and actress mother.

He earned his Master's in Playwriting from UCLA's Theatre Arts Department, later receiving a Drama-Logue Award for his scenic design of the Pilot Theatre production of "American Buffalo." After moving to New York and appearing in the off-Broadway production of "Lone Star" and a touring company of "Plaza Suite," he became a regular for two years on the daytime drama "Ryan's Hope."

Roles in Blake Edwards' "S.O.B.," "King Kong" and "Eat My Dust" in addition to guest starring credits on a number of episodic mainstays prompted an exclusive deal with NBC which led to his role as Arnie Becker, the shrewd and handsome divorce attorney, on "L.A. Law."

"L.A. Law" catapulted Bernsen to overnight stardom. During the late 80's and early 90's Bernsen appeared on over 50 magazine covers and earned both Emmy and Golden Globe nominations, hosted "Saturday Night Live," and appeared on "Seinfeld" and "The Larry Sanders Show." In the feature film arena, he starred in the motion picture comedy "Hello Again" followed by other critically acclaimed roles in "Disorganized Crime," Wolfgang Peterson's "Shattered" and as Cleveland Indians third baseman-turned-owner Roger Dorn in the extremely popular "Major League" series of films.

Corbin has also starred in an impressive string of films for television. Ranging from playing the role of civil rights lawyer Morris Dees in the NBC telefilm "Line of Fire: The Morris Dees Story" to a gumshoe ghost in the lighthearted NBC mystery romance "Love Can Be Murder" with Jaclyn Smith.

Corbin reprised his role as Arnie Becker in NBC's successful "L.A. Law Reunion" movie. Corbin can also be seen in the recurring roles of Congressman Henry Shallick on "The West Wing" and as Judge Owen Sebring on "JAG." Starring in the Christian based film "Judgment" has made Corbin Bernsen a household name.

Bernsen makes his home in Los Angeles with his wife, actress Amanda Pays, and their four sons.

Corbin Bernsen

Resume

FILM (Partial List)

MAJOR LEAGUE III	Director: John Warren
GREAT WHITE HYPE	Director: Reginald Hudlin
TALES FROM THE HOOD	Director: Rusty Cundieff
MAJOR LEAGUE II	Director: David Ward
SHATTERED	Director: Wolfgang Petersen
DISORGANIZED CRIME	Director: Jim Kouf
BERT RIGBY, YOU'RE A FOOL	Director: Carl Reiner
MAJOR LEAGUE	Director: David S. Ward
HELLO, AGAIN	Director: Frank Perry

TELEVISION MOVIES (Partial List)

THEY ARE AMONG US	Director: Jeffrey Obrow
TWO OF HEARTS (FAM)	Director: Harvey Froth
THE DENTIST (HBO)	Director: Brian Yuzna
THE DENTIST II (HBO)	
RIDDLER'S MOON (UPN)	Director: Don McBrearty
FULL CIRCLE (NBC)	Director: Bethany Rooney
HEADS YOU WIN	
TAILS YOU'RE DEAD (USA)	Director: Tim Matheson
VOICES FROM WITHIN (NBC)	Director: Eric Till
WHERE ARE MY CHILDREN (ABC)	Director: George Kaczender
I KNOW MY SON IS ALIVE (NBC)	Director: Billy Graham
GRASS ROOTS (NBC) 4 hr. miniseries	Director: Jerry London
LOVE CAN BE MURDER (NBC)	Director: Jack Bender
DEAD ON THE MONEY (TNT)	Director: Mark Cullingham
LINE OF FIRE:	
THE MORRIS DEES STORY (NBC)	Director: John Korty
BREAKING POINT (TNT)	Director: Peter Markle

TELEVISION SERIES

THE UNBELIEVABLES (Pilot)-Series Star	FOX
THE CAPE-Series Star	MTM PRODUCTIONS
A WHOLE NEW BALLGAME – Series Star	ABC/UNIVERSAL
L.A. LAW – Series Lead	NBC/20th CENTURY FOX

TELEVISION SPECIAL GUEST STAR (Partial List)

SEVENTH HEAVEN	WARNER BROS/SPELLING ENT.
TRACEY TAKES ON…	HBO/TAKES ON PRODUCTIONS

LARRY SANDERS SHOW   HBO/BRILLSTEIN-GREY ENT.
LOVE & WAR   CBS/SHUKOVSKY-ENGLISH ENT.
SEINFELD   NBC/CASTLE ROCK

Corbin with his mother Jeanne Cooper (*The Young & The Restless*) at CBS 75th Anniversary

Corbin Bernsen Contact:

James/Levy/Jacobson
3500 W. Olive Ave., Suite 1470
Burbank, CA 91505
Phone: 818-055-7070

Elon Gold

Favorite Quote:

"Youth may be wasted on the young, but retirement is wasted on the old."

Elon Gold

Profile

As a Boston University student at the tender age of 19, the *Boston Herald* hailed Elon Gold as "a comedy star on the rise." Ten years later that star continued to rise as Gold starred in the NBC/Paramount series "In-Laws" based on his stand-up comedy.

Growing up in the Bronx, a big fan of comedy, Gold has emerged into a naturally gifted stand-up comic, sketch performer, actor and writer. Having discovered at a very young age that he had an uncanny ability to do impressions, Gold went from mimicking his teachers to mastering truly unique voices like Charles Grodin and Howard Stern. In fact Gold got to do Howard on Howard Stern's show and Grodin on Charles Grodin's show. At 17 Gold began his stand-up career and one year later Gold's impression-infused routine led to his first television appearance on MTV's "Half-Hour Comedy Hour" where he appeared alongside Chris Rock, Ray Romano and Drew Carey. By the time he was an undergraduate student at Boston University—where he graduated cum laude with a B.A. in Economics—Gold was splitting his time between his studies and touring comedy clubs and colleges across North America. In 1993, Gold was invited to perform at the world-renowned Just for Laughs Montreal International Comedy Festival, where he appeared in a Showtime Network special hosted by the late John Candy. This Montreal appearance along with his work on the MTV sketch series "Comikaze," led to Gold's first television series on the ABC sketch show "She TV" which was hailed by *Time Magazine* as one of the year's Top Ten Shows.

His success in the comedy world provided the perfect segue to his career as an actor. His credits include playing Mary Richards' boss (the new "Lou Grant") on the highly-rated "Mary and Rhoda" movie of the week on ABC, a regular performer and writer on Dana Carvey's ABC sketch comedy series, star of the short-lived WB series "You're the One" and host of the Cable Ace Award-winning Nickelodeon series "Inside Eddie Johnson." Gold's career has taken a couple of dramatic turns with performances in the independent features "Restaurant" and "Origin of the Spaces" where he starred alongside Amanda Peet.

In 2000, Gold combined his stand-up, writing and acting skills to develop and star in the Columbia TriStar pilot "Good as Gold." Along with his co-creator and co-writer Ira Ungerleider ("Friends"), Gold assembled an all-star cast including Mary Tyler Moore as his mom, Elliot Gould as his father and Jonathan Silverman as his brother. Although the pilot did not become a network series, Gold learned the value of mining his real life for comedic inspiration. With that lesson learned, Gold took another one of his life experiences—he and his wife living with his in-laws—and pitched a series idea that soon found a home at Paramount and NBC. With "Frasier" star Kelsey Grammer executive producing, "Frasier" executive producer Mark Reisman writing and executive producing, acclaimed feature film star Dennis Farina starring as his father-in-law, and multiple Emmy-Award winning actress Jean Smart starring as his mother-in-law, once again Gold has mined comedy gold from his miserable existence.

Currently, Gold splits his time between New York and Los Angeles, and between the Friar's Club and time with his wife Sacha and son Brandon...and, of course, his in-laws.

Elon Gold

Resume

TELEVISION

In-Laws	Series Regular/Producer	NBC/Paramount
Good As Gold (Pilot)	Series Regular/Co-Creator	Sony
Mary and Rhoda (MOW)	Lead	ABC
Talk To Me (Pilot)	Series Regular	ABC/Disney
You're The One	Series Regular	WB/Castle Rock
The Dana Carvey Show	Recurring/Writer	ABC
She TV	Series Regular	ABC/Carsey Warner
Ned and Stacey	Guest Star	FOX
Anything But Love	Guest Star	ABC
The Wyatts (Pilot)	Guest Star	FOX
Late Night w/ Conan O'Brien	Recurring	NBC
Rosie O'Donnell Show	Guest	Warner Bros. TV
*Inside Eddie Johnson	Host	Nickelodeon
Talk Soup	Guest Host (Fall 1994)	E! Entertainment
4th of July Special 1995	Co-Host	Comedy Central
Pipeline	Featured	Comedy Central
Comikaze	Featured actor/writer	MTV
MTV Half Hour Comedy Hour	Featured '89, '90, '92	MTV
Stand-Up Sit Down Comedy- (Half-Hour Comedy Special)	Featured Performer	E! Entertainment
Montreal "Just For Laughs" Special	Featured Performer	Showtime

*Cable Ace Award Winner

FILM

Origin of The Species	Paul / Lead	Independent, Dir. A. Heinz
Restaurant	Kurt / Lead	Independent, Dir. E. Bross
Private Parts	Dial-A-Date Caller/Featured	Paramount, Dir. B. Thomas

FESTIVAL/CLUB APPEARANCES

2001, '99, '96, '93 Just For Laughs Comedy Festival   Montreal, Canada

Extensive list of appearances available upon request

Elon Gold Contact:

United Talent Agency
9560 Wilshire Blvd. 5th Floor
Beverly Hills, CA 90212
Phone: 310-273-6700

Melanie Mann

Melanie Mann

Profile

Melanie was born in Flemington, New Jersey. The oldest, by five minutes, of twins, she was always known as the more outgoing and dramatic one of the pair. She and her sister were always putting on wild plays with their stuffed animals, or involved in heated debates over whose Barbie got to date Ken more often. It was thanks to these and other adventures that primed her to be an actress. Mesmerized by a traveling group of skit performers, she was bitten by the acting bug at the tender age of twelve, and has never looked back.

After earning her high school degree through six years of home schooling, she continued her education at Point Loma Nazarene University in San Diego, California. There she trained in theatre under Dr. Paul R. Bassett at Salomon Theatre. She appeared in several university productions, including prominent roles in "The Actor's Nightmare," "The Children's Hour" and "Le Bourgeois Gentilhomme," as well as the lead roles in "The Foreigner" and "Servant of Two Masters."

Her off-campus productions included "The Man of La Mancha," "Blood" and the 100-year anniversary revival of the stage version of "Way Down East." In addition to appearing onstage, she earned the position of Technical Manager at Salomon Theatre and did the lighting design and stage management of countless on- and off-campus productions. She also studied voice at PLNU, dance at San Diego City College and Mesa College and film workshops at The Actor's Workshop in San Diego. She presided over and managed Alpha Psi Omega, theatrical honor society, and worked to create a theatre alumni society, earning her the 2000 Star Award, presented by the mayor of San Diego, for volunteerism in theatre. She earned her Bachelor of Arts degree in Theatre. She was thrilled to work with Jeanine Lim on "Stuck." While this was not her first film project, having appeared in "Millennium Bomb," "Street Girls" and "Every Fifteen Minutes," in San Diego, this was her first project on the east coast.

Her love and eternal thanks go out to her enduring and loving family and friends, her Salomon Theatre gang, and to the One who makes all things possible.

Melanie Mann

Resume

FILM & TV

Walter's Room	Walter's Mom	East Coast Pictures
Art of War	Lead	Joey McAdams, Director
Ellis Island	Ellis	Marcos Azevedo, Director
Two of a Kind	Madeline	Homebrew Productions
Stuck	Jennifer	Jeanine Lim, Director
Cowboys and Indians	Lolly	Luigi Scarcelli, Director
Millennium Bomb	Bambi	Tom Gerald, Director
Street Girls	Reporter	C.O.F.O., San Diego
Waiting on an Angel	Student	Stu Seagull Productions
Every Fifteen Minutes	Witness	San Diego P.D.
The Mikey Jay Show	Co-Host	Variety Show

THEATRE

Way Down East	Kate	Upstage Players
Blood	Roxy	Faultline Theatre
Le Beourgoise Gentilhomme	Nicole	Salomon Theatre
The Children's Hour	Helen	Salomon Theatre
Servant of Two Masters	Beatrice	Salomon Theatre
The Man of La Mancha	Undrstdy	La Jolla Stage Co.
The Foreigner	Catherine	Salomon Theatre
The Actor's Nightmare	Ellen	Salomon Theatre

TRAINING

Point Loma Nazarene University	4 Years
The Film and TV Workshop	6 Months
Mesa College	1 Year
San Diego City College	5 Months

Melanie Mann Contact:

Melanie Mann
P.O. Box 1572
Wappingers Falls, NY 12590
Phone: 845-380-0084
Website: www.melaniemann.com

Mike Messier

Favorite Quote:

"Live in the Moment, Die in the Memory."

Mike Messier

Profile

Mike Messier was born in the days of disco in the land of the suburbs. He grew up with a modern family background: one sister, divorced parents, and family cat. His escapes from his Northern Virginia childhood were television, movies, and Professional Wrestling. His parents indulged him in these interests. Messier was particularly fond of horror movies such as "Poltergeist" and "A Nightmare on Elm Street." A turning point in Messier's personal development came when he and a friend skipped school, "borrowed" his mother's car, and saw a "Goodfellas" matinee. Liotta and De Niro, the editing, the moral ambiguity, and the use of Clapton's "Layla" piano solo in the film awed Mike.

Inspired, Messier began editing VCR and Boom Box to VCR music videos in the privacy of his own home. Two of these videos were a tribute to the Pro Wrestling Tag Team "The Road Warriors" and a compilation of scenes from the movie "Faces of Death." Luckily, Messier's high school offered a TV Production class and Messier was then challenged to write his first screenplay; "World War 3 part 2," an account of a futuristic battle between Saddam Hussein and "George Bush Junior." The film featured characters "rapping" themselves into the narrative. Messier played 'Roddy Reagan' in the film.

Messier pursued Pro Wrestling early in his Rhode Island College career as a wrestler, ring announcer and wrestling beat writer. He developed the characters of "Mad Dog" a dog biscuit chomping, bark at the moon brawler and the more flamboyant "Smudge Baby," a cross dressing, lisping tactician who asked opponents to be the "new daddy" of "My little, little girl Lisa Marie" (a Cabbage Patch doll dime store knock off.)

Messier put acting and filmmaking on hold until his seventh and final year of college when he conceived a film inspired by a local rock 'n' roll vixen and the Devo song "A Girl You Want." Messier cast himself as Guy Smith, a stalker to a sexy muse in the film eventually titled "Man In You," an eighty minute digital video piece that took a year and a half to complete. Messier also collected music, character actors, locations and promoted viewings of the final film. Messier found this to be hard work; he preferred just to act.

After graduation, Messier took acting, improvisation and auditioning classes and stocked up on acting and trade books at a book outlet store, which took him a year to read. Messier worked in lead and character roles in independent and student films and a Pro Wrestling play "Baby's Changing," in which on closing night he was able to convince the audience and several co-stars that he had actually injured his opponent, beyond the scope of the play's script. Messier found steady work in Providence's Murder on Us dinner theatre where he learned that audience interaction often varied on the amount of drinks a particular audience had consumed. Messier also learned that female audience members who gave out their phone numbers usually didn't expect or appreciate an actual phone call in return. Then Messier got a call himself that he was happy to return.

Messier was one of 11 semi-finalists for an HBO show called "Candidate 2012" in which one "ordinary American" will run for President of the United States of America, all while being documented by HBO. Messier did not get cast, but he assumes that this is only the preview to the movie of his life, which Jim Morrison predicted for us all.

Mike Messier

Resume

TELEVISION

HBO's Candidate 2012	Semi-Finalist	Jay Roach-Producer
The Mike Messier Show	Star/Director	RI Public Access TV

FILM

I Deserve to be a Celebrity	Promotional Tape	Copies Available
Man In You	Guy Smith (lead)	Fuzzy Head Prod.
The Georges Aad Show	Georges Aad (lead)	RISD/Greg Kanaan
Jesus, Mary and Joey	Extra Work	Federal Hill Pictures

THEATRE

Baby's Changing	Fate – Wrestling Villain	Poor Man Productions

MURDER ON US DINNER THEATRE

A Deadly Christmas Carol	Tiny Tim, Young Scrooge	John Thayer- Director
Murder at the Irish Wake	Mary Margaret McFarty	John Thayer- Director
The Italian & Irish Wedding	Groom, Vinny, Momma	John Thayer- Director
Murder in the Court	Cannibal Rector	John Thayer- Director

PRODUCTION EXPERIENCE

Victorious (the play)	author and producer	The Call
Man In You	conceived, produced etc.	Fuzzy Head Prod.

PROFESSIONAL WRESTLING

Pro Wrestler	Smudge Baby, "Mad Dog"	RI, MA and CT
Ring Announcer, Commentator	Various Promotions	New England and NC

COMEDY EXPERIENCE

So Funny I Forgot to Laugh	Comedy Night Host	The AS220 Club
Writers with Drinks	Smudge Baby performance	Club Hell

TRAINING AND WORKSHOPS

Maine International Workshops	Actor in Residence	Rockport, ME
Providence Film Festival	Actor for Directors class	Richard Shenkeman
Perishable Theatre	Introduction to Acting	Fred Sullivan
Perishable Theatre	Scene Study	Kate Lester
Perishable Theatre	Auditioning for Film	Doug Wright
Community College RI	Improvisation	Jeff Butterworth
Community College RI	Acting 1	Doreen Bramley
Rhode Island College	Playwriting	Elizabeth Anderson

OTHER SKILLS B.A. in English from Rhode Island College, Visual Artist, Spoken Word Artist, Pro Wrestling, Writer, Chess Player, Intergender Thumbwrestling Champion.

Mike Messier Contact:

Email: maddogmikemessier@yahoo.com

Olivia Rosewood

Olivia Rosewood

Profile

Olivia Rosewood was seen in Cameron Crowe's critically acclaimed film "Almost Famous" as Beth from Denver, the long, red-haired "band aid." She can also be seen in "Orange County," opposite Colin Hanks, Chevy Chase and Lily Tomlin, for Paramount and MTV. Other credits include, "Hiding in Walls," and "Break A Leg."

Olivia began her career at the ripe young age of seven playing a young Bess Truman in the Off-Broadway play "The Buck Stops Here." Born into a family of entertainers, she was naturally drawn to acting and performed in various plays all over the country before landing her first role in a feature film at the age of seventeen. James Cameron's "Titanic" was a baptism by fire into the whirlwind of Hollywood. She can be seen in "Where's Marlowe?" a Paramount Picture, "Dirt," an award winning independent feature, and "In Quiet Night," another independent.

The Cast of _Almost Famous_

525

Olivia Rosewood

Resume

FILM | **DIRECTOR** | **STUDIO**
A MIDSUMMER NIGHT'S RAVE | GIL CATES JR. | INDEPENDENT
ORANGE COUNTY | JAKE KASDAN | PARAMOUNT
DIRT | MICHAEL COVERT | INDEPENDENT
ALMOST FAMOUS | CAMERON CROWE | DREAMWORKS
WHERE'S MARLOWE | DAN PYNE | PARAMOUNT CLASSICS
TITANIC | JAMES CAMERON | FOX

TELEVISION
L.A. DOCTORS | RICK BOTA | FOX

THEATRE | **LOCALE** | **ROLE**
LOVE AND MADNESS | THEATRE LAB | OPHELIA
THREE MUSKETEERS | THEATRE LAB | CONSTANCE
AGNES OF GOD | ROSE THEATRE | AGNES
SILK | USC | SILK

TRAINING
HOWARD FINE, SABAN EPSTEIN, DAVID MONTEE

Olivia Rosewood Contact:

Manager: Paul Nelson
Phone: 310-786-4900

Agent: Julia Buchwald
Phone: 323-602-2331

Robert Forster

Robert Forster

Profile

When pundits say that just being nominated for an Academy Award is tantamount to winning, they must have had actor ROBERT FORSTER in mind. His role as Max Cherry in Quentin Tarantino's "*Jackie Brown*" was a landmark performance and helped revive a career, which Forster has described as having "a five year upwards first act and a 25 year sliding second act." His performance garnered universally great critical acclaim, but even more importantly, he received an Oscar nomination for Best Supporting Actor. It has turned around a career that started over 35 years ago and put him suddenly in great demand.

He has not stopped working since he co-starred with Samuel L. Jackson, Pam Grier and Robert De Niro, as the innately decent bail bondsman in "Jackie Brown," performing in a roster of roles in films and television which run the gamut of both high profile and independent projects. He has won accolades from film critics including those in New York, Chicago, Los Angeles, Washington, D.C., Boston, and Philadelphia praising his work in David Memet's "Lakeboat," directed by Joe Mantegna, and the up coming "Diamond Men," with Donnie Wahlberg, as the traveling salesman forced to mentor his young replacement. Also Forster starred in "Strange Hearts" with Rose McGowan, a modern-day film noir. On the small screen he co-starred in the CBS TV film, "Like Mother, Like Son: The Strange Story of Sante and Kenny Kimes," with Mary Tyler Moore.

After "Jackie Brown," Forster starred in a quartet of independent films "Outside Ozona," "Family Tree," "The Magic of Marciano," co-starring Nastassja Kinski and "It's the Rage," with an all-star ensemble including Joan Allen, Gary Sinise and Andre Braugher, as well as the updated versions of Alfred Hitchcock's "Psycho," directed by Gus Van Sant and a television version of "Rear Window," with Christopher Reeve. In 1999 Forster was featured in the MGM sci-fi film "Supernova," co-starring Angela Basset and James Spader, and did an audio reading of the best-selling book, "Hit Man," for Dove Audio.

Forster blazed on the scene in his debut film, in 1966, in "Reflections in a Golden Eye," co-starring with Marlon Brando and Elizabeth Taylor, directed by John Huston. He followed this in 1968, with the seminal film, "Medium Cool," by Haskell Wexler, playing the TV newsman, whose carefully guarded objectivity is undercut by the events at the Democratic convention in Chicago. Forster also starred in several television series, including the TV noir series, "Banyon," which according to Forster, was filled with "fast cars and even faster women."

He figured that if he persisted, someday a young hotshot filmmaker, familiar with his work, would create a role for him. What he didn't realize was, there would be two young guys, anxious to cast him. One was Quentin Tarantino, who had thought of him for two earlier films, but then wrote the Max Cherry role with Forster in mind. The second young director was Englishman Paul Chart, who created the role of Dr. Jake Nyman, in the thriller "American Perfekt," for Forster, after carefully following his career. This film also stars Amanda Plummer, David Thewlis and Paul Sorvino.

A native of Rochester, N.Y., Forster began his acting career in local theatre, moving to New York City in 1964, where he made his professional debut in the two-character Broadway production of "Mrs. Dally Has A Lover." Other stage credits include "A Streetcar Named Desire," "The Glass Menagerie," and productions of "Twelve Angry Men," "The Sea Horse," and "One Flew Over the Cuckoo's Nest." Over the years, he has done consistently well-received work in small films, including his stand-out performances in "The Don Is Dead," "Stunts," "Avalanche," "Alligator," and "Delta Force."

On television, Forster starred in three series: "Banyon," "Nakia," and "Once A Hero," and numerous television films including, "Death Squad," "Standing Tall," "The Clone," and an Emmy Award winning episode of "Police Story."

In 1986, Forster produced and directed "Hollywood Harry," a detective film spoof, in which he starred with his daughter, Kate, then age 14. During his career, he created an actor's workshop and then expanded its range to become in demand as a motivational speaker. (www.robertforster.com)

"Never give up," Forster especially tells young actors. "If you can hang on to a good attitude, deliver the best stuff you've got, and don't quit, you can win it in the late innings." But it does help to have a Quentin Tarantino out there as one of your big fans.

Robert Forster at the premiere of *Like Mike*

Robert Forster

Resume

<u>**FILMS**</u>

2003 Cursed	Wes Craven	Dimension Films
2002 Grand Theft Parsons	David Caffrey	Swipe Films
2002 Charlie's Angels 2	McG	Columbia Pictures
2002 Infamous	John Leguizamo	HBO
2002 Confidence	James Foley	Lion's Gate Entertainment
2002 Like Mike	John Schultz	20th Century Fox
2002 Lone Hero	Ken Sanzel	Gunman Productions Ltd.
2001 Diamond Men	Dan Cohen	Panorama Releasing
2001 Human Nature	Michel Gondry	Fine Line Features
2001 Lakeboat	Joe Mantegna	Panorama Releasing
2001 Mulholland Drive	David Lynch	Picture Factory
2001 Roads to Riches (a.k.a. Strange Hearts)	Michell Gallagher	Gold Circle Films
2000 Family Tree	Duane Clark	Independent Artists
2000 Finder's Fee	Jeff Probst	Mystic Arts/Shavick Ent.
2000 It's a Shame About Ray	Ajay Sahgal	Shame About Ray Prod.
2000 The Magic of Marciano	Tony Barbieri	Lumiere International
2000 Me, Myself & Irene	Bobby Farrelly & Peter Farrelly	20th Century Fox
2000 Supernova	Walter Hill	MGM/United Artists
1999 It's The Rage	James D. Stern	New City Releasing
1999 Kiss Toledo Goodbye	Lyndon Chubbuck	A Pix Entertainment
1998 Outside Ozona	J.S. Cardone	Tri Star Pictures
1998 Psycho	Gus Van Sant	Universal Pictures
1997 Jackie Brown*	Quentin Tarantino	Miramax
1997 American Perfekt	Paul Chart	Nu Image
1997 Demolition University	Kevin Tenney	Demolition U Productions
1997 The Method	Kevin Lewis	Roundtable Productions
1997 Uncle Sam	William Lustig	Solomon Int'l. Pictures
1996 Hindsight	John T. Bone	Bruder Releasing Inc.
1996 Original Gangstas	Larry Cohen	Orion Pictures Corp.
1995 Guns & Lipstick	Jeno Hodi	No Goodbyes Productions
1995 Scanner Cop II	Steve Barnett	Showdown Productions
1994 American Yakuza	Frank Cappello	American Yakuza Prod.

Year	Title	Director	Studio
1994	Point of Seduction: Body Chemistry III	Jim Wynorski	New Horizons
1993	Cover Story	Gregg Smith	Arrow Entertainment
1993	Midnight Kiss	Jim Wynorski	Midnight Kiss Prod.
1992	Maniac Cop 3: Badge of Silence	William Lustig	Academy Video/HBO
1992	South Beach	Fred Williamson	Po' Boy Productions
1991	29th Street	George Gallo	20th Century Fox
1991	Diplomatic Immunity	Peter Maris	Fries Distribution Co.
1991	In Between	Thomas Constantinides	Monarch Home Video
1991	Night Vision	Fred Williamson	Night Vision Productions
1990	Peacemaker	Kevin Tenney	Fries Entertainment
1990	Satan's Princess	Bert I. Gordon	Paramount Home Video
1989	The Banker	William Webb	Virain Films
1989	Esmeralda Bay	Jess Franco	United Int. Pictures
1988	Committed	William A. Levey	World Wide Ent.
1987	Counterforce	Jose Antonio de la Loma	Counterforce Productions
1986	The Delta Force	Menahem Golan	MGM/Canon Films
1985	Hollywood Harry	Robert Forster	Canon Films
1983	Walking the Edge	Norbert Meisel	Empire Pictures
1982	Vigilante	William Lustig	Film Ventures Int.
1980	Alligator	Lewis Teague	BLC
1980	The Kinky Coaches and the Pom Pom Pussycats	Mark Warren	Summa Vista Pictures
1979	The Black Hole	Gary Nelson	Walt Disney
1979	The Lady in Red	Lewis Teague	New World Pictures
1978	Avalanche	Corey Allen	New World Pictures
1977	Stunts	Mark L. Lester	New Line
1973	The Don Is Dead	Richard Fleischer	Universal Pictures
1972	Journey Through Rosebud	Tom Gries	GSF
1970	Cover Me Babe	Noel Black	20th Century Fox
1970	Pieces of Dreams	Daniel Haller	United Artists
1969	Justine	George Cukor	20th Century Fox
1969	Medium Cool	Haskell Wexler	Paramount Pictures
1969	The Stalking Moon	Robert Mulligan	National General Pictures
1967	Reflections in a Golden Eye	John Huston	Warner-Seven Arts

* Academy Award Nomination – Best Supporting Actor

TELEVISION

Year	Title	Director	Studio/Network
2003	Karen Sisco	Michael Dinner	Universal/Jersey Films
2003	Fastlane – "Pop Dukes"	Josh Pate	Warner Bros. Television
2002	Fastlane – "Ray Ray"	Marcos Siega	Warner Bros. Television
2002	Murder in Greenwich	Tom McLoughlin	Columbia/TriStar
2002	Due East	Helen Shaver	Showtime
2001	Like Mother, Like Son: The Strange Story of Sante and Kenny Kimes	Arthur Alan Seidelman	CBS
2000	L.A. Sheriff's Homicide	Michael Fields	Paramount Pictures
1999	Spawn	Various	HBO Animation
1998	Rear Window	Jeff Bleckner	ABC
1993	Necessary Force		
1993	Sex, Love and Cold Hard Cash	Harry Longstreet	SLCHC Productions
1992	In the Shadow of a Killer	Alan Metzger	NBC
1990	Checkered Flag	John Glen & Michael Levine	ABC
1988	Mick & Frankie	Mark Tinker	ABC
1987	Once a Hero	Kevin Inch	ABC
1986	Adventures of William Tell	George Mihalka	Hallmark
1981	Goliath Awaits	Kevin Conner	Vidmark Ent.
1978	The Darker Side of Terror	Gus Trikonis	CBS
1978	Royce		CBS
1978	Standing Tall	Harvey Hart	NBC
1977	The City	Harvey Hart	NBC
1974	The Death Squad	Harry Falk	ABC
1974	Nakia	Leonard Horn	ABC
1973-1977	Police Story	Edward M. Abroms & Corey Allen	Columbia TriStar
1971	Banyon	Robert Day	NBC

THEATRE

Year	Title	Location	Venue
1996	In the Moonlight Eddie	Los Angeles	Pasadena Playhouse
1995	The Big Knife	Los Angeles	Stella Adler Theatre
1976	One Flew Over the Cuckoo's Nest	Various	On Tour
1975	The Sea Horse	Louisville	
1973	A Streetcar Named Desire 25th Anniversary	New York	Lincoln Center
1972	Twelve Angry Men	New York	Off Broadway
1970	The Glass Menagerie	Rochester, NY	
1968	A Streetcar Named Desire 20th Anniversary	Various	On Tour
1965	Mrs. Dally Has A Lover	New York	John Golden Theatre

BOOKS ON TAPE

Barbs from the Barb	by Francis K. DeNuit & Michael Viner	Dove Audio
Cat in a Jeweled Jumpsuit	by Carole Nelson Douglas	Dove Audio
Cat in an Indigo Mood	by Carole Nelson Douglas	Dove Audio
Cat on a Hyacinth Hunt	by Carole Nelson Douglas	Dove Audio
Dark Homecoming	by Eric Lustbader	Dove Audio
Everybody Dies	by Lawrence Block	Dove Audio
The Greatest Cat Stories of the 20th Century	Various authors	Dove Audio
The Greatest Mysteries of all Time	Various authors	Dove Audio
The Greatest Horror Stories of the 20th Century	Various authors	Dove Audio
Hit Man	by Lawrence Block	Dove Audio
Journey of the Dead	by Loren D. Estelman	Dove Audio
Malice Domestic 2	presented by Mary Higgins Clark	Dove Audio
Maps in a Mirror	by Orson Scott Card	Dove Audio

Robert Forster Contact:

Website: www.robertforster.com

Gloria Reuben

Gloria Reuben

Profile

Emmy-nominated Gloria Reuben has emerged as one of Hollywood's most sought-after actresses after having made her mark in feature films, television and music. Coming off a successful run with the legendary Michael Feinstein in the holiday show at Feinsteins at the Regency Hotel in New York, Reuben is now seen starring in Lifetime's "1-800-MISSING." Gloria stars as the no-nonsense FBI Agent Brooke Haslet who teams up with a psychic to find missing persons. Reuben also acts as associate producer.

Reuben has also starred on the CBS series "The Agency," opposite Gil Bellows. She was also seen starring in the Showtime movie "Feast of All Saints," and she starred in the CBS miniseries "Innocent Blood: The True Story of the Salem Witch Trials."

Starring as health care professional Jeanie Boulet on the critically acclaimed NBC series "ER" proved rewarding to Reuben, earning her multiple Emmy nominations and a Golden Globe nomination. During her time on the show, she enjoyed an enormous amount of respect and praise from critics and fans alike.

Reuben recently switched gears and embarked on a U.S. tour, singing backup for the legendary Tina Turner. She is currently pursuing a solo career.

She appeared on stage in the off-Broadway production of Eve Ensler's "The Vagina Monologues," and completed a starring role in Michael Almereyda's feature film "Happy Here and Now" opposite Ally Sheedy and David Arquette.

Born in Toronto, Canada, Reuben credits the early influence of her mother, an accomplished singer, for inspiring her to develop her performing talents. As a result, she began playing piano at an early age, and studied music technique and theory, as well as ballet and jazz at the Canadian Royal Conservatory. After a brief modeling stint, she moved to Los Angeles to pursue an acting career.

On film, she has starred opposite Johnny Depp in John Badham's "Nick of Time," and Jean Claude Van Damme in Universal's "Timecop." She also starred in the HBO world premiere of "Indiscreet" opposite Luke Perry, in director Greg Lombardo's independent film "Macbeth in Manhattan" and opposite Ray Liotta in "Pilgrim."

Her television credits include a regular role on the NBC series "The Round Table" and the television movies "Soul Survivor," and "Johnny's Girl" for ABC; NBC's "Confessions: Two Faces of Evil" and "Percy and Thunder" for Turner Network Television. She has also guest-starred on several television series, including three episodes of NBC's "Homicide: Life on the Street," "China Beach" and "The Young Riders," among others.

Reuben currently resides in New York.

Gloria Reuben Contact:

PMK/HBH
650 Fifth Avenue, 33rd Floor
New York, NY 10019
Phone: 212-582-1111

Tim Gato

Tim Gato

Profile

Tim Gato comes from a family of five brothers. His childhood was the first training ground for his acting career. The defining moment for him came in eighth grade when he played the role of Sherlock Holmes in a school play. Since that time he has wanted to become an actor and he enjoys nothing more than the thrill of making an audience laugh, cry and dream.

Tim's films are "Phoenix Minority," "Male's Tales" and "The Note" to name a few. On stage he has appeared in "Wait Until Dark," and in addition he was in "The Brady Gang" for The History Channel. Tim enjoys horseback riding and is very close to his brothers. All six enjoy hanging out with each other.

Tim Gato

Resume

FILM

The Perfect Storm	Extra	Wolfgang Peterson	Warner Brothers
Alias (spoof)	Security Guard/ Guest	Efram Potelle	Newborn Pictures
Phoenix Minority	Lead	Richard Meyers	Independent Film
Male's Tale's	Lead – Bucko	Lew-Ann Leen	Shanagan Productions
The Note	Lead-Probie	Kurt Metting	Emerson College
ATF'D	Supporting-Jones	George O'Connor	Midnight Chimes Prod
Into the Black	Supporting-Roger	Marc Powers	Green Monster Films

STAGE

Wait Until Dark	Supporting	Christopher Price	Biddeford City Theatre

TELEVISION

The Brady Gang	Clarence Shaefer, Jr.		The History Channel
Godsmack Video	Grillman		Cyclops Films

COMMERCIAL

Hardy, Wolf & Downing	Boxing Fan		Hardy, Wolf & Downing
AbForce-Infomercial			Groff Films

TRAINING

Acting for the Camera		Susan Shaw	Acorn
Workshop for Actors		Skip Peacock	JBST
Building a Good Voice		Dianne Holly	Acorn
Acting for Film		Richard Meyers	Independent
Workshop for Actors	Assistant Teacher	Skip Peacock	JBST
Acting Workshop		Drew Grindstaff	Four Winds Productions

ACCENTS

British, New York, French, German, Southern, Italian and Coastal Maine

SPORTS

Baseball, Football, Bowling, Frisbee and Volleyball

SPECIAL INTERESTS

Horseback Riding, Poetry and Writing

Tim Gato Contact:

Talent Management Agency
Phone: 207-251-0794

Rachele Leps

Favorite Quote:

"Luck is what happens when preparation meets opportunity."
Darrell Royal

Rachele Leps

Profile

Rachele Leps has performed all over the Central Florida area, won numerous contests and is one of the brains behind Spectrum, a dance company. She has appeared in "Jesus Christ Superstar," "Moulin Rouge" (Winter Park Racquet Club), American Diabetes Association's Walk for the Cure" (dance), Third Thursdays Shin-dig (dance), Amazing Grace (vocal soloist), and Auto Max commercials.

She studied Acting and Improv at Lisa Maile Image, Modeling and Acting, voice with Ron Feldman and has also studied guitar and piano. She has signed with Ward Productions as a vocal artist.

Rachele Leps

Resume

TELEVISION

Auto Max Boat Scene	Featured	KVG Productions
Auto Max Car Scene	Featured	KVG Productions
Jazzercise Salute to Fitness Half Time	Ensemble/Dancer	Jazzercise/FL. Hospital
Jazzercise Fitness	Ensemble/Dancer	Jazzercise/Ch. 9 News
Orlando Magic/Jr. Magic Girl	Ensemble/Dancer	YMCA/Orlando Magic
Peach Bowl Half Time	Ensemble/Dancer	Georgia Dome
Lake Howell Interview	Principal	Channel 9 News

LIVE PERFORMANCE

Third Thursday's Shin-dig (*Hard Rock Night*)	Ensemble/Dancer	Spectrum Dance Company
Third Thursday's Shin-dig (*Jazz Night*)	Ensemble/Dancer/Vocal	Spectrum Dance Company
Winter Park Racquet Club (*Moulin Rouge*)	Ensemble/Dancer	Spectrum Dance Company
American Diabetes Association (*Walk for the Cure*)	Ensemble/Dancer	Spectrum Dance Company
Amazing Grace (*Vocal Solo*)	Principal	Tuskawilla Methodist
Grown-up Christmas List (*Vocal Solo*)	Principal	Tuskawilla Methodist
"The Gift" (*Vocal Solo*)	Principal	Tuskawilla Methodist
Live News Reporter	Principal	Lisa Maile
Rollins Dancers	Ensemble/Dancer	Rollins College Org
"Party 4 U" (*Dance*)	Principal	Rob Labby
Wild Horse Saloon (*Sing to Win*)	Featured	Pleasure Island, FL
Hard Rock Oscar Night (*Universal Studios Florida*)	Model	Lisa Maile
Earthquake / Jaws	Principal	Universal Studios, FL
Auto Max Car Scene	Featured	KVG Productions
Twix Campaign	Featured	Lisa Maile
Jingle Bear	Principal	Lisa Maile
In My Life (*Vocal Solo*)	Principal	Orlando Arena
Harmonious Monks	Principal	Dennis Klee

THEATRE

Alexander and the Terrible Horrible...	Choreographer	Orl UCF Shake-speare Festival
Jack And The Beanstalk	Assistant Choreographer	Orl UCF Shake-speare Festival
Jesus Christ Superstar	Principal	Tuskawilla Methodist
Telling Tales	Principal	The TaleTellers Troup
Incense & Nonsense (A Night Of Religious Burlesque)	Principal	Act About Players

TRAINING

ADVANCED AUDITION TECHNIQUES	LISA MAILE ACTING SCHOOL	PATRICIA CLAY
TV AND COMMERCIAL ACTING	LISA MAILE ACTING SCHOOL	KEVIN O'NEILL/AL HUBBS
IMAGE AND CONFIDENCE DEVELOPMENT	LISA MAILE IMAGE MODELING & ACTING	VARIOUS
IMPROV	LISA MAILE ACTING SCHOOL	PATRICIA CLAY
VOICE AND MUSIC INSTRUCTION	ORLANDO, FL	RON FELDMAN
JO-LA-MAR (gymnastics/dance)	WINTER PARK, FL	VARIOUS
DANCE INSTRUCTION	WINTER PARK, FL	MARK DWYER

SEMINARS & WORKSHOPS INCLUDE

KIM CINQUE: FLORIDA STARS MODEL & TALENT AGENCY
BOB KAHN: CASTING
LISA MAILE: "BREAKING INTO THE INDUSTRY"
HELEN GITTENS: DIAMOND AGENCY

SKILLS

Lisa Maile/Children's Acting – Assistant Teacher, Singing (Christian, Broadway, Light Rock, Country), Guitar (basic), Dance (modern, hip hop, ballet, jazz, swing, salsa), Kickboxing (basic), Swimming, Mountain/BMX Biking (basic), Drive Stick Shift, Miss Orlando Pageant

Rachele Leps Contact:

Websites:
www.greenroomorlando.com under local talent
www.actingjobconnection.com
www.bandsinflorida.com under special events

Paul Tsoukas

Favorite Quote:

"When you board the train bound for success, never disembark until you reach your destination, regardless of how many stops there are along the way."

Paul Tsoukas

Profile

Paul Tsoukas was born in Coburg, an inner northern suburb of Melbourne, Victoria, Australia. His parents were both born in Greece and migrated to Australia in the 1950's. He attended a private school called Penleigh and Essendon Grammar School. His school offered a range of extracurricular activities such as sports, languages and drama. Throughout his teens he represented his school in tennis and basketball. He also studied Chinese for 6 years and became quite good at it, entering Chinese speaking competitions and placing very highly. However, from the very first time he was introduced to drama, he realized he had found his niche.

A year before he was to graduate he decided to quit school and enrolled in TAFE and started his apprenticeship as a cook. Those four years were the hardest years of his life. He realized you only get one chance at life and there should be as few regrets as possible. You have to do what makes you happy.

At the age of 20, he was accepted into a modeling agency and this was the first time he felt like he was moving in the right direction. He also completed a three- year acting course for stage, film and television. Over the next 5 years he would go from a small agency in Melbourne to an international agency in Tokyo, Japan. He was on his way to achieving his goal and it felt great!

Paul lived in Japan for 10 months and he worked as one of the top models landing jobs in *Tokyo Fashion Week* as well as doing TV commercials and working for big corporations such as Sony. Upon returning from Japan, he joined an acting agency in Melbourne and began auditioning for all kinds of roles. He is now actively pursuing his dream and it is his intention to travel to the United Kingdom and the United States to study acting and to audition for more roles. One of his main goals is to be part of the main cast in a feature film. He has two brothers, one is a Project Manager for Cisco Systems and the other is a Freelance Graphic Designer and Website Developer. Paul speaks Greek fluently and he is currently studying Russian because he lived with three Russian models while in Japan, and fell in love with their language.

Paul Tsoukas

Resume

EQUITY MEAA

TELEVISION

2001 The Eggs	TV Pilot	B&T Ent.	BLEARY
2001 Ponderosa	US Cable	Western Prod.	ADR

TELEVISION COMMERCIALS

2002 Target	TVC	The Film Business	GROOM
2001 Vidal Sassoon	TVC	(JAPAN)	LEAD SUPP.
2001 NTT-Docomo	TVC	(JAPAN)	LEAD SUPP.

VIDEO GAMES

2001 Final Fantasy X	PS2	Squaresoft Ent.	TIDUS

SHORT FILMS

2002 Fish and Chicks	SF	Kella Kokkinos	JAKE
2001 The Sting	SF	Yoram Simons	DOOGAL
2000 Tomorrow Dies	SF	VCA Project	JOHNNIE

PLAYS/THEATRE

2002 The Last Supper	T	A.R.C.	TODD
2002 Peter Pan	T	Hartwell Players	STARKEY

TRAINING

2002 Ultimate Screen-test Course	T.A.F.T.A.
2001 Voice Techniques	V.C.A.
2001 Character Analysis	V.C.A.
1998-2000 Advanced Acting for Film/TV/Stage	T.A.F.T.A.

SKILLS

LANGUAGES: Greek(f), Russian(g), Mandarin(b)
ACCENTS: American, English, Greek, Italian, Scottish
LICENSES: Car, Motorcycle, Forklift
ATTRIBUTES: Stilt walker, Juggler, Swimming, Rock climbing

Paul Tsoukas Contact:

Lilly Dawson
Email: lillydawsoncasting@bigpond.com

Donna Bigoski

Favorite Quote:

"Tribulation brings perseverance; and perseverance, proven character."

Donna Bigoski

Profile

Growing up in North Eastern Pennsylvania, Donna Bigoski had access to endless entertainment venues. Her interests were both in front of and behind the camera. In an effort to show her thought processes and problem solving capabilities, Donna took the production route first.

Various job titles including Production Coordinator, Producer and Set Designer, are positions she held while trying to figure out where she belonged. Out of the blue and almost by mistake, she appeared on a weekly entertainment show. After multiple on camera segments and her own weekly magazine show, Donna's confidence grew. It was evident that this production worker turned talent realized that the fun and challenging jobs were indeed in front of the camera.

In addition to perfecting her on-camera presence, Donna has tackled some interesting hobbies, including scuba diving, horseback riding as well as a few musical instruments including the guitar and keyboards. Today she continues to pursue the possibility of landing a role in which she can expand her acting experiences, grow professionally and give a remarkable performance not soon forgotten.

Donna Bigoski

Resume

TELEVISION

Out of Focus	Segment Host	FOX
Your Life	Host	WB
The Tonight Show	Extra/Skits	NBC
Jeremy Hall Music Video	Extra	Moser Brothers

STAGE

Lost and Found	Comedy Skit Member	Orlando, FL

SPOKESPERSON

Winston Cup Racing	Racing Host	Pocono, PA

TRAINING

Acting for Stage & Screen	Florida State University	Tallahassee, FL
Adult Acting ABC's I & II	Act III Acting Studio	Orlando, FL
TV, Film & Commercial Acting	Lisa Maile	Winter Park, FL
FMPTA Seminars	FMPTA	Orlando, FL

SPECIAL SKILLS AND INTERESTS

Dancing, Acoustic Guitar, Horseback Riding/Barrel Racing, Scuba Diving (certified), Snorkeling, Softball, Biking, Fishing, Yoga, Pool, Jet Ski, Computers.

WORK HISTORY:

June 2002 – Current

Marketing, Promotion and Public Relations – Highlife Farms, Orlando FL.
Responsible for all aspects of advertising and maintaining business contacts including International organizations and breeders. Create press releases, magazine ads and articles for local and national publications. Coordinate with surrounding businesses for every aspect of facility events and promotions.

March 2001 – May 2001

Assistant Sales Manager-Teranex Media Services, Orlando, FL.
Continuous contact with new clients to solicit Internet encoding and streaming business. Maintained phone and in person communication with existing clients worldwide regarding their video/Internet service related needs. Managed large revenue accounts, customer relations and client Internet project schedules. Company wide downsizing closed Media Services Division.

September 2000 – March 2001

Production Coordinator – Century III at Universal Studios, Orlando, FL.
Contract position for nationally aired production "Ron Hazelton's Housecalls." Various duties included coordinating and updating show rundowns, assigning and overseeing crews for production shoots, maintaining hectic deadlines, supervising postproduction and effectively staying within and often below budgets. Opportunity in Media Services and contract ending terminated responsibilities.

548

July 2000 – August 2000	**Production Assistant – Century III at Universal Studios**, Orlando, FL. Assisted show Producers and Directors with daily activities on pilot shoot of "Killer Golf" sports game show. Promoted to Production Coordinator for "Ron Hazelton's House Calls" at Century III, Universal Studios. Hired as full time Production Coordinator for national home improvement production.
January 2000 – March 2002	**Freedom Ride, Inc.**, Orlando, FL. Assisted with horse care throughout the day in addition to leading horses during therapeutic classes as well as local and state Special Olympics events. Also coordinated holiday gift and donation drives.
May 1998 – August 1998	**Internship – The Tonight Show with Jay Leno**, Burbank, CA. Continuously worked close to show producers and assistants with segment preparations from conception to completion. Conducted research on scheduled guests to enhance interview content. Observed control room activity during rehearsals and show tapings in addition to being talent in show skits.
August 1997 – December 1999	**Assistant Producer/Production – WFSU-TV**, Tallahassee, FL. Assisted in coordinating governmental affairs programming, including television and Internet broadcasts of the Oral Arguments of the Florida Supreme Court as well as hearings of the Florida Public Service Commission. Additional responsibilities for live and taped events include: Pledge Drive talent, Associate Producer, Director, Technical Director, camera operation, and set design. Relocated to Central Florida.
May 1995 – August 1997	**Promotion Director/Producer/Head of Affiliate Relations-WYLN-TV35**, Hazleton, PA Arranged all station promotions within broadcast area as well as on sight event activities for network. Produced all advertising strategies for outdoor, radio, and television campaigns. Maintained contact with local media, Chamber of Commerce and the Warner Brothers Network for specialized events. Contributed as on-air talent for weekly magazine program, camera operation for all sporting events plus talk/informational programs, as well as produced and directed live and taped events. Completing college degree and beginning a career in Florida ended employment.
EDUCATION:	50% completed, MBA program, **The University of Central Florida**, Orlando, FL. Bachelor of Science in Communication, Minor-Theatre, **Florida State University**, Tallahassee, FL. April, 1999-Deans List Associate of Applied Science in Broadcast Communication, **Luzerne County Community College**, Nanticoke, PA. May, 1995-Presidents List

Donna Bigoski Contact:
Phone: 407-579-2065

Marianna Romalis

Marianna Romalis

Profile

It all started for Marianna fourteen years ago when she landed a part in the play "Shayna Maidel" in Baltimore, Maryland. Her first real lead came in Heritage Players "Don't Drink the Water, " in which she played Susan Hollander. She has also appeared in the films "Major League II," "Home for the Holidays" and "Twelve Monkeys." She was in a pilot for Indie filmmaker, Michael Freeman, "Dead Laughing." She played the off beat character Angel in the dark comedy "BBQ Princess."

Marianna has written and performed on Fil Sibley's Rocklive Cable TV show. She dabbled in Shakespeare with Judith Shakespeare Co. and Instant Shakespeare doing readings and scenes from comedies and dramas. She was a riot playing the part of Deliah in "Is There a Comic in the House?" She has done a number of Industrials and regional commercials. In New York she took modern dance at Martha Graham School and jazz at Circle. Marianna was born in Russia and speaks fluent Russian.

Marianna Romalis

Resume

FILM

The Auditions-Grad. NYU	Actress	Dir. Kirill Mikhanovsky
BBQ Princess-NJ	Angel (lead)	Dir. Brett Rogers
Getting In-MD	Alice Taylor (lead)	Dir. Jimmy Trainer
The Bacchae-LA	Sister #1 (cast in featured role)	Dir. Brad Mays/Morgan Creek
Twelve Monkeys	Movie Box Office Attendant	Dir. Terry Gilliam

TV/VO

Fil Sibley Productions	Rocklive/MusicNight	BethAnne/others (wrote/performed)
Baltimore Cable Ch. 42		
Microprose	Computer Video Game	Voice of Ludmila
Towson University	WTSR	News/Music Announcer

OFF BROADWAY

John Houseman Studio Theatre	Two Small Bodies	Dir. Carl Andress/Warren Friedman (Saints Theatre Co.)

OFF-OFF BROADWAY/REGIONAL

LoveCreek	I Want to Touch the Statue of Liberty	Dir. Anne McKay
Tribeca Performing Arts Center	Is There a Comic in the House?	Dir. Elise Schield
Puerto Rican Traveling Theatre	The Sons of Juan Perez	Dir. Robert Delos
Instant Shakespeare Co.	Richard II	Dir. Paul Sugarman
Krane Theatre	Eh Joe	Dir. Cradeaux Alexander
Metropolitan Playhouse	The Coat	Dir.Paulina Shore
Judith Shakespeare Co.	Two Gentlemen of Verona	Dir. Joanne Zipay
Circle in the Square School	A Couple of White Chicks…	
	The Seagull	Dir. Bruce Katzman, Mark Hammer
Stella Adler Studio	The Three Sisters	Dir. Bruce Katzman, Mark Hammer
Towson U-Grad. Dirct. Workshop	Lion in the Streets	Dir. Kate Howard
Loyola College	Guys n' Dolls	Dir. Bill Finnegan
Heritage Playhouse	Don't Drink the Water	Dir. Kathy P.
Bowman Ensemble	Animal Farm	Dir. Russell Muth

TRAINING

Circle in the Square Theatre School	Therese Heyden, Alan Langdon, Jackie Brooks
Judith Shakespeare Co.	Shakespeare Workshop w/ Joanne Zipay
Stella Adler Studio	Chekhov Intensive w/ B. Katzman, M. Hammer, J. Edelmann
Speech and Voice	Harriet Bigus
Pulse Ensemble Theatre	Acting Apprentice: training and performance w/Alexa Kelly
Joy Newman Comedy Workshop	Improvisational Comedy
Loyola College	Marnie Nixon Master Class in Voice
Towson University Thr. Dept.	Theatre, Music, Voice- 1½ yrs.
Shakespeare Theatre, D.C.	Alexander. Tech.-Susan Cohen, Speech-Sarah Felder
Steve Yeager, dir. of Divine Trash	Acting for Film/TV
Walt Witcover	Acting
Barry Feinstein	Acting

Mark Joy

Favorite Quote:

"What you can do, or dream you can do, begin it.
Boldness has genius, power and magic in it."
Johann Von Goethe

554

Mark Joy

Profile

Mark has been an active member of the East Coast film community for over 18 years. His credits include co-starring roles in many films such as "Black Rainbow," "Pecker," "The Perfect Daughter," "The Memoirs of Sally Hemings," "Luv Struck." His next release as co-star will be John Grisham's "Mickey." Mark has worked on over 50 films and a dozen network series, such as, Legacy, Matlock, The Fifth Corner, Dawson's Creek and Alien Nation to name a few, and in countless commercial and corporate projects. After living and working in entertainment for a time in NY and LA, Mark made a lifestyle choice and has now lived in Virginia for many years.

Mark Joy

Resume

SAG/AFTRA/AEA

FILM: (Theatrical)		DIRECTED BY:
MICKEY (John Grisham)	Co-Starring	Hugh Wilson
BLACK KNIGHT	Principal	Gil Junger
DIVINE SECRETS OF THE YA YA SISTERHOOD	Principal	Callie Khouri
PECKER	Starring	John Waters
DOGMA	Principal	Kevin Smith
BRUNO	Principal	Shirley MacLaine
CHERRY FALLS	Principal	Jeoffrey Wright
CECIL B. DEMENTED	Principal	John Waters
MUPPETS FROM SPACE	Principal	Tim Hill
TAKEDOWN	Principal	Joe Chappelle
JOURNEY OF AUGUST KING	Principal	John Duigan
RADIOLAND MURDERS	Principal	Mel Smith
BACK STREET JUSTICE	Co-Starring	Chris MacIntire
LAST OF THE MOHICANS	Principal	Michael Mann
BLACK RAINBOW	Starring	Mike Hodges
CRAZY PEOPLE	Principal	Tony Bill
CITY HALL	Principal	Harold Becker

TELEVISION: (MOW)		
MEMOIRS of SALLY HEMINGS	Co-Starring	Charlie Haid
THE LOVE LETTER	Co-Starring	Dan Curtis
HOLY JOE	Principal	Larry Peerce
LOVE STRUCK	Starring	Larry Peerce
THE PERFECT DAUGHTER	Starring	Harry Longstreet
MIRACLE IN THE WOODS	Guest Star	Arthur Seidleman
MY STEP SON, MY LOVER	Guest Star	Mary Lambert
IN THE BEST OF FAMILIES	Guest Star	Jeff Bleckner
BEAUTY & THE BANDIT	Guest Star	Hal Needham
NIGHT WALK	Guest Lead	Gerald Freidman
BROKEN CHAIN	Co-Starring	LaMont Johnson
WHAT SHE DOESN'T KNOW	Co-Starring	Kevin Dobson
WHAT THE DEAF MAN HEARD	Principal	John Kent Harrison
VAULT OF LOVE	Principal	Marcus Cole
THE JIM VALVANO STORY	Principal	David Morris
BLIND SPOT	Principal	Michael Uno
IN A CHILD'S NAME	Principal	Tom McLoughlin
THE RYAN WHITE STORY	Principal	John Herzfeld
MY NAME IS BILL W.	Principal	Daniel Petrie
UNSPEAKABLE ACTS	Principal	Linda Otto
THE CHARLIE WEDEMEYER STORY	Principal	Roy Campanella Jr.

TELEVISION: (Episodic)

NAT TURNER (PBS special)	Principal	Charles Burnett
LEGACY (11 episodes)	Recurring	UPN/Atlantis
LAW & ORDER (triple episode)	Guest Star	Ed Sherin
QUANTUM II (13 episodes)	Narrator	The Learning Channel
AMERICAN GOTHIC	Guest Star	Michael Nankin
WALKER, TEXAS RANGER	Co-starring	Tony Mordente
TOUCHED BY AN ANGEL (pilot)	Principal	Jim Sadwith
MATLOCK (4 episodes)	Guest Star	Leo Penn
TWILIGHT ZONE SPECIAL	Principal	Robert Markowitz
THE 5TH CORNER	Series Reg.	John Herzfeld
ALIEN NATION	Guest Lead	Harry Longstreet
A MAN CALLED HAWK	Guest Lead	Mario D'Lia

THEATRE: (on request)

TRAINING: Episodic TV: Pro Artists Group, LA, Improvisation and On Camera workshops, The Acting Lab, Brody/Levy Open Stage NY

SPECIAL SKILLS: Weight Training, Certified Personal Trainer, Mountain Biking, Horseback Riding, Flat Water and Sea Kayaking, Limited Firearms, Some Stunts.
Languages: French, German. Dialects: British, Irish, French, German, Southern

Mark Joy Contact:

The Bullock Agency
Phone: 301-209-9598
Website: www.markjoy.com

Crystal Bernard

Favorite Quote:

"Don't listen to what a man says, listen to what he does."

Crystal Bernard

Profile

Actress singer/songwriter Crystal Bernard was born September 30, 1961 in Garland, Texas. Her father was a minister and she sang is his gospel group from a very young age.

Crystal has starred in the movies "Jackpot" and "Gideon." She has also been featured in many films such as "To Love Honor and Betray," "Secret Path" and "A Face to Kill For." Her early movie breaks were "Young Doctors in Love," "High School U.S.A." and "Master Ninja II."

Crystal's television credits include "Wings," playing Helen Chappel Haskett, "It's a Living," "According to Jim" and "Happy Days." Her theatre credits include "Annie Get Your Gun."

Crystal can also be seen in "Dying to be Perfect," "As Good as Dead," "Lady Against the Odds," "Miracle Child" and "Chameleons." She wrote and recorded "The Girl Next Door" and her latest CD is called "Don't Touch Me There."

Crystal loves racing and has raced in the Toyota Pro-Celebrity Race as part of the Long Beach Grand Prix. She also regularly competes in the Dodge Neon Challenge.

Crystal getting a lift from Fabio

Crystal Bernard

Resume

FILM

JACKPOT		Dir. Michael Polish
GIDEON	Independent	Dir. Claudia Hoover
YOUNG DOCTORS IN LOVE	20th Century Fox	Dir. Gary Marshall

TELEVISION

SINGLE SANTA SEEKS MRS. CLAUS	HALMARK CHANNEL	Dir. Harvey Frost
ACCORDING TO JIM	ABC	Guest Star
LOVE, HONOR & BETRAY	CBS	Dir. Peter Levin
THE SECRET PATH		Dir. Bruce Pittman
A FACE TO KILL FOR	USA	Dir. Michael Uno
WINGS	NBC	Series Regular
DYING TO BE PERFECT	ABC	Dir. Jan Egleson
AS GOOD AS DEAD	USA	Dir. Larry Cohen
LADY AGAINST THE ODDS	NBC	Dir. Bradford May
MIRACLE CHILD	NBC	Dir. Michael Pressman
CHAMELEONS	NBC	Dir. Glen Larson
IT'S A LIVING	ABC	Series Regular
HAPPY DAYS	ABC	Series Regular
HIGH SCHOOL USA	NBC	

THEATRE

ANNIE GET YOUR GUN – 'Annie'	Broadway	Limited National Tour

Crystal Bernard Contact:

IFA Talent Agency
8730 Sunset Blvd., Suite 490
West Hollywood, CA 90069

Nestor Serrano

Nestor Serrano

Profile

Nestor Serrano is a native New Yorker whose acting career spans more than two decades. While working as a computer operator for the Bank of New York, Nestor felt he needed to make a move. Not sure of where to go or what to do, he began taking classes at Queens College. While on his way to computer science class, Nestor spotted a long line of students waiting to audition for the drama department. Interested in meeting new people, Nestor auditioned for and got the role of 'Prince' in Don Peterson's "Does a Tiger Wear a Necktie?" That experience was enough for Nestor to make it his last semester at Queens College and his first at the famed Lee Strasberg Institute.

Nestor got his first professional break in Harold Prince's off-Broadway production of "Diamonds." He has over thirty off-Broadway productions to his credit. Naturally, Broadway was not far off when director Herb Ross cast Nestor in "The Boys of Winter," along side Wesley Snipes, Matt Dillon and Ving Rhames. "Cuba and His Teddy Bear," opposite Robert De Niro, followed that production. Nestor was seen back on the boards of Broadway with Patrick Stewart in "The Tempest." He made his debut on London's West End in the Olivier nominated play "Jesus Hopped the A Train," directed by Philip Seymour Hoffman.

Nestor Serrano has been seen in some of the biggest blockbuster features, from his first role as the charmingly annoying house painter, Jose in "The Money Pit" to "Bad Boys," "The Negotiator," "The Insider" and "Bringing Out the Dead." Nestor can also be seen in the films, "Runaway Jury," starring opposite Gene Hackman and Dustin Hoffman, "The Day After Tomorrow" starring opposite Dennis Quaid, and "Infamous," which was directed by and stars John Leguizamo. Interestingly enough, Serrano and Leguizamo starred in the cult classic film, "Hangin' with the Homeboys."

Serrano's film career has been augmented by constant work on television and has had series regular roles in "Witchblade," "True Blue," "Hat Squad," and "Maloney." He has also guest starred in many prime time programs including "24," "CSI Miami," "ER," "Law and Order," "Law and Order: Special Victims Unit," "Profiler," and "X-Files," among others.

Nestor loves New York and maintains his residence there with his lovely and charming wife Debbie, and his smart-as-a-whip son, Spike. He also has two faithful companions, Blackie and Elvis.

Nestor Serrano

Resume

FILM

Day After Tomorrow	Roland Emmerich, dir.
Runaway Jury	Gary Fleder, dir.
Infamous	John Leguizamo, dir.
Replay	Lee Bonner, dir.
City By the Sea	Tom Dey, dir.
Empire	Michael Canton Jones, dir.
After the Storm	Guy Ferland, dir.
Bait	Antoine Fuqua, dir.
Bringing Out the Dead	Martin Scorsese, dir.
The Insider	Michael Mann, dir.
The Negotiator	F. Gary Gray, dir.
Daylight	Rob Cohen, dir.
Indian in the Cupboard	Frank Oz, dir.
City Hall	Harold Becker, dir.
Bad Boys	Michael Bay, dir.
Hangin' With the Homeboys	Joseph Vazquez, dir.
Lethal Weapon	Richard Donner, dir.
Brenda Starr	Robert Ellis Miller, dir.
The Money Pit	Richard Benjamin, dir.
Girls in Prison	John McNaughton, dir.

TELEVISION

24	Recurring	FOX
CSI: Miami	Guest Star	CBS
UC Undercover		NBC
Witchblade	Recurring	TNT/WB
Law & Order: SVU		NBC,USA
Ready to Run (MOW)	Lead	Disney
JAG		CBS
The Profiler (2 episodes)		NBC
Partners		CBS
The X-Files		FOX
Early Edition		CBS
Promised Land		CBS
Dellaventura		CBS
Maloney	Series Regular	CBS
NY Undercover		FOX
Hat Squad	Series Regular	CBS
The Commish		ABC
Love, Lies & Murder (MOW)		ABC
Against the Mob		NBC
True Blue	Series Regular	NBC
Sonny Spoon	Recurring	Cannell Productions

THEATRE

Jesus Hopped the A-Train		London/West End-The New Arts Theatre
The Tempest	Antonio	Broadway -- Broadhurst Theatre
Cuba and His Teddy Bear	Red Light	Broadway – Longacre Theatre
Boys of Winter	Lt. Bonny/Sgt. Delapenya	Broadway – Biltmore Theatre
The Creditors	Adolf	CSC
The Learned Ladies	Tristan	CSC
Diamonds	Comic/Warner Wolf	Circle in the Square
Union City Thanksgiving	Comic/Warner Wolf	Intar

TRAINING

Lee Strasberg Institute	Scene Study	Barbara Covington, David Gideon
American Conservatory Theatre	Scene Study	Ray Reinhart
Shakespeare Studio		Raphael Kelly

Cast of *The Hat Squad*

Nestor Serrano Contact:

Allman/Rea Management
141 Barrington Ave.
Los Angeles, CA 90049
Phone: 310-440-5780

Robert Patrick

Robert Patrick

Profile

Robert Patrick's career has been marked by several standout performances and his work demonstrates an impressive range not often seen by many actors. He was seen starring in the film "Charlie's Angels: Full Throttle" opposite Drew Barrymore, Cameron Diaz and Lucy Liu, for director McG. You can also see him in the pilot for the FX Network's original series "Snitch" and the film "Pavement" opposite Lauren Holly.

He also starred as 'John Doggett' on the last two seasons of the now-classic television series, "The X Files." Prior to that, Robert was seen in the Robert Rodriguez box-office hit, Spy Kids, for Dimension Films opposite Antonio Banderas and in Miramax Films' All The Pretty Horses opposite Matt Damon and Penelope Cruz, directed by Billy Bob Thornton.

Additional roles for Robert include Universal Pictures' Detox opposite Sylvester Stallone and A Texas Funeral, opposite Jane Adams and Joanne Whalley. Patrick's performance in three high profile second season episodes of "The Sopranos" received him critical acclaim. He is best known for his performance as 'T-1000' in Terminator 2: Judgment Day opposite Arnold Schwarzenegger and The Faculty directed by Robert Rodriguez and written by Kevin Williamson. Patrick's additional film credits include From Dusk To Dawn 2: Texas Blood, the sequel to From Dusk to Dawn, with Quentin Tarantino and produced by Robert Rodriguez for Miramax; Copland opposite Sylvester Stallone and Robert De Niro for Miramax, as well as the independent film The Only Thrill starring opposite Diane Keaton, Diane Lane and Sam Shepherd.

Also, as a favor to John Singleton, Patrick made a chilling cameo appearance in Rosewood, and before that took a comedic turn in Castle Rock Entertainment's Striptease opposite Demi Moore, as her lowlife, thieving ex-husband. He's also starred in Paramount's Fire in the Sky, Double Dragon: The Movie, Decoy with Peter Weller, The Last Gasp, and Hong Kong '97 for TriMark Pictures as well as a Showtime episode of "The Outer Limits."

Born in Marietta, Georgia, Patrick has also lived in Dayton, Cleveland, Detroit and Boston. He played American Legion Baseball in high school and football at Bowling Green State University in Ohio, but after sitting in on drama classes, he decided to quit football and pursue acting.

In 1984 Patrick moved to Hollywood where a few weeks later, he was cast as a joint-smoking beatnik in the play *Go*. While performing on stage Patrick was discovered by a casting director for Roger Corman's production company and quickly won the role of a psychotic biker in Warlord From Hell. Patrick next starred in the futuristic western Equalizer 2000. Taking his talents to the stage, he co-starred in the Los Angeles premier of David Mamet's *The Shawl* at the Waterfront Stage.

While a partner in the now dissolved independent film production company, 360 Entertainment, Patrick produced, along with Stanley Isaacs, Within the Rock and The End of the Road, a film in which he had a starring role.

Patrick completed filming "Ladder 49" opposite John Travolta and Joaquin Phoenix. The film, directed by Jay Russell, tells the story of a firefighter who is trapped in a burning building, while hoping and waiting to be rescued. While there, he reflects upon his life and experiences. It was filmed in Baltimore, Maryland.

Robert Patrick resides in Los Angeles with his wife Barbara and their two young children.

Robert is currently starring in "Walk The Line" with Joaquin Phoenix as Johnny Cash's father Ray. As of this printing, "Walk The Line" is the second highest rated movie in the United States and is already being rumored as an Oscar contender for 2006.

Robert and wife Barbara at the premiere of *Walk The Line*

Robert Patrick Contact:

PMK/HBH
8500 Wilshire Blvd., Suite 700
Beverly Hills, CA 90211

Catching Up With The Stars

Adam LaVorgna during photo shoot for *7th Heaven*

April Weeden-Washington at the premiere of *Hair Show*

Billy Crudup promoting the new film *Charlotte Grey*

Brande Roderick and Carmen Electra at the premiere of *Starsky and Hutch*

Camille Winbush 2005's NAACP Outstanding Supporting Actress in a Comedy Series

Dennis with Jimmy Smits and Kim Delaney on the set of *NYPD Blue*

Dustin Nguyen with Pamela Anderson and Natalie Rataino at the *MTV Music Awards*

At home with Ed Asner

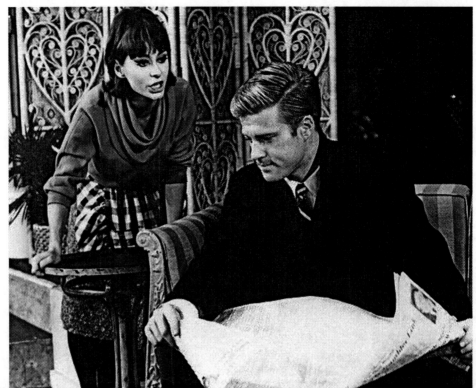

Elizabeth Ashley and Robert Redford in the stage production *Barefoot in the Park*

Elon Gold and Pamela Anderson promoting the series *Stacked*

Frances McDormand receiving instructions for the film *City By The Sea*

George O. Gore II at Teen People Magazine's *25 Hottest People Under 25* Party

Gloria Reuben and the cast of *ER* at the Screen Actors Guild Awards

Jack Plotnick and Sally Field in a scene from *Say It Isn't So*

574

James Caan with his son Scott and Brad Pitt at the premiere of *Oceans 12*

Janice Lynde at the 2005 Daytime Emmy Awards

Jorja Fox at the 2004 Emmy Awards

Joyce DeWitt at TV Land's *TV Greatest Hits* Reception

Keith David won an Emmy in 2005 for narrating *Unforgivable Blackness*

Kyla Pratt at the 2005 Vibe Awards

Michael Rosenbaum at the premiere of *Batman Begins*

Natashia Williams at the Soul Train Music Awards

Niecy Nash in attendance as Women in Film and the Hallmark honor Dr. Maya Angelou

Paula Jai Parker at the premiere of *Hustle and Flow*

Shirley MacLaine with Joan Collins and Debbie Reynolds in Las Vegas

Stuart Pankin in a scene from *Honey, We Shrunk Ourselves*

Tami Anderson at the Divine Design Fundraiser

Tom Bower and Sir Ian McKellen at the After-Party for *The Laramie Project*

Tommy Lee Jones receiving the 2005 Best Actor Award at the Cannes Film Festival

To Be Continued...

If you are an actor or actress who would like to be included in my future volumes, send an 8X10 photo, short biography and resume.

I will contact you, or call 559-594-4533.

<u>**Mailing Address**</u>

C. Elizabeth Lalla
P.O. Box 873
Exeter, CA 93221

E-Mail – celebwriter@earthlink.net
Website – www.celizabethlalla.com

C. Elizabeth Lalla

Celebrity writer C. Elizabeth Lalla was born in Salisbury, North Carolina. Her family moved to California when she was five years old, settling in Exeter, a small town in the San Joaquin Valley. Elizabeth has always held an interest in Hollywood and the stars. As a celebrity writer, Elizabeth loves to write about the accomplishments of actors and actresses. She doesn't concentrate on just the stars. She wants everyone to be noticed for their talent. She has dreamed of putting together volumes of books with the stars, the established and the aspiring. Her sense of humor and outgoing personality has opened many doors for Elizabeth. She loves meeting and talking with celebrities and enjoys associating with people who know how to laugh and have fun. She has traveled all over the world, is down to earth, easy to talk to and open to new adventures. Her home base now is the town she grew up in, which is nestled in the foothills below Sequoia National Park.

CPSIA information can be obtained at www.ICGtesting.com
Printed in the USA
BVOW06s1442080115

382229BV00004B/3/A